SCIENCE AND CULTURE SERIES
JOSEPH HUSSLEIN, S.J., Ph.D., GENERAL EDITOR

QUEEN ELIZABETH

QUEEN ELIZABETH
A version of the "Armada" portrait, by an unknown
artist. National Portrait Gallery.

QUEEN ELIZABETH

BY

THEODORE MAYNARD

The Bruce Publishing Company :: Milwaukee

To

Leo Harlow

and

Caroline Giltinan Harlow

Preface by the General Editor

THE sphinx of modern history, elusive puzzle of historian and psychologist, such is Elizabeth, resplendent Tudor Queen of England.

In her very portraits we always find something to bring us up short. Only perhaps in the death mask do we see her natural features. But she died in old age, haggard, after a most fierce struggle, and the mystery remains.

Yet all is not mystery. Of the facts themselves of her reign we have ample certainty. Her rather attractive features and strongly marked Tudor characteristics, won the hearts of her subjects. Her spiritual lineaments were truly known to God alone.

With his genial humor (so important in this book), his generous sympathies, and his intelligent comprehension, Mr. Maynard has perhaps brought us as close to a correct understanding of her as we well can hope to attain. If in a book of this compass he cannot quote documents *in extenso*, he carefully cites chapter and verse. Nor does he challenge tradition without offering proof.

The most significant contribution of this work is its judicious treatment of the religious aspect of the reign of Queen Elizabeth. Important and absorbing though this question is, and the key to the entire situation, yet it has been dealt with inadequately and even superficially in standard biographies. The time, then, has come to present it fairly and fearlessly, assigning praise or blame impartially, as the facts shall warrant. Truth is after all the best defence of a deserving cause. It has been the author's touchstone.

Preface by the General Editor

Yet the religious interest of this volume in no way interferes with a proper record of the age. Nothing of its romance or significance, as definitely related to the subject of this biography, has here been overlooked: its plots and pseudo plots, its perils and adventures, its dramatic episodes and mighty undertakings, its reckless wickedness and hidden virtue, its basest perfidy and sublime heroism — all are spread out in living colours on the author's canvas as they existed side by side in that tumultuous period. It was an age which has exercised and will continue to exercise a fascination over men, though their concept of it is more often gathered from poetry than from sober history.

Thus Virginia Woolf, after quoting an especially extravagant passage, quite naturally throws up her hands in delighted consternation at the entire Elizabethan drama, where we "wander in the land of the unicorn and the jeweller among dukes and grandees, Gonzalos and Bellimperias, who spend their lives in murder and intrigue, dress up as men when they are women, as women if they are men, see ghosts, run mad, and die in the greatest profusion on the slightest provocation, uttering as they fall imprecations of superb vigour or elegies of the wildest despair."

That indeed was the world of which the poets dreamed, but the real flesh-and-blood men and women of the day were not so far different from ourselves, though their emotions then found more free expression and the brightly coloured life of the Middle Ages had not yet been reduced to the comparative drabness of our times. Even Elizabeth herself, amid all the radiance of her court, a demigoddess on a gilded throne, had something not a little preposterous about her. And yet no one would deny her to have been one of the world's most splendourous appearances on the stage of history. For the legend of Gloriana there was some foundation.

Dramatic, certainly, she was, and that to an extent disguising still further the real woman. With consummate ease she could impersonate at any moment the very opposite of all her true qualities, thoughts, and sentiments. But as in the case of Shakespeare's strolling player, when her part was acted out, her

Preface by the General Editor

audience departed and her purpose gained, what then was Hecuba to her or she to Hecuba: the character she had assumed to the woman she actually was! Something of the Elizabethan poets, too, ran in her blood and they in turn could draw fresh draughts of inspiration from her fountain. Quill in hand, Elizabeth herself was no mean poet. As for prose, in that she was almost among the masters.

No wonder, then, that few persons have ever been spoken of in such superlatives. Yet quite independently of all the iridescent adulations poured out before her and indulgently accepted by her as a matter of course, much of the praise more judiciously accorded her was well deserved. That holds true particularly when there was question of her superb intellectual brilliancy, her classical attainments, and her literary deftness.

Qualities of a less estimable kind, but on which she perhaps plumed herself even more greatly, were those displayed by her in the diplomatic field. Throughout the whole of Europe there was no single hand to match her own on the political chessboard. Combined with natural cleverness and a shrewd knowledge of the game was a Machiavellian cunning that reflected in a startling way the teachings of the Florentine guide in deception. Ambiguity, as a cultivated art of expression, reached in her a degree of virtuosity. Truly, the sphinx of the Thames!

In an age of contradiction she was the center of contradictories: by turns fascinating, playful, hard, abhorrent, disgusting even, savagely cruel, and again almost tender. Magnificent and yet the most pathetic of women if we know ever so little of the heart that beat within her bosom. Mercurial though of iron. Brave as a lion in personal perils, yet easily terrified into committing the most bloody excesses through apparent dangers to her position. Such situations, adroitly staged or climaxed by the very men most near to her, invariably made of her an easy tool for their nefarious designs.

It was part of the great pathos of her life that failing to receive genuine human affection at any period, such as the girl or woman in her craved to have, and thwarted in her deepest natural desires, she allowed her soul to become shrivelled up by endless plottings and intrigues. Secular-minded in the extreme, the artistic forms of piety and elaborate prayers resorted to by her on occasion never reached deep enough to bring her lasting comfort. Hers was a devious and tormented mind. Her external conduct may often doubtless be explained as a reaction against such conditions. That may in part explain the puzzle confronting her biographer. Perhaps, in fact, he has largely solved it by acknowledging it as a puzzle.

And here be it said, as a more immediate introduction to this book, that since the "spacious" days of Queen Elizabeth there has been no period in the English-speaking world so propitious as the present for the appearance of this volume.

Old prejudices, it is true, are not dead and old enmities still rankle in the souls of many, yet new problems and issues of numerous kinds have obliterated to a large extent these unhappy survivals of the past and lessened the passions they were calculated to arouse. More than at any earlier period, readers are willing to give fair hearing to a sincere, unbiased, and convincing story of Elizabeth, Tudor Queen of England, as here set down in these stirring pages.

Joseph Husslein, S.J., Ph.D.,
General Editor, Science and Culture Series

St. Louis University,
April 16, 1940

Contents

xiii

Contents

List of Illustrations

1

Harry's Daughter

O N SEPTEMBER 7, 1533, Anne Boleyn, since January 25 of the same year Queen consort of England, lay in labour in the palace of Greenwich in the room known as the Chamber of the Virgins. During the weeks before the birth was expected, her husband, distraught between anxiety and hope, consulted astrologers and soothsayers. They extolled the virtues of a magical jewel and the skin of a snake which, laid on the thighs, ensured an easy delivery. They were also careful to foretell that a male child would be born. Henry, as though to force the hand of fate, had caused a proclamation to be drawn up announcing the birth of a Prince. It may still be seen with the addition of an "s" in Henry's own script. That was all he could squeeze in, and it was written in bitter disappointment that the child was only a Princess. If there was public rejoicing that day in London, much of it was due to a malicious satisfaction that Anne had failed to produce a son. She was anything but popular among the people, whose sympathies were with Katherine of Aragon. Those who had often shouted after her "Nan Boleyn, the whore!" understood what a setback this was for the upstart's ambition.

It was with such a sour welcome that Elizabeth Tudor came into the world between 3 and 4 that afternoon. She was named after the mother of Henry and the mother of Anne, being baptised the following day with Cranmer as her godfather and the Duchess of Norfolk and the Marchioness of Dorset for godmothers.

There is no need to revert here upon the causes of the royal divorce. But it may be admitted that, however much Henry was moved by a base passion for Anne — some set the extraordinary infatuation down to witchcraft — dynastic considerations weighed heavily. He had persuaded himself that Katherine's inability to produce any but stillborn sons, or a son not viable, like the one who had died shortly after birth, was a judgement on him from God for his having married his brother Arthur's widow. Obviously only a strong male heir could preserve the Tudor line. In the dark cloud upon Henry's face, the Queen probably already perceived the shadow of her doom. Her only chance was that of bearing again, and in short order — this time a male child.

There were several reasons why an heir was needed. Though the Salic Law was not formally recognised in England, a common argument among lawyers was that one existed in effect. Certainly the sole previous instance of a Queen Regnant, that of Matilda, was hardly of happy omen. In view of the doubtful legitimacy of the infant girl now whimpering at Greenwich, Anne knew that, if she could, she must mother a future King of England.

It was not merely that Henry's marriage to Anne was denied validity both by canon law and the common law of Europe; all the circumstances of the marriage raised a question of its validity even according to English law — circumstances that Henry was himself going to invoke a couple of years later.

We may dismiss the reports spread later by Nicholas Sanders that Anne was Henry's daughter.[1] There is, however, reason for believing that Anne's mother had once been Henry's mistress, as there is no doubt at all that her sister Mary had been such. This presumably was the ground of Cranmer's pronouncement of invalidity in 1536, just before Anne's execution.

In addition there were enough legal deficiencies. Anne had been privately married to Henry on January 25, 1533, when she was already with child. But Henry had to wait until Cranmer could receive the Papal brief appointing him Archbishop of

---

[1] Sanders derived the story from Rastell's Latin *Life of Sir Thomas More* and from Nicholas Harpsfield. Cardinal Allen, who was to call Elizabeth an "incestuous bastard," went to the same sources.

Canterbury before Cranmer could divorce Katherine. The consecration of the King's pliant instrument occurred on March 30; on the following Whitsunday, May 23, the divorce between Henry and Katherine was promulgated. Not until then, it might be noted, was Anne crowned. Under ordinary circumstances a coronation of a queen consort was not regarded as necessary and was, in fact, often dispensed with. In the case of Anne it was intended to be an affirmation of the legitimacy of the child she was to bear. But though she could not be crowned until after the decree of divorce, the absence of that decree had not prevented the secret marriage four months earlier. Punctiliousness had to be dispensed with because of the desperate emergency. Henry had counted upon the birth of a son as sufficient to offset any irregularities. Now Anne had failed him — and had ruined herself. The King, whose pedantic mind was fertile in finding legal pretexts for the impulsions of his passions, even now had ready to hand, should he ever wish to use it, a complete case against her.

He had long resented Anne's having driven him so hard. Before consenting to become his mistress she had exacted a solemn promise that he was to divorce Katherine, and that she was to be Queen. Such was the King's infatuation that he agreed to all her demands, increasing thereby her power over him, while at the same time making inevitable a fierce reaction as soon as his infatuation began to decline. Had she borne a son she would not, of course, have insured Henry's fidelity, but she would at least have insured the security of her own position. Now she was obliged to witness the King's attentions to Jane Seymour.

In the hope of heading him off she went so far as to encourage affairs with ladies less dangerous to her than the meek Jane. When Henry showed that he preferred to pick his mistresses for himself, she tried to interest him in his old hobby of theology. And when this failed, too, she upbraided him in cold storms of indignation, alternating these with futile attempts to regain her lost sway over his appetites. The satisfaction of sensuality proving insufficient to allow her to forego the satisfaction of being a shrew, her rages resulted in a miscarriage — of a boy. Her fate was now sealed. In a spasm of greasy tenderness after the birth of Elizabeth, Henry had attempted to console the weeping woman, vowing, "I would beg from door to door rather than forsake you" — an easy promise for a king to make. It was different this time: instead of blaming himself for his wife's miscarriage, he blamed her. For her sake he had battled against the Papacy during 1534, and in 1535 had sent Sir Thomas More and Bishop Fisher to the block for refusing the Oath of Supremacy. Though they had been careful not to raise the question of Anne's title, she had understood the implications and had shown remorseless spite. Yet when in September of the year of the martyrs the Queen found herself with child again, there was a flickering up, along with Anne's hope, of some part of the King's former affection. After the miscarriage the end of the tether was reached.

To make the catastrophe all the more cruel, it came just at the moment when Anne thought that, after all, she was going to be safe. For on January 7, 1536, old Queen Katherine died, writing a noble and beautiful farewell letter to Henry, ending "Mine eyes desire you above all other things." Then on the 29th Anne miscarried.

Henry's response to Katherine's death was characteristic. Upon the arrival of the news, he went the rounds of his courtiers gleefully, carrying little Elizabeth in his arms to show her off. The child, who had been living in a separate establishment with a governess and nurses, was brought to Court specially for the occasion. Further to parade his exultation, the King dressed from head to foot in yellow, except for a white plume in his cap. The scene lived in the seared memory of those who witnessed it; fortunately upon the memory of a child of two and a half no impression could have been left.

Nor could any impression have remained upon her mind of what so swiftly followed. Three months later the Queen was in the Tower, charged with adultery and incest. On May 19 the expert French headsman brought over specially from Calais cut off her head with his sword. With astonishing levity she had jested with Sir William Kingston about the slenderness of her little neck, and he had explained that she would not feel the stroke, it was "so subtle." Though at the first impact of terror her Catholic feelings had momentarily welled up and she had asked to have the Blessed Sacrament in her apartments in the Tower, she soon steeled herself into insensibility. One wonders, indeed, whether she felt her situation to be other than that of a desperate gambler who had lost the last throw.

We must surmise that there was, even in her cold heart, some pang at leaving her little daughter, though we have no record of any scene of farewell between mother and child. It is likely that, mingled with whatever maternal tenderness may have touched her, was an obscure grudge against Elizabeth for having been a girl. Anne had seen very little of her since her birth.

The charges of adultery against the Queen had, at any rate in some of the instances cited, sufficient foundation, although it seems improbable that her brother, Lord Rochford, who died on the scaffold as one of her paramours was really among them. Anne's enemies — in particular Henry's boon companions, the ambitious Seymours, and those who, hoping for reunion with Rome, worked for her downfall — were determined that she should not escape for lack of evidence. The shouts of "Nan Boleyn, the whore!" grew louder than ever. However innocent she may have been with regard to some points in her indictment, there can be no doubt of her general guilt.

The adultery of the Queen was in a very different political (though, of course, not moral) category from the promiscuous love affairs of her husband. For the Queen's infidelities could have foisted upon the throne one who was not the King's son.[2] Yet in Anne's political (though again, not moral) extenuation it might perhaps be said that only in a forlorn hope of bearing a son and so retrieving her position did she do what she did. Katherine before her had had a series of miscarriages of male children. Anne may have believed Henry incapable of siring a son who should live. What had doomed Lord Rochford was his

[2] Afterwards it was suggested by the Spanish Ambassador and others that Norris or Lord Rochford, and not Henry, was Elizabeth's father. This we may dismiss; Elizabeth was an unmistakable Tudor.

reading aloud at his trial a question so delicate that it had been handed to him written in French: it was whether the Queen had ever told Lady Rochford that the King was impotent. On the other hand, Rochford's action may have merely indicated that he knew he was already lost, and that this was the Boleyn way of taking revenge. Henry was extremely sensitive to any hint that he was lacking in virility.

Prior to Anne's execution Cranmer's ecclesiastical court pronounced her marriage to Henry invalid from the beginning, for reasons carefully not committed to writing but about which we can be morally certain. If, in face of them, the illogicality of sentencing this woman to death for adultery is obvious; so, too, are the political consequences that might have arisen from the faithlessness of one who, whether or not she was validly married to the King, had hitherto been accounted his true wife. Yet though Anne deserved what she got, Cranmer's subservience is of the slimiest character. He must have known at the time he delivered the sentence of Katherine's divorce, of the impediment to Henry's marriage to Anne. Nevertheless he had acted so as to clear the way for this marriage, and now, upon Anne's fall, had crowned his infamy with a letter of incredible baseness in which, in alarm for his own head as the contriver of the marriage, he accused his former patron while pretending to defend her.

There is one rather comic fact in the sordid business: so quickly did Anne's crash follow upon her elevation, that in the Parliament at Dublin an act declaring her "the most dear and entirely beloved wife" of the King, and making it misprision of treason "to utter anything to the prejudice of this marriage," was passed a few days after the marriage had, in London, been declared null and void. This, however, was due merely to the slow communications of the time and the dilatoriness of legislative bodies. The main point to bear always in mind is that according to canon law — even according to canon law as received in England after the schism — Anne could never have been the wife of Henry, unless a dispensation had been given of a kind Canterbury would not admit.

Harry's Daughter

The King immediately proceeded to bastardize his daughter Elizabeth by act of Parliament — as he had already bastardized his elder daughter Mary — in order to make her forever incapable of the succession. Mary, when she came to the throne, had that insulting statutory stigma removed. It was never removed in Elizabeth's case. As Queen she took legal advice on the point, and was told that it would be safer not to raise the issue. Her claim therefore rested upon nothing except her acknowledged Tudor blood and the will her father drew up.

That she resembled Henry in many ways came later to be apparent to everybody. She had his imperiousness and quick temper and (as some would say) his cruelty. But apart from her red hair, she did not look like him in figure or features. Her likeness to him lay in interior disposition. She had his intellectual ability, though in her case it was far more practical and less abstract than his. If she did not share her father's interest in theology, she inherited some part of his artistic gifts. She was a skilful musician, though she was without the faculty for composing any of the admirable music Henry has left; and her verse does not rise to the level of his best lyrics. This, however, may have been due to the circumstances that she had little time to devote to such amusements. Her prose, when not deliberately involved (and sometimes when it is), shows a fine command of style. The main difference between father and daughter is that where Henry, in his indolent and expansive fashion, delegated most of the details of administration to Wolsey, More, and Cromwell, each in his turn, Elizabeth, though served by the Cecils, who were quite as astute as any of their predecessors, devoted close attention to affairs of state. For all that, the similarities between them were strong enough to warrant Elizabeth's describing herself, whenever she got the chance, as "Harry's daughter." It was so good a card to play that she even cultivated her father's bluffness. The people of England were never allowed to forget that she was a Tudor.

We may see, side by side with her Henrician traits, much that stemmed from that mother whom she is never recorded as having mentioned, whom she may have thought it discreet not

7

to mention. Anne Boleyn's were her inordinate vanity and her trickiness and her obstinacy, though two of these qualities were equally Henry's. The dissimulation for which Elizabeth became so famous, in so far as it did not spring from the difficulties of her position, we must think of as derived from Anne: Henry never deceived anybody except himself. But the strain of vulgarity that was always liable to betray itself was found in both parents. And Elizabeth had little pride, for this goes with a sense of honour and has nothing to do with its imitation, vanity. On the other hand, she was rarely vindictive; such cruelty as she showed was no more than the manifestation of fear. When free from this she was upon the whole good humoured, at times to the point of boisterous camaraderie that many thought unseemly. Her rages were merely hysterical; they passed quickly and she bore no grudges. They were, however, a constant strain to those whose business in life it was to manage the unaccountable woman.

One characteristic — perhaps the most important of all — was derived from her grandfather, Henry VII. This was her parsimony: something so absent from Henry VIII's make-up that it would have been better for him and England had he had enough of it to temper his prodigality. Despite having been left by his skinflint father the unheard-of fortune of £2,000,000 (a sum whose actual value we hardly reach even by multiplying it by ten), yet to satisfy his personal extravagance and his wish to make the monarchy impregnable by virtue of its economic bastions, he debased the coinage and so swindled his subjects, and he committed the still worse blunder of looting the monasteries. In doing so, he was forced to enrich the lay proprietors to such an extent that, diametrically opposite to his designs, he created an oligarchy that was destined a hundred years later to destroy effective kingship in England. That oligarchy proved an incubus bequeathed to his son; it contrived to hamper the Marian reforms; and it was the determining factor in Elizabeth's reign. In this respect, above all others, Elizabeth was Harry's daughter.

The little girl about to develop into the extraordinary

HENRY VIII
From the painting by Hans Holbein, in Warwick Castle.

woman who, more than any other of English blood, has most profoundly influenced the destinies of the world, was a shamefully neglected child. Nobody suspected what was in store for her; nobody suspected it for a long time. She slipped into an obscurity which was only broken, some years later, with a scandal and her own imminent personal danger. There was no reason at all to think that she would ever be Queen of England, still less to imagine that she would be the greatest of England's queens.

Her father did not want to be bothered with her, or even to be reminded of her existence. When he remembered her at all, he thought of her, quite simply, as a disappointment. Accordingly she was bundled off to Hatfield, where she was put under the charge of Lady Margaret Bryan, a Boleyn connexion.

Until her mother's disgrace and death, however, she was the "Princess Elizabeth," her sister, seventeen years older than herself, being accorded, because of her statutory bastardy, only the title of the "Lady Mary." To the credit of Katherine of Aragon's daughter it must be said that she steadfastly refused to admit that Elizabeth took precedence over her or that her own blood was base. Loving and dutiful to her father as she was, on the rare occasions when she saw him, on that point she long remained adamant. It was her mother's honour that she was upholding. Under threats and in an agony of soul she yielded in the end to the extent of acknowledging Henry to be head of the English Church. But when Anne Boleyn tried to humiliate her by making her take her meals in the public dining room, Mary fought and won. However much Henry might neglect Katherine's daughter, it now and then occurred to him that she was also his own.

It was hardly to be expected that Mary, now a grown woman and keenly conscious of her own and her mother's wrongs, should feel any special affection for the child of her mother's supplanter. However, she was too good a Christian to show any resentment toward the infant who had been put over her. That her attitude was as kind as could be expected in the circumstances is shown by her letter to Henry: "My sister Elizabeth is in good health (thanks to Our Lord), and such a child toward as I doubt not but your Highness shall have cause to rejoice in time coming."

Soon they were to be sisters in misfortune as well as in blood. After the ruling of Cranmer's court in May, 1536, Elizabeth was herself declared illegitimate, and this was further emphasized by special act of Parliament, under which she, with Mary, was debarred from the succession. It was now, in fact, made treason for anyone to assert that either of the "Ladies" was of legitimate birth. And the statute affirming their bastardy, and imposing the penalty of treason on whoever denied it, remained unrepealed even after they had been named by Henry's will as in the line of succession. If the English have a rather poor reputation for logicality, the explanation may perhaps be found in the bewildering inconsistency introduced among them by the Protestant revolution.

After Anne Boleyn's execution Elizabeth, now close to three years, was sent to Hunsdon Hall in Hereford. Mary went with her, and after the birth of Edward the boy joined his sisters. Perhaps if his mother had lived he might have been kept at home with her; more likely not: the age was little addicted to the modern cult of childhood. Besides, there was less danger from contagious diseases in rural districts, plague elsewhere being sporadic. In the house on the hill, with its pleasant view of the River Stort, life could be agreeable enough.

No doubt it was agreeable for the King's children, though their regimen was severe according to our notions. The dominant idea in the bringing up of the young seems to have been to get them out of their childhood as soon as possible. Thus Wriothesley, visiting them in 1539, wrote in high praise of the Lady Elizabeth that at the age of six she conducted herself with the gravity of forty. It was the greatest compliment he could pay.

But Lady Bryan had her troubles. Hardly before Elizabeth was out of her infancy, and at a time when she was having "great pain with her great teeth," the governess had to write to Cromwell, who was then ruling everything in England, protesting against the orders that had been issued that the child was to take her meals at the adult table. "Alas, my lord," she says, "it is not meet for a child of her age to keep such rule yet. I promise you, my lord, I dare not take it upon me to keep her Grace in health an she keep that rule. For there she will see divers meats, and fruits, and wine, which it would be hard for me to restrain her Grace from. Ye know, my lord, there is no place of correction there; and she is too young to correct greatly. I know well, an she be there, I shall neither bring her up to the King's Grace's honour, nor hers, nor to her health, nor to my poor honesty." It is a sensible letter, and what Lady Margaret asked was granted. But it makes one shudder at the complaint that there was no "place of correction" available. The right sort of dark hole, suitable for the chastisement and confining of refractory infants, was the one defect in an otherwise suitable establishment.

What is still more startling is to learn from the same letter of the poor provision that had been made for the King's daughter in the matter of clothes. Perhaps it was due to this early experience that she displayed in later life so inordinate a love for every sort of finery. At all events, Lady Bryan had to appeal to Cromwell that the Lady Elizabeth "May have some raiment; for she hath neither gown, nor kirtle, nor petticoat, nor no manner of linen, nor smocks, nor kerchiefs, nor sleeves, rails, body-stychets, mufflers, nor biggens. . . . I have driven off as long as I can, that by my troth I can drive it off no longer." The appeal did not go unanswered. Though he was at the time conducting such a terror that, as Erasmus put it, men felt "as if a scorpion lay sleeping under every stone," he found time to deal with so unusual a piece of business as a little girl's wardrobe. Outside the scope of state affairs he was kindly; in some incomprehensible way he contrived to combine with his ruthlessness a charity that fed a large number of poor every day at his door. Elizabeth's tatterdemalion condition was due to nothing worse than masculine thoughtlessness. She was promptly sent for and measured for new clothes.

We need not ascribe to parsimony what we hear of Elizabeth's making a shirt for her brother when he was six. This was merely an indication that she was getting the training in needlework then, very correctly, considered part of every girl's education. We may also suppose that this glimpse of Elizabeth in a domestic moment indicates the tenderness felt by both sisters for their delicate, white-faced, precocious, and rather priggish brother. With that frigid acidulousness that was so disagreeable a feature of the diary he was soon to keep, he records that his whole life until he was seven was spent among women. On the women's part, natural affection was entwined with pity, and both were entwined with and heightened by awe. For though Edward was not robust, his sisters looked upon him as destined to be King of England and the father of a line of kings. Almost the last thing in the world the six-year-old shirtmaker could have looked for was her own long career of turbulence, chicane, and glory.

2

Ascham's Pupil

HENRY VIII, though given to making disparaging remarks about women, had a much better opinion of their intelligence than he allowed to appear. It may be that the disparaging remarks took their origin from his perception of the fact that, quick as his own intelligence was, that of several of his wives was at least as good. This was especially true of Katherine of Aragon who, as his first wife, probably had a good deal to do with awakening his antifeminism: for nearly twenty years it was she who conducted state affairs while the King played and hunted. This might have been readily forgiven had she not been tactless enough to remind Henry that the greatest victory of his reign — that of Flodden — was won by her while he was in France. She touched him there at one of his most sensitive points: his vanity demanded that he be famous as a conqueror of men as well as of women, virile in all respects. The response of his hopelessly immature character was to affect a contempt for women's brains. It came out in the famous sneer of the last years of his life when Katherine Parr dared to disagree with him on a point in theology. He got even by calling her a "great clerk"; surely she ought to have remembered who, while Arthur was still Prince of Wales, had been destined for the see of Canterbury!

The truth, however, is that Henry — the friend of Sir Thomas More, that father of learned women — had advanced ideas about feminine education. He brought over Vives, the Spanish scholar, to draw up a minutely detailed pedagogical plan for Mary, and the King was immensely proud of the Princess's linguistic and musical accomplishments, though he would not have been Henry had he not flattered himself that her talents were paternally derived. So now with the education of Elizabeth. The series of celebrated tutors — William Grindal and Richard Cox (afterwards Bishop of Ely) and Roger Ascham and Sir John Cheke (upon whose name Milton permits himself a somewhat facile rhyme in the sonnet about "teaching King Edward Greek") — were quite the best men for the purpose Henry could have secured.

In Elizabeth they were fortunate in having a first-class mind to develop. Even before they took over the tutoring she was unusually well prepared for what they had to impart. Ascham, for instance, has been generally credited with teaching the girl her exquisite script. But however much he may have improved it, that script was beautiful before either Ascham or his predecessor Grindal took her in charge. We can still gaze admiringly at the manuscript of the translation she made when eleven of Margaret of Navarre's dull poem *The Mirror of the Sinful Soul* (a composition in very different vein from that Lutheran's *Heptameron*). Even if in this translation, as in the others with which she occupied her leisure moments in later life, Elizabeth did not always take the trouble to be strictly accurate, at least it was a notable achievement for a girl of her years. One is left wondering where a child could be found today capable of so much.

The forcing process must have begun early, as was customary in those days of ruthlessly driven precocity, and presumably it was entrusted in the beginning to Katherine Ashley, who was to remain with Elizabeth until her death in 1565. If Mrs. Ashley was, as events were to prove, a not very wise friend, she must have been a highly competent governess.

After Katherine Parr, at the age of thirty-one, married the King in 1543 (as her third husband), she took Elizabeth under her wing and brought her to Court. There she supervised the girl's education. There, too, Lady Margaret Douglas, the King's Scottish niece who was to be the mother of Darnley, lived with the royal children.

The arrangement did not prove very successful and came,

before long, to an abrupt end. The new Queen — the "great clerk" — was a Lutheran in her sympathies and we may surmise began to instil her ideas into Elizabeth's head. The Queen evidently took a fancy to her stepdaughter and was indiscreet enough to venture the prophecy that the "bastard" would yet wear the crown. That — quite apart from any Protestant sentiments that the child's prim little mouth may have echoed — would have been amply sufficient to account for the animosity the King showed his daughter. But it may also have been, in part, that Henry could not bear to have near him one who was in so many ways like Anne Boleyn. If we want to look for a still subtler reason we may find it in Elizabeth's resemblance to himself: Henry was no man to endure the sight of his real face in such a mirror. Probably all these factors operated. At all events, Elizabeth was soon packed off to Hatfield.

Henry grew, with the advance of age, increasingly orthodox and devout. His devoutness made him grieve that the ulcer in his leg had now made it impossible for him to genuflect to the Blessed Sacrament; his orthodoxy (to his own schism) made him burn Friar John Forest for the heresy of affirming the spiritual supremacy of the Pope. All the same Henry was not very careful about the orthodoxy of the tutors provided for his children. Cheke and Grindal, however, no doubt found it prudent to conceal, for the time being, their Protestant leanings. As for Cox, he was a refugee abroad from 1544 to 1548 and was not appointed tutor until Somerset's protectorate. Ascham began to teach Elizabeth at the same time; but he had directed Grindal in his work as, after he had given up his tutorship, he continued to exercise a general supervision over Elizabeth's studies. The bending of her mind toward heresy could not have been avowed while Henry lived, yet it was surreptitious and insidious, and may be set to the score of Katherine Ashley. Nevertheless we rightly think of Roger Ascham as the teacher who had most to do with the developing of Elizabeth's intellectual gifts.

At this time Elizabeth showed a strain of adolescent piety. It passed, and few more secular-minded women have lived than the great Queen; but at least she went through a pious phase. Thus we find her at the age of twelve writing out an Italian sermon as a gift for her brother, and busily translating prayers into all the languages in which she was being instructed.[1] If these prayers and sermons were not always of a strictly orthodox character, they could be explained away as being mere exercises if the King should ever happen to look over his daughter's copybooks, which in the case of a man so careless about details was not likely to happen.

Though the masculine tutors provided for the royal children were hardly of the genius of the ribald Skelton who had had charge of Henry in his youth and to whom the Prince owed the development of his own streak of genius, they were at least learned and able men — possibly more learned than Skelton and certainly more thorough. Ascham was in addition a man of remarkable versatility. He was to become Latin Secretary to Queen Mary in 1553 (with special permission to remain a Protestant), a diplomat, and, in the end, a prebendary. As a teacher he was no doubt all the better for not being entirely a bookworm. One remembers his treatise on archery, an attempt to revive that declining sport in England; and his humanity is revealed by the not altogether creditable fact Camden records of him, that he was always in financial straits because of his passion for dicing and cockfighting. This little weakness, we may suspect, served to endear him further to the Lady Elizabeth.

There was no difference whatever between the course of studies followed by Edward and that followed by his sister. In the *Scholemaster* we have Ascham's own account of his brilliant pupil. It was written after Elizabeth had become Queen, and we might discount it as the kind of flattery she expected to receive, were it not amply borne out by all the facts. "Point forth six of the best given gentlemen of this court," he says, "and all together they show not so much good will, spend so much time, bestow so many hours daily, orderly, and con-

---

[1] Her study of Melancthon's *Loci Communes,* a kind of compendium of Protestant theology and political theory, belongs to a later period.

stantly, for the increase of learning and knowledge, as doth the Queen's Majesty herself. Yea, I believe, that beside her perfect readiness in Latin, Italian, French, and Spanish, she readeth here now at Windsor more Greek every day, than some prebendary of this Church doth read Latin in a whole week. . . . Amongst all the benefits that God hath blessed me withal, next the knowledge of Christ's true religion, I count this the greatest, that it pleased God to call me to be one poor minister in setting forward those excellent gifts of learning in this most excellent prince." Ascham had sound cause for pride in his pupil.

It was a day when Greek had suddenly become all the rage in learned circles in England. That Latin was not neglected is attested by the version Elizabeth made of the *Consolation of Philosophy* of Boethius and her translations from Horace. But Greek was the all-important study in the eyes of the Humanists. Therefore we find Elizabeth, under Ascham's direction, turning Plutarch and Xenophon into English, and we may be sure that the surviving manuscripts do not represent the whole of her output. For Greek we hear of Isocrates, Demosthenes, Sophocles, the New Testament, and St. Cyprian as among her textbooks. She also studied Hebrew, though of this she probably got only a smattering.

Along with a close study of the classics went an equally close study of modern languages. As Queen, Elizabeth used to boast that, when she was a girl, she knew six languages better than English itself. And toward the close of her life, speaking to de Maisse, the French Ambassador, she could afford the joke, "It was no marvel to make a woman talk; it were far harder to teach her to hold her tongue." Though she did not have a good French accent, she was very fluent, as she was also in Italian and Spanish. Indeed, she used to parade her proficiency, talking loudly so that everybody might admire. Sometimes, it is to be suspected, they admired in the Latin sense, but they never failed in compliments: much can be condoned in royalty. Yet after making all due allowances, it must be fully admitted that Elizabeth had a very wide culture. Her solid knowledge of ancient and modern tongues was to be one of her greatest

Queen Elizabeth

assets in the tortuous diplomatic intrigues, the endless foreign correspondence of her reign. She could supervise all the details of such matters herself.

As valuable an asset was her extraordinary English prose style, one never equalled for meaning as little as possible, while seeming to say a great deal and to be packed with significance. And the same virtuosity in the ambiguous is to be found no less in the Queen's French, Spanish, and Italian state papers. This she could hardly have derived from Ascham, whose own style was, for those days, notably lucid. More probably his influence is to be found in her other literary manner: nobody could be more direct and to the point than Elizabeth when it suited her purpose — that is, when there was no object in dissimulation. In so far as anybody can be taught to write — to write in a vivid and personal style, as compared with the wooden correctness which is all a pedagogue can impart — Elizabeth owes the crown of her education to Ascham.

His method of instruction was to make his pupil translate from (say) Greek into English, and then from English back again into Greek or some other language. No better device for acquiring lordship over words is to be discovered, though few teachers could be found today so hardy as to use it. More than once it has been suggested that it was because of this that Elizabeth's English often reads like a translation, by which it is meant that her English is studied and stilted. The criticism is to some extent just. At the same time we should never forget what I have already mentioned — that other Elizabethan style of a vigorous vernacular. Whenever she is involved it is because she found it convenient to be so.

We have no right to expect in state papers an attention to prose cadence. Yet in them, along with much that shows an indifference to literary niceties — for they had often to be written in a hurry — there are many instances of the fall, the artful coiling, and the mounting climax of phrase and sound possible only to one of genuine literary parts. Even as a child she displayed, perhaps even a trifle ostentatiously, the talents she already possessed. Thus, writing to her brother, when he was

Ascham's Pupil

king, a letter accompanying a portrait of herself, her choice of
words and her rhythm unmistakably indicate an artist. "For
though from the picture the colours may fade by time, may give
by weather, may be spotted by chance; yet the other [she is referring to her affection] nor time with her swift wings shall over-
take, nor misty clouds with their lowerings may darken, nor
chance with her slipping foot may overthrow." However artificial the sentiment, the style could hardly be better. Elizabeth
encompassed within the scope of her versatility the power to
have been a great writer. For to her masterly handling of language she added imagination and a wealth of ideas and wit
and force and, perhaps most important of all, the special con-
junction of the brain and nerves required. All she lacked was
pity of heart, and even that might have been permitted its
flowering had hers been another lot. If Elizabeth had not been
a Queen she could have become a famous author.

In poetry, too, she showed some talent, though less talent
than in prose. The challenge to the authenticity of some of the
pieces attributed to her is, I suspect, unconsciously based for
the most part upon the inability of bookish men to understand
how a woman of action could also be a poet. Such pedants
might read again Carlyle's profoundly true argument that the
great poet is potentially great in any capacity: that Shakespeare
could have led armies or built cathedrals as well as he constructed plays. Leonardo da Vinci, however much he may seem
to stand alone in actual performance, is really the typical artist
and was unique only in his opportunities for rounding out his
gifts. Elizabeth stands as an instance of the opposite type of
genius. A poet *manqué*, but a poet, wrote the lines opening
with "The doubt of future foes exiles my present joy." A poet,
without any qualification to the title, wrote the lyric whose
first stanza is:

When I was young and fair, and favour graced me,
  Of many was I sought, their mistress for to be;
But I did scorn them all, and answered them therefore,
    Go, go, go, seek some otherwhere,
      Importune me no more.

19

And if that despite its admirable management of verbal music is dismissed as conventional, at least the lyric she wrote after the departure of Alençon in 1581 has a personal and sincere note. The whole poem will be quoted in its proper place later; at the moment, as a sample of its quality, I quote the central stanza:

> My care is like my shadow in the sun —
> Follows me flying — flies when I pursue it;
> Stands and lives by me — does what I have done;
> This too familiar care doth make me rue it.
> No means I find to rid him from my breast,
> Till by the end of things it be suppressed.

All the extant poems, however, belong to a later period; there is no indication that the Lady Elizabeth ever tried her hand at verse. The regimen of the worthy Ascham was too strenuous to permit anything beyond the business in hand. What he did, following Grindal and Grindal's predecessor, was to provide a broad general culture. He drilled Elizabeth to habits of study; he sharpened her intelligence. He considered that enough.

Neither he nor anybody else (unless we believe the story of Katherine Parr's prophecy) had any expectation that Elizabeth was to be Queen. For though King Edward, who succeeded to the throne at ten, was not robust, there was no reason as yet for anticipating his early death, as is shown by Somerset's invasion of Scotland to compel that country to yield her Queen to be England's bride. In any event the bar of Elizabeth's illegitimacy remained and was sufficient to prevent any serious attempt to marry her off as a pawn in the diplomatic game. She was left alone with her books. Her future for the first eighteen years of her life held so little promise as not to be worth consideration by statesmen engrossed in much more important affairs.

What went on in her mind we do not know, except that we can be sure that a mind so acute and so interested in political happenings was busy with its secret thoughts. She may well have brooded over her mother's fate; if so, the tight-lipped girl of thirteen who appears in the first picture of her was careful not to let anyone know what was in her thoughts. Of them we know nothing, though we can infer a precocious development of judgment and of cunning that was soon to stand her in good stead. She was on the verge of a crisis that was to make her ill for four years and to leave a permanent scar upon her soul. Steeled by this experience, she steered successfully past the shoals of high treason and matrimony. And if such an experience was not a part of her formal education, she learned from it something not to be found in books: it was the determining factor in the formation of her character.

3

~~~~~~

The Admiral

HENRY had made all his dispositions for the succession.
Edward, of course, was to follow him. About the Prince's
legitimacy — Katherine having died before Henry married Jane
Seymour — no question could be raised. But the unheard-of
step was taken of getting Parliament to concede the King the
right to name his son's successors, if the boy died childless; and
the successors named were the two Princesses, who had previously been declared illegitimate and debarred from the throne
by statute. The alternative was to admit the rightful claim of
the little Queen of Scots, granddaughter of Henry's sister
Margaret.

But all those who stemmed from Margaret were ruled out.
Upon the death of her husband, James IV, she had married the
Earl of Angus, only to get a papal annulment later, and to take
a third husband. Henry wrote sternly to inform his erring sister
that marriage was indissoluble; though he later gave what
amounted to justification of her conduct by divorcing Katherine, he regarded his as a special case, and vented his displeasure
upon Margaret by disinheriting Mary Queen of Scots and the
child his sister bore to Angus. She was Margaret Douglas, and
was to be Darnley's mother.

Henry turned instead to the descendants of his younger
sister Mary, who had married Charles Brandon, Duke of Suf-
folk. Their daughter Frances had married the Marquis of
Dorset (who was to be created Duke of Suffolk in 1551), and
Lady Jane Grey was one of the three girls born of this marriage
who were now put into the line of succession — though only after
Henry's own children and in the event of the Marchioness of
Dorset's not bearing a son.

The Admiral

It is useless to look for anything like logic from Henry's passionate and confused mind. Before Edward was born, and while the King was still without a "legitimate" heir, he had actually toyed with the idea of declaring his bastard, Henry, Duke of Richmond to be his successor. But Richmond had died at the age of seventeen in 1536, poisoned, it was suspected, by Anne Boleyn and her brother.[1] Had he not died and had Edward not come into the world, the dangerous plan would probably have been followed, and would certainly have resulted in civil war. For though the King's will would no doubt have had authority, even in so monstrous a decision, with many people, at least as many others would have supported the rightful claims of Mary.

That contingency, fortunately, did not arise. Edward was recognised as heir by everybody, though before long intrigues began as to who should be the delicate boy's successor in the event of his dying without issue. To get him under his thumb, and so master any emergency that might arise, Edward Seymour, Earl of Hertford and the young King's uncle, persuaded the Council to declare him Protector, though under Henry's will he had been put only on an equality with the other fifteen executors.

Hertford's brother, Thomas Seymour, who had only been appointed to the board of advisers to the executors, was placated — or so it was hoped — by being created Lord Admiral and Baron Seymour of Sudeley. As his ambition was quite as great as his brother's, he was from the beginning bitterly disappointed.

He had, indeed, plans of his own — plans formed even before Henry's death. His first idea had been to marry the Lady Mary, but as Mary would not so much as listen to his proposal, he offered his hand to Elizabeth, almost before the King's body was cold.

Elizabeth, though only fourteen, was prudent. She was aware

[1] Anne may have hoped to save herself by removing a male claimant and so leaving the way still clear to her own daughter: that was the only basis for suspicion. But the poison charge was not established.

that the Council would never agree to such a marriage, and that if she and Seymour took the bit between their teeth they would be liable to a charge of high treason. Yet she did not refuse him outright; all that she asked was that he wait two years.

That period was much too long to suit Seymour's schemes. He at once went to Katherine Parr — who was an old "flame" of his — and persuaded her to marry him. As he could not get the King's daughter, he took the King's widow. Their secret marriage occurred thirty-four days after Henry's death. Then, having accomplished his purpose, he "got round" his brother and the Council to sanction a marriage which, altogether unknown to them, already existed. The wealth of Katherine, and her rank, for the moment contented him. But perhaps this jovial and devious scoundrel was merely purposing to use Katherine as a means of obtaining Elizabeth. Subsequent events would suggest as much. In the meanwhile he consolidated his position. His pickings as Lord Admiral were plentiful. Sent out to exterminate a nest of pirates in the Scilly Isles, he came instead to an understanding with Thomessin, their leader, that he was to receive a share of the spoils. It was an admirable little arrangement that provided Elizabeth with a model when she became Queen.

He had contrived to get Elizabeth into his own household at Chelsea. And there she was to complete her education — though in ways that nobody bargained for. As a minor point it might be mentioned that it was from the Admiral that she acquired her rich vocabulary of oaths — some of the fo'castle variety, others theological, all salty or sultry. Seymour had been considered, after Henry, as the most consummate artist in profanity in the kingdom. Elizabeth showed herself an apt pupil, and may have been in Shakespeare's mind when he created Hotspur's wife.

The marriage of the Queen Dowager did not improve relations between the Seymour brothers. The Admiral's wife claimed precedence over the Duchess of Somerset, and the Protector was naturally incensed at the march the Admiral had stolen upon him. Even so, Thomas Seymour was not satisfied. Though piracy was lucrative, it offered nothing compared to the loot Edward Seymour was obtaining. The great pile of Somerset House going up in the Strand, for the building of which several London churches were demolished to provide materials, was itself an affront. Not that the Admiral was scandalised by sacrilege; it was merely that he had an obscure feeling of having been wronged.

He was a finely built, handsome man of thirty-eight with a big auburn beard, a notable rider in the tilting yard and a famous lady-killer. If he had not married before this, it was because he had found irresponsible dalliance so much more to his taste. He had the good looks and the false kind of affability that many women find irresistible. Even the shocking language which made them put their fingers to their ears was, with some of them, an additional grace, a proof of bluff manliness. But Edward Seymour, though a simple, soldierly man, knew Thomas too well not to be vaguely suspicious. He had reason to be more suspicious than he actually was.

At once the Admiral began to work upon Edward the "Codlin and Short" device for all that it was worth. The Protector was inclined to be a bit brusque and dictatorial with the young King; accordingly the Admiral cultivated his nephew in a different style. The jolly and freehanded uncle used to tip the boy lavishly, thinking the money well spent. On one occasion we hear of his quietly passing £40 to Sir John Cheke, the tutor, telling him to keep half of it for himself. It was a shrewd provision: Cheke's mouth had to be shut. We also hear that Edward, though a frigid little prig, used the tips for making bets. His gratitude to the Admiral was expressed in surreptitious notes left in an agreed-upon place under a rug. Edward was apparently quite won over by the avuncular charms.

Thomas Seymour needed to win him over: he had a dangerous game to play. Having failed to marry Elizabeth, a possible successor to Edward, he concocted a new scheme. It was that Edward should marry Lady Jane Grey; and Lady Jane was, according to the terms of Henry's will, the next in line for the throne after Mary and Elizabeth. To round out his plans the Admiral managed to get the consent of Jane's father, Dorset (afterwards Duke of Suffolk) to his own wardship over the girl. The fact reveals what must have been in Seymour's mind: he was to get control of the King, then, in the event of Edward's early death, Lady Jane was to be proclaimed Queen in her own right, and Mary and Elizabeth ousted.[2]

To be on the safe side, the Admiral lured Elizabeth to Chelsea, where he could keep his eye on her and seize her person in case of necessity. He would not have hesitated to kill her had the situation called for murder, but as he always had several alternative designs in his mind, he may have still hoped that a chance would come for his marrying her. Here he overshot the mark. His amorous propensities got the better of his judgment; he began to make love to Elizabeth.

It was all done in a spirit of good clean fun, so that the Admiral, when the talk began, protested that nothing more than a little playful romping had been intended. Indeed, some of the defenders of Elizabeth still insist that it was nothing more. Everybody knew what a lively fellow the Admiral was. Against this, however, we have both the true character of the man and acts that could have been dictated only by a cunning ambition. There is no villain quite so wicked as the one who wears a mask of bland innocence — unless it be that other type of villain who pretends to be a high-spirited playboy.

When the goings on at Chelsea came out in 1549 the following was the reluctant deposition of Katherine Ashley upon being sent to the Tower. She said as little as possible to incriminate Elizabeth, but she knew that it would not do to attempt a complete denial. She therefore admitted that "At Chelsea, after my Lord Thomas was married to the Queen, he would come many mornings into the Lady Elizabeth's chamber when she was ready, and sometimes before she was ready, and

---

[2] We must remember that Northumberland's later plot also called for the ousting of Elizabeth no less than Mary. The Protestant heroine would have got short shrift from these Protestant champions, among whom was Cecil. The gang in control were completely indifferent to anything except their own advantage.

sometimes before she did rise;[3] and if she were up, he would
bid her good-morrow, and so go forth to his chamber, and
sometimes go to her maidens and play with them. And if the
Princess were in bed, he would open the curtains and bid her
good-morrow, and she would go further into bed." At the same
time Mrs. Ashley added, what may have been true enough, that
on two mornings the Queen was with the Admiral and that they
both tickled Elizabeth while she was in bed. That, of course,
made it all very harmless. For good measure she related how on
one occasion, "he romped with her in the garden, and cut her
gown, being black cloth, into a hundred pieces." And to show
how innocent even that really was she went on to say that when
she scolded Elizabeth for permitting this "she answered, she
could not strive at all, for the Queen held her while the Lord
Admiral cut her dress." The witness revealed, in short, only
what was already partly known. Yes, there *had* been barge trips
at night made by the Admiral and the Lady Elizabeth; nor
could Mrs. Ashley altogether deny "other light parts." But her
artful loyalty minimised the significance of everything. Elizabeth was duly grateful and, in her turn, loyal. One is left
wondering to what extent she learned her first lessons in
duplicity from her clever governess. Yet baffled as the examiners
in the Tower found themselves to be, they could hardly have
believed that Seymour's wife regarded these escapades with the
indulgence attributed to her by Mrs. Ashley. They were, however, unable to question her themselves, because by the time
the enquiry was made, Katherine Parr was dead.

One of the admissions dragged from Mrs. Ashley was that the
Admiral had been jealous of the manservant who used to carry
baskets of coal to Elizabeth's room. Once he had been there, it
appears, for three hours with the door shut. The only reason
the Council did not probe more deeply into that matter was
that they were only faintly interested in the question as to
whether or not Elizabeth had misconducted herself with a

---

[3] It is easy to deduce from the phrasing of all this how these admissions were
drawn out piecemeal, each bit being in response to a question following up the
last answer. We must admire at the same time how Mrs. Ashley stressed anything
that could be made to seem innocent.

groom; after all, the founder of the family, Owen Tudor, was a servant of Catherine of Valois, Henry V's widow, before he married her — if there ever was a legal marriage. What the Council was investigating in 1549 was Elizabeth's relations with the Lord Admiral. For in that there might be involved a dynastic plot.

The upshot of the enquiry was to leave little doubt that there had been unseemly behaviour, to say the least, at Chelsea; on the other hand, it could not be proved that Elizabeth had aimed at anything beyond a momentary amusement. Her youthful inexperience was in her favour; so also was the common knowledge that the Admiral could never resist making love to a woman. All that can be said with any certainty is that the strange Seymour *ménage* broke up, and that it did so because the complaisant Queen Dowager at last put her foot down. She had seen Elizabeth kissing a man — possibly the groom — in the gallery of the house and, still worse, had caught her husband with Elizabeth "in his arms." Just what was meant by that ambiguous phrase we do not know; at all events Katherine took a serious view of the incident. Elizabeth was sent in May, 1548, to Cheshunt to get her out of the way of the dangerous attentions of admirals and grooms.

Yet there was no open quarrel between the girl and the woman; Katherine wanted no scandal. Elizabeth probably had a plausible explanation of the matter: she was good at such things, and the Dowager found it advisable to accept the explanation. Seymour continued to write to her, and she to him and Katherine. We have a letter from Elizabeth to the Admiral's wife on the subject of her approaching confinement, wishing her a "most lucky deliverance" and signed "Your most humble daughter." Katherine had been six months gone with child at the time of the girl's departure — her first pregnancy in four marriages. One cannot help surmising that Henry VIII had married her in order to prove his questioned virility. If he could succeed where two previous husbands had failed, that would indeed have been a triumph. Such was the constitution of that vain and immature mind!

The Admiral

It was the Admiral who enjoyed the triumph, though it hastened his undoing. On August 30 Katherine bore a daughter and died a few days later. On her deathbed she spoke wildly saying that "those about her" — clearly meaning her husband and Elizabeth — would be glad to see her die. "Why, sweetheart," protested the Admiral, "I could you no hurt." She looked at him sadly and answered, "No, my Lord, I think so. But, my Lord, you have given me many shrewd thrusts."

With Katherine gone, the Admiral made the mistake of beginning to woo Elizabeth again. At once the early morning romps at Chelsea, the river excursions, and the "other light parts" — concerning which we may be sure gossip had previously come to the Council's ears — took on a new significance. The Council had been tricked once before at the time of Seymour's marriage to Henry's widow; they did not propose to be tricked a second time by a marriage between Seymour and Henry's daughter. The Admiral was arrested and charged with high treason.

Despite all his cunning, he had not been sufficiently cautious in his enquiries about Elizabeth's property. His own estates being in the west of England, he had put enquiries afoot as to whether her patrimony could not be drawn from western property. And when an investigation was started it was learned that he had bribed the controller of the Bristol mint to supply him with £10,000. What could this be for except to finance a rebellion? People who had hitherto been inclined to smile at his dreams of grandeur — at that dream of his, for instance, of carving out a kingdom for himself in America — now were convinced that he was a dangerous man. They remembered that he had obtained the wardship of Lady Jane Grey with the object of marrying her to the King. But they knew that the boy was only twelve and so unable to marry for some years, and that his increasing delicacy had begun to make it seem likely that he would never live to be married at all. Evidently the Admiral now considered Elizabeth a vastly stronger card to play than Lady Jane. As he had command of the navy, he could proclaim Elizabeth Queen and become King as her husband.

With the Protestant interest behind him he anticipated scant difficulty in dealing with Mary.

Upon his fall, his friends dropped away or became his accusers. His design of ingratiating himself with the King by means of tips and a clandestine correspondence came out. Everything fitted together to damn him. Even his dealings with the Scilly pirates, hitherto winked at, were put into the list of thirty-three offences with which he was charged.

Everything fitted in, indeed, against the Admiral, most beautifully. But was not Elizabeth guilty, too? That was why the Council arrested Mrs. Ashley and Thomas Parry, afterwards to be Sir Thomas and a member of Elizabeth's own Council. It was at this time that the gay doings at Chelsea in the previous year were gone into. Now Sir Thomas Tyrwhitt, supported by a group of lawyers, went to Hatfield to question Elizabeth. The moment was one of extreme danger to her, because if it could have been proved that she had listened favourably to the Admiral's proposal of marriage she could have been arraigned for high treason. She understood her danger; she circumvented it.

Of her own capacity to lie her way through anything she could be sure. Could she be sure of what Parry and Mrs. Ashley would say? Luckily they proved to be staunch. They had all agreed to tell the same story and stick to it; as Tyrwhitt wrote, "They all sing the same tune." Parry, however, threatened with the rack, made certain admissions; and Mrs. Ashley, confronted with these, had to admit them too. But loyally she took the blame upon herself. There *had* been some playfulness liable to misconstruction during the old days at Chelsea; she was a truthful woman and could not deny that. But as for the talk about marriage it all came to this: she had made jokes to the Lady Elizabeth about her marrying the Admiral; and she and her young charge had told fortunes with cards, and the "man" was the Admiral. All of which was merely a game to beguile the long evenings. Of course it was impossible for her to speak of what might have been in the Admiral's mind; as to the Lady Elizabeth she could testify that *she* at least had never seriously entertained the thought of marriage.

The Admiral

All this may be true enough as far as it goes; but we are left with a strong suspicion that Mrs. Ashley knew a great deal more than she told. When the examiners could extract no more information from the prisoners in the Tower, Tyrwhitt took their depositions to Hatfield. "False wretch!" Elizabeth exclaimed when Parry's testimony was read to her, though with a quick realisation that he had said nothing sufficient for a charge of treason. Her gratitude to the "false wretch" and to Mrs. Ashley was shown by the fact that she kept them both close to her after her accession.

The sixteen-year-old girl had shown a masterly duplicity and a steely calm that one cannot help but admire. Tyrwhitt could wring no admission from her. The outburst against Parry, "False wretch! he promised not to confess to the death," was as adroit a piece of fencing as can be imagined. Had she *not* burst out, Tyrwhitt would have been sure there was much more concealed. That seeming inadvertency saved her: what was really a sigh of relief she knew would be taken as a cry of dismay. To her credit it must be added that when the questioners suggested that she confess, and throw the blame on Mrs. Ashley, Elizabeth refused. It was loyal of her, and all her life long she showed this kind of loyalty to her friends; but it was also, of course, the safest thing she could do. She guessed that a trap had been set for her, and dextrously she avoided it. Tyrwhitt had to write back to the Council that his inquisition had failed. "And yet," he added, "I can see from her face that she is guilty."

But looks, however guilty, are not evidence. It was precisely evidence against her of the kind wanted that could not be produced. Ladies' heads cannot be cut off merely because men have kissed and fondled them. Even on this point Tyrwhitt blundered. When he tried to frighten Elizabeth by telling her that it was generally believed in the country that she was with child by the Admiral, she instantly perceived the weak point in the attack. So that was what people were saying! She sat down and wrote in high indignation to Protector Somerset: "My Lord, these are shameful slanders, for the which, beside

31

the great desire I have to see the King's Majesty, I shall most heartily desire your Lordship that I may come to the Court after your first determination, that I may show myself as I am." After such a challenge the matter had to be dropped. It did not prove that Elizabeth's relations with the Admiral had been innocent, but Tyrwhitt had been manoeuvred into putting Somerset in the wrong. Elizabeth followed up her advantage by insisting that a proclamation of her good conduct be issued and that Parry and Mrs. Ashley be released from the Tower.

There was nothing, however, she could do to help the Admiral. Yet he was not greatly disturbed by his situation, for he counted upon a well-tipped nephew coming to the rescue. When brought before the Council he acted with disdain and refused to answer their questions. Their response was to give him no trial but to condemn him by bill of attainder. It was passed on February 25, 1549, and on March 20 he was executed, Edward readily signing the warrant, and cold-bloodedly noting down the fact in his journal. Elizabeth's comment was "This day died a man with much wit and little judgment." On the eve of his execution Seymour wrote letters to Mary and Elizabeth urging them to work for the Protector's downfall. On the scaffold he whispered to his servant, who had the notes sewn between the soles of his shoes, to be sure that they were safely delivered. Latimer described him in the official sermon as the man "most free from the fear of God that ever he knew or had heard of in England."

Despite Elizabeth's seeming indifference the affair was a profound shock to her, one that perhaps marked her for life. One historian has used the picturesque expression that she was ever afterwards married to Thomas Seymour's ghost. And von Klarwill has written: "A branch of modern medicine has imposed upon itself the task of fathoming such prostrations of the soul and their reactions. It has not ventured to draw under observation Elizabeth of the House of Tudor, because it would find itself face to face with a soul that was stronger than all the dogmas of psycho-analysis, which hold that it is impossible to bear up against such convulsions." It is not my intention to

ELIZABETH, AS PRINCESS
From the painting at Windsor Castle.   Artist unknown.

play the psychiatrist, but it must be recorded that there was a nervous breakdown following the Admiral's execution, one that lasted four years. We must call it that, though the doctors of the time had no name for the disease.

In this connexion it is necessary to enquire a little — reluctant as I am to go into such unsavoury matters — into the truth of Elizabeth's alleged sexual abnormality. If she really was, as Lady Shrewsbury years afterwards put it, "not as other women," it may well be that she made the discovery during her "rompings" with the Admiral. Though there can be no decision on the fact itself, however much such a fact would serve to explain much of her career, I must note the historical evidence, such as it is. Ben Jonson informed Drummond of Hawthornden that Elizabeth "had a membrana on her, which made her incapable of man, though for her delight she tried many." Brantôme said "she was unfit to be a wife," and added some explicit anatomical details which I need not reproduce. The Scotch Ambassador, Sir James Melville, wrote that she was "incapable of bearing children." And there are other contemporary documents to the same effect.[4] What may be significant is that after her death her body was not embalmed, as was customary. The Council must have been aware that there was a good deal of talk and wished to avoid a *post-mortem* examination. But the circumstance can be taken to prove no more than the existence of the gossip — and that the Council were afraid that it might be proved to be fact. Further than that we cannot go. No medical testimony exists.

As an instance of the kind of gossip that floated around, there is, in the manuscript life of Jane Dormer (afterwards Duchess of Feria), a story that Elizabeth during her stay at Cheshunt bore a child to Seymour. Later we hear of supposititious children by Leicester. One young man — if not one of Walsingham's spies, an adventurer playing his own hand — even presented himself at the Court of Spain as Elizabeth's son.

[4] These are noted in Pollard (p. 181). They include statements by Feria, Philip II, and Noailles. But they all, of course, merely record gossip. None of these witnesses was in a position to *know*.

Queen Elizabeth

There is not a particle of truth in any of these stories. The Virgin Queen probably died a virgin — in the technical sense. It is unlikely that she was, as ordinarily understood, anybody's mistress, though a whole string of lovers have been supplied for her. But it is even more unlikely that she lived chastely. I am inclined to believe that she went further with the Admiral than with any of the other men with whom her name is associated. I am also inclined to believe that at this time she made the discovery that true marriage could never be for her. Hence her endless chatter about virginity.

Mr. Lytton Strachey's suggestion that though there may have been no physical obstacle to marriage a psychological one may have been created by the Seymour affair strikes me, as do others of his suggestions, as altogether too subtle. Nor could the execution of the Admiral, I think, in itself have caused a nervous breakdown: this was something that was the possible conclusion of every political career in those days; it involved hardly more disgrace than being beaten in an election in ours. However distressed she was by it, Elizabeth was too hard and cold a person to lose her health on that account. But to have discovered that she could never live the life of a normal woman — she with her more than normal desire to prove her womanhood — would have sufficed to account for the long period of prostrations, as also for the frequent hysterical outbursts of her later life. Ben Jonson's version of her condition, though it cannot be confidently accepted, at least provides a working hypothesis.

Eventually and by degrees she pulled herself together. Her courage was too great to allow her to give way finally. She therefore hymned virginity, and in due time used her various marriage projects in the diplomatic game. Yet she repeatedly gave herself away, getting furious when anybody — man or woman — connected with the court married. Her objection to the marriage of her bishops was, I am convinced, due to this and not to any remnant of Catholic sentiment. By cruel mischance, impotence had condemned her to virginity. For that reason, as Sir Walter Raleigh (who should have known) said, "Her minions were commanded to uncomely employments." Elizabeth's, it is to be feared, was a case history for Krafft-Ebing.

So far this chapter has been concerned with Elizabeth's private affairs. It is necessary at this point to indicate briefly the chief events of Edward's reign, as they bear upon her own. Edward Seymour, having gained command of the Council, had himself created Duke of Somerset. He crushed the Scots in 1547 at the bloody battle of Pinkie Cleugh (or Musselburgh) in an effort to force a consent to the betrothal of their young Queen to Edward;[5] and he proceeded to the spoliation of the Church and the guilds and the endowed schools and to the establishment of Protestantism.

The principal matter to consider is the change in religion. Henry, it must not be forgotten, was a strong upholder of the Mass and the doctrine of the Real Presence. The party now in power saw their chance of consolidating their material gains by extirpating the Mass. Yet they had to proceed slowly. The Prayer Book issued in 1549 did little more than translate the Mass into English. In fact the first move of the government was merely to have the Communion administered in both kinds. Until 1549 they left the Latin Mass intact.

The liturgical use of the vernacular was, upon the whole, popular, as it would probably be among the majority of Catholics today. So far from denying essentials, it appeared to reaffirm them. If there were protests in Cornwall this was mainly because the Cornish still had their own language. Latin was more intelligible to them than English.

But even in the Prayer Book of 1549 there were phrases that were significant to theologians — Protestant implications. Having insinuated these the government felt strong enough in 1552 to issue another Prayer Book and forty-two articles, several of which were decidedly offensive to all Catholics. These articles, reduced in number and slightly modified, and that Prayer Book, slightly revised, formed the basis of the subse-

[5] It must be granted that politically the main lines of Somerset's Scotch policy were eminently sound. What he was aiming at was the union of the two kingdoms.

quent Elizabethan settlement. It was the work of Cranmer and was the greatest of all achievements of English prose.

The second Prayer Book, however, was not universally received. In many of the remote parts of the country Mass was said in Latin to the end of Edward's reign. And there was a rising in Devonshire and Cornwall which demanded the restoration of the Mass and the reservation of the Blessed Sacrament over the high altar in a hanging pyx. But this did not imply any general wish for the restoration of the Papal supremacy; on the contrary, the demand was specifically for the Henrician Six Articles.

The rebellion was put down, mainly by Italian and German mercenaries — a fact worth remembering. Sir Anthony Kingston, son of old Sir William, and a man who in his youth had been in the Pilgrimage of Grace, was one of the chief butchers. He had decided that Catholicism did not pay. By him recalcitrant priests were hanged from their steeples, and a special vengeance was taken on Exeter and Bodmin, the main centres of disaffection. Kingston possessed an unusual sort of humour. For he sent word to the Mayor of Bodmin that he was coming to dine with him, and that he would like to have a gallows prepared, as he had a man to hang. After dinner Sir Anthony took his host to look at the gallows. "Do you think it is strong enough?" he asked the mayor, who assured him that it was. "Then get you up," the guest said, "because it is for you." When the mayor protested against this sort of justice, Kingston blandly answered, "Sir, there is no remedy, for you have been a busy rebel." And up the mayor had to go.

With such ferocious pleasantries was the Edwardian religion imposed. The best that we can say of the government is that it made no active attempt to punish those who remained Catholic in belief, unless they resisted the official mode of worship. The chief martyr of the reign was Joan Bocher, who was condemned by Cranmer for heretical views on the Incarnation and burnt at Smithfield, another of the Protestant bishops who was to suffer under Mary assisting in the proceedings.

The people in the country parts, especially in the north and west, were still sincerely attached to their religion, even if they were not very well instructed in it. They did not understand what was going on and so fell an easy prey to the Reformers. For that matter, the majority of priests were not sufficiently well grounded in theology to grasp the significance of the Protestant moves. Catholicism rested more largely than now upon traditions that nobody so far had seriously questioned rather than upon strictly defined dogma: the work of the Council of Trent was still to be done. At this stage, therefore, Protestantism could be represented as being the bold, the enterprising, even the definite thing. But it had not yet come to be looked upon as specially English. Precisely those parts of the country that were most free from foreign influences most strongly resisted it — if only because they thought it outlandish.

If the mass of the people was almost unanimously Catholic (however vaguely), the governing classes were mostly indifferent to religion, looking upon it as serving a useful purpose in keeping the lower orders in subjection, but believing that any religion would serve equally well. Irreligious themselves, and yet wanting an established religion which they were not prepared to invent personally, they found it convenient to import a religion from abroad.

Those whom they did bring over — Italian, German, Swiss, and Polish heretics, men like Bucer; the ex-Dominican, Peter Martyr; and John à Lasco — were by no means favourably impressed with what they found. Thus Bucer wrote at Whitsuntide, 1550,[6] to Calvin to tell him that there was no religion in England; that of repentance, faith, and good works no one thought at all; that the ministers who professed the Evangelical doctrines held four or five livings at the same time and officiated in none; and that the lords were plundering the Church. With ill-concealed contempt for the morals and muddleheadedness of most of the English reformers, the foreign theologians set to work to fashion an official religion — the Anglican estab-

[6] The date of this letter might be noted. It was written while England still had the Mass of the 1549 Prayer Book. Nothing could indicate more clearly that a drastic Protestantism was already about to be thrust on the country.

lishment. But they were employed at all only because the governing classes saw that the extension of Protestantism would extend their own opportunities for loot. The cynics and the fanatics combined their forces.[7]

The theory was that the excess wealth of the Church was to be confiscated by the Crown only to be put to better social uses. For this theory, plausible arguments could be given: in but too many instances the Church was too rich for its own good. In practice, however, very little of the confiscated wealth found its way to the Crown. Even under Henry the King's servants were too strong to allow him to keep more than a small proportion of the spoils. Under Somerset and his gang, the King was a child who did whatever the Protector told him to do. Now as there were no monasteries left to loot, they turned their attention to the endowments of the bishoprics, of the guilds, and of the schools, pouching the proceeds themselves. Eighteen of these schools were refounded upon another basis and still bear King Edward's name. But as William Cobbett remarked in his vigorous way, the King Edward grammar schools are merely the ones that were spared. Among other results of the spoliation was an almost complete breakdown of the universities. Under the furious impact of the Reformation, as Green puts it, "The intellectual impulse of the New Learning died away."

It would perhaps be too great a simplification to describe the Reformation in England as a conspiracy of the rich; but it was certainly an economic revolution. The more enlightened — Somerset among them — therefore made a belated attempt to check the rapacity which was ruining the country for the benefit of a few; so laws against the inclosures of communal lands were passed. It proved, however, impossible to stem such a tide: laws could always be got around. Though it was enacted that

[7] The clear-sighted foreigners, though fanatical in their objects, were often cynical enough in their methods. Thus both Peter Martyr and Bucer told the honest, if rather stupid, Hooper, that he was making an unnecessary fuss about the use of vestments. So far from objecting to outward forms, he ought to welcome their retention because under their cover radical theological changes could be all the more easily made.

the landlords should leave sufficient land for their tenants, the question raised by Latimer remained: "Who shall judge what is sufficient?" The answer was only too plain: the landlords judged. They cared very little as to how many laws were passed, so long as those laws could not be enforced. Had a certain proportion of land to be returned again from pasture to the plough? Then a single furrow driven across a field made it arable land. And it must be admitted that of the men who were perpetrating these wrongs, most were still Catholic in belief, however lax they might be in practice. Not a passion for theological reform but naked greed was the motive. Catholic gentlemen were disinclined to make any strong protest against a government whose economic policy gave their class such boundless gain. Kett's rebellion — in which the grievances were material not spiritual — occurred only to be suppressed. In England alone in all Europe there was deliberately and violently destroyed all connexion between the peasantry and ownership. Long before the English Reformation, Sir Thomas More had seen that, under the system of inclosures, "sheep were eating men." Now his prophecy was fulfilled: The sheep had become tigers.

Things reached such a pass that Somerset had to be got rid of. But it was a serious error of judgment that those of Catholic sympathies on the Council — men like Wriothesley and Arundel — joined the cabal that was to make John Dudley (now Earl of Warwick and soon to be Duke of Northumberland) Protector. They knew Dudley to be a Catholic at heart and hoped that his coming into power would eventuate in a Catholic restoration. The man, in fact, did die protesting upon the scaffold his firm adhesion to the Catholic Faith, but the pressure of events forced him now further along the Protestant path than the declared Protestant Somerset had ever ventured to go. It was during Northumberland's administration that the relatively Catholic Prayer Book of 1549 was discarded in favour of the aggressively Protestant one of 1552.

The most that one can say in extenuation of the pusilanimity of the English Catholics is that they regarded what was happening in the religious sphere as merely ephemeral. By now they were expecting Edward to die, and they knew that if that happened Mary, about whose sincerity there could be no doubt, would bring back the Mass. She was holding out valiantly under pressure, however much her brother might be disturbed in conscience at having to tolerate "idolatry" in her case. Yet she was able to maintain her ground only by taking up the position that, until the King was of age, he could not rightfully exercise his supremacy over the Church. Nevertheless that technicality, for the time being, sufficed. Mary's real position was well known. The Catholic lords could afford to wait. In the meanwhile there was an opportunity not likely to occur again for enriching themselves.

The main factors that brought about the fall of Somerset were political and personal. He had managed affairs badly. The war with Scotland had cost £1,500,000, and had brought no results. Internal financial conditions were in a hopeless muddle, so that loans at the rate of 14 per cent had to be made and the currency further debased. In addition there was a sense of resentment against an arrogant man. Indeed, some of the members of the Council are suspected of having supported Somerset's execution of the Admiral in the crafty expectation that fratricide would recoil upon his own head. They had long wanted to get rid of him. Warwick's triumph over Kett made him strong enough to be successfully backed as the Protector's supplanter.

In all this Cecil played the part of a traitor to the man whose secretary he had been. He did not, it is true, appear publicly against his patron, but there exists a memorandum in his writing (Cotton Manuscripts: Titus B. 11) in which he had drawn up nineteen leading questions to be put to Somerset. There was in those days only one end to such a career: Somerset's head fell upon the same block upon which Northumberland was to lay his own eighteen months later.

Some reforms were, it is true, effected by the new administration, but in the large the internal situation remained unchanged. Though Edward was now betrothed to the daughter of the French King, in the hope of strengthening England's diplomatic position, it grew more and more evident that Edward was destined for an early death. Northumberland's standing at the same time grew increasingly precarious. He was even less popular than Somerset among people who remembered his base origin, that he was the son of Edmund Dudley, Henry VII's extortioner. Even those landowners who had hitherto acquiesced in the establishment of the "Gospel" had begun to turn wistful eyes in the direction of Mary. They were sick of upstart and greedy Protectors.

It was in such a situation that Northumberland decided upon his last desperate throw.

4

~~~~~~

Traitor's Gate

BEFORE Northumberland finally decided on the plot which brought him to a traitor's end, he toyed with another. How seriously we do not know; in any event it was soon discarded. The scheme was to marry Elizabeth to his eldest son, whose wife was to be divorced to clear the road. If Elizabeth was ever approached about it, she was, as usual, too wary to commit herself. Probably it was no more than one of those vague projects which a fertile mind easily formulates and then drops as impracticable.

The matter of the succession had to be decided at once, for Edward was now seen to be dying. If Mary was to be discarded under statutory law as illegitimate (which was the ground Northumberland came to take up), so also was Elizabeth. That left Mary Queen of Scots, whose accession would mean the long-desired union of the two kingdoms. But she was a Catholic; she was a foreigner; and it was feared that the close association of Scotland and France would mean French domination.

Yet the only means of keeping her out was the will of Henry VIII, and this had named Mary and Elizabeth to follow Edward. That will therefore must be discarded and Edward make a new devise. The consent of the Privy Council was forced by its master to the nomination of Lady Jane Grey, and she was married, by way of consolidating Northumberland's position, to his son, Lord Guildford Dudley. It was an extremely dangerous plan, but its dangers had perforce to be accepted if English Protestantism were to be maintained. Cranmer willingly signed the document, knowing the accession of Mary would mean his own ruin. Cecil, being more astute politically than either the Protector or the Archbishop, perceived that the plan was not likely to succeed and so signed unwillingly. He tried to get out of doing it at all by feigning illness. Nevertheless he was compelled to affix his signature, though afterwards he explained that he did so merely as a "witness."

Edward was now in a terrible condition. His hair and nails were falling out; eruptions were all over his wasted body; and, in the final stages of his illness, his fingers and toes began to drop off. These were the symptoms of the syphilis he had inherited from his father. The general breakdown of his constitution resulted in a galloping consumption.[1]

Over his early death one cannot shed many tears. Edward was one of the most objectionable youths of whom history holds any record. Except for his gambling, he did not have — to use Disraeli's unkind description of Gladstone — a single redeeming vice. His pious cant and his coldness of heart appear on nearly every page of his journal. In his passing England was spared much.

In the spring he began to spit blood. At the same time his legs were swelling and he was a mass of putrefaction. In the summer a report circulated in London that the King was dead; and when, on July 4, he was lifted from his bed and carried to the window of the palace at Greenwich, so that the people could see for themselves that he was still alive, he looked so much like a corpse that the crowds outside believed they had seen one, that this was another of Northumberland's tricks. Two days later he actually did die. It was the eighteenth anniversary of the execution of Sir Thomas More. But with the strange faculty that the English have of inventing a legend that a famous person reported dead is still really alive, some continued to hold, even into Elizabeth's reign, that Edward was concealed in the depths of a state prison. As against this, other rumours spread that Northumberland had poisoned the King in furtherance of his own ambition.

---

[1] Too much has been made of the fact that the illegitimate Duke of Richmond also died at Edward's age, and that Mary and Elizabeth had poor health all their lives. Elizabeth lived to be old, upheld by her indomitable vitality; and if Stukeley and Perrot were actually Henry's sons, as was reputed, their constitution was notably vigorous.

At once the conspirators acted. Before any announcement of the death was given out — it was suppressed for two days — Northumberland tried to lure Mary and Elizabeth into his clutches. Messages were sent them that they had better come at once to Greenwich if they wished to see their brother alive. Somebody, however (probably Cecil), sent private word to Elizabeth at Hatfield that she had better stay away; and somebody else (it may have been Arundel) gave Mary a similar warning.

The message reached Mary at Hunsdon in Hertfordshire. At once she took horse and rode toward the Norfolk coast, only just succeeding in breaking through the cordon that was being spread to cut off her escape. Her first impulse was apparently merely flight; but as the coast was being watched by the fleet, she turned inland again, and as she turned the tide turned with her. The sailors of the ships threatened to throw their officers overboard if they did not come to the assistance of their rightful Queen, and the people in the Eastern counties — in spite of the fact that those were, London excepted, the parts of England most infected with Protestantism — also rose to help her. Though she was refused admission to Cambridge and Norwich, at the aged Duke of Norfolk's residences of Kenninghall and Framlingham she was welcomed. The Duke himself, who had been under sentence of death since 1547, was still in the Tower. The old nobility, almost to a man, were in Mary's favour, for they were sick of upstart and arrogant Protectors; and with the common people Mary was popular, both on account of her own ill usage and her mother's. By the ninth, the same day in which Northumberland officially admitted the King's death, she felt secure enough to write a letter to the Council demanding their allegiance.

Lady Jane Grey had now been proclaimed Queen. Therefore upon the arrival of Mary's letter Northumberland was obliged to act openly. Distrusting the Council, however loud their protestations of loyalty, he would have preferred to remain in London so as to prevent intrigues against himself, and to have put the Duke of Suffolk in command of the army. But as Lady

44

Jane would not let her father go, there was nothing for it: Northumberland had in person to march against Mary.

As soon as he had left London, the Council, seeing how the wind was veering, made their first cautious moves in support of Mary. When Northumberland, to whom reports were coming in of how she had been enthusiastically proclaimed Queen both in the east and the west, sent a desperate appeal to the Council for reinforcements, excuses were found for not supplying them. Against him thirty thousand loyalists had been mustered, and he had only two thousand men. Falling back upon Cambridge, he received news of the Council's having declared for Mary, of how Suffolk had told his daughter that her dream of sovereignty was over and had with his own hand torn down her royal regalia. Now in an equally desperate, and equally unsuccessful, effort to save his head, the Protector tossed his cap into the air at Cambridge and swore allegiance to Mary. The next day Arundel arrested him.

We might note, in view of the horrified indignation shown during Elizabeth's reign at foreign interference, that Northumberland's plot had been furthered by Noailles, the French Ambassador, and that the letters concerning this had passed through Cecil's hands. It was not that the French wanted Lady Jane to be Queen; their object was merely that of excluding Mary Tudor: they counted upon the breakdown of Jane's weak administration, when they intended to put forward their own candidate, the Queen of Scots, who had been kept for safety in France since 1548.

Upon the collapse of Northumberland's conspiracy, Cecil was lucky at not being sent to the Tower along with his friend, Sir John Cheke. But, as Professor Pollard has said, "His conduct had been a miracle of evasion." Though one of the Lansdowne Manuscripts contains his defence of himself, in which he asserts, "I eschewed writing the Queen's Highness bastard, and therefore the Duke wrote the letter himself, which was sent abroad in the realm" — this by the bye served the useful purpose of giving evidence against Northumberland — there is in the same collection a document in Cecil's holograph, dated July 10 (the day

45

before Mary's summons to the Council arrived) which was drawn up to be sent to the Lords-lieutenant of the counties ordering them "to disturbe, repell, and resyste the fayned and untrue clayme of the Lady Mary, bastard daughter . . . of Henry VIII." It was this very proclamation that Northumberland had issued on the twelfth. We can only conclude that its original draft did not then come to light. In any event, Cecil cast himself on Mary's mercy, pleading that he had acted as he had done only under compulsion. He did all he could to exculpate himself further by an ostentatious practice of the Catholic religion. Although he was excluded from the Council, papers exist which show that he was given a certain amount of state employment during Mary's reign. Having come so near the scaffold, he was extremely careful to avoid even the shadow of complicity in subsequent plots.

There is no need to enter at length here into the political events of the years 1553–1558. Suffice it to say that there were two rebellions — both of them backed by the French — of which the one that was led by Wyatt, the son of the poet, almost succeeded, and would have succeeded had not Mary shown an iron courage. Even when Wyatt's men were under the walls of her palace of Whitehall, and Stephen Gardiner in a panic was advising flight, telling the Queen that her barge was all ready, she stood firm. And the rebellion was crushed.

What must be gone into is the part, if any, played by Elizabeth in this affair.

When Mary entered London as Queen for the first time her sister rode by her side, a lissom, redheaded girl whose youth appealed to everyone who saw it in contrast with the dowdy and dumpy figure of the prematurely aged Mary. Elizabeth had what her sister lacked, a sense of showmanship, and she used it then, and always, to the utmost. She had also a sense of political reality: Northumberland's conspiracy had been directed as much against her as against Mary; there was nothing she could safely do except join forces with the rightful Queen.

She must, nevertheless, have been somewhat cast down by her sister's accession. For now Mary, at the age of thirty-seven, announced that she intended to lay aside the celibacy which was her private preference and to marry for the sake of producing an heir. It seemed the end of Elizabeth's hopes for the crown.

It was in her choice of a husband that Mary made her most serious political mistake. All England wished her to marry an Englishman, knowing that there were two husbands of royal descent available. One was Reginald Pole, the son of that racily outspoken old Countess of Salisbury whom Henry VIII had beheaded; the other was Edward Courtenay, Earl of Devonshire, who since his father's execution in 1538 had been imprisoned in the Tower.[2]

Mary, however, soon dismissed Courtenay as a possible husband. To make up for his long imprisonment, he at once began to lead a highly dissolute life. The pious Mary would not entertain the thought of such a man.

In spite of this — as she had accepted the idea of marriage only for political reasons — she would have been well advised to have accepted him. The marriage would have been popular, and might have resulted in an heir. If it had accomplished nothing else it would have avoided the disaster of the Spanish marriage.

The other available English husband of royal blood was Cardinal Pole. He had recently had a good chance of being elected Pope, and probably would have been elected had he not decided to make no active candidature but to leave everything to the guidance of the Holy Ghost. That fact reveals his character: though he has been given a bad name in history, he was one of the noblest and most disinterested of men.

He showed that disinterestedness again — and his bad political judgment — by not only discouraging all efforts to make him King of England but by writing to Mary advising her to retain her single state. Yet his marriage to the Queen was quite feasible, for though a Cardinal, he was at this time only in deacon's orders. Even had he been a priest, a dispensation,

[2] Pole was a grandson of the Duke of Clarence, and so grandnephew of Edward IV. Courtenay was the same King's great-grandson.

for a cause of such gravity, would have been obtainable. Almost the same situation was to arise later in Poland, when a Jesuit Cardinal, succeeding to the throne, was released from his vows of celibacy. Pole's ambitions, however, were entirely of the spiritual order. Moreover, it is likely that Mary was shocked at the suggestion that she should marry a cardinal. It was made only to be dropped.

Yet it is one of the piquancies of history that Mary might have saved the Church in England by this marriage. Pole understood the English temper, being very English himself. He would have kept the fires of Smithfield low, had he not been able to quench them altogether. That Canterbury furnished a large proportion of martyrs indicates only that it was, after London and Norwich, the chief center of heresy — and that Pole was conscientious. He had no zest for persecution.

In her dilemma Mary put herself in the hands of her cousin, the Emperor Charles V, asking him to nominate a husband. He, thinking mainly of his political advantage, nominated his son, the Prince of Spain, afterwards Philip II. It was a tragic decision for England and the Church.

We need not make the usual error of supposing that the Spaniards were particularly unpopular in England; on the contrary, Spain was the traditional ally against the traditional enemy, France. It was this very fact that dictated Charles's wish to consolidate the alliance. The same fact made England, with whatever reluctance, accept a foreigner as king. It is nearer the truth to say that the English, being already narrowly insular, had a suspicion of all foreigners. In this case, at least, their suspicion was justified that the marriage was designed to benefit Spain rather than England.

Then, too, there came to arise in the national mind a belief — one that was entirely unfounded — that it was at the instance of Philip that English men and women were burnt at the stake. Actually, Philip did his best to restrain the persecution. The Inquisition was never set up in England. But people who heard of the holocausts in the Spanish dominions could not be brought to believe that Philip was not egging Mary on, though

Traitor's Gate

Castro, Mary's Spanish chaplain, preached against the terror. And when Philip dragged England into a war with France that resulted in the loss of Calais — a calamity that seemed as enormous as the loss of Gibraltar would today — men's minds confusedly identified Catholicism with Spanish domination, and Protestantism with Englishry. After Calais fell, Feria records (though no doubt with exaggeration), two thirds of the people began to stay away from Mass. It was not a question with them of reason but of nationalistic passion. As so often happens, men imagined they were thinking when they were merely excited.

Mary, on gaining the throne, repudiated her supremacy over the English Church. But as it was not yet legal for her to do so, her proclamations, until Parliament had met, dodged the issue by putting at the end of her titles a vague "&cetera" — a formula that Elizabeth found it convenient to employ, in her turn, during the early — and officially Catholic — months of her reign. It was, of course, seen from the beginning that Mary would be content with nothing less than reunion with Rome.

What is noteworthy is that she was unable to bring this about until after the impropriators of monastic property had been legally confirmed in their possession, and an understanding reached with the Holy See that no disgorging would be insisted upon. Until that was settled Cardinal Pole, the Pope's Legate, was kept waiting in Flanders.[3] Then a delegation was sent to bring him over, among whom was Cecil, displaying, as was customary with him, a prodigious rosary. The barge of the Legate, a cross gleaming at its prow, rowed up to the steps of the palace at Greenwich, and Pole (according to the story) greeted his Queen and cousin with the angelic salutation: *Ave Maria, Dominus tecum!*

At the beginning of her reign Mary had shown herself

[3] It went very much against the grain for Pole to accede to this. The Pope had condemned, though only in general terms, such spoliations as sacrilege. Much of Mary's "unpopularity" was due to the fact that she was known to wish the restoration of Church property. Out of her own purse she refounded the abbey at Westminster and the house of the Friars Observant at Greenwich. Under her the robbers would not feel quite safe, though they had been powerful enough to force, for the moment, a recognition of their claims.

extraordinarily lenient to those who had conspired against her — a leniency with which she was to be reproached later, when it was pointed out that she burnt heretics but spared traitors. Northumberland, indeed, had to suffer, and, whether from policy or in sincerity, made most sweeping confessions of Catholicism in the days while he was awaiting execution and on the scaffold itself. Lady Jane Grey and Lord Guildford Dudley, on the other hand, were merely kept in precautionary confinement. Though Renard, Charles V's ambassador, protested that the Queen would not be safe until she had cut off the heads of all the principals in Northumberland's conspiracy, Mary remained resolute in her reluctance to shed blood, in particular the blood of her cousin Lady Jane. It was Wyatt's rebellion that brought about their doom — that and the fact that the untrustworthy Suffolk, though pardoned in 1553, was implicated in the new conspiracy.

The nine days' Queen has been made into a Protestant heroine. That she would not recant is certain, for which, I suppose, she is entitled to whatever credit is due any kind of constancy. The most she would do was to accept the ministrations of the gentle Feckenham, Abbot of the restored Westminster, on the scaffold. She suffered, not because of any real crime of her own, but because of the ambitions of others. But she was a little prig. I confess to feeling chilled, not edified, by her refusal to have a parting with her husband, on the ground that they were so soon to meet in heaven.

Mary now proceeded to move through a series of blunders toward the ruin of Catholicism in England. She had accepted Philip, "sight unseen" and against the advice of her Council, including that of her Chancellor, Bishop Gardiner. It was like a woman of her deeply religious character to ratify her promise in a midnight visit to her oratory where, with Renard and a lady in waiting as witnesses, she vowed before the Blessed Sacrament to take no other man as her husband. Once this decisive step had been taken, all the floodgates of her natural emotions were opened. Probably no King has ever been loved so much as this admirable and pathetic woman loved Philip.

Traitor's Gate

The Pope's marriage gift was that of the sovereignty of Ireland. Hitherto that country had been a Papal fief and the English kings "Lords of Ireland," until Henry added its kingship to his honorifics. Now that title was confirmed by the Holy See. It was little more than a recognition of the fact that feudal concepts had become merely theoretical. With her right everywhere acknowledged, with rebellion crushed, with the son of the Emperor for husband, with England restored to the unity of Christendom, Mary had nothing more to wish for than an heir — which she was now confidently expecting. Her fortunes appeared to be at their height at the very moment when they were about to decline. It makes a sad story.

It is all the sadder because the worst blows struck at Catholicism in England were those dealt by the champions of the Church. What Philip of Spain and Mary Tudor left undone was to be completed by Mary Queen of Scots, and some — though I am not among them — would include Pius V as those who blundered worst in dealing with the affairs of England. At the moment, however, I am concerned only with Mary.

Her burning of heretics, taken alone, would probably not have been sufficient to cause a Protestant reaction, though it must be considered a bad error of judgment, if nothing worse. The heretics were burned, it is true, under existing laws, as they had been burned under Henry and Edward and as they were to be burned (though most historians slur this over) under Elizabeth. Even the number of those who suffered — something under three hundred, among whom were several who were criminals, despite their enrollment in Foxe's *Book of Martyrs* — though it was large, does not wholly account for the revulsion of popular feeling. What did most harm was the general (though baseless) conviction that Philip, a foreigner, had instigated the burning of Englishmen. If he had not been liked before, he now became hated. And as people increasingly identified patriotic and Protestant sentiments, Philip's unpopularity created new Protestants and made them vocal. Their antagonism was due, in many instances, really to Spain rather than to the Church. Their angry confusion concealed this from their minds: they thought themselves Protestants. I do not want to press the point too far, because, after all, we do not know to what extent this operated. But we may be sure that it operated as a powerful contributing factor.

Yet the burnings would not have occurred except with the consent of the Privy Council, many of whose members were (as subsequent events showed) personally indifferent to religion. They thought it advisable to humour the Queen's fanaticism as a fair exchange for the concessions she had made them in the matter of monastic property. There was always a possibility that the question of restitution would be raised again. So rather than lose their lands they were perfectly willing to let heretics go to the stake. Meanwhile they made loud protestations of their own orthodoxy, even if they were not always punctilious in religious practice.

In Mary's extenuation it should be said that when she embarked upon persecution she had no idea how far she would have to go. Furthermore she had had extreme provocation. Scurrilous pamphlets against her were being circulated. The dog, shaven like a priest and with a placard round its neck saying that it was the Pope, thrown through one of her windows is a sample of the sort of thing that warned her of the need of drastic action. It was believed that a few salutary examples would suffice. Several times there were pauses in the persecution while the Council waited to see what effect Smithfield had had; the burnings were reluctantly resumed only when it became evident that the object had not yet been achieved. Mary was a kindly woman, but she accepted the proposition — in logic an inescapable one — that the destruction of Faith, the most precious heritage of man, being the worst of crimes, should be treated accordingly. But practically every Protestant of the time accepted the same proposition. Archdeacon John Philpot, who was himself burned, had been a notable upholder of this principle.

So also had Cranmer; he had condemned Joan Bocher during Edward's reign. If he had any right to complain of his treatment it was that, unlike other bishops, who were quietly allowed to leave the country, he was given no such chance, but was reserved for punishment not so much on account of his heresy as because he was the one man the Queen could not forgive on other scores. His share in Northumberland's conspiracy could have been passed over; men fully as guilty were pardoned. But it was he who had divorced Katherine of Aragon and had declared Mary a bastard. If the Queen had to execute him, however, she should have sent him to the block instead of the stake.

He was not played with fairly — at least such is my opinion — we are inclined to say, and for after he had made his series of abject recantations the rules of the game demanded that he be spared. Although some attempt has been made to justify Mary's action on the grounds that he was condemned for perjury and adultery, the manner of carrying out his death sentence was one normally attached to heresy only. In any case Mary decided his crime was inexpiable in any other way. In so deciding she gave him the opportunity of taking a spectacular revenge. Brought out to make a final public recantation in St. Mary's, Oxford, before he went to the stake, he astonished everybody by repudiating all his recantations and by dying with his offending hand in the flames. The gesture has filled the imagination of the world. Though one can understand the bitterness of Mary, she should have pardoned him out of policy if not out of mercy.

The worst feature of the persecution was that — with the exception of the five Bishops, Cranmer, Latimer, Ferrar, Ridley, and Hooper, and a few other high ecclesiastics — the Protestant martyrs were poor and obscure people. Those who should have been executed were the rich robbers, who were making a hypocritical pretence of Catholicism. Mary must have known that the really dangerous heretics were escaping; she connived at their escape.[4]

[4] However, she had really no choice in the matter. As for the heresy law, its actual application was in the hands of the bishops. Some condemned nobody. Gardiner, who was Bishop of Winchester as well as Chancellor, had no martyrs in his diocese. Bonner was the worst offender, though we must remember that he had, in London, the worst of the Protestant hotbeds to deal with. Even so, he often exercised himself to save the accused, and stretched points when he could. He was a rough, tough, but not a cruel man. And he bore himself nobly under the Elizabethan persecution.

Queen Elizabeth

But what of Elizabeth while all these events were in progress. What, in particular, was the truth about her suspected implication in Wyatt's rebellion?

His scheme had turned on effecting a marriage between her and Courtenay, since Mary had rejected him, and their elevation to the throne. It was natural to suppose her to be a principal in a plot whose object was her own advantage. There will always be some to suspect her, for this if for no other reason.

Something more definite than suspicion, however, is needed for conviction. And though documentary evidence was produced against Elizabeth, it did not prove her complicity beyond all shadow of doubt. A copy of a letter she had written the Queen was found in the intercepted mailbag of the French Ambassador, who was working with the rebels though with the intention of "dishing" them afterwards. A letter was also found from Wyatt himself in which he advised Elizabeth to move further west so as to be in touch with the rising expected there.

What can be said in Elizabeth's defence is that no letter from her to Wyatt was found; that Wyatt affirmed her innocence; that she did not follow Wyatt's advice and move to a place where she could be in touch with the western rebels; and that, finally, she had a keen sense of what was due to established authority.

This last is perhaps a rather intangible matter. Elizabeth held, quite sincerely, to the principle that a crowned head was sacrosanct. Yet in later life she did not always act upon that principle, but countenanced rebellion in Scotland and France and the Netherlands (while pretending not to be responsible for what her subjects did), and executed, however reluctantly and again with disclaimers of responsibility, Mary Queen of Scots. But at least there is no indication that she ever wished to marry Courtenay — assuming that she was capable of marriage at all. And she was too shrewd a judge of affairs ever to commit herself to a course of action unless she could be sure of its success. If she had been informed as to the plans of the conspirators she must have perceived them to be badly coordinated. Finally, she might have guessed that a man of Courtenay's weak character would somehow ruin everything — as in fact he did by yielding under pressure and confessing to Gardiner.

If Gardiner spared Courtenay it was probably with the purpose of shielding Elizabeth. There is reason to suspect that the Chancellor quietly disposed of incriminating documents. As for the letters actually found, Elizabeth could only say that she had no idea how the copy of her letter to the Queen had reached the French Ambassador and that as for "the traitor Wyatt, he might peradventure write me a letter, but on my faith I never received one from him."

The explanation was not very convincing, and on much slenderer evidence many a man has been sent to the block. Yet though it is likely enough that Elizabeth had been in touch with what was going on in order to make the most of eventualities that might turn up, it is unlikely that she did more than that. Even so, Renard, the Imperial Ambassador, pressed for her execution, and Mary, knowing Elizabeth's tricky character, guessed that she knew more about the Wyatt affair than she would admit. But she could not bring herself to shed a sister's blood in the absence of complete proof of guilt, and had she attempted it, the Council would have overruled her. For though Elizabeth was still officially illegitimate — so that the Duchess of Suffolk and her surviving daughters, as well as Lady Lennox, claimed precedence over her — she was nevertheless in the general estimation heiress presumptive. Therefore nothing worse happened to her than a period of incarceration.

When she was ordered to come from Ashridge to the Court she was ill, or pretended to be. Mary, however, was not to be put off with excuses. The royal physicians were sent down, who pronounced her well enough to travel. Under the custody of her uncle, Lord William Howard, she took five days to travel thirty-three miles. Then on March 18, 1554, after nearly a month in London trying to obtain an interview with the angry Queen, she was sent to the Tower. She contrived to get an extra day by making a frantic appeal to be allowed to write a last letter to Mary, and by the time it was written the Thames tide had turned and it was too dangerous to attempt the shooting of the rapids under London Bridge. Her letter was ignored: on Palm Sunday, a wet and dreary day of the kind England is famous for, the Lady Elizabeth disembarked at Traitor's Gate.

At first she sat down on a wet stone and refused to move, until she saw a kindhearted gentleman weeping over what he supposed was her inevitable fate. Upon this she got up and, turning her eyes to the dull skies, said for everybody to hear: "O Lord, I never thought to come in here as a prisoner; and I pray you all, good friends and fellows, bear me witness that I come in no traitor but as a true woman to the Queen's Majesty as any is now living." Elizabeth could always rise to such occasions and extract the full dramatic value from any situation. But if her plight was dangerous, she may have had good reasons for knowing that it was not nearly so dangerous as it seemed to be. After all, she could comfort herself with the thought of the lack of evidence and of Mary's merciful nature. Years afterwards, indeed, she told Castlenau de Mauvissière that she believed her entrance into the Tower spelled her end, that she had determined to ask nothing of her sister except that her head be cut off with a sword instead of an axe, and that a Frenchman be sent for from Calais for the purpose. But this may well have been more dramatisation. Even had Elizabeth's guilt been proved beyond all question, it is extremely improbable that Mary would ever have brought herself to sign her death warrant.

Elizabeth was now on the point of gaining a most powerful friend. This friend was Philip of Spain. The threat of Wyatt's rebellion — motivated by the Spanish marriage — had defeated its own object: it had served to frighten Parliament into consenting to that marriage. As it was necessary that the Queen bear a child as soon as possible, the country swung to the belief that she be allowed to marry the husband of her own choice, Courtenay having thoroughly discredited himself. One of the incidental but most important consequences of Mary's marriage to Philip was that Elizabeth's fortunes were re-established.

It would be an exaggeration to say that Philip saved her life: that was already saved. What Philip did was to secure her claim to the succession, in order to further Spanish policy. Though Elizabeth was illegitimate, Philip preferred to have her nominated as heiress to the crown, since the alternative was Mary Queen of Scots and a French domination. And it is curious to record that Renard — the very man who had once urged Mary to send Elizabeth to the block — made a right-about turn under instructions and drew up an elaborate paper to demonstrate that it was much more likely that the Queen of Scots would become a Protestant than that Elizabeth would. He must have known that this was not so, for we have letters by him showing that he was not deceived as to which religious party Elizabeth at heart belonged. His arguments were nevertheless solemnly advanced, and though they convinced nobody they at least justified the refusal of admitting the Scots Queen's title.

But as it was impossible to keep Elizabeth in the Tower without bringing her to trial, and equally impossible to allow her to go to Court as though nothing had happened, she was sent to Woodstock and put under the charge of Sir Henry Bedingfield, a Privy Councillor about whose Catholicism there could be no doubt. He was to remain a staunch recusant when Elizabeth came to the throne — when she, for her part, showed him no ill will, despite the somewhat pedantic strictness with which he had guarded her.

Tradition tells us that at Woodstock Elizabeth wrote with a diamond upon a windowpane:

> Much suspected of me;
> Nothing proved can be.

It is hard to believe that she did anything of the kind; she was far too canny to commit such an incriminating admission even to paper, let alone so imperishable a substance as glass. But the couplet does exactly express her situation.[5] That this continued to be ambiguous is shown by the revival in 1556 of the project of marrying her to Courtenay. Though the plot this time did

[5] Years later Elizabeth told the French Ambassador: "I learned by experience to keep silent during the time of Queen Mary, when had anything been proven against me I should have lost my life."

not get so far as open rebellion, it had many ramifications, several peers and a dozen members of the House of Commons, being implicated. There were three executions and Kingston (the butcher of Cornwall in Somerset's days) died — just in time to escape the scaffold. Kate Ashley was one of those sent to the Tower — her second visit! — where she was questioned along with Castiglione, Elizabeth's Italian tutor. They were, however, soon released. Elizabeth was not, this time, accused, though once more she was suspected of much.

At Woodstock, under Bedingfield's lynx eye, she lived quietly, studying and planting trees, and studiously keeping aloof from politics. The Bodleian Library still possesses the ornamented copy she made of St. Paul's Epistles, signed by her "E. C." — *Elizabeth Captiva*. And she appends as a note to her work: "I walk many times in the pleasant fields of Holy Scripture . . . and lay them up at length in the high seat of memory." Spent in such occupations her life could not have been unpleasant, and her reported remark, "The milkmaid's lot is better than mine," may be discounted. Elizabeth was not addicted to self-pity, and in any event she had cause to congratulate herself upon a punishment no worse than an easy confinement.

Mary was, with good reason, anxious about her sister's faith. So that when at last release from Woodstock came — for with the death in September, 1556, of Courtenay in Padua the immediate danger was removed — Elizabeth was summoned to court and invited to show that she was a Catholic. She therefore consented to attend Mass, as she continued, in fact, to attend it during the first months of her reign. All the same, Mary was not satisfied as to the genuineness of the conversion and insisted upon knowing whether the attendance at Mass was due to "conscience or policy." Challenged in this forthright way, Elizabeth swore that it was conscience alone that actuated her. Further to convince the doubting Mary, she asked her to supply the vestments and plate necessary for the celebration of the Divine Sacrifice. As if that were not enough, she wrote to Charles V, begging him to send suitable ornaments for her private chapel. Elizabeth wanted to impress the Emperor with the devoutness of her Catholicism.

In all this we have nothing but adroitly played politics. As she now found it advisable to conform to the practice of the Catholic faith, she did so with a flourish — and her tongue in her cheek. She still contrived, on due occasion, to convey that her position was not quite what it seemed. Thus when Mary sent some clerics to question her on the subject of the Real Presence — and it must be remembered that the decisive question put to all those charged with heresy was that of whether there was or was not more than the elements of bread and wine in the Eucharist — she made up, on the spur of the moment according to the legend, the following quatrain:

> Christ was the Word that spoke it;
> He took the bread and broke it;
> And what His word doth make it,
> That I believe and take it.

The solemn conviction with which some Protestant historians have put this forth as ascertained fact is amusing. One would like to see any of them boil down so much theology into impromptu verse! It is still more amusing that none of them seems to know that this is only a somewhat free rendering of a stanza in the *Adoro Te* of St. Thomas Aquinas. Whether or not Elizabeth ever quoted it, the translation is, of course, susceptible of a meaning consonant with Protestantism. Elizabeth was an adept at giving adroit answers to awkward questions.

Mary continued to be as suspicious of Elizabeth's politics as of her religion. When the sisters met and Elizabeth on her knees asseverated that she had never conspired against the throne, Mary, still doubtful about one whom she knew to be an accomplished liar, had to let the assurance pass with a muttered "God knows!" That she perfectly understood with what kind of a person she had to deal is revealed by the instructions she issued while Elizabeth was still at Woodstock, that she would receive no more of her "disguised and colourable letters."

Queen Elizabeth

When Elizabeth had been taken back into mistrustful favour, marriage projects began to be put on foot for her. One was that she marry the Earl of Arundel's son. This was not seriously pressed because Philip thought of the eleven-year-old Don Carlos or, more definitely, of his cousin Emmanuel Philibert, the Duke of Savoy, who could be trusted to look after Spanish interests in the event of Elizabeth's ever succeeding Mary. But Elizabeth would not so much as meet Emmanuel Philibert when he visited England, so that projects were entertained of sending the obstinate girl to Flanders, or, even to Hungary, to get her where she could give no trouble.

Had a foreign marriage ever taken place it is as certain as anything can be that Elizabeth would never have become Queen of England. The country, disgusted with its Spanish King, would have refused to accept another. This Elizabeth understood perhaps more clearly than anyone else. Even apart from Mary Queen of Scots, there were several other candidates to the throne, among them Lady Margaret Clifford and the two sisters of Lady Jane Grey. All of them were ready to profess either Catholicism or Protestantism, as circumstances and their own interests demanded. At the moment they were, of course, ostentatiously Catholic — like Elizabeth herself.

The problem of the succession was now becoming more urgent every day. Mary lived in a state of perpetual pregnancy, which each time was diagnosed as dropsy by the doctors.[6] It was becoming increasingly plain that the Queen would probably die before long, and that in any case it was impossible that she bear a child. It was also plain that the country wanted Elizabeth. Some wanted her because she was expected to turn Protestant; all wanted her because she was a Tudor. Her illegitimacy was looked upon (as Mary's had been) as merely technical.

There was nothing that Mary could do except bow to the national sentiment, especially as this was strongly supported by

[6] Competent medical opinion now believes that Mary's primary trouble was that of an ovarian tumor. She did have one genuine pregnancy — followed by an early miscarriage. (Cf. Chamberlin's *Private Life of Queen Elizabeth*, where the evidence is examined in detail.)

Traitor's Gate

the husband with whom she was so infatuated. Yet she did so with misgivings, and again questioned her sister as to the orthodoxy of her beliefs. Jane Dormer (soon to be Countess and eventually Duchess of Feria, a lady very close at this time to Mary) records Elizabeth's answer. It was explicit enough to satisfy even the Queen: "I pray God that the earth may open and swallow me up, if I be not a true Roman Catholic!" What more could be said? Elizabeth had to be publicly acknowledged as Mary's successor.

It was, from one point of view, fortunate for her that she had been obliged to wait so long. Had she succeeded Edward (supposing the previous death of Mary), the reaction against the corrupt Protestant administrations of Somerset and Northumberland would probably have forced her to declare herself a Catholic. This, of course, she would have done willingly enough. But hers would have been a Henrician Catholicism, not capable of sustaining itself. England had not yet come to perceive that there could be no real Catholicism except in union with Rome. Mary grasped that perfectly, but her Spanish marriage and the loss of Calais and the burnings of heretics had induced something that cannot be quite correctly described as Protestantism but which was unquestionably a mood of irritation against the ecclesiastics imagined to be responsible for the national calamities. These factors made possible a Protestant *coup d'état* — and Elizabeth's career.

She had for some time past been in surreptitious communication with Cecil. A letter exists to him from Parry, written in September, 1549, which proves that even then there was a close understanding. "Her Grace commandeth me to write thus," reads a sentence in it: " 'Write my commendations in my letter to Mr. Cecil that I am well assured, though I send not daily to him, that he doth not, for all that, forget me.' " And Camden tells us that Cecil was Elizabeth's constant adviser, although he managed matters so dextrously, that he was not so much as suspected at the time of Wyatt's rebellion.

The end now came for Mary. She was surely the best woman who ever sat upon the English throne, one absolutely devoted to what she believed to be right, and unflinching in carrying it out. But she was, because of her very honesty, a poor politician. We can regard her sallow, sickly face and her disappointed heart only with compassion. But we must also say frankly that, despite her unselfishness and kindness and loyalty and piety, she made a series of catastrophic blunders. On November 17, the Feast of St. Hugh of Lincoln, as she was lying in bed and hearing Mass, she died. She had been a little delirious previously, but even her delirium showed what sort of woman she was: she had visions of angel children around her.

On the afternoon of the same day, in the palace of the Archbishop of Canterbury at Lambeth, there died Cardinal Pole. He, too, had largely failed, not due to lack of ability, but rather through unacquaintance with recent developments among the Catholic body in England. He had further been obliged to sanction the retention of the impropriated lands, something that went much against his grain. He had also been strangely oblivious of his duty in filling vacant bishoprics, a fact that was to have an untoward effect in the new reign. Some of his reforms, however, were admirable. Even before the Council of Trent decreed the establishment of seminaries he had set them up, realising that the fundamental necessity was the systematic education of both priests and people in their faith.[7] Like his cousin, the Queen, he was utterly selfless and devoted to duty as he saw it. But he had not lived long enough to complete his work, and he lacked genius for leadership. The greatest mistake of his life was not that he had failed to take the Papacy when it was within his grasp, but that he had not married Mary. By doing so he might have saved Catholicism in England. Such is the strange judgement one is obliged to pass upon him.

The two embalmed bodies lay in state for a month. Then on December 13 that of the Queen was buried in the Westminster Abbey she had refounded. It was the most splendid funeral

[7] In fact it was Pole's idea that was taken over at Trent along with the word *seminary* itself. (Cf. Pastor's *History of the Popes*, English translation, Vol. XIV, p. 392.)

England had ever seen; that last grace was offered her. But her husband Philip did not attend. The following day the Cardinal was buried. With him and Mary there passed away Catholic England.

5

"The Oil Stinks!"

PHILIP of Spain had already befriended Elizabeth in several ways — including one of which he was quite unconscious. He had given England an experience with a foreign king that made it all the more ready to greet with enthusiasm one who boasted of being "mere English." Even the war with France, into which he had dragged the country — and which was still going on — though it resulted in the loss of Calais, was fortunate for Elizabeth: it put out of the running for the English throne Mary Queen of Scots, for the sufficient reason that she was now married to the Dauphin and was therefore to be Queen of France. In later years Cecil himself was to say frankly enough what he would never have admitted earlier: that Mary was considered by the overwhelming majority of the people to be the rightful claimant. It was not so much her Catholicism as her French marriage which made it i   her candidacy. England was afraid of being reduced to a dependency upon France even closer than that dependency upon Spain of which everyone was heartily sick. If the word *Calais* had been written on Mary's stricken heart, the same word might with justice have been blazoned in jewels upon Elizabeth's diadem.

The Count of Feria, the Spanish Ambassador, went down a week before Mary's death to Hatfield to see Elizabeth, to remind her of what she owed to Philip. She was polite but noncommittal. On the subject of religion she used ambiguity: when the Ambassador advised her to be careful about it, she put him off with a "It would indeed be bad for her to forget God who had been so good to her." As for the alliance with Spain, her policy was to be that of using Philip's friendship for all that it was worth; but she had no intention of acknowledging her obligations to him or of allowing him any voice in English affairs.

Nevertheless, it was Philip's support that proved decisive. England needed the Spanish alliance against France, which otherwise might have invaded England to assert the right of its Dauphiness. And Elizabeth needed the invaluable service that Philip rendered in keeping the English Catholics quiet. He did it by sending them private assurances time after time during these early years that religious matters would satisfactorily settle themselves. A still greater service he rendered Elizabeth was that of persuading the Pope to withhold his fulminations.

Elizabeth from the beginning, however, took a high and mighty line. When Mary had sent word that she was to be acknowledged as her successor, Elizabeth made answer, "I am very sorry to hear of the Queen's illness, but there is no reason why I should thank her for the intention of giving me the crown of this realm, for she has neither the power of bestowing it, nor can I lawfully be deprived of it, since it is my peculiar and hereditary right."[1] The argument was not very sound: both Mary and Elizabeth ascended to the throne by virtue of Henry's will, yet both were by statutory law illegitimate, and Elizabeth was in addition illegitimate by the canon law of the Henrician Church, as well as by the canon law of Rome and the common law of Europe. Her only valid argument — apart from Mary's devise, and her father's — was that Anne Boleyn had, after all, been crowned. The real strength of her position — apart from Philip's support and the fact that Mary of Scotland was the Dauphiness of the enemy — lay in the English lack of interest in what they would have considered legal technicalities. Henry's matrimonial affairs had become so tangled that people were, for the most part, content to accept anybody who was an authentic Tudor. That bastardy, even bastardy about which there could be no question, was not regarded as an insuperable bar-

---

[1] When she announced her succession it was to say: "The crown of this realm is by natural blood and lawful succession descended unto us as the only right heir thereof" — thus skilfully making her claim to the throne under Henry's will appear to prove the legitimacy of her birth. But under any circumstances she would, of course, have asserted her legitimacy.

rier is shown by Henry's having seriously thought of declaring his base-born son, the Duke of Richmond, his heir. What had a weight that we can hardly conceive of today, was the ruling monarch's nomination of his successor. It was not a formally defined right at all, yet Edward's right to bequeath the crown had been disputed only on the ground that, as a minor, he was incapable of exercising his royal privilege. Elizabeth herself was to exercise this right forty-five years later. Mary's nomination was therefore an extremely strong point in Elizabeth's favour.

Feria was not Elizabeth's first visitor, promptly as he went to Hatfield. The road was crowded with office seekers even before Mary's death, and of these, Cecil was perhaps the earliest to arrive. Mary had been known to be dying since August 17, when she was taken ill at St. James's. The three months before her death gave Elizabeth and Cecil ample leisure to complete their plans. Even before she ascended the throne it was upon his astute intelligence that she relied.

Her doubtful claim gave him and his faction a hold over her. But they were well aware that in this young woman of twenty-five they had by far the ablest candidate available. Her masterly handling of the Seymour scandal and of her suspected implication in the Wyatt conspiracy had been noted with admiration. Cecil selected her with unerring instinct, and there at once began a lifelong partnership, the most successful partnership of its kind the world has ever known.

There was another weakness, besides those already pointed out, in her position: a doubt occupied many men's minds whether a woman could hold the sceptre sufficiently firmly; and this doubt had been increased by the events of Mary's reign, so filled with plots. On the other hand, all the other candidates, except those whose descent from collateral lines made their claim shadowy, were also women. Of these women — or for that matter, of all the men in question — the one who unmistakably had the most talent for sovereignty was Elizabeth. And she was known to be, if not precisely a Protestant, one who would accept Protestantism. Cecil and the group with whom

66

he worked balanced all the factors and reached their decision. From their own point of view it was much the best they could have made.

On the day after Mary's death (November 18) Cecil drew up memoranda in which he listed the potentates who were to have messengers sent them announcing Elizabeth's accession. At the head of that list stands the name of the Pope. The next day the list was rewritten, and the Pope's name left off. The fact suggests that this omission came after Cecil had consulted the new Queen. I may as well express my belief at this point that Elizabeth was more directly implicated in the permanent breach with Rome than is commonly supposed. This is by no means to acquit Cecil of responsibility, but I think that both contemporary and modern historians have been a little too kind to Elizabeth in this matter. About which more will develop as we proceed.

It is argued in all the Protestant histories that the circumstances of Elizabeth's birth, and therefore her title to the throne, necessitated the repudiation of the Pope's authority. This, however, is not the case. No Pope could, of course, have given an explicit acknowledgment of her legitimacy; but there was no inclination at Rome to raise that awkward issue. Paul IV showed himself not unfriendly, and had Elizabeth not shown heretical tendencies, no difficulties would have been put in her way. Both Paul and his successor proved themselves lenient, much too lenient, in fact. As subsequent events were to make plain, it would have been better had the Papacy struck at Elizabeth as soon as she had avowed and established heresy. At it was, Paul IV did *not* declare Elizabeth a bastard, great as was his provocation. Such a declaration did not come until twelve years later, and then from Pius V, at the time of her too long-deferred excommunication.

What is true enough is that it would have been embarrassing for Elizabeth to have asked the Pope for his recognition of her right, as this could only have been given in guarded terms. It is certain that such a recognition would have been accorded, had it been asked for, and had religious guarantees been offered.

67

As it was, Elizabeth, for the moment, did nothing. She left her agent, Sir Edward Carne, at Rome, but furnished him with as little business as possible. She and Cecil were probably not yet sure of the precise lines of the religion they were to introduce — or they may have been playing for time.

There is one thing of which we may be virtually sure. Had Elizabeth been entirely free to make her own choice, she would have preferred a return to the Henrician system — that is, Catholicism without the Pope. Mass would then have been said in England, and by a validly ordained priesthood, though it would probably have been a Mass in English instead of Latin. Elizabeth, in short, had no great devotion to the Elizabethan settlement. She liked an elaborate ritual and detested the extreme forms of Protestantism. Sometimes in the years to come she permitted herself sneers at Cecil's "brethren in the Lord." Had she been sufficiently interested in theology, she might have insisted upon the restoration of Henry's Six Articles. Being secular-minded, she accepted a larger amount of Protestantism than she wanted for the sake of political convenience.

In any event it is perhaps more than questionable whether the Henrician compromise could have endured. The cutting off of England from communion with Rome a second time destroyed the sole authority capable of ensuring orthodoxy. Henry had succeeded in maintaining a precarious fidelity to the doctrine of the Real Presence only because England, in his time, all but universally accepted that doctrine. Since then Protestantism had increased in England. It was now impossible, short of a continuation of Mary's religious policy, to arrest the growth of the cancer. A strong and sincere Catholic monarch could have eradicated it. But the new masters of the country feared that this might involve an ultimate restitution (if only in part) of the monastic lands they had stolen, as it would involve the restoration of a large number of spiritual lords to the Upper House. And these lords would have been on their guard to prevent any repetition of Cromwell's orgy.

Though it is necessary to admit the difficulties of Elizabeth's political and economic position — or rather that of the group who had now got her into their hands — those difficulties were not insuperable. The Church would probably have been content with a partial restitution; indeed, one that was complete was perhaps already impossible, since the spoils had already, in many instances, changed hands several times. A concession could have been made as to Mass in English. Nor was it impossible that the Pope might have dispensed the Anglican clergy from their vows of celibacy. Large privileges of ecclesiastical appointment and control could have been invested in the Crown. The one thing the Pope could not tolerate was heresy. And it was heresy, followed by an attempt to extirpate the Mass, that was decided upon. No feelers for compromise were put out. On the contrary, when the Council of Trent began its sessions England, though invited to send delegates, refused to do so. All the acts of religious aggression came entirely from the side of Elizabeth, and largely depended upon her own will. As Feria was soon to write to Philip, "This country has fallen into the hands of a woman who is the daughter of the Devil, and the greatest scoundrels and heretics in the land." He knew England well, and had recently been married to Jane Dormer, who was, by the way, Philip Sidney's cousin, the godson of the Spanish King.

At first, Elizabeth, though a daughter of the Devil, did not act too precipitately. Neither she nor Cecil was sure, as yet, as to how much the country would stand. And they first wanted to get the coronation safely over. The government, therefore, proceeded with caution.

The second day after Mary's death there was issued a proclamation, startling in view of what followed, but which was at the moment taken (as it was intended to be taken) by the Catholics as reassuring. It read: "The Queen straitly charges and commands all manner of our subjects of every degree not to attempt upon any pretence, the breach, alteration, or change of any order or usage, presently established within this our realm upon pain of our indignation, and the pains and penalties which thereto may in any manner belong." On the face of it, that seemed to indicate no change. Only such people as were skilled at reading between the lines caught a hint that, though all *unauthorised* change in religion was prohibited, one that was *authorised* was coming. The "pains and penalties" could even be taken as meaning the fires of Smithfield, even if these had been extinguished some months before Mary's death. What the proclamation really meant the whole country was soon to know. But no move was made while the dead Queen's body was lying in state, all the churches resounding with requiem Masses for the repose of her soul.

There was, however, a new Privy Council appointed, one whose make-up must have been disquieting to Catholics. In Mary's Council there had been thirty-five members, far too many, it must be granted, for serviceable use. Of these only eleven were retained, among whom was Archbishop Heath of York, who had formally proclaimed Elizabeth Queen in his capacity of Chancellor. To have summarily dismissed him just then would have been highly impolitic. But eight new men, all of them known to be Protestant in sympathies, were brought in. To those excluded, apologies were given: no slight was intended, it was explained; but a smaller Council was necessary for efficiency. It is worth recording the names of the eight: they were Parr, the Marquis of Northampton, the Earl of Bedford (one of the greatest beneficiaries of the monastic loot), Edward Rogers, Sir Thomas Parry, Sir Ambrose Cave, Francis Knollys (a Boleyn cousin), and Cecil himself. The eighth name was that of Sir Nicholas Bacon, the father of a famous son, who before long replaced Archbishop Heath, though only with the title of Lord Keeper. All of which makes clear that the main lines of Elizabeth's religious policy were already decided upon.

It was still too early, however, for Elizabeth to show her hand. The first thing was to get her crowned and anointed; then there would be attaching to her the sacrosanct character of majesty. Yet of eventual religious changes there already appeared signs that were ominous. For instance, when Elizabeth entered London on November 23 and was met at Highgate by a delegation of bishops, she went out of her way to be discourteous to Bonner, refusing him her hand to kiss. Still, this could be interpreted as nothing more than disapproval of his part in the burnings, or mere personal dislike. But four days later William Bill, whom Mary had deprived for doubtful orthodoxy, was put up to preach at Paul's Cross. He reproved the excesses of the Protestant mobs who had begun to disturb the saying of Mass, but the rest of his sermon was not at all Catholic. Then when Christopherson, the Bishop of Chichester, preaching the following Sunday at Paul's Cross, refuted Bill, he was at once committed to prison. Nevertheless all this was still discounted by the Catholics. Christopherson, they argued for their comfort, had flouted the Queen's authority in confuting her preacher. The incident, they hoped, meant no more than that.

While Mary's body was lying in state it was hardly seemly for Elizabeth to do anything definite. But eleven days after the funeral, the Queen, choosing Christmas day, ordered Oglethorpe, the Bishop of Carlisle, who was to say her Mass, to omit the elevation. Oglethorpe very properly refused to comply on the ground that he had no right to depart from the established rubric, so Elizabeth walked out at the consecration.

It should be noted that the Queen gave this order on her direct personal authority. No official alteration had yet been made in religion. Parliament had not yet met. England was still in communion with Rome. The only indication so far given that the Queen might resume the Royal Supremacy over the Church was that, while she did not put that Supremacy among her titles (since it was not yet legal for her to do so), she had begun to employ the "&cetera" which Mary had found a convenience until such time as Parliament allowed her to renounce the Supremacy. The implication was unmistakable: Elizabeth believed that the mere fact of her being Queen gave her authority over the Church, and that the function of Parliament was limited to a declaration of an authority which was inalienably inherent in kingship. But still she refrained from any open declaration; she had to be crowned first.

Now comes a curious fact: the monarch whom Pastor describes as "within the boundaries of England . . . more king than a Charles V, and more Pope than a Gregory VII or an Innocent III" was superstitious enough to consult the astrologer, Dr. Dee, about the most lucky day for her coronation. We shall perhaps do the doctor an injustice if we look upon him merely as a charlatan. A fellow of Trinity College, Cambridge, and a lecturer at Paris on Mathematics, he was an astronomer, hydrographer, geographer, and crystallographer. Before dying at the age of eighty-one he wrote seventy-nine books, among which was an autobiography where we are introduced to his eight children and their mother, "painful Jane." Among his discoveries was the philosopher's stone for invoking angels. Shakespeare probably had him in mind when he wrote of summoning spirits from the vasty deep. The handsome young Welshman — of Arthurian descent, as he claimed — was perhaps a genius, but as his alchemical experiments were not productive of much gold, he was obliged to seek it by other means. After all, he did have eight hungry children and painful Jane to provide for. Then as now the intellectually emancipated were among the easiest of people to humbug. So Dr. Dee drew his horoscopes, consulted his crystals and the stars, and pocketed the Queen's fee. Having done which, he selected January 15.

Even under these auspices, a serious hitch in the coronation plans very nearly occurred. Archbishop Heath should have done the crowning; he flatly refused. And all his fifteen colleagues — several bishoprics were vacant — also refused to officiate. Even Kitchen of Llandaff, the only one among them who eventually conformed to the Elizabethan settlement, was resolute in his refusal. In the end, however, Oglethorpe of Carlisle consented.

It is interesting to note the reason he gave, according to Sanders: "Lest the Queen should be angry if no one would anoint her, and be more easily moved to overthrow religion." Sanders adds, "Nor were things at this time so desperate but that many hoped it might still be possible to turn her from her purpose." In other words, all the bishops knew (or guessed) what was in Elizabeth's mind. The best that Oglethorpe could hope for was the bare chance that, by his avoiding provocation, the Queen might prove amenable. It was a serious error of judgment. Had he stood firm with the others, Elizabeth would have been forced to show her hand at once by sending for one of the deprived Edwardian bishops, or to give satisfactory guarantees to the Catholics. She would probably have adopted the second course, though this does not mean that she could have been counted upon to have kept her word. As it was, she had gained her main point: it was sufficient that one bishop be found to do what was required of him. Afterwards she could settle scores with the hierarchy.

The coronation procession was a tremendous success. Elizabeth had all the arts of the actress and the showman at her command, and she employed them to the full. Her stage managers saw to it that little performances should be put on at various points in the route that would make clear to the cheering public her true religious sentiments. The government had a magnificent opportunity for catching the populace of London in its mood of most exuberant loyalty, and of making patriotism seem synonymous with Protestantism. At one place a child was let down from a triumphal arch to present the Queen with a copy of the English Bible, and, as Holinshed relates, Elizabeth "as soon as she had received the book, kissed it, and with both hands held up the same, and so laid it upon her breast, with great thanks to the city therefor." At another place there was stationed a young woman arrayed as a queen, and over her head was the inscription, "Deborah, the judge and restorer of the house of Israel." The procession was turned into a Protestant demonstration.

Elizabeth looked a splendid figure that day riding in her open litter with its gold embroidery matching the cloth of gold of her gown. The guards on either hand were in uniforms of crimson and carried gilded battle-axes. Her footmen wore on back and breast the white and red roses of York and Lancaster and the initials "E. R." On her red hair was the coronet of a princess. When she put her foot to ground, her erectness and slimness gave the impression that she was tall. Everybody felt that the young Queen had a smile specially for him, or was waving to him personally. One especially radiant smile, given while she was going up Cheapside, made one of the attendants ask what it was that so pleased her. She answered, "Because I have just overheard one say in the crowd, 'I remember old King Harry the Eighth.'" The chronicler exclaims delightedly, "How many nosegays did her Grace receive at poor women's hands: how ofttimes she stayed her chariot, when she saw any simple body offer to speak to her Grace!" Though some Catholics considered the whole affair rather vulgar — the Mantuan agent wrote that in his opinion the Queen "exceeded the bounds of gravity and decorum" — all this depends upon the point of view. For the attaining of her object — the roar of the crowd — Elizabeth must be admitted to have behaved with the utmost cleverness. It was her personal triumph; the best stage management in the world might have let the whole show fall flat had there not been at the centre of the stage the most consummate actress in the world.

Unfortunately, one must add that she was also the world's most consummate liar. Having cajoled Oglethorpe into crowning her, she committed, shamelessly in the sight of all and without any fear of God, cold-blooded and monstrous perjury. To make it, if possible, worse, she committed the offence at a moment when she and her councillors had already (though secretly) decided upon the proscription of the religion the Queen was vowing to defend.

Lingard says that the bishops, except for Oglethorpe, absented themselves from the ceremony. This is an error; they were present in copes and mitres and met her singing *Salve, festa dies*. There was no point in their staying away after Oglethorpe had yielded under pressure. Perhaps they clung to a faint hope that what was to happen would not prove to be so bad as they feared, for nobody yet, except Elizabeth and her closest advisers, knew precisely what was going to be done. As loyal subjects of the Queen they wished to show their loyalty. They showed their loyalty to the Church by withdrawing when at the Mass, said by the royal chaplain, the elevation was omitted. Understanding the significance of this — that it implied a denial of the Real Presence — they must have looked at one another with dismayed faces.

Edward, like his sister Mary, was crowned after a Mass in Latin, and, of course, took the same oath that Elizabeth took. But as Edward was only ten at the time, he cannot be blamed for perjury. No such extenuation can be offered in Elizabeth's behalf.

The terms of the coronation oath should be set down. When Oglethorpe, following the prescribed ritual, asked, "Will you grant and keep, and by your oath confirm . . . the Laws, Customs and Franchises, granted to the clergy by the glorious King St. Edward, your predecessor?" Elizabeth did not blush to answer, "I grant and promise to observe them." The Bishop went on, "Will you keep peace and godly agreement entirely according to your power, both to God, to the Holy Church, to the Clergy, and to the People?" And Elizabeth returned, "I will keep it." Then there was, according to the liturgy, a formal request: "We beseech you to grant us pardon, to preserve unto us and to the churches committed to our charge all canonical privileges and due law and justice; to protect and defend us, as every good king in his kingdom ought to be the defender of the bishops and churches under his government." The solemn promise was made: "With a willing and devout heart, I promise and grant my pardon, and that I will preserve and maintain to you and to the churches committed to your charge all canonical privileges and due law and justice, and that I will be your protector and defender to my power, by the assistance of God, as every good king in his kingdom ought in right to protect and defend the bishops and churches under their government." The ritual concludes, "This done, the King (or Queen) doth confirm that he will observe the premisses of his oath, taken immediately upon the altar before all."

It is painful to write these words down even four hundred years after the event. But they are needed if the story of Elizabeth, and Elizabeth's own character, are to be comprehended. When she retired with her ladies in waiting to the withdrawing room, she wiped off the sacred oil of anointing and with a grimace muttered, "Pah, it stinks!" But she had got what she wanted that day in the chrism. She was now fully Queen of England. She could now proceed to the breaking of her oath. One wonders whether her disgust with the holy oil may not really have been disgust with herself.

The oil still stinks.

6

∞

The Elizabethan Settlement

AFTER the coronation, events began to move swiftly. It is likely enough that Elizabeth and her advisers were still far from certain as to all the details of their religious policy, and indeed the Thirty-Nine Articles, the official body of doctrine of the Church of England, were not sanctioned until 1563 and did not become fully operative legally until 1571, but the chief features of the settlement must have been determined as soon as Elizabeth came to the throne, if not before. It was, however, her method always to seek Parliamentary sanction for what she had decided to do. So Parliament was summoned to meet ten days after the coronation.

On that day (January 25) Elizabeth was met at Westminster by a procession of its monks carrying lighted candles. Having now no further use for Catholic rites, she could afford to be rude, even about so indifferent a matter as a procession. "Put away those torches!" she snarled in her deep harsh voice. "We see well enough without them." If nobody could be more affable when it suited her, nobody could be more brutally and (as in this case) gratuitously boorish. Professor Pollard has said of Henry that he was every inch a king — and no gentleman. With the sex transposed, the same might be said of Elizabeth. The coarse streak in her emerged again. She went out of her way to insult those whom she was about to strike down. It was safe now: she had a packed Council and a packed Parliament; and she was crowned.

The packing of the House of Commons has been denied. It is true enough that — judging from the incomplete list of the membership of her first House of Commons — about half of its members had already sat in one of Mary's Parliaments. But the

77

Queen Elizabeth

subservience of these men was well known: they could be safely counted upon to pass Protestant legislation in the same way that they had obediently upheld Catholic laws in the previous reign. Not all strong Catholics were rooted out from among them; there was no need for that. Only the new members were hand-picked. Father John Hungerford Pollen, the author of the most sober and accurate book on Elizabethan ecclesiastical matters, has said that "it was not necessary in those days to bribe very heavily." I might add that it was not necessary for the excellent reason that many of them had been bribed already: they belonged to the class that had profited by the loot under Henry and Edward and had consented to the Marian restoration only on condition that their monastic holdings were to be left to them. But as the events of Mary's reign had made them fear that, if Catholicism were allowed to grow in strength, they would, sooner or later, have to make some sort of restitution, they were only too willing to insure their property by a profession of Protestantism.

This was still more true of the Privy Council. Even after its reconstruction, half of its personnel was Catholic in belief. But these Catholics had also been enriched by the spoils of the Church and would offer no effective opposition to anything that the inner "kitchen cabinet" of Cecil and Knollys and Bacon and Bedford proposed. Like the majority of Englishmen of the time, they were weary and bored by religious conflict. Such dogmatic convictions as they had were not allowed to interfere with their private profit.

We must disabuse our minds, moreover, of the idea that a Tudor Parliament acted with anything like the independence of those that met under the Stuarts, or, for that matter, under the mediaeval kings. While they were not like the assemblies of modern totalitarian regimes, whose function is merely to register decisions already made by their dictators, little liberty of discussion was allowed them. It was the Privy Council that was the effective engine of government, and to that body all appointments were made directly by the monarch who, indeed, was free to act in disregard of the Council's advice. Parliament was summoned as rarely as possible and only to vote supplies or when an additional colour of legality was needed by the Queen.

Further, we should remember that the House of Lords had far more legislative influence than the Commons. And the House of Lords could always be packed by the simple device of creating new peers, or by some trick by which the members in opposition were for the moment excluded. Elizabeth combined both methods in this Parliament. Bishop Christopherson was already in jail; two other bishops were soon to join him there; several other spiritual peers were prevented from voting;[1] and, to make sure that the scales were weighted on the right side, five strong Protestants were sent to the Upper House. These were William Parr, the brother of the late Queen Dowager, who was made Marquis of Northampton; Somerset's son, whose earldom of Hereford was now restored; Henry Carey, the son of Anne Boleyn's sister Mary, now created Baron Hunsdon; Howard of Bindon; and St. John of Bletso. Well might Feria write to Philip, "The Queen has entire disposal of the Upper Chamber in a way never seen before in previous parliaments." Elizabeth and Cecil had the situation "in the bag" before they began.

The House of Lords since the destruction of the monasteries had been a very small body, the abbots no longer being there. Even so, the spiritual lords were fewer by six than they should have been because of Pole's negligence in filling vacant bishoprics[2] — rightly described by Feria as "fatal." It was known that the voting would be close. Of the eighty-four lords, thirty-seven were reckoned as resolutely Catholic. But if those whose Protestantism was open and vigorous numbered only twenty-one, the seven who were classified as "trimmers" and the sixteen "uncertain" were likely to fall in line behind the administration. To be on the safe side, the government packed the Upper House, and on the crucial vote got a majority of three. In the House of Commons the majority was somewhat larger.

[1] Feckenham, the sole abbot left in the kingdom, was refused his seat, along with the Prior of the Knights of St. John. And the Bishop of St. Asaph, on the ground that his translation to Oxford was still in process, was at first excluded.

[2] The vacancy caused by Pole's own death brings the total to seven.

But a majority of three is still a majority. That Elizabeth was quite sure of the outcome is shown by the fact that on February 1, long, long before Parliament passed the Supremacy Bill, relations with Rome were broken off. This also indicates that the English government was not — as is usually represented — acting defensively against the Papacy. Rome had done nothing; England was still part of the universal Church. The aggression came entirely from the side of Elizabeth's administration. They did not wait to see what the attitude of the Pope might be; they did not want union and refused all attempts at reconciliation; they were out to eradicate Catholicism. The same men who had previously supported Mary's restoration of the Mass now united to destroy it.

The question arises as to what proportion of the English people were in favour of this revolutionary change. To ask it is perhaps rather academic in view of the fact that the people were not consulted nor had any way of making their wishes known. For that matter, they had no idea as to just what the government proposed doing, nor were they, as a rule, capable of forming any clear concept of the significance of the official moves. The adhesion of the governing classes counted infinitely more than the opinions of the mob who, without the gentry, were leaderless. Majority was not in those days a determining factor in politics; even in our own time we have seen in Germany and Russia what an organized minority can accomplish.

What we know, however, is that the Convocation of the Clergy, which met a day before the opening of Parliament under the presidency of Bonner, spoke in unmistakable terms unanimously reaffirming belief in all Catholic doctrines, including that of the Pope's Supremacy and the Real Presence — the two fundamental issues. They were ignored: the Elizabethan settlement was wholly a lay affair against which the voice of the pastors was raised in vain. Even such Protestant extremists as John Knox and John à Lasco denounced the imposition of doctrine and liturgy on the Church by laymen, the one as "carnal wisdom and worldly policy," the other, as "parliamentary theology."

The Elizabethan Settlement

But if England was now governed in religious matters by lay politicians — men enriched by the loot of the monasteries — there was undoubtedly a good deal of anticlericalism among the masses. Clerical exactions had long been odious, and though the Marian persecution had been approved by Parliament and the Privy Council, the sentences on the heretics had been passed by ecclesiastics, who thereby had increased their odium.[3] This anticlerical and antiprelatical sentiment was a powerful motivating force in early Protestantism. Elizabeth expressed it in her own fashion when she said of her parsons, "Two or three of them are enough for a whole county." So high an ideal proving to be impracticable, at least the clergy were to be kept under subjection to the civil power.[4] Of a more positive Protestantism there was relatively little, outside of London and those southern and eastern seaports that had been most infected from abroad. The doctrines of the reformers were a foreign product, from which the more English parts of England were almost totally free.

This is not to say, however, that any part of England — even the north — was specially enthusiastic about the continuance of the union with Rome. Thomas Percy, for instance, the Earl of Northumberland, who was later executed by Elizabeth (and eventually beatified as a martyr), and his brother, who was to be murdered in prison, were both on the commission for administering the Oath of Supremacy to the clergy. They may have accepted their office reluctantly; that they did so at all is typical of the times. The lines were not yet clearly drawn: few understood that union with Rome was necessary if England was to preserve the Faith. We may therefore say that the majority, like Elizabeth herself, would probably have preferred a return to the Henrician system of the Mass without the Pope.

[3] The Elizabethan persecution of Catholics escaped this by condemning the recusants in the civil courts, not on religious grounds but on those of treason. The new method was disingenuous but shrewd.

[4] A late example of what I have in mind is to be found in Froude. He is anti-clerical rather than anti-Catholic, his animosity extending almost impartially to parsons as well as priests. This animosity was slightly modified in favour of parsons only because they were, to a great extent, under lay control and because the Reformation meant the triumph of the layman over the cleric.

Queen Elizabeth

The situation was perplexing. Four times in twelve years — in 1547, 1549, 1552, and 1559 — there had been alterations in the established religion. And these alterations had brought about confusion in men's minds. That they could not have been very zealous in their religious life to have permitted them to occur without vigorous protest is obvious. But the changes themselves had served to increase indifference, while among those who deplored them most a comfortable illusion was created that there was no need to worry, that the new settlement would prove to be as impermanent as those that had preceded it.

What I think must be discounted are the extravagant statements made as to the number of Catholics in England at the beginning of Elizabeth's reign. When Feria said that two thirds of the people ceased to attend Mass after the fall of Calais, that could have been only a fashion of speaking. On the other hand, when some of the *emigrés* quite late in Elizabeth's reign assured Philip II that three quarters or (according to some of their estimates), nine tenths of all Englishmen were Catholics at heart, that was merely wishful thinking. Something had to be done to convince Philip that England was only waiting a chance to throw off Protestantism; otherwise he would not be spurred to attack.

It would be safer to estimate that in 1559 two thirds of the English people — including even the noble robbers — were vaguely Catholic in sympathies. Unfortunately few were found sufficiently attached to their faith to fight for it; and in the beginning, as we shall see, various ingenious compromises in the matter of practice allowed them to believe that it was not necessary to fight at all. For they were able to retain Catholicism as a private conviction, and the surreptitious saying of Mass was for a number of years winked at. The remaining one third of the people were perhaps about equally divided into camps so definitely Catholic and Protestant as to admit no compromise. We must remember, however, that no reliable statistics exist, only reports on local conditions and subjective impressions.

The attitude of the clergy provides the best index, though

The Elizabethan Settlement

even here we are on uncertain ground. The strong Catholic affirmations of Convocation have been noted. They represented the attitude of the abler and more intelligent of the clergy, who were — we must gather from this — Catholic almost to a man. The bishops, with the solitary exception of Kitchen of Llandaff, refused the settlement. He had been Abbot of Eynsham, and had been rewarded for his complaisant surrender at the time of the dissolution of the monasteries with a royal chaplaincy and, in 1545, with a bishopric. That he, too, was a Catholic at heart is shown by his refusal to crown one whom he suspected of the intention of perjury and by his later refusal to take part in the consecration of Matthew Parker as Archbishop of Canterbury. He was eighty-one in 1559, too old for resistance. If he conformed, none of his colleagues did.

When we come to the parish priests, the story is different. Camden, the annalist, says that there were 9,400 living in England, and that less than two hundred of the incumbents were deprived.[5] That statement still appears in most histories of the period, though, since the researches of Dom Norbert Birt, it has become open to serious question. Fathers Birt and Pollen — and they are upon the whole supported by the German Protestant historian, Arnold Oskar Meyer — contend that Camden's figures are misleading. Of the nine thousand odd benefices many were held by pluralists, so that the number of priests may be reasonably reduced to eight thousand, which figure Pollard accepts. Of these Birt estimates, after an exhaustive examination of such registers as exist, that seven hundred were deprived and that eleven hundred and seventy-five gave up their livings. Those who continued to work actively as missionaries were few; so also were those who went abroad. But we have no means of knowing how many were kept privately as chaplains or secretaries in the houses of the wealthy; and there were undoubtedly many who, rather than take the Oath of Supremacy, lived as best they could as farmers or artizans. But again we

[5] Many who were not deprived suffered sequestration, that is, suspension, not a deprival of their benefices. Some of these, no doubt, conformed later. But even when they did not, they are not numbered by Camden among those who refused the Elizabethan settlement.

have no figures for England as a whole. What we do know is that of the eight hundred priests in the London diocese who conformed at first, twelve at least — probably more, but we have records of twelve — later repudiated their conformity. As against this it is likely enough that some who at first refused conformity were afterwards obliged to give in their adhesion.

In any case, even supposing we adopt the largest estimate — which is probably too large — only a quarter of the clergy declined to compromise with conscience. Of the remaining three quarters not many were convinced Protestants; they yielded to force of circumstances, hoping that better days would come. Elizabeth might die or marry a Catholic. God in His good time would right the wrong. Comforted by such considerations, the average priest accepted the Prayer Book and said his Mass in private. In the severest judgement passed upon them it must be allowed that at least they showed far more courage than the Henrician clergy.

One strong inducement held out to them was the permission to marry. Some of them had done so during Edward's reign, and these had been given their choice under Mary of putting away their wives or of being deprived. But the tradition of clerical celibacy had been weakened: there was new weight in the argument that marriage was preferable to the secret concubinage that had too often been practised.

The strongest inducement of all was that conformity secured them in their livings. Like the laity, the clergy had been shaken by the successive revolutions in religion, and hardly less than the laity had an excessive reverence for the Crown. Some of their members had already shown themselves past masters in pliancy. The Vicar of Bray of the song is mythical; but the Vicar of Blisland in Cornwall, who was inducted in 1529, lived through all the changes under Henry, Edward, Mary, and Elizabeth, to die in possession in 1581 — a triumph of subservience to the powers that be! Men of this unheroic stamp were not of the metal to withstand the redoubtable Elizabeth. If so large a proportion of the clergy showed themselves to be of the willow rather than of the oak, we may justly infer that the proportion was still higher among the laity to whom they set an example. Against such feeble opposition Elizabeth and Cecil could ride roughshod.

In magnificent contrast stands out the action of the bishops. It is true that they might have done more than they did. Perhaps they should have launched against the Queen the excommunication a minority of them proposed, even if this could have been no more than a valiant gesture. In other respects, too, a greater vigour could have been shown. Archbishop Heath, for instance, when making his speech in the House of Lords against the Royal Supremacy, based his argument on the ground that no woman could be head of the Church because no woman could preach or administer the sacraments. It opened the door to the rejoinder that it was an admission that then an English King *was* capable of such functions. In any event Heath's argument lost much of its weight owing to the fact that Elizabeth was, after all, making no such Caesaro-papal claims for herself as had been asserted by Henry. She was too clever not to avoid that absurdity, and contented herself with the title of "Supreme Governess," with the implication of limited instead of unlimited powers over the Church. Nicholas Heath would have done better to have said boldly all that he meant — namely, that no law of man could override the law of God and the authority conferred by Christ upon His Vicar on earth. Heath, however, was not an inspiring leader, as appears in his answer to Feria when he asked the Archbishop what could be done: "Nothing can be done but we can suffer whatever God wills." Bonner, as a far more resolute man, might have successfully captained the English Church in the crisis had he not made himself extremely unpopular by his share in the burnings under Mary. The hierarchy could therefore make no more than a dignified protest and go down to defeat.

The government, however, was not content with a demonstration of its power to impose Protestantism; it decided to demonstrate also the weakness of the Catholic case. Accordingly the Westminster Conference was called for a series of public debates between the reformers and the bishops.

It is worthy of note that these debates began on March 31, 1559, and that the Act of Supremacy did not finally pass until April 25 or receive the royal assent, making it law, until May 8. Yet the outcome being already foregone, Sir Nicholas Bacon, who presided at the Conference, did not hesitate to use his chairmanship as though the Queen's Supremacy over the Church already existed. But, of course, his position and that of the government was that this Supremacy was, and always had been, inherent in the monarchy.

Again the Catholic champions were tricked into a false position. They had been given to understand that, as the defenders of the doctrine still legally established, they had certain rights. Yet these rights were steadily denied them. Though they were told that they should begin and that Jewel and his confrères make the rebuttal, Bacon changed the rules of debate from day to day so as to give the Protestant disputants the advantage by putting the Catholics on the defensive. At first, too, it was agreed that Latin should be used; then, without notice, English was adopted. And though it had been arranged that the debates were to be in private, they were thrown open to a lay audience before which the Protestants could declaim.[6] Finally, Bacon ruled that only the reading of written arguments was to be allowed, and when the Catholics protested against this, saying that they had not been notified in time, the fat Lord Keeper roared at them, "For that you will not that we shall hear you, you may perhaps shortly hear from us." That same afternoon two of the Bishops, those of Winchester and Lincoln, were thrown into the Tower, and so could not vote upon the Supremacy bill still before Parliament. The rest of the Bishops were fined £3,000 and ordered to present themselves daily before the Council until their fate could be determined.

Tricks of this sort ensured the legal establishment of Elizabeth's Supremacy. This was the essential point to secure; from

[6] Bacon permitted (perhaps he instigated) the blasphemous discourtesy of a Protestant controversialist who, as soon as a Catholic had finished speaking, offered a prayer, ostentatiously turning his back meanwhile upon the Blessed Sacrament.

it everything else would follow.[7] Henry, as has been said by someone, claimed to be the Pope, the whole Pope, and something more than the Pope. Though precisely what was involved in Elizabeth's title of "Governess" was not yet clear — since the Thirty-Nine Articles were not issued until four years later — it might be as well to set down the article dealing with the Supremacy. It reads: "We give not to our princes the ministering either of God's word or of the sacraments, the thing which the injunctions [of 1559] also set forth by Elizabeth our Queen do most plainly testify, but that only prerogative which we see to have been always given to all godly princes in Holy Scripture by God Himself; that is, that they should rule all estates and degrees committed to their charge by God, whether they be ecclesiastical or temporal, and restrain with the civil sword the stubborn and evil doers." This limitation was not, however, indicated at the outset: the term *Governess* could be interpreted, by those who wanted so to interpret it, as of practically unlimited application, while on the other hand, Catholics who were looking for a loophole for their consciences were able to maintain that nothing so radical as Henry's position was implied and that they could take the oath. The paragraph just quoted was a later gloss; at the time Protestants who pushed the Erastian theory to its logical conclusion could argue (and did argue) when the question of the validity of Archbishop Parker's consecration was brought up, that even if it could be proved to be insufficient, the royal sufficiency would cover everything.

This argument, however, was only the thinly spun theory advanced by the more ingenious of the extremists. What counted much more was the pragmatic argument of *Cuius regio, eius religio*, a position incomprehensible today, though totalitarianism seems prepared to take up similar ground. In the sixteenth century it was widely accepted as a truism.

Yet even at this early stage disruptive forces were already

---

[7] We need not, however, stress too much the majority of three in the House of Lords. Even had they been defeated, the government would have found some means of passing their bill — perhaps through a conference of both Houses or, if necessary, through further packing of the Upper Chamber.

at work upon Anglican unity — if it can be said ever to have existed. Calvinism, which was widespread in England, asserted a theocracy — which was a good reason for Elizabeth detesting the Puritans. At the same time we should, of course, remember that many Elizabethan theologians — Archbishop Whitgift for example — accepted the Calvinistic system in its main lines and yet were strong upholders of the episcopacy. We must also remember that among the supporters of the Settlement were not a few who held that, while bishops should be left as a useful convenience, they should be stripped of their endowments and be paid directly out of the royal treasury. Arma il Wade — clerk of the Privy Council — considered a pittance of five hundred or a thousand crowns ample. As a matter of fact some episcopal endowments were taken away, Cecil blandly explaining, "I like no spoil, but I allow to have good things put to a good use" — the good use being to hand them over to the courtiers. His own estate of Burghley had once been monastic property.

The Prayer Book soon followed the Supremacy. In this matter Elizabeth and her advisers have often been praised for their moderation — which consisted, for the most part, in the removal from Edward's VI's second Prayer Book of some of the passages most calculated to be offensive to Catholics. The people were, for example, no longer invited to pray to be "delivered from the Pope of Rome and his detestable enormities." And the Thirty-Nine Articles, when they appeared, were only the Edwardian Forty-Two, with the scurrilous bits omitted. What the new liturgy provided was a service in the vernacular — something that was popular — and one of incomparable majesty and charm. Cranmer had achieved the feat of making his translations even finer than the originals.

Though what the Anglican Church got in the end was the Order of Morning and Evening Prayer, from which the Communion Service was carefully separated and still more carefully reduced to nothing but a memorial of Christ's death, it was by no means certain, until the last moment, that the Mass in English would not, after all, be retained. On December 29,

1558, no more radical change had been introduced than that of having the Gospel and Epistle read in English. And as Easter approached a proclamation was drawn up and printed (British Museum, G. 6463) legally enjoining an English Mass with Communion in both kinds.[8] Only at the last minute did Elizabeth change her mind, and the proclamation was withdrawn. Instead, an absolute prohibition (as from June 24, 1559) of the saying of Mass was issued. Only then did the full intentions of the reformers appear. The breach with Rome was to be a breach with Catholicism as well.

Elizabeth would have preferred to keep the Catholic forms. She by no means approved the Protestant excesses that broke out after her accession; and even after the Settlement, when Nowell, the Dean of St. Paul's, preached in her presence against images, she called out in a loud voice, "To your text, Mr. Dean! To your text! Leave that; we have had enough of that. To your subject!" In her own chapel she was "High Church," displaying a crucifix and candles. And to Quadra, Feria's successor in 1559, she said, "I long to be a nun, and to pass my days in a cell," adding that there was no difference, except of phraseology, between her beliefs and those held by Catholics. Though there is no need to take this sort of thing too seriously — the cynical Ambassador commented, "This woman must have a hundred thousand devils in her body" — it is probably true that, in so far as her secular mind occupied itself with religion, she had a Catholic taste.

Unfortunately it went no further than being a taste, and that taste was not shared by large groups of her subjects. Even before 1558 was out, mobs of rowdies in London were incited to make attacks upon images and to create disturbances at Mass. One man, a printer, on Ascension Day, 1559, snatched the processional crucifix away in St. Paul's Cathedral — where Bonner was still stoutly holding out — and showed the broken fragments of the figure of Christ to his Protestant friends as "the Devil's guts." In January the Venetian Agent wrote to the Doge to tell him, "The greater part of the people have entirely re-

[8] It may be seen in Gee's *The Elizabethan Prayer-book* (1902 ed.), p. 235.

nounced the Mass," but said there was no interference with those who attend. A month later Il Schifanoya, the Mantuan Agent, writes that Mass is still being said in the London churches, "the Host being elevated as usual in the presence of large congregations who show much devotion." But on April 14 we find Jewel writing to Peter Martyr: "The Mass in many places has of itself fallen to the ground, without any laws for its discontinuance." He offsets this, however, by telling the same correspondent on March 20 that at Oxford University there are scarcely two men "who think with us," adding bitterly, "Two famous virtues, namely ignorance and obstinacy, have wonderfully increased at Oxford since you left it."

In view of all this no generalisation can be safely attempted. The contradictions that appear in Jewel's own letters reveal that conditions varied in different parts of the country, and among different classes of men. The universities, especially Oxford, were still Catholic in the main; so also were the professional classes everywhere. But there was a vociferous Protestant group in London, and it was this group that chiefly attracted the attention of English and foreign observers. London's adhesion to the new religion — though this is not to say that there was anything like a majority of Protestants even there — ensured the success of the English Reformation, just as the fidelity of Paris to the Faith during the later wars of religion saved it in France. The Catholics were at a disadvantage: they kept quiet because they wished to provoke no strife, while their enemies used all the arts of propaganda without check. The roaring mobs made London seem to be more Protestant than it actually was.

The Catholic bishops were now summarily dealt with. Bonner was several times during May urged to resign. He refused to do either that or to take the Oath of Supremacy; therefore, on June 11 the Blessed Sacrament was removed from his cathedral of St. Paul's and he was deprived. When the Council warned him that he would have to consider carefully how he was to live if this happened to him, he made the noble reply: "It is true nothing else remains to me, but I trust in God who will not fail me, and in my friends. . . . I shall be able to gain my living by teaching children, which profession I did not disdain to exercise, although I was a bishop; and should I not find anyone willing to accept my teaching, I am a Doctor in the Laws, and will resume the study of what I have forgotten, and will thus gain my bread; and should this not succeed, I know how to labour with my hands in gardens and orchards as well as any gardener in this kingdom; and should all this also be insufficient, I desire no other grace, favour or privilege from her Majesty than what she grants to mendicants who go through London from door to door begging."

The Council had tried to win him over, as they tried to win all the bishops over. As he would not budge, he was imprisoned, and died ten years later in the Marshalsea. From the point of view of the administration it was impossible to allow him to be at large, even as a beggar. Nor were they ready to make him the martyr he was quite ready to be.

None of the deprived bishops were given their liberty, though Goldwell succeeded in escaping to the continent, where he died in 1585. They were, however, treated upon the whole with what, considering the methods of those days, was no undue rigour. Elizabeth could have proceeded against those who refused the oath as traitors, as her father had done. She was too shrewd to do so. It was enough to keep them in custody so as to prevent their becoming centres of Catholic reaction. And though bloody laws against "Papists" were passed, they were for some time held merely *in terrorem*. It was hoped that these laws would never have to be enforced, but that Catholicism in England, deprived of its bishops, and with its priests forbidden to say Mass, would quietly and painlessly fade away. It was this expectation, rather than an inclination to mercy, that saved the recusants, for the time being, from the severe persecution they were eventually obliged to endure.

The extremists howled in vain for the putting to death of the "caged wolves"; Cecil was content to keep them caged. And though the treatment given them varied, in most instances their caging was not uncomfortable, however irksome and humiliating it may have been. The usual procedure was to give the bishops an easy confinement in the palaces of their successors. Archbishop Heath, the best treated of all, after a short imprisonment, for form's sake, was permitted to retire to his estate in Kent, where Elizabeth now and then visited him. She bore him no grudge; perhaps she was even grateful to him for having advised against the excommunication proposed by several of his more hotheaded colleagues. All parties, with good reason, respected the former Lord Chancellor: he had fallen, but was not disgraced. His pious, if not particularly heroic life, came to an end in 1578. Of course Bonner, and one or two other bishops who were regarded as dangerous men, were never released from jail.

But if Elizabeth retained some personal affection for Archbishop Heath, she made a palpable hit against him in her address to the deprived bishops on December 6, 1559. She said, "As for our father being withdrawn from the supremacy of Rome by schismatical and heretical counsels and advisers, who, we pray you, advised him more, or flattered him, than you, good Mr. Heath, when you were bishop of Rochester? . . . Nay, further, who was more an adviser of our father than your great Stephen Gardiner, when he lived? Are ye not then those schismatics and heretics? If so, suspend your evil counsels."

The argument could have been met, but it would have done no good to argue. The decisive answer that Heath and Bonner and Tunstall (had he not just died) could have made was that they had erred in accepting the Henrician schism, and had long since repented. They saw more clearly now what a breach with Rome led to, and were not going to repeat their mistake. The reformers often noted with surprise that it was precisely the men who had been most compliant under Henry and Edward who were most resolute under Elizabeth. They need not have been surprised; those who had been closest to old King Henry had the best opportunity for taking the clearest and fullest survey of the question and therefore now, if belatedly, stood firmest.

The Bishops might have pressed home the rejoinder, when

The Elizabethan Settlement

Elizabeth twitted them with their previous acceptance of the Henrician system, that she — and all her advisers — had accepted the Marian restoration. They might have gone even further and pointed out that their own defection could be to some extent extenuated as a mere error in judgment. They had shown weakness, but they had not perceived all that was involved; this was something that had grown clear only with the passage of time. The apostacy of Elizabeth and Cecil, on the other hand, was deliberate and followed a hypocritical profession of Catholicism. If one can perhaps say that Elizabeth's Catholic conformity was known at the time to be merely perfunctory, and that she did no more than the bare minimum required of her, what can justify her perjury at her coronation? As for Cecil, his Marian Catholicism was positively unctuous, as the Catholic controversialists took malicious delight in reminding him. His great enemy, Father Persons, was to describe him as having "frequented Masses, said litanies with the priest, laboured a great pair of beads which he continually carried, preached to his parishioners at Stamford, and asked pardon for his errors in King Edward's time." And Verstegen, in his *Declaration of the True Causes of the Great Troubles* (published at Cologne in 1592), completes the picture by showing Cecil "Creeping to the cross" in an "exterior show of devotion before the high altar." (He, like Persons, also gibes at the famous Cecilian rosary.) Should all this be challenged as exaggeration, it is at least possible to produce the list of those who confessed and communicated at Easter, 1558, in the parish of Vembleton: the first two names on it are those of Sir William and Lady Cecil. But, indeed, the same sort of oily piety was displayed by him during Elizabeth's time — with a Prayer Book substituted for a rosary. It often got on the nerves of Elizabeth, who indulged herself in sneers on the subject. Yet there is reason to suspect that the Secretary's private views about religion were almost as latitudinarian as those of the Queen herself: both were less interested in Protestantism as a doctrine than as a political weapon.

It was this man, however, who became so relentless a persecutor. If Mary and Bonner also persecuted, they at least passionately believed in their cause. Bonner had now proved that he was ready for martyrdom, and when Mary said, during Edward's reign, that she would willingly lay her head on the block rather than renounce her faith and its practice, we know that she meant it. Cecil was of a vastly different stripe. On him Macaulay has delivered the scathing sentence, "The deep stain on his memory is, that for differences of opinion for which he would risk nothing himself, he, in the day of his power, took away without scruple the lives of others." If at first he did not persecute to the death, this was merely because he believed that threats and fines and imprisonment would suffice. From the beginning he dangled a noose over every Catholic head and, when that did not prove enough, he came to make a free use of the hangman.

The early Cecilian "moderation" was, as we shall see as the story progresses, of a very spurious sort. Apart altogether from subsequent butchery, Cecil managed almost at once to place English Catholics in so cruel a position that their lives became a daily martyrdom. For they, who so deeply loved England, were made to appear England's enemies. We may admire the adroitness with which this was contrived; we can feel nothing but loathing for such a refinement of cruelty.

Moreover, when the execution of Catholics commenced, instead of honestly admitting that he killed them on account of their religion, Cecil sent them to their deaths for "treason," refusing them the glory of dying for their faith. The Marian method, however much one may deplore it, was at least straightforward. As for the form of the cruelty, I fancy that many will agree with me that, if a choice must be made between a clean death at the stake and the bloody horrors of Tyburn, Smithfield would be in every way preferable. For at Tyburn the Catholic martyrs were at once cut down from the rope, to be castrated and to have their hearts and their bowels cut out and burnt before their eyes — all this in the knowledge that their heads and quartered bodies would be allowed to rot in public places without burial. It is hard to write with restraint of Cecil. Elizabeth was not cruel except when she was frightened: sometimes she showed mercy; Cecil never. He followed a consistent policy of using any means for de-Catholicising England under the pretext of enforcing loyalty to the Queen.

One more word needs to be said about that concept of loyalty. Mediaeval Catholicism had consistently inculcated the principle that Caesar should have his due. But the authority of the monarchy was held to be subordinate to the law of God, whose custodian was the Papacy. The power of the Crown was also limited in practice by a large number of charters to townships and guilds, as well as by feudal rights. The Renaissance, on the other hand, aggrandised the scope of royal authority, removing from it all previous restraints. The Papacy was denounced; the guilds were destroyed, the charters abrogated; and Parliament was reduced to subserviency. Nevertheless, the tradition of Catholic loyalty persisted, making Catholics an easy prey. Many men found it impossible not to confuse the subjection which was the mark of the new age, with that dignified loyalty which had been the mark of the old. The loyalty of Catholics to the monarchy, therefore, became the most powerful weapon in the hands of the reformers. Only the better educated — the higher clergy, the lawyers (the Inns of Court remained one of the strongest Catholic fortresses during Elizabeth's reign) and university men — seemed to be able to make the necessary distinctions. The mass of the people, despite their loose attachment to Catholicism, were hopelessly bewildered. Out of loyalty to the Queen they felt themselves obliged to conform to the Queen's religion. And when the enemies of England were foreign Catholics, patriotic fervour, among the unthinking, fanned the flame of Protestantism.

Even with all this, the creation of a distinctively Protestant culture was only gradually achieved. The bulk of the clergy was, during the early years of the reign, Catholic in sympathy, and often secretly Catholic in practice. As for the new parsons who were ordained to take the places of those who had refused to take the Oath of Supremacy, they were, in many instances, ignorant artizans whose sole qualification was that they could stumble through the Prayer Book. Landowners who had livings in their bestowal often appointed their domestic servants. Ministers of this sort were obviously not capable of giving any religious instruction. Only in the larger centres was a theological Protestantism to be found, and there it was as a rule fanatical rather than spiritual. It took time to develop parsons who were educated, and still longer to develop those who had a higher idea of religion than that of ranting diatribes against Papists.

Nor were the first Elizabethan bishops men of whom the government could feel particularly proud. In Jewel they had a scholar, though not a very ingratiating character. The others were, for the most part, politicans or protégés of politicians. It is hardly to be wondered that the Puritans had a low opinion of these "successors of the apostles." Matthew Parker, who was chosen for the primacy, was an exception, yet even he was a man of no remarkable brilliance in spite of his pleasant antiquarian hobbies. He possessed, however, genuine piety and was a wise administrator. To his credit it must be said that he showed a reluctance, unique among his fellows, for accepting office. Nobody else said *nolo episcopari;* nobody else could show an episcopate of such dignity and charity and moderation. He was an incarnation of all that was best in Anglicanism. Cecil, who had been his friend at Cambridge, picked him with unerring instinct for the see of Canterbury.

If great shrewdness dictated Parker's appointment, one is tempted to call another of the government's actions a stroke of genius. Perhaps it would be more accurate to say that the effect of that action was what one might associate with a stroke of genius, were not the motive behind it marked by blatant vulgarity. The government used a book for the dissemination of Protestantism, or rather for the increasing of anti-Catholic prejudice. It was Foxe's *Book of Martyrs,* which had been written in Latin during Mary's reign; now translated into English it created a prodigious sensation. No stone ever hurled against the Catholic Church in England ever did so much damage.

It is (or used to be) the fashion to account for the Reformation on the ground that the Scriptures were issued in the vernacular.[9] And they must be admitted to have been a powerful influence over uninstructed minds who were told that here was the sole guide of faith, but who could hardly do other than accept the Bible in the sense that the accompanying notes put upon it and the sense in which they heard the Protestant preachers interpret it. The Bible, however, while it could be made to further the cause of the Reformation, could be no less effectively used by Catholic controversialists, which was why a small group of refugees on the continent produced, as speedily as possible, for the aid of the missionary priests and their flocks, the Douay version of the Scriptures.

The Bible, though translated in a Protestant sense, and buttressed by Protestant notes, was, therefore, as an instrument of propaganda, less important than *The Book of Martyrs*. The government saw to it that Foxe's "Golden Book of Legends," as the Catholics called it, was chained in every church for the people to read. Catholic critics — Cope and Harpsfield, for instance — at once began to point out its many distortions of fact. But it was in vain that the witticism was spread abroad that "many who were burnt in the reign of Queen Mary, drank sack in the reign of Elizabeth." It was in vain that Persons listed "more than a hundred and twenty lies uttered by John Foxe, in less than twenty pages of his *Acts and Monuments*." It was in vain that a man named Grimwood, of Higham in Suffolk, brought an action against the parson of the parish for citing Foxe's account of how this very Grimwood had brought false testimony against John Cooper, one of the martyrs, for which Grimwood — still very much alive — was described by Foxe as having died suddenly and disgustingly under God's judgement. The people crowding into the churches to hear the most let-

[9] There had been many translations of various books of the Bible into English during the Middle Ages, and even secular writers (Chaucer, for example) show how steeped they were in the Scriptures. For those who could not read, there were plays and the pictorial representations in the churches. Middle English was less intelligible to the Elizabethans than it is to us; therefore most of the vernacular translations were by now, in effect, in a dead language. The reformers had the advantage of providing what was, for the moment, the most complete English version so far available — one made in English as it was then spoken.

tered among them read aloud, never heard of the refutations. Nor did they hear of Foxe's own ludicrous defence: that he was not the first historian to make mistakes. Simple, ignorant, and kindly folk — they were stirred and horrified by the account of the sufferings of those whom Mary had sent to the stake. Not unnaturally their indignation made them believe that the Catholic martyrs who were so soon to suffer under Elizabeth got no more than their deserts.

It is not necessary here to make any further exposition of Foxe's fables. That has been done over and over again with great thoroughness, especially by Gardiner and Maitland. One judgment will suffice: it is from J. S. Brewer's Introduction to the first volume of the *Letters and Papers, Foreign and Domestic, of the reign of Henry VIII:* "Had Foxe . . . been an honest man, his carelessness and credulity would have incapacitated him from being a trustworthy historian. Unfortunately he was not honest; he tampered with the documents that came into his hands." Nevertheless, his statements were swallowed without question. They were used by the Elizabethan government precisely in the same way that a modern government uses atrocity stories as war propaganda. All this was, quite literally, part of the Cecilian war against the Catholic Church. The administration must have known the book to be full of lies; they did not regard it as less useful on that account.

It must be admitted that, even today, the best informed reader finds difficulty in resisting the admirable prose style and the astonishing gifts for narrative possessed by the Martyrologist. Though we are well aware that everything in his pages must be taken with at least a grain of salt, we cannot help being moved. And there is, of course, the incontestable fact that, however much Foxe may have exaggerated and lied, Mary did burn close on to three hundred victims. An uncritical audience was then completely at the mercy of such fascinating mendacity.

Until Foxe's book appeared, however, there seems to have been no great public horror at the Marian burnings. Most people probably considered that the persecution had gone too far; hardly any of them objected to the principle of persecution. What Foxe did was to present vivid scenes in such a way as to make them appear more real than the same scenes as they had been beheld by many who were afterwards to read about them. Here, before there was any drama worth talking about, and before there were any novels or newspapers, a tremendously exciting popular literature was provided. It was much more widely read than the Bible. But many of those who were appalled by the account of Catholic cruelties went off to seek, as best they could, in the Bible a justification for Protestantism. It is one more proof of the ability of art to triumph — for a while — over truth.

Again we must applaud Cecil's cleverness, however much we may deplore his unscrupulousness. Though the sharpest weapon that the Elizabethan government was to use against the Church was that of a steadily applied and bloody persecution, and though we must insist that the Catholic England of 1559 and the generation that was to follow lost its faith mainly because that faith was forcibly suppressed, we cannot minimize the effect of propaganda upon the national mind. It is true that Harding (at any rate in the opinion of Catholics) decisively routed Jewel in controversy. But Jewel and Harding did not have one reader where Foxe had a hundred. In so far as the English people were persuaded to become Protestants — in most instances it was not so much that they became Protestants as anti-Catholics — the main credit has to be given to Foxe. Every revolutionary movement is made possible by a book — whether it be the *Contrat Social* or *Das Kapital* or *Mein Kampf*. The Protestant revolution was no exception. Its book was the *Acts and Monuments*.

7

Manoeuvering for Position

THE settlement of religion, though it was destined to succeed, did not succeed at once. All through the long reign
there were threats against it, and the triumph of Protestantism
in England was not secured until a hundred years after the
defeat of the Armada. Especially during the first years of Elizabeth, it was expected that she would fail in what she was attempting, which was one reason why Catholics kept quiet. They
kept quiet until it was too late.

Even apart from religion — if any of the political events of
that time can be so separated — the position of Elizabeth was
sufficiently precarious. She had obtained, indeed, the backing
of a powerful party; but there was no guarantee that their backing would continue indefinitely. Though there was on the
surface an abject subservience, there was an underlying instability. A sixteenth-century ruler always stood in danger of
assassination, as was shown by the cases of Henry III and of
Orange. And every politician was in danger of suffering eclipse,
not at the polls but on the scaffold.

Against Elizabeth there was the damaging fact of her illegitimacy — under statutory as well as English canon law, not
to mention law as received throughout Europe. That she was
exercised about this is shown by her consulting Sir Nicholas
Bacon as to whether she should do what her sister had done
and have the bar sinister removed by act of Parliament. He advised that it would be safer to leave the matter alone — advice
which speaks volumes. What she did have as a tower of strength
was Philip's undeviating support. It preserved her from ex-

ternal attack; it also prevented her Catholic subjects from giving trouble. They were repeatedly assured by the King of Spain
that things would right themselves as both they and he desired.
As for any danger of a French invasion, the official view was
expressed by Cardinal Granvelle: "Spain must defend London
as it would Brussels." Philip even went so far as to make a
proposal of marriage through his ambassador, Feria. Had he
come to England for Mary's funeral and proposed in person, the
whole story of Elizabeth might have been quite different. As it
was, he not only failed to come, but framed his offer in terms
hardly flattering to Elizabeth's vanity: his motive, he said, was
the service of God.

Elizabeth considered the proposal for a month before rejecting it — or rather, before putting Philip off. She, too, had a
motive: if she married her sister's widower, his case and hers
would be precisely parallel to that of Henry and Katherine. For
Philip could marry her only on condition that she apply for a
dispensation from Rome (as her father had done), and for her to
do so would be a virtual admission that Katherine's marriage
was valid, which would involve the further admission that Anne
Boleyn's was not. At once the fatal rock of her own illegitimacy
was run upon.

This was her ostensible reason for declining Philip. Whether
it was the real reason, nobody knows. After all, an application
for a papal dispensation (which would have been granted as a
matter of course) would also have elicited a papal acknowledgement of her right to the throne — something well worth pocket-
ing a little pride to obtain. However, as we shall see, Elizabeth
was fertile in finding excuses for rejecting every one of her
numerous suitors in turn. In each case there rises a question
as to whether this was not due to her incapacity for marriage.
But there were, no doubt, sound political reasons for her not
marrying Philip. His marriage to her sister had been extremely
unpopular; her own marriage to him would have been even
more so. She therefore preferred to keep his friendship. That
would have political advantages with no political drawbacks.
Only it was a little disconcerting when, upon being refused by

Queen Elizabeth

Elizabeth of England, he promptly married Elizabeth of Valois. Could he not have waited four months for an answer? Such, she sighed, was the fickleness of men! To the Count of Feria's ears those sighs sounded more like mocking laughter.

There remained urgent reasons why Elizabeth should marry someone. In the first place, marriage was then regarded as the duty of all women who did not enter religion: those who had neglected to perform that duty would be doomed to lead apes in hell. But in the second and more important place, there was only Elizabeth's life — and her health was not good — as a barrier to the incontestable claim of Mary Queen of Scots.[1] It is true that Mary had not as yet come to be looked upon by Catholics as their sole hope; on the contrary, her orthodoxy was at this time suspect. But unless England was prepared to accept the not very impressive Lady Catherine Grey as a claimant, or the Earl of Huntingdon (who was supported by Norfolk and Bedford and Pembroke), the only alternative was the Queen of Scots, which meant French domination. The surest barrier against all this would have been a child of Elizabeth's own body.

It was against Mary that Philip's support was invaluable. He was all his life actuated by a fear of France that amounted to positive mania. Even his marriage to the French King's sister did little to dissipate it. A settled point of his policy was to keep one who so soon (in July, 1559) became Queen of France from becoming also Queen of England, with an empire from the Pyrenees to the Orkneys. In such circumstances there was nothing for him to do but to back Elizabeth.

The traditional view as to Philip's relations with Mary Queen of Scots is not well based. It was only after Mary had been reduced to the status of Dowager of France that Philip felt any friendliness toward her. And only toward the end of her life, after her sufferings had excited pity and her constancy to Catholicism admiration, could Philip be induced to help

[1] The only argument against it was that she had been barred by Henry's will. There remained, however, a question as to whether that will had ever been signed. Mary asked for its examination, which Elizabeth promised but without fulfilling her promise. The will has, in fact, a signature — though a disputable one. In any event Mary's claim on the grounds of blood overrode everything else.

her.[2] Even that was largely due to thirty years during which Elizabeth had abused his friendship and had at last goaded him into retaliation. So far from Spain's ever backing Mary, policy ruled it out. Thus, when at the beginning of Elizabeth's reign Feria and Quadra thought that something ought to be done for the persecuted English Catholics and advised Philip to support the claim of Lady Catherine Grey, who, as a move in her private political game, was letting it be understood that she was prepared to restore the Faith if put upon the throne, not even with that inducement was he willing to listen to the suggestion. To let Lady Catherine in would, he knew, be to play into French hands. *She* would never be able to maintain herself against Mary. Elizabeth, therefore, had to be strongly supported, whatever she did, as a means of keeping Mary out. What seems to be a miracle of patience was really only a piece of political calculation. It was the price that had to be paid for an advantage for which hardly any price could be thought too high.

For this reason Philip persuaded the Pope to withhold his hand when France was pressing for Elizabeth's excommunication. The French motive was, of course, political; what was really sought was a declaration in favour of the Queen of Scots. The Spanish motive was equally political: what was really sought was the prevention of a declaration in favour of Mary. Philip gained his diplomatic point. Though it is often said — it was said even by Lingard and Tierney — that the Bull *Cum ex apostolatus,* issued by Paul IV, involved Elizabeth's condemnation, it actually merely laid down the broad principle that all sovereigns who supported heresy *ipso facto* lost their right. But according to fixed Papal procedure it would have been necessary, had Elizabeth been directly aimed at, to have named her and to have summoned her to submission, before proceeding to give a judgement in her case. So far from this being done, Paul showed himself willing for any reasonable compromise.

[2] This is the broad truth. It must, however, be added that at moments of irritation against Elizabeth, Philip entertained other ideas. His letter to Alva of December 16, 1569, for example, was written in a mood of exasperation.

The same thing may also be said of Pius IV, who was elected on Christmas Day, 1559. As he was about to summon the Council of Trent, and as Protestants everywhere were loudly calling for such a council, he sent invitations to all Christian countries to send representatives. In April, 1560, he appointed Abbot Parpaglia to go to England to arrange matters with Elizabeth.

The choice was an unfortunate one. Parpaglia was suspected by Philip of being in the French interest. Therefore difficulties were put in the Nuncio's way and he had to be recalled to Rome when he had got only so far as the Low Countries.

Pius's second choice was acceptable to Spain. This time he appointed Abbot Martinengo as Nuncio, and Elizabeth professed herself willing to receive him, as we know from a letter Quadra wrote to Cardinal Granvelle on April 14, 1561. "She said to me, of her own accord," he says, "that she would be pleased at his coming, but that . . . in conformity with the laws of this kingdom, he would be styled Ambassador of the Roman Pontiff only, as it is forbidden to give the title of Universal or Supreme Pontiff." Even that technical discourtesy raised no real obstacle, though it is unlikely that any good could have come of Martinengo's visit. The English Protestants might shout for a "free" Council; Elizabeth's own opinion, as expressed to the French Ambassador, was that "two Christian sovereigns, acting in unison, [could] settle everything on a better principle." Religion was, to her Erastian mind, something for Kings not the Church to determine.

At the bare possibility that a Nuncio (under whatever title) should come to England, Cecil was thrown into a convulsion of panic. In spite of all the provisos that might be made for a Church council in which English Protestant bishops should sit on an equality with the other delegates, there was here a serious threat to the whole Anglican establishment so recently set up. For the deprived English Catholic Bishops could hardly have been prevented from attending, and had they done so, the falsity of the Elizabethan establishment would have been all too evident.

Cecil met the danger in characteristic fashion. He employed

a device he was going to use many times again when his position
was threatened. He deliberately manufactured a plot against
Elizabeth in order to scare her. The chaplain of Sir Edward
Waldegrave was arrested, and admitted that he had been saying
Mass. A letter from one of the imprisoned bishops was intercepted. It contained the expression of the hope that the Nuncio
would be able to secure the release of himself and his colleagues. As neither fact could be construed as "treasonable,"
Cecil ingeniously linked both to some disturbance that was
going on in Ireland — where there was always some disturbance
— and further connected it with the arrival in Ireland of the
Jesuit Father Wolfe as the Pope's representative. To clinch the
matter, Cecil made a calculated scene in the Council, declaring
that anyone who voted for Martinengo's admission was guilty
of treason. Sir Nicholas Bacon backed him up, as he always did
on such occasions, and the Council, terrified at so much as the
imputation of treason, at once gave way.

This refusal to admit a Papal Nuncio would of itself have
been sufficient for a sentence of excommunication upon Elizabeth. But still it was not issued — and again largely because of
Philip's dissuasion. If the matter was raised at the Council of
Trent, it was raised only to be decided against. Though
Nicholas Sanders, who was present as the theologian for
Cardinal Hosius, drew up a memorandum urging what he
called the "easy measures" of absolving the English from their
allegiance to Elizabeth, of confirming Mary's title, and of
sending some of the Louvain exiles to Scotland with an offer
of the crown, the Emperor's representatives argued that Elizabeth's condemnation would mean the rebellion of his Protestant subjects. Besides, there was a Hapsburg marriage to
Elizabeth in the offing. As for Philip, he was alarmed lest the
condemnation of Elizabeth would, by clearing the way for
Mary, bring an extension of French influence — the thing of all
things he most dreaded. He therefore urged that the resources
of moderation were not yet exhausted. Persuasions in favour of
"practicability" prevailed in the end: the only result of the discussion was that the Emperor wrote to Elizabeth asking that

the imprisoned bishops be released and that Catholics be allowed to have the same sort of toleration accorded the Huguenots in France. To which Elizabeth replied that toleration was contrary to the laws of England.

At this point it might be worth noting that the action taken by Dr. Sanders, though nothing came of it, was no doubt reported in England, to be remembered against him when he was sent by the Pope to Ireland in 1580, and to serve for the further discomfiture of the Jesuit missionaries who arrived in England at the same time. As for the proposed visit of Martinengo in 1561, Cecil prevented it by acting as though the life of Elizabeth were threatened. On May 8 he complacently writes: "When I saw this Romish influence toward, about a month past, I thought it necessary to dull the Papists' expectations by discovering of certain Mass-mongers and punishing them. . . . I take God to record that I mean no evil to any of them, but only for the rebating of the Papists' humours, which by the Queen's lenity grow too rank. I find it hath done much good." By "intending no evil" he presumably meant that he did not intend to execute any of those he had arrested. Many of these sixty or seventy men, however, were kept in prison for years, some until they died. Yet we have Cecil's own admission that this was only a diversion to prevent Martinengo's visit to England.

How mild Rome was by comparison with the English government appears in the curious Sackville incident. Young Thomas Sackville, afterwards Lord Buckhurst (and Lord Treasurer), and already joint author with Thomas Norton of *Gorboduc*, the first English tragedy in blank verse, was in Rome in 1563. He had voted in Parliament for the Elizabethan Settlement of religion and was now apprehended by the Inquisition. At once Bishop Goldwell, the one Marian Bishop who had escaped from England, came to his rescue, and the Pope sent for Sackville to tell him that he would make the path smooth for Elizabeth if she would return to the Church. He was instructed to make private enquiries as to whether, even at this late hour, a Nuncio would not be received in England. But again the conciliatory Papal move was blocked. Sackville's father, Sir Richard, was Undersecretary of State and was so alarmed by even the appearance of being mixed up in so dangerous a business that he ordered his son to say nothing about it and to stay abroad until the tempest had died down. That such an attempt was made proves once more the desire of the Papacy to heal the quarrel, as it also proves the determination of the English government to keep the quarrel alive. Even as late as 1565 we find Pius IV saying in consistory that all hope of Elizabeth should not be abandoned, though by then the only hope lay in her making a Catholic marriage, and though events were to show that the most Elizabeth was prepared to concede to her Catholic suitors was a toleration of strictly private devotions from which the all-essential Mass was to be excluded. Meanwhile she continued to use Philip's friendship and protection, to dangle herself from time to time as a marriage prospect before the Emperor or France — according to the political situation — and to play her own crafty hand.

For her success — perhaps the most brilliant and the most continuous enjoyed by any ruler in history — she was equipped equally by her gifts and her defects. The parsimony and the hesitation so often noted in her were not the least of the factors contributing to her eventual triumph, for these were powerful brakes upon her impulsiveness and hot temper. Her scintillating intelligence would hardly have sufficed had she not had a dullard's habit of hard work, the willingness to give attention to details. But above all she succeeded because she was devoid of principle.

Hers was an age of political chicane; but as Green remarks, "In the profusion and recklessness of her lies Elizabeth stood without a peer in Christendom." The lies, however, were not always so reckless as they appeared to be. There were occasions, indeed, when one cannot but feel that Elizabeth took a perverse pleasure in deceiving people: it was the main pleasure she extracted out of the numerous marriage negotiations. But though she delighted in the exercise of her virtuosity in falsehood and was a thoroughgoing Machiavellian — even if it is questionable whether she had made any systematic study of the Florentine — her mendacity usually served a useful political purpose. She was too clever to indulge her propensity gratuitously — at any rate, too often. For she would have defeated herself had she allowed foreign princes and ambassadors to become convinced that she *never* spoke the truth. The amazing thing is that, while they all came to look upon her with suspicion, they were all repeatedly taken in by the air of innocence she could assume at will. She sounded so plausible, and she had so much personal fascination that they continued to believe — with reservations. They discovered, too, that sometimes she could be very candid, as they also discovered that she sometimes made a diplomatic use of truth — when she knew it would be supposed that she was merely practising duplicity. They all in turn were tricked by her, and knew themselves to be tricked; they consented to be charmed.

Philip of Spain she consistently, and over a long term of years, hoodwinked. As consistently, he remained her friend. He was himself given to intrigues, for his position was difficult, but his slow, laborious mind had a fundamental honesty and an underlying disinterestedness that made him incapable of understanding Elizabeth. How she repaid his kindness in shielding her from both Rome and France, we shall see.

Cecil was the perfect instrument for carrying out Elizabeth's devious policies. Though perfidious and cruel, he seems almost honest when compared with most of the men with whom he worked. Perhaps this was, in part, because he could afford to refuse bribes; he was already immensely rich.[3] All the same it is to his credit that he did not avail himself of some of the opportunities for plunder that were open to him. It was enough that he should exercise and keep his power, and that he should protect what he already held. We find, it is true, that Sir John Shirley, upon the death of Sir James Croft, who was Comptroller of the Household, asked Cecil to use his influence with the

---

[3] He had obtained by one means or another, no less than 300 separate estates; and most of these had belonged to the Church. Macaulay, a little quaintly, remarks, "We must not, however, suppose from this that his gains were exorbitant, or his fortunes greater than his services had merited."

Manoeuvering for Position

Queen to obtain his appointment to the vacant office, adding, "My thankfulness to your Lordship shall be £500, beside my everlasting service, which I am already bound to do your Lordship." But this sort of jobbery was common in those days, and after all Shirley did not get what he was after. It must be remembered, too, that Cecil was virtually alone among the high officials of Elizabeth's Court in refusing the valuable presents Drake offered upon his return from the most lucrative of his piratical raids.

Concerning Cecil's vast ability there is no need to dilate here. The fact that he was able to retain power until his retirement (when he managed to introduce his no less able son, Robert, as his successor) demonstrates Elizabeth's confidence in him. And though his power was several times challenged by highly placed rivals — by Norfolk, by Essex, and by Leicester (if Leicester really was a rival) — he emerged each time with his power stronger than ever. On the basis of his principles, such as they were, he made hardly any mistakes, none perhaps of a purely political sort. If he misjudged military affairs, these were outside his special province. There was nothing bold or dashing about him; had there been, his career would not have lasted long. His character was timid and mediocre; none of his policies was heroic; his caution and deceitfulness are anything but attractive qualities; and his lack of amiability, streaked with occasional spitefulness, kept him from being liked. But the temper of his mind exactly suited Elizabeth who, in general, put herself in his hands. Her confidence was not misplaced.

Though his was not a lofty intelligence — as a statesman he was definitely inferior to Richelieu and Bismarck — he was a past master in the art of political manoeuvering. Nothing happened at home or abroad without his knowing it, and his grasp both of the whole tangled scheme of things and of all its details is attested by his enormous extant correspondence. But as his descendant, Lord Algernon Cecil, says of him in his life of Robert Cecil, "Everywhere the principles of Machiavelli were shamelessly practised, and, beside the profound and passionate sense of spiritual things which may be found in the dying

109

prayer of Machiavelli's earliest pupil,[4] we may find the most unblushingly direct, the most insidious guile, the most perfidious cruelty."

As to the extent of Cecil's influence over Elizabeth there has been disagreement among historians, and perhaps this is a matter that can never be definitely determined. Phrases such as *Regnum Cecilianum,* "Cecil rules everything," "Cecil is king," frequently occur in the correspondence of the ambassadors. At other times, however, there are similar expressions that indicate that Leicester was — at any rate for the moment, and perhaps only because Cecil found it convenient to allow it — paramount in the Council. Probably the real truth comes closest to being stated by Naunton when he said that Elizabeth ruled by factions she herself created and played off against one another.

Froude steadily advances the thesis that it was Cecil who was the master of Elizabethan England: to the Queen he grants no more than enough good sense to follow her Minister's advice, and amazing good luck to save her when she did not follow it. Mr. Hilaire Belloc advances the same thesis with the difference that, where Froude considers Cecil's domination fortunate, he considers it a calamity. There were, indeed, many occasions when Cecil altered the Queen's letters, or sent privately different written instructions, or (when that was not sufficiently safe) a private message that was different from both the royal letter and his own. It is, however, quite possible that this was done with Elizabeth's knowledge and consent; it would be fully in accord with her own tortuous character.[5] What Cecil controlled were the sources of information. He could withhold it when it suited his purpose to do so. Or he could supply the Queen with false information. This being the case, he was able to frighten her into whatever action he thought desirable.

At the beginning of the reign the administration was looked upon as tentative and provisional. Several times it seemed that Cecil would fall; several times he threatened to resign. Only gradually and by cautious steps did he fully establish himself.

---

[4] Thomas Cromwell.

[5] Many official letters, too, in those days were written for no other purpose than to have them intercepted — and so throw the interceptors off the track.

Manoeuvering for Position

Yet it is, I think, an exaggeration to talk about the *Regnum Cecilianum* or, as Mr. Belloc does, about the "Cecil dynasty." The continuance of any Minister in office depended upon the will of the Queen. What we may safely say is that Elizabeth was, as a rule, eventually persuaded of the soundness of Cecil's judgment. Her mind and his were beautifully in tune. While she might disagree with this or that detail of the proposed policy, or the best means for reaching the desired end, there was no serious disagreement as to the ends themselves. She cannot be absolved for responsibility for any of the happenings of her reign.

The first important happening in foreign affairs was the Treaty of Cateau-Cambrésis, signed on April 2, 1559. By it England left Calais in the hands of France, though on the face-saving condition that the French were either to return it in eight years or pay half a million crowns. Elizabeth can hardly be blamed for yielding to circumstances at a time when she was in no position to fight a war. To have continued would have imperilled her position at home. Yet the fact should be remembered, for what it is worth, that it was Elizabeth and not Mary who actually gave up Calais. Had Mary lived, the ultimate issue might have been different.

The French Commissioners put their case with devastating logic. They were not "annexing" Calais but merely "holding" it until its rightful possessor could be determined. They were ready enough to return it to the English Crown, but the question was: to whom did that Crown belong? In their opinion it belonged to Mary Queen of Scots, Dauphiness of France.[6] Once more we have an instance of how logic can be a double-edged weapon. The French believed that their ingenious move would strengthen Mary's position. Actually it had the contrary effect: it stiffened English opposition to her. As Elizabeth could not recover Calais, she had to see if something could not be done to undermine France in Scotland.

In May, John Knox, having served his time in the French

---

[6] They could not have taken this line of argument had Mary Tudor still been upon the English throne, though no doubt they would have discovered some other reason for keeping Calais now that they had captured it.

galleys and having sat at Calvin's feet at Geneva, returned to his native country, which was ruled, in Mary's absence, by the Regent, her mother, Mary of Guise. Almost immediately (on July 10) the King of France, Henry II, died of an accidental wound in the tilting yard, and his son succeeding to the throne as Francis II, Mary was now Queen of France as well as of Scotland. As she was also rightful Queen of England — and asserting her right — Elizabeth decided to do what she could to weaken her. The arrival of Knox was timely: fiercely as Elizabeth disapproved of him on personal grounds, his identification of the "pure gospel" with opposition to a French (and strongly Catholic) Regent was going to be all to her advantage.

The Scots Lords of the Congregation, who had broken into rebellion, quickly appealed to England for help, shrewdly calculating that it could not be refused, as it would damage Elizabeth's rival. Before August was out, Mary of Guise began to complain of the English backing being given Scotch rebels, whereupon Elizabeth assured the French Ambassador, who was instructed to make the protest, that she knew nothing of the matter. She asseverated that she detested all rebels against a lawful sovereign, and that if any Englishmen had any hand in what was going on across the border, she would punish them when she knew who they were. As a final artistic touch she led the Ambassador into the gallery at Hampton Court and showed him the portrait of Mary of Guise hanging there. The poor man, half (but only half) convinced by Elizabeth's assurances and her air of innocence, wrote to the Regent conveying the love of England's Queen and added, "If one could judge from outward show, it would seem, Madam, from her words and other demonstrations that she has none but good intentions to keep peace and friendship between your Majesties."

Things did not go well with the Scottish rebels, despite the fact that the fleet carrying reinforcements from France was wrecked. The Regent's existing forces proving sufficient to hold their own, the Lords of the Congregation appealed to Elizabeth again.

The help she sent was given in a way very characteristic of

her. It was her principle throughout life, as she said herself, to "wage war underhand" whenever possible. She could not openly declare herself on the side of the rebels, for that was likely to be taken by potential English rebels as their justification. Besides, she had no wish to involve herself in a war with France by invading Scotland. Accordingly she sent her young admiral, William Winter, to the Firth of Forth, but gave him strict instructions that whatever he did was to be entirely on his own responsibility.

Philip of Spain made a perfunctory protest against this breach of international law, while his envoy dropped the hint to Cecil that Spain had no objection to English intervention in Scotland. And the Duke of Alva quoted a Spanish proverb to the English Ambassador: "If thy enemy be in the water to the girdlestede, lend him thy hand to help him out; if he be in to the shoulders, set hold on him and press him down." Such being Spain's real attitude, France was in no position to move directly against England, and Winter's ships effectually cut off all possibility of new French troops reaching Scotland. The Lords of the Congregation were encouraged to persist against the Regent.

There was another card Elizabeth now thought of playing. Before 1559 was out she arranged through Throckmorton, her Ambassador in France, that the Earl of Arran, who was in the line of succession to the Scots throne, should be smuggled out of France into England. There seems to have been a question whether the English Queen should not marry him and oust Mary. That course, however, was decided against as too risky. Moreover, one look at Arran was enough. So he was sent off to Scotland (his visit to England being kept secret) to help the rebel lords. Shortly afterwards his feeble mind gave way, and he remained insane until his death forty years later.

Cecil's point of view was expressed clearly: "If controversy of religion be among them, to help to kindle it . . . and especially in Scotland, to augment the hope of them that incline to good religion." A Catholic Scotland would always have been a danger to Protestantism in England. But if the French were kept occupied with Scottish affairs, they would be hampered from giving English Catholics any assistance. Cecil was therefore inclined for an intervention more open than Elizabeth wished and unbosomed himself to Throckmorton, "God trieth us with many difficulties. The Queen's Majesty never liketh this business of Scotland."

But, while avowed assistance to the Scotch rebels was never given, Elizabeth reaped the fruits of victory. The French garrison valiantly defended the fortress of Leith, but as the summer opened it grew certain that they would have to surrender owing to the lack of provisions. As Mary of Guise was dying, the French decided to retreat while they could and get the best possible terms. Elizabeth claimed a right to take part in the negotiations — she who had always insisted she was not helping the rebels! — and so sent Cecil to Scotland. The treaty of Edinburgh was signed on July 6. Under its terms the French bound themselves to withdraw from the country, and a clause was inserted in a phrasing capable of an interpretation that Mary Queen of Scots renounced all claims to even so much as the English succession. Angrily she refused to confirm such a provision, and when, most unluckily for her, the sickly young Francis II died on December 5, she was left with no position in France except that of a Dowager. In view of this she was advised by her Guise uncles to return to Scotland.

Her first step was to ask Elizabeth for a safe-conduct through England. It was refused on the grounds that she had not ratified the treaty of Edinburgh, but also (for the unexpressed reason) that it was thought unwise to allow the legitimate English claimant into the country. Later — too late — Elizabeth changed her mind about this, or perhaps she merely wished her consent to arrive too late. But she may have decided that a personal meeting with Mary might solve many problems. Or perhaps she was meditating treachery. We know for certain only this much: that when Mary went by sea, Winter received secret instructions to intercept her if he could. As Cecil wrote of the waiting English ships, "I think they will be sorry to see her pass."

Manoeuvering for Position

Pass, however, Mary did, thanks mainly to a thick fog. And when she protested against Winter's being in her waters, Elizabeth blandly explained that the English fleet was merely looking out for some Scotch pirates. It was a palpable lie and deceived nobody. Elizabeth continued to give surreptitious aid to the Lords of the Congregation.

Even apart from all obligations of honour (something that never weighed very much with Elizabeth), it was monstrously cruel to increase the difficulties of an unprotected young girl among men who were as ruthless as wolves. It is a wonder that Mary was able to hold out as long as she did. Her failure to maintain herself must be laid at the door of the Elizabeth who was always professing strong affection and solicitude for her. There was no longer, since the withdrawal of the French, the excuse that Scotland could be a danger to England. It was only because Mary was a Catholic and the rightful claimant to the English throne that she had to be remorselessly ruined. The rest of her story will have to be deferred. All that need be recorded at this point is that when Cecil returned from Edinburgh he advised Elizabeth to make some of the Scots lords her pensioners. A thousand pounds spent then, he told her, would save ten thousand later on. It would be better still to spend two thousand; the ultimate savings would be in proportion. Especially did he mention Glencairn as "poor, honest, constant, and wise." Maxwell, too, was "a very wise and religious man." Hume and Maitland had "good qualities" and could be bought cheaply. "The Lord James would be gratified." And Kirkaldy "had reason to be remembered." All these saints apparently had itching palms.

Elizabeth's next adventure was in France. Her motives for intervention — again an unacknowledged intervention — were twofold, one positive, the other negative. Cecil persuaded her, and perhaps himself believed, that there was coming into being a Catholic League for the extirpation of Protestants.[7] She had to

[7] We now know this to be a myth. All of the archives have been searched in vain for a single document about this famous League. But as a man so much "in the know" as Bacon assumes in his essay "Of Seditions and Troubles" that this league existed we must conclude that it did — in Protestant imaginations.

defend herself while she could. Yet rather illogically she considered that, by supporting the Huguenots in the war of religion which broke out in 1562, she was putting her money on the winning horse.[8] It was a bad miscalculation, yet even ten years later we find Walsingham reporting from Paris (just before the Massacre of St. Bartholomew's Day) that French Protestantism was destined to triumph. Had it done so, England would at once have allied itself with France against Spain. But immediate advantage could be extracted by weakening the French government through stirring up internal strife. Elizabeth had, nevertheless, the effrontery to write to Philip II on September 22, 1562, saying, "We have been much troubled and perplexed from the beginning of these divisions in France, and upon divers causes: first, because we had great compassion to that young King, our brother, so abused by his subjects, as his authority could not get them to accord." In the same letter she tells Philip that while she intends to live at peace with the French King, "We mean to direct all our actions . . . to save to our realm in this convenient time our right to Calais." However hypocritical she may have been in her "compassion" for the boy, Charles IX, she was honest enough in her intention of recovering, by fair means or foul, her lost foothold in France.

It was understood by the English volunteers that they must be pretending to act on their own responsibility. If they won, Elizabeth would have the benefit; if they lost, they must accept the consequences. When some of them were captured by Guise he hanged them with the ironical inscription over their heads that this was on account of their "having come to France against the will of the Queen of England to the service of the Huguenots."

Intervention in France proved a costly mistake. The English gave their assistance on condition that Condé and Coligny hand over to them the towns of Rouen and Havre as security for the restoration of Calais. The agreement united France in a resolve

[8] On December 31, 1560, Throckmorton wrote to Cecil, "The true religion is very likely to take place in France, and so consequently throughout all Europe where Christianity is received."

to expel the English invaders. Rouen fell on October 25, and though Guise was shot in the back the following February, his spirit continued to animate the nation; Havre was recaptured on July 28, 1563. Elizabeth had, in the end, nothing to show for her adventure. By breaking the treaty of Cateau-Cambrésis she had forfeited all claim to Calais. Nor did she succeed in recovering the money she had lent the Huguenots.

Elizabeth, in truth, was a universal troublemaker. She had already begun to play her tricks upon Philip II. And though there is no need to pity him as one must pity Mary of Scotland — for he was the richest and most powerful monarch in the world, and it would never have occurred to him that he needed pity — Elizabeth's actions in his case have a special tinge of meanness. He was her benefactor, and she systematically took advantage of his kindness, repaying it with wrongs — which, of course, she denied perpetrating. For his part, he was like a mastiff that gazes disdainfully at the cur yelping at his heels; he thought he could afford to ignore the wretched animal. Finding herself secure by the very circumstance of his haughty might, Elizabeth traded upon the fact right up to the undeclared war of 1588.

His forebearance is simply astonishing. He had not only held off the Pope from excommunicating Elizabeth and France from attacking her, he had actually gone so far — very foolishly and with a complete blindness to the real issues — as to get Quadra, his Ambassador (who was also a bishop), to represent to the Pope that, though the Elizabethan Prayer Book admittedly left out much that a Catholic would like to see included, it at least contained no positive heresy. Because Philip wanted to keep the English Catholics quiet, he tried to get Rome to say that they might with a good conscience attend the Protestant services. The Communion, Quadra obediently wrote, was "entirely made up from the Scriptures and the prayers of the Church, without any false doctrine or impiety." What was the Pope's answer we shall hear later. The point at the moment is Philip's unremitting efforts on Elizabeth's behalf.

Quadra's successor, Don Guzman de Silva, was selected because of his optimistic friendliness of disposition. He could be counted upon to put the best construction on everything. Thus we find him writing to Philip on October 9, 1564, to say that "circumstances had at first obliged [the Queen] to dissemble her real feelings with regard to religion." It was a subject on which Elizabeth was habitually very specious. When it suited her she could always convey — to Catholic quarters — the idea that she was a Catholic at heart. The candles and the crucifix on her private altar doubtless accorded with her aesthetic taste; they also served to suggest a vague impression of Catholicism. For the same reason she ostentatiously washed the feet of a poor woman on Maundy Thursdays. All this, she knew, would be reported abroad. It enabled Philip to believe that there was, after all, hope for her conversion. So he continued to be her protector during the first difficult years of her reign, though by doing so the result was achieved (sincerely deplored by him, but not fully perceived until too late) that he had allowed the fostering of what had been in the beginning the delicate and exotic plant of heresy. That Protestantism was permitted to make headway in England while it was still weak was largely his fault. And when at last it had become strong, Philip was again to blame for so behaving as to play into Cecil's hands. The English government, therefore, were able to picture Catholicism as synonymous with the Spain which by degrees they came to treat as an enemy.

Yet quite gratuitously Elizabeth began, almost from the beginning of her reign, to sow dissension in the Netherlands. She was actuated by the fear that if Spain was too strongly secured on the other side of the North Sea, it would be a menace to England. As Spain — like France and Scotland — had to be weakened, anti-Catholic pamphlets were smuggled over, and with them went English agents, seeking to fish in troubled waters. Cardinal Granvelle wrote to Philip complaining of this, but as usual there came from Elizabeth a surprised protestation of innocence. How completely Philip was sunk in his infatuation is shown by his letter to Granvelle of August, 1559: "If the new Queen" — he is referring to Mary who had recently become Queen of France — "were to die — and her health, you say, is very bad — it would relieve of us of many embarrassments, and of the right which they assert to England." He went further than the expression of such pious hopes: he demonstrated repeatedly that, rather than have Mary as Queen of England, he would go to any lengths in his support of Elizabeth.

The importance he attached to this is indicated by his patience in suffering depredations upon his commerce. Here, however, I think we cannot consider Elizabeth the main offender: though she came to take shares in the later piratical expeditions in the Atlantic and Pacific, she disapproved of the Channel pirates. It is true that she was an adept at spinning fine distinctions; so that, after 1572, she for a while allowed La Marck, the leader of the Dutch "sea beggars" the use of her ports as bases of operations. But even this permission was withdrawn, and in the early years of her reign she made some efforts, which were probably sincere enough even if they were not notably vigorous, to suppress piracy. The difficulty encountered was that her vice-admirals were sometimes in league with the pirates (as her old friend Thomas Seymour had been), and that juries were reluctant to convict. She did, after all, hang some pirates, though she was often obliged to wink at their misdeeds.

But what shall we say of that enormous act of piracy of her own — the seizure in December, 1568, of the Spanish treasure ships with their half million ducats?

First, in justice to the English side of the case, we must recall certain facts. John Hawkins, with his cousin Drake as his second-in-command, had made several slaving expeditions to the west coast of Africa, selling at a huge profit the negroes they captured. Though this was in flat defiance of the humane Spanish law which forbade the importation of negroes, except in small numbers and under government control, Hawkins, who knew Philip personally, may have believed that Elizabeth's investment in the enterprise, and the friendly relations existing between England and Spain, would suffice to cover any technical irregularities. Perhaps the very fact that the prohibition law was drawn against Spanish slave traders made him feel that he was exempt. The colonists certainly welcomed the traffic, although, to square themselves with their own government, they made a show of buying slaves only at the point of English guns. And Hawkins felt himself secure enough to try to sell in Spain the cargoes he had purchased in the Indies with the proceeds he obtained from the sale of his blacks. He seems to have counted upon being allowed to continue without molestation, and to have felt injured when his goods were confiscated.

Then on September 16, 1567, he was surprised by Mendenez, the famous admiral, in the harbour of San Juan de Ulloa and attacked, though he had with him two ships of the royal navy, one of them named the *Jesus*. Two other ships had to be abandoned with the *Jesus* — which in any case was so rotten that her loss was fortunate, as the syndicate would have had to repair her at their own expense. But Hawkins in the *Judith* and Drake in the *Minion* got away safely.[9] and in the view of the Elizabethan "sea lawyers" Hawkins was entitled to redress. It was his brother William who wrote to Cecil on December 3, 1568, suggesting that Philip's treasure ships be held by way of reprisal.[10]

This was Cecil's case. That it was not a very strong one is shown by the fact that the government did not proceed to extremities at once. On the contrary, Elizabeth had already promised the Spanish Ambassador that she would see that the money was safely delivered to Alva. Mr. Belloc sees in this an instance of Cecil's overruling the Queen. It may be so; though in face of Elizabeth's habitual indifference to her pledges, I do not think the point can be confidently pressed. When she shifted her stand it was to say that the money had not been "seized"; it was merely being held for safety because of the pirates infesting the Channel. How insincere this plea was, is indicated by

[9] Drake in the *Minion* abandoned Hawkins to his fate. Sir Julian Corbett has attempted to defend this treachery, which was afterwards brought up against Drake, on the ground that the ships missed one another in the darkness. More recent investigation, however, has shown that Drake fled in daylight.

[10] Though Hawkins himself did not reach England until a month later, the news of what had happened had already arrived, though the first report was that Hawkins himself had been killed.

another shift in argument: the money would not actually become the property of Spain until it had been delivered in the Netherlands; until then it belonged to the Italian bankers who had made the loan. Very well; that being so, Elizabeth announced that she would borrow it herself. It was in vain that Don Guerau de Spes, the new Spanish Ambassador, a man of fiery temperament, stormed and threatened war. Elizabeth knew that it was quite outside his province to declare it and so could smile at his rage. And when he induced Alva to make counter reprisals by cutting off English trade with the Low Countries, the imposition of the embargo hurt Spain far more than it hurt England. The proper course of procedure would have been for Hawkins to have presented a bill of damages to Spain if he believed he had a just claim. Instead, Elizabeth stuck to Philip's money.

She did more, or Cecil did it for her. The government, knowing that it now had Hawkins's head in a noose, made him pretend to go over to Philip with an offer of service in the event of an invasion of England. Cecil consistently used men whom he had got into his power, compelling them to act as his spies and *agents provocateurs*. And so plausible was Hawkins and so gullible was Philip, that the famous pirate and slave trader was made a grandee of Spain and advanced no less than £40,000. One cannot but gaze astonished at the craft of Cecil and his agent.

Elizabeth had scored more heavily than she imagined when she first made her seizure. She and Cecil were perfectly aware that Alva needed this half million ducats for the payment of his troops, and they had hoped merely to embarrass him by their action. They could hardly have had the foresight to perceive what the outcome would be. Alva was obliged to impose new taxes in the provinces under his administration, and the taxes he devised were of a kind peculiarly obnoxious to a mercantile country. It was these taxes, more than anything else, that brought to a head the gathering discontent in the Netherlands and led to an open revolt. Elizabeth had never been, so far, in any danger from Spanish attack from across the North Sea; on the contrary, Philip had been a buttress against France. It was because he might become, at some future time, a danger that she wished to provide for any contingencies by weakening him just sufficiently to keep him occupied. She could now congratulate herself on her success. Morally considered, she had committed an infamous crime; politically, she had achieved a master stroke.

Indeed, all through these years, with the exception of the solitary blunder of intervention in France, the Queen and her advisers had played their cards with supreme skill — even if they often behaved like cardsharpers. Their lack of conscience was really incredible. Thus when Sir Thomas Gresham, Elizabeth's financial agent at Antwerp, managed to rob the Spanish arsenals of their supplies and send them over to England, that, too, was applauded as much as his financial ability. And it happened a year or two before the events of 1567–68 gave even the shadow of justification for such unfriendly acts.

And still Philip never struck, though constantly urged to do so. This was not because he was afraid, but because he was forebearing, and because he lacked both foresight and insight. It had not yet dawned upon him — or for that matter, upon the world — that English sea power was to be taken seriously. He knew, of course, that when he and Mary had fought France together, England had possessed the best equipped navy in the world. But he had observed how little that navy accomplished. As for the English land forces, their weakness was pitiable. Lord Paget at the beginning of the reign shared the generally prevailing view and told Cecil that, if France should invade from Scotland and Philip come to the help of Elizabeth, England would be turned into a "Piedmont" by the contestants. Only with the growing sense of national security did Elizabeth venture upon unveiled attack. Until then she counted upon her security, which consisted in the reluctance of Spanish pride to attack an opponent so weak as herself — on that, and on Philip's settled policy of overlooking her misdemeanors and upholding her against France.

8

The Dudley Affair

LORD ROBERT DUDLEY, better known by his later title of the Earl of Leicester, was of the worst blood in England. His grandfather, Edmund Dudley, infamous as Henry VII's extortioner, was executed to please the people by Henry VIII in 1510. His father, who made himself Duke of Northumberland, and his brother, Guildford Dudley, perished on the scaffold at the opening of Mary's reign. And Lord Robert, who had proclaimed his sister-in-law, Lady Jane Grey, as Queen at King's Lynn, deserved a traitor's death but was pardoned by Mary.[1] The saying was that his brother had been a king, his father a duke, his grandfather an esquire, and his great-grandfather a carpenter; but that the carpenter was the only honest man of the lot and the only one to die in his bed.

This, however, is by no means the worst that can be said. Though the murder of Amy Robsart cannot be definitely brought home to her husband, he was strongly suspected of the murder, which was certainly to his advantage, or which he believed would be. In the same way he was suspected of the murder of Walter Devereux, Earl of Essex, the father of Elizabeth's favourite. During his absence in Ireland, Devereux's wife, the precious Lettice, had born Leicester several children and, when she was a widow, married him. Again there is no sure

[1] Ambrose Dudley, made Earl of Warwick in 1561, was also condemned — and also pardoned — after the same conspiracy. He was among the few who dared to be a Catholic when Elizabeth came to the throne, though he soon discarded his religion in favour of political advancement. But he was a brave, if not very fortunate, soldier, and had enough reputation for decency to inspire Mary Queen of Scots to appeal to his sense of justice when he sat as one of the judges at her trial. He died in 1590.

proof, for the Earl was an adept at covering up his tracks. But time after time the word "poison!" was whispered in connexion with this man. At least we have his letter to the Council suggesting that Mary Queen of Scots be got rid of by these means.[2]

But even this is not all. When Arundel and Norfolk, the leaders of the old aristocracy, nearly succeeded in pulling down Cecil in 1568, Leicester pretended to be upon their side — in order to betray their plans to the Queen. The same thing happened in the rebellion of the Northern Earls, and in the Ridolfi plot, which resulted in Norfolk's execution. One is left with a feeling that Leicester was a high-class *agent provacateur*.

His military talents may not have been so despicable as most historians say. His father was an excellent soldier, as was his brother Ambrose, who made so brave and fruitless a defence of Havre in 1563. If Leicester did not shine when in command of the army in Netherlands, this may have been because he was hampered by the insufficiency of his supplies. Another explanation is that Elizabeth appointed him with a private understanding that he do as little as possible. Her policy did not call for great victories but merely for the hampering of the Spanish administration.

It is noteworthy in this connexion that it was he who was put in command of the levies at Tilbury in 1588. Perhaps he was chosen because he could be counted upon to make terms with the Spaniards in the event of their landing. Surely had there been any serious intention of resistance, an abler and more vigorous general could have been found than the then fat and ailing Leicester, who died before the year was out. Henry Carey, Lord Hunsdon, who was such a man, was given only a paper army.

Dudley's whole career is a tissue of treachery and lack of principle. Later in this chapter we shall see how he was ready, if only he could obtain Spanish support for his marriage to the

[2] Mr. Chamberlin, in his recently published *Elizabeth and Leycester*, attempts an elaborate but not very convincing defence. The Earl had enemies, and calumny was a favourite weapon of the time. There can be no doubt, however, that Leicester's reputation among his contemporaries was definitely and deservedly bad.

The Dudley Affair

Queen, to become a Catholic himself. Yet later he set himself up as a leader of the Puritans. He used any cant that served his purpose. Naunton was to write of him, "I never saw a style or phrase more seemingly religious, and fuller of the strains of devotion, and were they not sincere, I doubt much of his well being, and I fear he was too well seen in the aphorisms and principles of Nicholas the Florentine, and in the reaches of Caesar Borgias." Quadra's opinion of him was, "Lord Robert is the worst young fellow I have ever encountered. He is heartless, spiritless, treacherous and false." I am afraid that there will be few people met in these pages who shine with a moral and spiritual light; there are none so wicked as Dudley. It may be true that Elizabeth was grateful to him for having lent her money when they were prisoners at the same time in the Tower. And no doubt the man admirably fulfilled the functions of a Master of the Revels who took care that the Queen was kept amused. But these reasons hardly suffice to explain his long term in favour. Dudley alone of all the men whose fortune Elizabeth made, aspired to marry her, and seems to have come closest to doing so.

It was assumed by the councillors, as it was assumed by Parliament, that the Queen would lose no time in marrying. It was also thought virtually certain that she would marry a subject, England being by then sick of a foreign king. But nobody thought of Dudley in this connexion. Elizabeth's infatuation with such a man could be counted upon to pass. In any event there was the consoling reflection that he had been married since 1550 to Amy Robsart. Already other names were being mentioned. Lord Arundel, whose son had been proposed as a husband for Elizabeth during Mary's reign, offered himself. He was of a semiroyal family, forty-seven, and though not of any striking capacity, a man who would not have been objectionable to the old nobility. At once he returned home from the continent, weeping with joy at the accession (and perhaps at the prospect of his good fortune); the sardonic Feria remarking that his tears "floated the ship in." Elizabeth, however, seemed to prefer Sir William Pickering, a handsome and dashing lady-killer, though he too was in his forties, until his candidacy, like Arundel's, faded away. Rumours had already begun that she might be able after all to marry Lord Robert, whom she had made her Master of the Horse. His wife was reported to be dying of cancer and the lovers to be waiting, not too patiently, for her death.

Even in the country at large, and even before Amy Robsart was dead, gossip was busy about the relations between Dudley and Elizabeth. Thus in the summer of 1560, an enquiry was made into a case of *lèse majesté*. A Mr. Coke, it appears, had met an old woman named Mother Dow upon the road and had asked her "What news?" Her reply was that Lord Robert had given the Queen a new petticoat that had cost twenty nobles. Mr. Coke's ribald comment was, "Thinkest thou that it was a petticoat? No, no; he gave her a child, I warrant thee!" Having said which he gave Mother Dow a swig of the wine at his saddlebow and rode on, both of them shaking their sides with laughter.

The germ of truth in that story was that Dudley, being one morning in the Queen's bedroom when she was about to dress, had gone so far as to hand her her chemise. The Council, furious at the incident, had called him to account; naturally the ladies in waiting had talked. But there were other incidents of a similar sort. Once Dudley had kissed the Queen in public off-hand, without asking her permission, as though to proclaim his conquest. Another time, when he was hot from playing tennis, he had taken her handkerchief and had wiped his face with it. Men like the Duke of Norfolk and his brother-in-law, the Earl of Sussex, were most indignant. Stormy scenes occurred, and Quadra reported that the favourite was likely to get a dagger in his ribs one day.

It is impossible to say just what the relations between Elizabeth and Dudley actually were. Even some very cautious historians, judging the matter by their experience of the world, suspect that the Queen was Lord Robert's mistress. Others, holding as Mr. Belloc does, that Elizabeth's was a case of what he calls "lacivious impotence," see something still more sinister.

The Dudley Affair

While I incline, upon the whole, to the second opinion, I do not venture to pronounce. In view of what Quadra observed and reported, that the Queen had put her Master of the Horse in a bedroom connecting with her own, and that he was there at all times of the day and night, it is difficult not to believe that there was an impudent intimacy between them. Its precise nature is another matter: this is a case where the ordinary inferences are not safely to be drawn.

What is to be said on the other side is that Elizabeth, when she was thought to be dying of smallpox in 1562, protested to the Council that though she loved Lord Robert as a brother, "nothing dishonest had passed between them." Such a statement made under the shadow of death ought to be decisive. Unfortunately, we know only too well how the most solemn oaths were taken by Elizabeth with the greatest glibness and an air of injured innocence. The fact that she asked, on the same occasion, that Dudley be appointed Protector, in the event of her death, with a salary of £20,000 a year did not add, it would appear, to the Council's conviction of her blameless behaviour.

What at least is certain is that there were none of the children concerning whom stories of a most circumstantial sort were nevertheless spread. For instance, the Bishop of Padua wrote to the Cardinal of Como in 1575 that the English Ambassador at Madrid had said that Elizabeth had a daughter thirteen years old whom she would marry to anyone Philip II selected. But the Bishop adds cautiously, "I have heard talk of this daughter, but the English say they know nothing of the matter." A little later there appeared in Spain an Arthur Dudley, who pretended to be Elizabeth's son and a Catholic. Englefield wrote to Philip about this youth, "I consider him a very feigned Catholic." The Spaniards, who were by now used to English tricks, looked upon him as a spy. He may, however, have been merely an adventurer playing his own hand and looking for Spanish support to the English throne if Elizabeth died. There had been two such imposters during the reign of Henry VII, and in Mary's a young man appeared who claimed to be the supposedly dead Edward VI.

But to dismiss all the fantastic stories about Elizabeth's children, by no means proves, of course, that there had been "nothing dishonest" in her relations with Dudley. The point to remember is that the English courtiers and the foreign ambassadors believed those relations — whether honest or not — were so intimate as to make it likely that Elizabeth would marry Dudley if she got the chance.

Such a chance soon came, but in such a way that the marriage project (if there ever really was one) had to be dropped. On September 8, 1560, Amy Robsart, Dudley's wife, was found dead at the bottom of the staircase of her house, Cumnor Place, where she lived in retirement; and a malodorous scandal broke.

Froude, though he rejects the thesis of murder, draws particular attention to a letter written by Quadra on September 11 to the Duchess of Parma. In it Quadra relates how Cecil, who had just returned from negotiating the treaty of Edinburgh, was depressed at finding Leicester in the ascendant. The Secretary confided to the Bishop that he perceived "the most manifest ruin hanging over the Queen through her intimacy with Lord Robert," who had made himself not only master of the business of state but "of the person of the Queen." In this conversation, which occurred, according to Quadra, on the day of Amy Robsart's death — but before news of it had arrived at Court — Cecil had said that "they were thinking of destroying Lord Robert's wife. They had given out that she was ill; but she was not ill at all: she was very well, and taking care not to be poisoned."

The following day — still before news of the death had arrived — Elizabeth had a conversation with Quadra. "She told me," he writes, "that Lord Robert's wife was dead or nearly so, and begged me to say nothing about it." The Bishop goes on to tell the Duchess that popular feeling was running so high about the Dudley affair that the Queen was in danger of being sent to the Tower. Then Lord Huntingdon would probably be declared King: "Cecil himself told me that he was the true heir to the throne."

It must be insisted upon that the prospect of Elizabeth's

ROBERT DUDLEY, EARL OF LEICESTER
From the painting of an unknown artist,
in the National Portrait Gallery.

downfall was anything but wishful thinking on Quadra's part. On the contrary, he showed that he regarded the situation as highly detrimental to Spanish interests. Huntingdon, he says, is a "great heretic," and Cecil was intriguing with the French. "It may be," he sums up, "that I am over-suspicious; but with such people it is always prudent to believe the worst. Certainly they say openly that they will not have a woman over them any more; and this one is likely to go to sleep in the palace, and to wake with her lover in the Tower."

Now, that letter would seem to be quite decisive both as to Dudley's having arranged for the murder of his wife, and to Elizabeth's having been privy to it. Yet there still remain some doubts. Maitland thinks that the Bishop made up the whole story — though why he should have done so is not at all clear; he obviously thought the affair a calamity. And Professor Pollard argues that Quadra's postscript — "Since this was written the death of Lord Robert's wife has been given out publicly" — was not the only part of the letter written on the 11th, but that the body of the letter was composed after and not before word had come that Amy Robsart was dead. For this, however, he offers no proof, contenting himself with a mere expression of opinion. The answer to such gratuitous suppositions is that though Quadra may have conceivably juggled with dates, or even have been a downright liar, the letter itself indicates that he had no motive for lying. He was very much upset by the news he had to pass on, for the end of Elizabeth would have meant the end of all Spanish influence in England.

Everything now looked black indeed. Abroad it was universally believed that there had been foul play. The French made caustic remarks about the religion of the wife-murdering English, and Mary Queen of Scots dipped her tongue in Gallic malice to say that Elizabeth was about to marry her Master of the Horse who had murdered his wife. Dudley found himself obliged to institute some sort of an enquiry.[3] The coroner's

[3] His political enemies tried to make use of an accusation of murder brought against his steward by Amy's half brother, whereupon the obliging Cecil put the man in jail and kept him there until he retracted.

jury brought in a noncommittal verdict of "death by misadventure," and it must be admitted that it is, in the face of deficient evidence, a tenable theory that this woman, neglected by her husband and distraught, should have thrown herself down the stairs. We hear, however, no more about the cancer of which — so it had been given out — she was dying. Unless we are to reject Quadra's letter, it is plain that Dudley, Elizabeth, and even Cecil, were expecting something to happen in Cumnor Place.

Despite the scandal, most people took it for granted that the Queen would now marry Lord Robert. Even if Elizabeth had a physical impediment that made a true marriage impossible, she may have thought that an ostensible marriage was better than none at all. For more than a year after the "misadventure" she behaved as though that were her intention, and Dudley went swaggering about as though he were sure of the "Crown matrimonial." So much did the courtiers look for the marriage that on one occasion a rumour sprang up that it had taken place, secretly, while the couple were staying in Lord Pembroke's house.

Quadra, in the meanwhile, found that his apprehension as to what would happen to Elizabeth gradually proved groundless. Most surprisingly he decided that it would be best after all to back Dudley, for though he occasionally continued to describe Elizabeth as "this woman," "this Jezebel," he wrote to Philip on January 22, 1561, "The Queen and Lord Robert are lovers; but they intend honest marriage, and nothing wrong had taken place between them which could not be set right with your Majesty's help." The last phrase is a little mysterious, but the reason for the Bishop's change of front is that they had assured him that they were "determined to restore religion by way of a general council." At all events that was the message brought by their go-between, Sir Henry Sidney, who was cousin to the English Countess of Feria as well as brother-in-law to Dudley himself. "Cecil," writes Quadra, "who was the greatest obstacle, has given in, being bribed by a promise of the offices vacated by Sir Thomas Parry, who died a few days ago of mere

The Dudley Affair

ill humour."[4] Quadra explodes splenetically in the same letter: "This woman is generally believed to be out of her mind; and it is thought she can never have a child. Some say she is a mother already, but this I do not believe."

It is, however, unlikely that Cecil had really been won over; Elizabeth's marriage to Lord Robert would have destroyed his own ascendency. There may be an even darker tinge to the whole affair than we imagine. We know that Dudley, in a great panic over the scandal of his wife's death, had written at once to Cecil, for among the Hatfield Manuscripts there is a letter from him endorsed by Cecil himself that breathes a grovelling gratitude to the Secretary for the help he had promised to give in the predicament. Can it be that Cecil had undertaken to suppress what he knew, and had by this means got Dudley into his power? Can it be that he was ever afterwards in a position to practice blackmail upon him? Such a hypothesis would explain much in Dudley's subsequent career. All was grist that came to the Cecilian mill. It may be that he ground out from murder a further security for the Protestant cause.

What Cecil's secret thoughts were may be learned from the balance sheet — he habitually used this method — drawn up by him in 1566 when the project of Elizabeth's marriage to the Archduke Charles was being considered. It is not necessary to reproduce his estimate of Charles as a husband, except to say that it was favourable to the Archduke's character. But of Dudley, Cecil lists among the disadvantages under the heading "Likelihood to love his wife:" *Nuptiae carnales a laetitia incipiunt et in luctu terminantur.* As for Dudley's "Reputation" the curt judgement is: "Hated of many. His wife's death."

But to go back a little way: Philip, upon getting word from Quadra that Elizabeth and Lord Robert were prepared to make a Catholic restoration as payment for his support, promptly accepted the offer and instructed his Ambassador to further the marriage. His mills, too, could turn anything to grist. So the

[4] In other words, of a broken heart. He had gone down on his knees to Elizabeth, begging her to give up so shameful a project. Nobody knew better than himself how close she had come to ruining herself in the affair with Thomas Seymour.

Bishop, who had so recently called Dudley "the worst young fellow in the world," now told Elizabeth that she had the King of Spain's blessing, and that "he well knew the high character that was borne by Lord Robert." Elizabeth was no longer "this Jezebel" in his letters. With such support it is not at all impossible that the marriage would have taken place, upon a guarantee being given to restore Catholicism, had not the English Catholic nobility refused to buy their freedom at the shameful price of accepting Dudley.

The Bishop, cynically, and with no illusions, went on playing his not very edifying political game. He was accepted as the confidant of the lovers and smiled his sly avuncular benediction upon their pretty billings and cooings, while reporting carefully to Spain everything that happened. Elizabeth prattled to him in 1561, "I wish to confess to you" — we may picture her going through the gestures she remembered making in her Catholic days, and Quadra's lifted eyebrows! — "I wish to confess to you and tell my secret, which is that I am no angel, and do not deny that I have some affection for Lord Robert for the many good qualities he possesses. But," she hastily went on, "certainly I have never decided to marry him nor anyone else, though I daily see more clearly the necessity for it." On another occasion (it was in June, 1561) the couple were with the Bishop in a barge on the river watching some water sports when Lord Robert said that, as they had a priest at hand in Quadra, there was no reason why they should not be married then and there. To which Elizabeth only made the enigmatic reply that perhaps the Bishop did not understand enough English. Having let them trifle in this way for a while, Quadra thought the opportunity had come for his suggesting that they should shake off "the tyranny of the men who were oppressing the realm." They could then restore religion and he would be very glad to marry them. But he sadly concludes that, though the Catholic party was gaining strength, the Queen was not inclined to marry anyone who was not approved by Cecil. Dudley had been so indiscreet as to talk in his exultation about the re-establishment of Catholicism.

It was characteristic of Elizabeth that while all this love-making was going on she was conducting negotiations for a marriage with the Archduke Charles. A Hapsburg marriage was, of course, what Philip really wanted; he had accepted Dudley merely as a possible second string. In the beginning it was not clear — and Elizabeth jested on the subject — as to whether she was expected to take Charles, or his elder brother Ferdinand. But soon the Hapsburg field narrowed down to Charles, and we have amusing letters from the series of ambassadors and special envoys employed in the business, most of which have only recently been published by von Klarwill. For instance, Count Helffenstein writes to the Emperor as early as February 25–26, 1559, as to how Elizabeth had overheard a group of ladies and gentlemen of her court discussing which of five or six Englishmen she was likely to marry. "The Queen answered that they were forsooth all intelligent people to propose such a magnificent match among her compatriots, but in the number of candidates they should have included one of her halberdiers." Again, Breuner writes to the Archduke Maximilian, King of Bohemia, in December of the same year, to say that he is "rather inclined to believe" that the affair between the Queen and Dudley was "but the innocent love which at times subsists between young men and maidens, though it be unseemly for such a princess." And Ahasuerus Allinga reports from London in January, 1564, that after he had made a speech extolling matrimony in which he had recommended it as a desirable evil, Elizabeth laughed at the teutonic tactlessness and had exclaimed "Desirable!" Then on June 4, 1565, Zwetkovich tells a pleasant story to the Emperor — this was at the time when a marriage with the youthful Charles IX of France was being discussed: "The Queen's jester spoke the truth when he said in English (the Queen interpreted it in Italian), 'She should not take the King of France, for he was but a boy and a babe; but she should take the Archduke Charles, and then she would be sure to have a baby-boy.'" The jest may well have sounded bitter in Elizabeth's ears. It was, however, in the vein of her own humour.

As the lovers and suitors came and went, Elizabeth indulged

herself as usual — and rather more than usual — in praising virginity. To her first Parliament she had said, when they raised the subject of her marriage (as did nearly all her Parliaments): "In the end this shall be for me sufficient, that a marble stone shall declare that a queen, having reigned such a time, lived and died a virgin." They relished the turn of phrase, and they humoured her pose without taking it too seriously: of course, she would put all that nonsense out of her head and marry. When she delayed, and appeared to be so much in love with Dudley, even a man like Sussex smothered his contempt for the upstart and, thinking it best to accept a bad situation for want of a better, wrote to Cecil to say that he believed the marriage ought to be encouraged — on the ground that such ardent love as the Queen showed Lord Robert was the surest guarantee of progeny.

One factor in all this must never be lost sight of: the country could not afford to wait indefinitely for the Queen to bear a child. Her health was so poor that at any moment she might die, as in 1562 she very nearly did. We happen to know that the toughness of her constitution — or, if the doctors object to that term, let me offer one that they will object to even more — that the vitality of Elizabeth was destined to overcome the ailments that should have killed her; the people around her who saw the ailments did not expect her to live long. A few words on this subject should perhaps be said at this point.

Mr. Chamberlin has garnered in his *Private Character of Queen Elizabeth*, a book strongly partial to her, all the available facts, and has obtained from such an authority as the Royal College of Surgeons, as well as from a number of distinguished practitioners, a long-range diagnosis of the Queen's various diseases. They report her as highly neurotic, tormented with nerves, so that "what we have always believed in, and joked about, as Elizabeth's violent temper, was not really temper at all." Dr. Spencer Wells, in an address before the British Medical Association, asserts that the root of her trouble was ovarian dropsy. But she also had jaundice, swellings in the face and other parts of her body, constant headaches, and a syphilitic sore in her leg inherited from her father. Salviati, the Nuncio in Paris, wrote to the Cardinal of Como on January 6, 1578: "They say that she hardly ever had the purgations proper to women, but that instead nature had come to the rescue by establishing an issue in one of her legs, which has never been scanty of flow." In short, the evidence seems to indicate that what was wrong with Elizabeth's health — both of mind and body — was a sexual abnormality aggravated by syphilis.

Mr. Chamberlin expresses the opinion, which strikes me as plausible, that this very abnormality was an asset to Elizabeth as a politician. A woman ordinarily constituted would probably have broken down under the strain of being obliged to play at being in love with one suitor after another. But then, of course, no ordinarily constituted woman would have acted in this way at all. She was obliged to console her vanity by methods which — apart from the moral issues involved — could only have increased the appalling tension of her mind. Sir Walter Raleigh (who is generally supposed to be one of the men who figured in what Mr. Belloc calls the Queen's "imperfect amours") is credited with the devastating remark that "her minions were not so happy as vulgar judgments thought them, being frequently commanded to uncomely and sometimes unnatural employments." If this rests on an authority not quite beyond question, there is no question at all but that it expresses a view widely held by Elizabeth's contemporaries.

I dislike dilating upon so unsavoury a theme, but there is no way of honestly avoiding it. The matter recurs so constantly that it has to be considered, for it is closely connected with the political happenings of the time, to which it provides a possible clue. Nor is the personality of Elizabeth to be truly discerned except in a lurid light. Yet that light flares up so fiercely and dies away so suddenly, that one cannot be sure as to just what it is that one has seen. As far as Dudley is concerned, I am tempted to throw out a suggestion that I marvel that nobody else, so far as I know, has made before. Can it be possible that the strong facial likeness between Lord Robert and Elizabeth was merely accidental? The existing portraits of the man in youth and of the woman might be compared again. And there is the fact that in his later life those about him commented upon Leicester's resemblance to Henry VIII. He was by then corpulent and red of face. If there is anything in this, it might serve to modify our judgement of Elizabeth's conduct — at any rate her conduct with Dudley. Perhaps she permitted him the familiarities that so scandalised her courtiers, not because he was her lover, but because he was her half brother.[5] I am not advancing any thesis: I am merely venturing upon a wild surmise, confessing as I do so that it is something that floats as no more than a shadow now and then before me. But is it not barely possible that Elizabeth may have been laughing up her sleeve all the time? It would have been like her to have taken a perverse pleasure in mystification.

There was little consistency in the strange character of the Queen, even in her relations with Dudley. When the patent for his earldom was first presented to her for signature, she happened to be in a bad mood (perhaps in a lover's quarrel), and so slashed it with her penknife, making a sarcastic reference to his forebears. Then when another patent was drawn shortly afterwards she fondled the new earl's neck during the ceremony of investiture. Melville, the Ambassador of Scotland, who was present described it as a "tickling." Nobody could have considered the procedure seemly; it was, all the same, very characteristic of Elizabeth.

Whatever be the truth of the relations between the pair, it is, I think, unlikely that Elizabeth ever had a settled determination to marry Dudley. Even supposing that she wished to marry him — that she was capable of marriage — cool reflection must have made her see the grave dangers that such a marriage would entail. As Baron Breuner said in his letter, already quoted from, to the Emperor: "If she marry the said My Lord Robert, she will incur so much enmity that she may one evening lay herself down as Queen of England and arise the next morning as plain

---

[5] At the same time we must remember that Elizabeth scandalised her Court by permitting similar familiarities to others — to Simier and Essex, for example. However, there is no certain record of even their being permitted so much as was Dudley.

The Dudley Affair

Mistress Elizabeth." It is almost word for word what Bishop
Quadra wrote, nine months later to the Duchess of Parma. But
though no certainty can be reached concerning the facts behind
this curious affair, Lingard's sober, if severe, sentence justly
covers it, as it also covers subsequent incidents of a similar sort:
"The woman who despises the safeguards, must be content to
forfeit the reputation of chastity."

9

The Evasive Virgin

IN THE preceding chapter I have been obliged, as I shall be obliged in some of the subsequent chapters, to introduce a certain amount of gossip and conjecture. I am well aware that neither can be considered history. Yet even when gossip is baseless — as much gossip is — it shows, at any rate, what was believed at the time, and to that extent has a historical nature. In the case of Elizabeth most people will always believe that so great a quantity of smoke could not have existed had there been no fire. Further, conjecture, though never to be confused with certainty, is forced upon one who is dealing with evidence from which it is clear that material facts have been abstracted. To make Elizabeth's story intelligible to one's own mind, one is obliged to construct some sort of bridge between the proved and the possible. Inference is indispensable unless the historian is content to be a mere chronicler, or unless his case is so complete — and how often does that happen? — that he can get along without it. The so-called impartial historian is almost always colourless and fails to focus his story. All that can be asked of the historian is that he be fair, that he indicate what is to be said on the other side. This I am trying to do; but so far from pretending to be "impartial," in the sense of having no personal convictions, I believe a point of view is necessary to the production of any sort of a pattern. In spite of Elizabeth's faults, I admire and even like her. But, if many things in her character as exhibited here — and still more in the character of many of the men by whom she was surrounded — are, because of my exhibition of them, likely to bring upon me a charge of cynicism, all I can say is that I have a much better opinion of humanity in general than may appear. I am dealing with particular people and their actions and the motives for their actions. It seems to me that a moral standard that would exculpate them would be cynical indeed. However great my indignation may be at what was done, I can often — especially in the case of Elizabeth — make due allowances. Her difficulties were great, so that some of the divagations of her politics were, no doubt, hardly avoidable in a world where principles were so little regarded, or where the principles were other than our own. Above all, I feel compassion for a woman so tortured in body and soul as often not to be held responsible. If pity for her abnormality dims to some extent the romantic picture of Gloriana, we may still fully grant that she was, nevertheless, richly endowed. In fact, genius is, according to one large group of psychiatrists, the fruit of neurosis, and Elizabeth was assuredly a genius. To deny her neurosis (whatever may have been its cause) would only be to accentuate the imputation of her guilt. In any event, truth must be served.

When we come to Elizabeth's marriage proposals we have a mass of documents, though probably not all that were written and certainly not the complete body of facts. In von Klarwill's collection, for instance, there are included only four letters previously published. Yet even with these documents before us, we cannot be sure as to what Elizabeth's intentions really were. It must be remembered that the most seemingly reliable witness may be ill-informed, or prejudiced, or charitably giving the best colour to a given situation, or, maliciously, the worst, or that he may see only what he wants to see, or reports only what he thinks he is expected to report, or that he is a downright liar. We have, therefore, a tangle of conflicting evidence before us. Having no other, we must do the best with it that we can.

There are two schools of thought with regard to Elizabeth's projected marriages — or rather, three. One of these holds that she did not want to marry, that she deliberately fooled her suitors to the top of their bent. Nobody in her own day believed in her profound (at all events, loudly expressed) love for virginity, though it became a sycophantic fashion to praise the "Virgin Queen." Still less does anybody today believe in her love of virginity. A Scotch Ambassador considered himself very canny in telling Elizabeth, "Madam, I know your stately stomach: ye think if ye were married, ye would be but Queen of England, and now ye be King and Queen both; ye may not suffer a commander." Such a consideration doubtless entered into the matter — at least sufficiently for the facile explanation to be accepted by Elizabeth with a grim smile. Doubtless, too, Elizabeth found it convenient to play off her suitors one against the other in the diplomatic game. But was this the whole truth? Was it not rather that Elizabeth, as she could not have any husband, decided to use her disability as an asset?

The second school of thought holds that she did want to marry, but could never make up her mind. Nobody could ever bring her to the decisive point, because the nearer she drew to it, the more clearly she perceived the disadvantages of the particular marriage under consideration. This would certainly have applied to the marriage with Dudley. The scandal would have been too devastating for a woman of her cautious temperament, and, even without the scandal, there was the danger of making implacable enemies of the old nobility that hated Dudley. Similarly in the proposed foreign marriages, the diplomatic losses which would have had to be incurred along with the diplomatic gains forbade her committing herself. Again there is something in this: only we should remember that similar considerations enter into almost every important human action. Elizabeth was indeed a vacillating woman; she weighed everything over and over again before reaching any conclusion. But, except on the marriage question, she always made up her mind in the end.

The third school of thought holds the working hypothesis (undemonstrable, but one that explains much that is otherwise inexplicable) that she would have liked to have married had she been able to do so, but was incapable of a true union. It was obviously to her disadvantage not to produce a son; to have done so would have been to have consolidated a position that was never too secure against the claim of Mary Queen of Scots. This enormous advantage would have assuredly more than offset any repugnance Elizabeth might have had to sharing her power with a husband. And a husband's influence — it need not have been domination — would, in turn, have brought with it the compensation of freeing her from the pressure of the politicians upon whom she was obliged to depend. Even if there were nothing else to go on, these reasons, I believe, would be enough, in themselves, to force upon us the moral — though not the absolute — certainty that Elizabeth did not marry merely because she could not.

As it was, she made the best of a bad job. She got a queer kind of artistic pleasure out of the deviousness of diplomacy; and she got a perverse kind of satisfaction in having suitors around her who were from the beginning doomed to sigh in vain. She knew that she was not going to marry any of them, but she enjoyed the wooing. Her defect served to extract the maximum of political profit out of the protracted courtship, while for her personal delectation she carried on a series of extremely intimate "flirtations" with less eligible gallants. It became a joke in the chancelleries of Europe, one that Mendoza set in circulation, that the Queen of England plighted her troth every year but never went to the altar.

Let me give, at this point, a list of those whose names were canvassed as husbands — exclusive of the supposititious lovers. While Elizabeth was still in the cradle, Henry VIII discussed the possibility of her marrying the Duke of Angoulême, Francis I's third son. He also thought of the Earl of Arran, who applied again when she was Queen. Philip of Spain, too, was proposed. These negotiations never got very far: Elizabeth was soon made illegitimate and barred from the succession.

In Edward VI's reign, the son of the Duchess of Ferrara, the Duke of Florence, and Hans Frederick of Saxony were mentioned as possibilities. Again her bastardy and uncertain prospects were no very powerful inducements.

Under Mary there was the treasonable design of Courtenay, Earl of Devonshire. There was also some vague idea that the Earl of Arundel's son might do. By no means vague was Philip's idea of disposing her to his cousin, Emmanuel Philibert, Duke of Savoy. Elizabeth fought against the project. She knew by then that Mary was not likely to live long; she also knew that with a foreign husband she would stand scant chance of being accepted by England as queen.

We are mainly concerned, however, with those who proposed for her after she ascended the throne. These are the Earl of Arundel (whose son had been offered previously), Sir William Pickering, Lord Robert Dudley, Philip of Spain and the Earl of Arran (both for the second time), Prince Eric of Sweden, the Duke of Holstein, Henry Neville, Earl of Westmoreland (whose son was to rebel against her in 1569), the Hapsburg Archdukes Ferdinand and Charles, De Vere, Earl of Oxford, the Duke of Anjou (afterwards Henry III) and his brothers Charles IX and the Duke of Alençon, later known as Duke of Anjou.

Some of these candidates, of course, were never considered seriously. Even Eric of Sweden and the Duke of Holstein, though they were politely listened to, were hardly worth bothering with. A marriage alliance with any available Protestant prince could not be weighed in the same scales with what the royal house of France or the Hapsburgs might offer. Nevertheless, John, Duke of Finland, came over in his brother Eric's interest, arriving with a rich train and servants whose livery showed on the lapels of their red velvet coats an emblematic pair of hearts pierced by an arrow. As though this pretty touch were not enough, he distributed money lavishly among the populace, telling them that where he gave silver the Prince would give gold. To impress Elizabeth with Eric's wealth he presented her with eighteen piebald horses and several chests of bullion. But she, though having no objection to accepting presents, suggested that Eric postpone his visit until she could resolve to submit to matrimony. The Duke wrote to his brother, "I see no signs of an immodest life, but I did see many signs of chastity, of virginity [how he could have seen these is not clear], and of true modesty, so that I would stake my life itself that she is most chaste." It is evident that Eric had heard some talk in a different strain. And, soon becoming jealous of the impression John was making, he recalled him.

The Evasive Virgin

The English suitors we may briefly dismiss. The Dudley affair cooled off, so far as any prospect of marriage was concerned, toward the end of 1561, though Lord Robert remained in the running for some time afterwards. None of his compatriots ever had any real chance.

Of the early marriage projects the most significant was that affecting the Archduke Charles. (His brother Ferdinand was soon withdrawn.) In October, 1559, when Quadra asked Elizabeth whether she wished the Archduke to come to England, she answered with an evasive "I hinder no one's coming." A few days later she amplified this. She hesitated about sending an invitation for fear of putting an affront upon the Emperor by having to reject Charles. She would not consent to marry a man whom she had not seen, nor would she insult him by asking him to allow himself to be inspected first. With that the matter hung fire. Later, however, we hear from the report of Zwetkovich to the Emperor Maximilian (June 4, 1565) of Elizabeth's ingenious solution: "She would argue that if she were to reject such a prince as the Archduke, people in general would say that she had been disdained by him and not he by her." So Charles need fear no humiliation by coming to England. This not proving altogether satisfactory, Maximilian two years later (September 30, 1567) offered another formula to Elizabeth's special envoy, the Earl of Sussex. As the important question was religion, and as the Queen had undertaken that no insult was to be offered the House of Hapsburg, "If mutual personal acquaintance bear mutual affection, the marriage can be solemnized. . . . If not, the Archduke would in full accord with the illustrious Queen return to his provinces, and neither would be lowered in any way." The blame could be thrown on credal differences.

There were sound political reasons for the marriage, though the Spanish Ambassador writes in 1565: "[Arundel] told me not to believe that Cecil wanted the Queen to marry. He was ambitious and fond of ruling, and liked everything to pass through his hands, and if the Queen had a husband he would have to obey him." As against this, which no doubt was a factor

143

to be reckoned with, was a still more important one. If the Netherlands were subdued — as everybody expected — and England found herself facing a large Spanish army across the North Sea, a marriage with Charles would avert all danger.

Financial questions, too, were involved, Elizabeth wanting the Archduke to support himself, while he thought himself entitled to support from England. But these were capable of solution: what eventually proved the great stumbling block, or was made into one, was religion. Here the Archduke conceded a good deal. He was ready to accompany Elizabeth to the Anglican services, so long as he was allowed to have Mass privately in his room. Yet even this proposal was agreed to with such reservations as to make all concessions from the other side meaningless. For if there should be any disturbance on account of the private Mass, the privilege was to be withdrawn — which, of course, it would have been on some pretext or other. A mob could always have been incited to riot against "Popery."

The Emperor Maximilian was perfectly willing that his brother go over to the Protestants rather than miss so rich a matrimonial prize. He himself, though officially a Catholic, was primarily an Imperialist. His total personal indifference to religion is shown by his refusal of the Last Sacraments on his deathbed. If he did not go so far as to advise Charles to commit apostasy, he made it sufficiently plain that he would raise no objection to it. "We only believe that if community can be obtained on this point, the two others [as to status and financial provision] will present no further difficulties." He could not understand why Charles was making all the fuss about such a trifle. Yet he suspected that it was Elizabeth who was deliberately erecting obstacles for some other reason, and petulantly remarks in the same letter that she "seems to regard it as profitable to create delays somewhere or somehow in order to gain advantage." On January 11, 1568, he is still complaining, "[Her] answer is most obscure, ambiguous, involved and of such a nature that we cannot learn from it whether the Queen is serious and sincere or whether she wishes to befool us." It was everybody's experience in dealing with Elizabeth.

The Evasive Virgin

All this dragged on from 1559 to 1570 — Elizabeth kept Charles dangling all those years, taking up the matter of the marriage and dropping it again, though it was she who made the last approaches — until the Archduke, disgusted with the whole business, married a Bavarian Princess. It is still impossible to be sure as to how sincere Elizabeth was, for in 1563 (in which year the project had been revived), she told the German envoy, "If I disclose to you what I should prefer if I followed the inclination of my own nature it is. this: Beggarwoman and single, far rather than a Queen and married!" Yet immediately she demanded most minute particulars as to the Archduke's personal appearance and qualities. However much she wavered, there were times when the marriage appeared to be practically settled. It came to nothing because she wanted to let matters drift. If Philip could not wait four months for her answer to his proposal, Charles had waited patiently for eleven years — and then suddenly had found his patience exhausted. To his credit it must be said that, though he went as far as he could to be accommodating about religion, he would not budge on essentials. However much his portraits suggest that he was a weak and disappointed man, he remained faithful to his Faith, and a daily attendant at Mass.

Elizabeth now turned to France for a husband. In 1564 Catherine de' Medici had put forward her son, Charles IX. He was a boy of fourteen, and the English Queen a woman of thirty-one. In spite of this, the absurd project was gravely discussed for a while. Charles was succeeded, as Elizabeth's suitor in 1570, by his brother, the Duke of Anjou, then nineteen when Elizabeth was thirty-seven.

Anjou's candidacy indicated a change in England's foreign policy. The queen felt herself now able to dispense with Philip's help. Or rather, as relations with Spain were getting progressively worse, she decided upon seeking a French alliance. Whether or not she meant to take a French husband is another story. In any event it was expected that Anjou would prove compliant about religion. Catherine de' Medici was notoriously inclined toward Protestantism, and her sons were supposed to be infected. Cecil and Walsingham both supported the new scheme for the reasons that France would stand between Elizabeth and the Pope, that Anjou was wealthy, and that he "would accommodate himself to the religion of England." The English Catholics received the news with consternation. They had pinned their hopes upon Elizabeth marrying a loyal Catholic.

Anjou turned out to be anything but enthusiastic about the marriage. He described Elizabeth as "an old hag with a sore leg" — a remark his brother's Ambassador had great trouble in explaining away. To soothe the Duke, the French agents reported to him in 1571 that Elizabeth was "the most perfect beauty that God had made during the last five hundred years." To Elizabeth the Ambassador ingeniously explained that the eighteen years' disparity between her age and Anjou's was — if only looked at in the right light — in her favour: Anjou was ten years older than his years, she was ten years younger than hers!

As for religion, the apostate Cardinal of Châtillon (Coligny's brother) told Elizabeth that Henry was very close to Calvinism. He ought to have known: his own Calvinism — and his wife's — were very much in evidence. But events did not confirm this. As a further argument, Paul de Foix, the French envoy, reminded Elizabeth that the mother of the Emperor Constantine had converted him, and that the wife of the King of Navarre had done the same. In the same way, Elizabeth might convert Anjou. She replied, "Although it were a great glory to imitate the Empress Helena in so great a thing, yet it by no means follows that such will be the case with regard to Monsieur, for there are fully as many wives converted by their husbands as husbands by their wives."

But this was not the only reason why Elizabeth hesitated. She spoke to la Mothe Fénelon about Henry's mistresses: what chance had she against such famous beauties? He responded with suitable flatteries: what a question to ask! Yet Elizabeth continued to wonder: "She did not wish for a husband who would honour her as a Queen without loving her as a wife." If he ceased to love her she would die.

The Evasive Virgin

Oh, but that was impossible! la Mothe assured her. Besides, the Valois were famous for their marital fidelity. As proof he instanced Charles IX — who had been married two months! Therefore, he said, "I would recommend a princess who wishes for perfect happiness in marriage to take a husband from the House of France."

Meanwhile Catherine de' Medici was having violent scenes with Henry because of his reluctance, and Elizabeth was remarking that "a certain person of high rank in France had said that Monsieur would do well to marry the old hag who last year had had an ulcer in her leg, which was not cured and probably never would be cured. . . . He might administer a poison which would make him a widower six months after marriage, and leave him free to marry the Queen of Scots, in whose right he would reign peacefully over the whole island." It is hardly to be wondered at that a courtship full of charming tendernesses like these did not prosper.

In the end the negotiations broke down because of the religious problem, though likely enough this was again merely used by Elizabeth as a pretext for avoiding what she had never had any intention of doing. Be that as it may, Anjou surprised everybody by refusing to apostatise. Mass was absolutely refused him — even Mass in private. The most the Queen conceded (which, of course, was nothing at all) was that Monsieur should supplement his Anglican devotions with "such rites, prayers, and ceremonies as are not repugnant to the Scriptures." To make sure that Anjou would not venture beyond them, he was told that everything would be withdrawn "if the Council avow of their honours that troubles do grow by reason of the said permission."

Here the Council overshot the mark, though possibly intentionally. All the efforts of Guido Cavalcanti, the mysterious Italian agent of Catherine de' Medici, who flitted to and fro between London and Paris, came to nothing. Anjou's mother made a tremendous scene about his throwing away the Crown of England — had not Nostradamus himself prophesied that all her three sons were to be kings? — but Anjou refused to renounce the Mass. It is the best thing one can record of his life, but it is a great deal. Elizabeth made the handsome comment: "I should be sorry if I thought Monsieur was willing to give up his religion, for if he had the heart to forsake God, he might also forsake me." Less handsomely she told la Mothe Fénelon in 1574: "When all was agreed upon, and I had arranged that he was to have the exercise of his religion in private, and had sent a councillor to signify my acceptance, it was found that he had taken a directly contrary course." As usual, she was, to put it mildly, disingenuous. Catherine de' Medici's version of the affair (in her letter to la Mothe of February, 1571) was: "My son has let me know by the King that he never wishes to marry her, even if she wishes it; so much has he heard against her honour, and seen of it in the letters of all the ambassadors there." Alençon, who must be left until a later chapter, was not so squeamish.

The Queen was now middle aged. Once again she had disappointed the Parliament that had petitioned her to marry. In 1559 she had evaded the issue by drawing off her coronation ring and saying, "When I received this ring I solemnly bound myself in marriage to the realm." They had naturally taken that to imply that she would marry a man. In much the same way she had put off the Parliament of 1563. As time went on, and Parliament grew increasingly restive with the unpredictable woman, she assumed a higher tone. In 1566 Parliament got a severe wigging when it ventured to bring up the question again. She told them that she was not surprised at the Commons: "They had small experience and acted like boys; but that the Lords should have gone along with them filled her with wonder." Then swinging on the Bishops she remarked: "And you doctors I understand make long prayers about this business. One of you dared to say in times past that I and my sister were bastards. . . . Go home and amend your lives and set an honest example in your families. The Lords in Parliament should have taught you to know your places; but if they have forgotten their duty I will not forget mine. Did I so choose I might make the impertinence of the whole lot of you an excuse to withdraw my promise to marry; but for the realm's sake I am resolved that I will marry; and I will take a husband that will not be to the taste of some of you. . . . Think you that the prince who will be my consort will feel himself to be safe with such as you, who thus dare to thwart and cross your natural Queen." She had carried the war into the enemy's country, and they were cowed. On she raged: "I am your anointed Queen. I will never by violence be constrained to anything. I thank God that I am endowed with such qualities that if I were turned out of the realm in my petticoat I am able to live in any place in Christome." That was the most she would give them for comfort — an angry renewal of her promise that when it pleased her, and not a moment sooner — she would marry. Let them beware of bringing up this question again. As for even naming a successor, she said: "I know too well that if I allow a successor to be named there will be found men to approach him or her with the same encouragement to disturb the peace of the realm. If I pleased I could name the persons to whom I allude." With which threat she swept out in an awed silence.

Throughout all these marriage negotiations Elizabeth had pretended to be not so Protestant as she was painted. She had to do something to placate the Catholics. Besides, if she were finally obliged to accept a Catholic husband — on conditions however humiliating to him — it would be to her interest to restrain extreme Protestant feeling. Thus, during her visit to Cambridge University in 1564, she showed in public her distaste for a play that had been put on for her. Bonner was introduced as a character, carrying a lamb in his arms and gnashing his teeth at it. That, though in bad enough taste, she allowed to pass. But when a dog entered carrying a host in his mouth, Elizabeth stood up and stopped the performance. It would not do to let Catholic foreigners hear of such blasphemy. And she probably was genuinely disgusted. She had some decent instincts. Her Protestantism was, in the main, a political convenience. If she had no strong attachment to the Catholic Faith, she had no strong dislike for it either. Even as late as 1588 observers on the continent believed that she would be willing to revert to Catholicism if Parma's army landed. However that may be, she disapproved of unseemly exhibitions, such as the Cambridge play. When she reached her apartments she relieved her feelings by swearing with more than usual vigour.[1]

Two final words should be said about Elizabeth's marriage projects. The first — and it casts a light upon the problem of Elizabeth's personal make-up — is that she frequently showed spite against those who married when she did not. Her dislike for a married clergy — and especially for married bishops — has sometimes been attributed to the remnants of her Catholic tradition. But celibacy is not a matter of Catholic faith, but merely of Catholic discipline. A married clergy for England might conceivably have been tolerated by Rome. Elizabeth's preference for a celibate clergy was rather due to her objection to the whole idea of marriage — for anybody at all. This could hardly have been due to an abstract admiration for virginity. Catholic priests and religious, though accepting celibacy themselves, never have a hatred for marriage as such; it would be heresy if they had. One questions the sincerity of Elizabeth's prating about virginity, not only because she talked far too much to be convincing, but because she always flew into a rage with the ladies and gentlemen of her Court who entered matrimony. We may set on one side her indignation when Lady Catherine Grey secretly married Lord Hertford, for the son she bore him was in line to the succession, and Elizabeth was something of a queen bee.[2] She was naturally still more

[1] I believe that Elizabeth on this occasion was really angry. But we must always remember that she rarely lost an opportunity for making scenes or for showing off. Thus at Oxford in 1566, while Dr. Westphaling was preaching in St. Mary's Church, the Queen became impatient with his long-windedness and sent word to ask him to cut his sermon short. This the poor man, having learned it all by heart, was unable to do. On the following morning, when Elizabeth had to address the University in Latin she saw her chance. As Cecil was standing on his gouty feet she broke off, perhaps partly out of consideration for him, until he was brought a stool, but mainly, as the cynical courtiers who knew her thought, to show her superiority to the parrotlike Dr. Westphaling.

[2] Elizabeth could not forget that there had been a project to set the couple up as king and queen at the time she was expected to marry Dudley. Lady Catherine remained a potential threat; that offered by her children was removed by Archbishop Parker's declaring her marriage null and void on the grounds of clandestinity.

angry when the erring Countess and her husband, who had been committed to the Tower, contrived to meet privately, so that another son was born. Lady Catherine's sister, on the other hand, Lady Mary Grey, who married Keyes, the serjeant porter of the Queen's water gate, could be laughed at: the *mésalliance* freed her from consideration, and the Court roared with laughter over so diminutive a woman marrying the gigantic serjeant. It appealed even to Elizabeth's not oversubtle sense of humour. What gave the virgin Queen away was the spite she showed the most harmlessly married people. An instance of this that comes to mind is that of the young lady in waiting who was asked by Elizabeth if she wanted to be married. Unsuspectingly the girl said, "I have thought much about marriage, if my father will consent to the man I love." Upon this Elizabeth promised to sue in her behalf, and later sent for the delighted child to tell her that her father had given his consent. "Oh, now I shall be happy, and thank your Grace!" came the cry, only to bring the cruel remark, "So thou shalt — but not to be a fool and marry. I have his consent given to *me*, and I vow *thou* shalt never get it into thy possession." There are so many cases of this dog-in-the-manger attitude. Even Leicester — perhaps most of all, Leicester — had to keep his second marriage a secret. And Essex fell out of favour for a short time for the same reason. Though, as she told the Duke of Würtemburg, she considered "the wedding ring the yoke ring," there is only one reason why she tried to prevent other people from accepting the yoke: it is that she turned against others the fury of her own frustration.

The other final word refers to the belief prevalent during the reign — and still generally prevalent — that Elizabeth's marriage to a Catholic would have resulted in a Catholic restoration, or, if not that, at least in a measure of tolerance. This would, of course, have been the case had Elizabeth married Philip of Spain: his first condition was that Elizabeth become a Catholic herself. But the most any of the proposed husbands could have effected would have been some slight amelioration of the lot of their coreligionists. At the same time a Catholic husband would have destroyed all chance of the Faith returning to England — that is, supposing Elizabeth had borne a child, which would, of course, have been brought up as a Protestant. Yet so desperate was the plight of the English Catholics, that for many years all that they and the Pope and Philip could do was to hope and pray for a Catholic marriage.

Even here, however, secular interests prevented unanimity among Catholics. For instance, when there seemed a possibility that Elizabeth might select one of the Valois, Philip instructed his agent in England to spread the idea that this would be injurious to the Church. By trying to head England off from France, he succeeded only in damaging the concept of himself as the great Catholic champion. However, he probably had persuaded himself of the doubtful orthodoxy of the House of France. What Philip should have done was the one thing he would never do until too late: that is, support the rightful claim of Mary of Scotland. But to that claim all the Hapsburgs were opposed. The instructions issued by the Emperor to Count Helffenstein in 1559 recognized Elizabeth as Queen of England, and added, "We are not aware that there remains another heir or successor." This attitude, though modified by the pressure of changing circumstances, remained part of the Imperial and Spanish policy. Elizabeth was to be married to a Hapsburg; out of fear of France, the Catholic Church in England was left to its fate in furtherance of secular ambitions. When at last Philip struck, the day for striking was past.

10

The Ruin of Mary

THE crucial issue of Elizabeth's reign was not her relations with Philip of Spain — important as these were — but her relations with Mary of Scotland. Philip, indeed, turned upon Elizabeth only after thirty years of provocation. He had held off so long because he believed, with some justice, that Mary's accession to the throne of England would mean that English alliance with France which was his bugbear. Even in his case, therefore, the determining factor was Mary Queen of Scots.

From the beginning it was Elizabeth's purpose to ruin her. But as such an avowed purpose or any attempt at naked conquest would at once have aroused France, she adopted the no less effective (and much safer) method of fomenting disaffection in Scotland. To her hand for this purpose there were the rebellious Lords of the Congregation.

We have seen how, when Cecil returned from the signing of the treaty of Edinburgh in the summer of 1560, he advised the buying of the Scotch Protestant nobility: they were going at bargain prices. It was they and not Knox — or rather, it was their support of Knox — that made the Reformation in Scotland possible. As Mr. Henderson, the biographer of Mary Queen of Scots, puts it, "The nobles listened to Knox because they had special worldly grievances against the Catholic clergy." Those grievances, of course, were that the clergy had wealth which the nobles coveted. Without the Lords of the Congregation Protestantism could have made little headway; it could hardly have survived even as the eccentric opinion of a few extremists had it not secured a preponderance of armed force.

That preponderance was secured only because of help from outside — from Elizabeth. She gave it surreptitiously and with frequent denials on oath that she was giving it at all. She went so far as to make a great show of disapproving of the Scotch rebels, so that when they were driven to take momentary refuge in England, they had to submit to a public wigging — which they and all the courtiers understood to be merely a matter of form. How did Moray dare to come into her presence? Before God she had not instigated his taking arms against his lawful prince! Yet on June 30, 1568, Elizabeth could unblushingly write to Mary, "I love no dissimulation in another, nor do I practise it myself." It is the hypocrite's favourite trick — to accuse another of the crime of which he is himself guilty.

That the condition of the Church in sixteenth-century Scotland was deplorable need not be denied. It was perhaps worse there than anywhere in Europe. The richer abbeys and priories were for the most part held *in commendam* by royal bastards, who, of course, made no pretence at living like ecclesiastics.[1] The bishoprics were filled by the younger brothers of the greater nobles. Clerical morals were everywhere at a low ebb. The Archbishop of St. Andrews, for instance, the base-born brother of the Duke of Châtelherault, who was the head of the numerous Hamilton family that was in the line of succession after the Stuarts, had five or six children by Lady Stonehouse. According to popular report the mistress of the Bishop of Dunblane was his own daughter. Reformation was obviously urgently needed — the reformation which was to come from the Tridentine decrees. Knox, however, backed by the Lords of the Congregation — men who were out for what they could grab from the endowments of the Church — took another line. Even before the arrival of Mary in Scotland the Scotch Parliament had met (in August, 1560, just after the treaty of Edinburgh) and abolished the Mass, imposing a death penalty upon anyone who, after a third conviction, said or heard it. That the laws of such a Parliament — which could only be summoned by the

---

[1] Lord James Stewart, afterwards Earl of Moray, is a case in point. This natural son of James V was made Prior of St. Andrews when he was seven.

Queen — were invalid troubled neither Knox nor the Lords: they calculated upon the moral effect; Mary would either have to accept Protestantism or be deposed.

They did not even have the excuse that they were acting as patriots. On the contrary, their policy meant the bringing in of their traditional enemies, the English, and of placing Scotland under the virtual suzerainty of Elizabeth. But from the point of view of Knox — and in this respect at least he was at one with genuine Catholics everywhere — religious truth was more important than nationality. The only disagreement was as to what constituted religious truth.

Mary landed at Leith from France on August 19, 1561, in a fog that had enabled her to escape from the English fleet instructed to intercept her. Knox, though disappointed at her safe arrival, announced that the "dolorous face of the hevins" indicated the divine displeasure, ignoring the fact that such fogs are a common feature of summer in the Firth of Forth. Further to console himself, he had the Queen serenaded in her palace that night by Calvinists groaning out their psalms.

Knox did not take long to show his hand. He had (to do him justice) published three years previously his *First Blast of the Trumpet against the Monstrous Regiment of Women,* whose title indicated that other blasts were to follow.[2] Less to his credit is his attempt to soften Elizabeth's anger by letting her know that what he had written was merely of general application; she was an exception; part of the divine dispensation — like Deborah. She was not mollified by the explanation.

John Knox's spiritual dictatorship, to which he felt he was directly appointed by God, was more thoroughgoing than the authority claimed by the Pope. For it applied to every detail of politics as well as religion. Under his scheme, if there was little place for any queen, there was certainly none at all for one who refused to submit to his brand-new Kirk. He made this abundantly clear in an interview with Mary.

[2] On April 6, 1559, Knox wrote to his friend, Mrs. Locke: "The Second Blast, I fear, shall sound somewhat more sharp, except men be more moderate than I hear they are." (Moderate!)

"My subjects, then," she said, "are to obey you and not me! I am subject to them and not they to me."

"Nay," he returned, "let prince and subject both obey God. Kings should be the foster fathers of the Kirk and Queens its nursing mothers."

"You are not the Kirk that I will nurse," she is reported to have answered. "I will defend the Kirk of Rome, for that I think is the Kirk of God."

To which Knox said "Your will, Madam, is no reason; neither does your thought make the Roman harlot the spouse of Jesus Christ."

He left her in angry tears. He had a susceptibility toward women, in his own grim way, but he was proof against Mary's charms. For that matter, Mary's power over men is largely a legend: it reposes mainly upon her three marriages, nor does she seem to have been endowed with the fascinations that enable some women who are not beautiful to bring men to their feet. Her quick wit and courage made many men admire her; none, I think, fell deeply in love with her. She has found most of her lovers since her death in those moved by pity for her sorrows and indignation at the treatment she received. At any rate the stern Knox was adamant; Mary might as well have tried to enchant a tiger.

Yet Knox, however consistent he may have been, was very unjust. So far from Mary's making any effort to re-establish Catholicism, she showed remarkable tolerance and nothing of the spirit of the Guises. This actually caused embarrassment to Elizabeth and Cecil who had counted upon her providing them with an excuse to intervene for the protection of Protestants. Here was Mary turning out to be a *politique!* That the intolerance was all on the Calvinist side may be seen in the proclamation Knox caused to be put up in Edinburgh on October 2, 1561, charging "all monkis, freris, preistis, nonnys, adulteraris, fornucatours, and all sic filthy personis, to remove themselffis of this toun and boundis thairof within XXIIII houris." All that Mary asked was that she and her fellow Catholics be allowed to retain Mass.

The Ruin of Mary

To allow her to have even so little as that was considered altogether too much. A few faithful nobles stood beside her, including some of the Protestants, like Bothwell. The rest went out of their way to give her trouble, and even one or two of the Catholic lords who had grievances against the Crown took advantage of the disorder to win redress. She soon found herself confronted with an impossible task, in which all that sustained her was her indomitable heart. "To know what life it is to lie all night in the field or to walk on the cawsy with a Glasgow buckler and a broad-sword" — that was a wish she had once expressed, and it was, in part, to be fulfilled. It was with this valiancy that she now confronted the wild beasts who were her enemies.

Perhaps worse than the tigers and wolves among them were men like Moray and Maitland of Lethington. The Lord James (soon to be Earl of Moray) was her father's natural son, and as such should have been her protector. Instead he became the most crafty of her enemies. As for Maitland, though he would have continued to support her had he been able to do so, he was too much of a Machiavellian politician not to change sides when he found this furthered his plans; and he loved the intricacies of deceit for their own sake. For a time, however, his diplomatic subtlety was at Mary's service. His dream was of an ultimate union of the Crowns of England and Scotland under a Stuart; but he abandoned Mary's cause, when he deemed it lost, for that of the infant James, and lent himself to besmirching his Queen until, too late, he made a last effort for her. He was a man indifferent to religion, one who indeed viewed the Kirk with contempt. But he made a sufficiently politic use of its phraseology, though not to the same extent as did the prim, pedantic, treacherous, and hypocritical Moray. Maitland's private opinion was pithily expressed — "God was a bogy to scare bairns."

It was Mary's misfortune that the man upon whom she had chiefly to rely was the one who eventually ruined her. This was James Hepburn, Earl of Bothwell, a ruffian border baron with a tincture of Renaissance culture but with nothing of the far-sighted political wisdom of those Italian despots whom he took for model. It was with such untrustworthy help that Mary sustained herself for several years.

She was not yet nineteen when she arrived in Scotland, but she conducted herself wisely and attended to affairs of state as quietly as was permitted her, and with conciliation to all parties. She did not interfere with the Calvinists, though she made an unostentatious (if not notably devout) practice of her own religion. For the rest she amused herself with music and dancing and hunting; and she continued the study of Latin under George Buchanan.

Buchanan merits a word at this point. Whether or not he had any hand in the forging of the Casket Letters (supposing that they *were* forged), he wrote the most venomous of all the attacks on Mary in his *Detectio* of 1571. He was an apostate priest (like Knox), and had taught Latin in the Collège de St. Barbe in Paris at the time St. Francis Xavier and St. Ignatius Loyola were there. It is amusing to record that an occasion arose when the founder of the Jesuits was about to run the gauntlet for some fracture of discipline (he was saved at the last moment, and his action received praise instead of punishment), and that then Buchanan was one of those who must have been waiting for him belt in hand. He was an excellent Latin poet, and a malevolent and unscrupulous man.

In spite of the difficulties confronting Mary, there came a moment when it seemed that the differences between her and Elizabeth might be solved. With their solution, the tension would have greatly decreased in Scotland. A meeting of the two Queens at York was proposed in the summer of 1562, and probably would have occurred had not Elizabeth begun her intervention in France. It may have been very fortunate for the Catholic cause that it did not. For Elizabeth was preparing to offer a league with Scotland and the recognition of Mary as her successor (in the event of her not having a child herself) on condition that Mary accept the English settlement of religion. To the extreme position of the Calvinists, with their theocracy, Elizabeth was, of course, inflexibly opposed, however much she used Calvinists in her political manoeuvres. And at this stage in Mary's career, when she was worn out with struggles with the Kirk and yet was striving for the great reward of the English throne, a *politique* might have been willing to accept the proposed compromise. She must have known that her claims had little support from the English Catholics at this time.[3] She was therefore most anxious to win over the English Queen.

It was of even greater political importance that Mary should marry. A union with a powerful husband would have enabled her to deal with her rebels; to bear a child, since Elizabeth was childless, would have been to make irresistible her claim to succeed Elizabeth. Catherine de' Medici, however, did not look with favour upon the proposal that her son Charles IX should marry his sister-in-law: that would have involved the return of the Guises to power. Nor was Philip enthusiastic about her marrying the Prince of Spain, Don Carlos, though this might have come to pass had not Quadra, who favoured it, died in 1563. Even so, Mary continued, almost up to the moment of her marriage to Darnley, to strive to win whatever diplomatic advantages might have accrued from taking this greedy, vile-tempered epileptic as her husband. Horrible as such a marriage would have been, it would at least have secured her political salvation.

But Elizabeth stood in the way: she considered that she had the sole right to select a consort for her cousin. Most astonishingly she put forward Dudley, making him the more eligible by conferring at last his deferred earldom.[4] As an inducement, she instructed Sir Nicholas Throckmorton to say that "if the Queen of Scots would accept Leicester, she should be accounted next heir to the throne as though she were her own born daughter."

Mary was naturally cool to the suggestion. Apart from the

---

[3] This appeared at the end of the year, when Elizabeth was thought to be dying and her possible successors were under consideration. The Catholics, for want of anybody better, were prepared to throw their support to Lady Catherine Grey, or even to Lord Huntingdon. Both were Protestants; either was ready to revert to Catholicism — or to embrace Islam if political advantage was to be obtained from doing so. As for Mary, it was only later that she was regarded by the English Catholics generally as their candidate.

[4] She also offered the Duke of Norfolk as an alternative.

ridiculous figure she would have cut in accepting Leicester — who was being disposed of like a castoff mistress — she suspected a trap. And it is still far from clear what Elizabeth had at the back of her mind. Perhaps she merely wanted to head off Don Carlos. Or perhaps she wished to recompense Dudley with the throne of Scotland, as she had not dared to make him King of England. More probably she calculated that such a marriage would remove the threat of Mary's claim. What she wrote to Bedford and Randolph (though it is hardly ever safe to take Elizabeth's words at their face value) was: "The Earl would bring with him no controversy of title to trouble the quietness of the Queen of Scots, and I prefer him to be the partaker of the Queen of Scots' fortune, who, if it lie in my power, I will make owner with him of my own kingdom." (The guarantee of the succession, it will be noticed, is now given only conditionally.) But Leicester, when he learned from Melville that Mary did not want him as a husband, quickly assured the Ambassador that the project was not his own, but Cecil's, and that he knew that if he accepted it he would fall out of favour with both Queens. Maitland, with pawky Scotch humour, made the suggestion that, as Elizabeth was older than Mary, she should marry Leicester herself; then Mary could marry the widower when she succeeded to the English Crown.

Instead, Mary married Henry Stuart, Lord Darnley. It seemed an eminently sound political move, for though Darnley was less of a catch that Don Carlos would have been, he was a strong claimant to the English succession — a much stronger one than Mary herself was at that time, as he was an English subject.[5] Therefore the marriage at once removed much of the prejudice against Mary as a "foreigner." Had the marriage been even tolerably happy, and had Darnley lived, the game would have been safely in Mary's hands.

There is some mystery as to why Elizabeth allowed Darnley to go to Scotland at all in these circumstances. His going, however, received the approbation of such men as Cecil and Lei-

[5] Mary Tudor had seriously considered nominating his mother, Lady Lennox, to succeed her.

cester, perhaps because they considered that it would be as well to keep in the good graces of one who might eventually become their king. But it may be that they, too, believed they had discovered a way of diverting Mary from Don Carlos. The opinion of Castelnau de Mauvissière and Silva was that Elizabeth had deliberately lured Mary into this marriage because she knew Darnley's character. In this, surely, the Ambassadors were being a little too clever.[6] Darnley was an unformed boy still, and Elizabeth, shrewd as she was, was no prophet. Nobody could have foretold the youth's degeneration. Nor can one easily believe that Elizabeth would have been so dastardly as to effect Mary's ruin by means like these.

Ruin, however, it was. Elizabeth peremptorily forbade the marriage — when it was too late to prevent it. Mary and Darnley had not been expected to rush things so fast. But, though Darnley arrived in Scotland only in February, he and the Queen were married in June, their haste being such that they would not wait for the dispensation necessary for the marriage of cousins to arrive from Rome. The action does not suggest a very scrupulous Catholicism.

For a couple of months Mary was apparently happy with her pink-cheeked young husband. Then she turned against him with loathing, having discovered his debauched habits and his drunkenness. But even these might have been condoned had they not been joined to a mental incapacity that made him contemptible in the eyes of all. His insufferable insolence set the Scots nobles against him. And his vanity was incurably wounded by Mary's refusal to give him — though he bore, by courtesy, the title of King — any share in the conduct of affairs.

In his jealous rage he plotted the murder of David Rizzio, Mary's secretary. This young Italian is usually said to have gone to Scotland as a paid musician, on evidence not very trustworthy. It is certain that he was not a Papal agent, for no

---

[6] This suggestion sounds shockingly cynical, as do many of the things said by Ambassadors of the period. We must remember, however, that they were accustomed to seeing human nature at its craftiest among Elizabethan politicians. As Quadra put it in a letter already quoted, "With such people it is always prudent to believe the worst."

single document in the Vatican archives has been found to support his supposititious position. But he did make himself useful to the Queen, and before long a good deal of state business came to pass through his hands. Often he was preferred as an adviser to any of the Scots nobles — and any of them was preferred as advisers to the King.

This was what infuriated Darnley — as it also infuriated men like Maitland and Moray. The "King," who had once been so intimate with Rizzio as to have shared the same bed with him, now began to plot his murder. Not having the courage to attempt it singlehanded, he contrived to effect the pardon of the rebel lords whom Mary had driven out. On their return they whispered in his ear, further to inflame him, that Rizzio's relations with the Queen were those of her lover, and the child she now bore in her womb was the Italian secretary's. This decided Darnley, and he and all the conspirators committed themselves — in the distrustful Scotch fashion — with a signed "bond." Cecil was privy to what was intended, for Maitland had already written about "chopping at the root; you know where it lieth," and Randolph and Bedford sent on a copy of the bond to London.

The murderers came upon Rizzio on Saturday evening, March 9, 1566, as he sat at supper with Mary and her half sister, the Countess of Argyle. Ruthven had proposed that they seize David in his room, try him before an improvised court, and hang him in the market place. That did not suit Darnley's idea of dramatic justice, and was moreover too dangerous: Rizzio must be killed in Mary's presence. Suddenly armed men burst into the little room — Ruthven, Darnley, George Douglas, Ker of Faldonside, and two others. Ker held a pistol at Mary's breast while the others took hold of Rizzio where he was crouching behind the Queen's skirts and dragged him outside. His body was found with nearly sixty wounds. Mary, who faced the assassins with scornful bravery, was in the seventh month of her pregnancy. John Knox, when he heard of what had been done (he had probably been informed in advance), called the deed "most just and worthy of all praise." Elizabeth felt somewhat differently. She said that in Mary's place she would have taken away her husband's dagger and stabbed him with it.

The Queen of Scots acted with decision, though in such a fashion as to give a handle later to her enemies. In order to detach Darnley from his fellow conspirators, whom she intended to deal with one by one, she pretended a reconciliation with him, then escaped from Holyrood in a furious horseback ride. On June 19 she bore her son James.

To Darnley, who was still suspicious of Rizzio, Mary showed her babe, saying, "My lord, he is so much your son that I fear it will be the worse for him hereafter." But calumnious reports as to his real parentage persisted for many years. The wittiest of the coarse jests on the subject was made a long time afterwards by Henry IV of France when he said that James I's claim to be the modern Solomon rested upon his being the son of David the harp player. There is, however, no longer any question as to Darnley's being his father; Mary's words have too much sad truth in them.

When the news reached Elizabeth she cried, "The Queen of Scots is lichter of a fair son, and I am but a barren stock!" She must have guessed that this child was destined to be King of England. For his christening she sent a font of gold, and the ceremony was performed by a Catholic bishop in mitre and cope, the despised Darnley lurking in the shadows of the royal chapel.

Something now had to be done about the "King." Divorce (or rather, annulment) was first suggested but was ruled out by Mary as involving the illegitimacy of her child. A decree, however, could have been obtained from Rome on the ground that the marriage had taken place before the arrival of the necessary dispensation. Then (according to Lennox) someone advised that Darnley be arrested for high treason and, when he resisted, run through with a sword. Nothing was decided. But those who had signed the bond with Darnley — using him for their purposes, as he had used them — had a new contemptuous grievance at his denial that the murder of Rizzio was of his contriving. In the Queen's hatred of her husband they perceived that they might get rid of him with impunity. Perhaps they already calculated that upon a hatred so undisguised they might afterwards throw the blame.

There is no need to write at length here about the tragedy of Kirk o' Field. Suffice it to say that Darnley was in that house instead of in the city because he was recovering from smallpox, and that on Sunday evening, February 9, Mary, though she had planned to return to Kirk o' Field late the same night, went to a dance at Holyrood for the celebration of a wedding of two of her servants. She said an affectionate farewell to the husband whom she was never to see again. At two the next morning the house where Darnley was staying was blown up by gunpowder. His body, and that of an attendant, were found near by, not injured by the explosion but strangled.

This remains one of the most celebrated of historical mysteries, one that is probably insoluble. There is no need for me to enter into the controversy about it. I will, however, express the opinion — the obvious one — that the circumstantial evidence against Mary seems rather strong. Regarded from that angle it might look as though she had left Darnley that night by design. Her staying at Holyrood, though it can be explained by the lateness of the hour, is also suspicious. On the other hand, it is likely enough that she was persuaded to stay there by somebody who knew what was brewing. There is nothing to show that the murderers did not intend to dispose of her along with Darnley; her room was just under his. The strangling proves fairly conclusively that the victim must have heard men in the house and that he tried to escape, but was caught and killed outside.

That Mary may have been implicated in the murder is, of course, by no means impossible, but no such implication necessarily flows even from the circumstantial evidence. It was for this reason that documents were afterwards brought forward by her political enemies — many of whom were known to have been themselves implicated. In the next chapter I shall touch briefly on the Casket Letters. At this point I need only remark that they prove altogether too much. The case is too complete not to make one suspect a "frame-up." It tends, therefore, to recoil upon the heads of those who first advanced it. Drury wrote to Cecil on November 28, 1567, to assure him that all the compromising papers had been burnt — with the exception of those affecting the Queen. The letter is damning — to Cecil.

Mary's subsequent actions have often been used against her reputation. She must be admitted not to have been very vigorous in bringing to justice the reputed murderer, who was Bothwell. But other facts should be remembered. She was for a while so stunned and bewildered as to be hardly capable of doing anything at all. If she was innocent and believed the blow to have been directed against her as well as against Darnley, she must have been giving all the thought she could collect to warding off the next blow. Further, it was well-nigh impossible for her to proceed against the powerful Bothwell. And, finally, she had all around her men who, if less guilty than Bothwell, were nearly all guilty to some degree, if only as accessories. A web so tangled was quite beyond the skill and strength of Mary's fingers just then.

When at last Lennox, the murdered man's father, insisted upon Bothwell's being tried, the accused came to court, accompanied by Maitland and Morton (who was to be executed in 1581 for his part in the murder), and several thousand retainers. Under these circumstances Lennox asked for a postponement, which was refused; and as no accuser dared to appear against him, Bothwell obtained a verdict by default. But everybody believed him to have been guilty, as everybody still does.[7]

What we might pause on a moment here is a curious defence of Mary recently made by General Mahon. His thesis, developed in several ingenious books that carefully marshal the existing evidence, is that Mary was indeed marked down for death — but that it was by Darnley! The General argues that Darnley did not know that his wife had failed to return from Holyrood, and that, having set the fuse to the gunpowder, he

[7] It might be noted that Lady Lennox, though she at first believed that Mary was implicated in the murder, came eventually to a conviction of her innocence.

was escaping from the house when Bothwell caught him and strangled him outside. The people, however, who were really at the bottom of the affair were Jesuits![8]

I believe I am correct in saying that there were no Jesuits in Scotland at the time, but that does not greatly matter: perhaps the General uses the word "Jesuits" in a generic sense, as meaning Catholic priests as a body. His thesis is that the assassination was designed abroad and was intended to remove Mary because she had not been sufficiently active in the suppression of Protestantism, or in advancing the Counter Reformation. Darnley, according to this thesis, was prepared to re-establish Catholicism in Scotland; but to do so he first had to get rid of the Queen. That accomplished, he was to be proclaimed King, or perhaps merely regent for his son, and then stamp out Calvinism. To quote Mahon: "The Counter Reformation movement, aimed against the Protestant Lords and the Queen, was the basis of the tragedy of Kirk o' Field; and Darnley and Lennox [a Protestant, by the bye, though Lady Lennox was not!] were the moving spirits, encouraged by foreign envoys who came over to represent Philip of Spain and the Nuncio."

There are of course no documents that support such a contention, except Darnley's spiteful and unmanly complaints against his wife in which, seizing on any weapon to hand, he threw doubts upon her Catholic zeal. He wrote in this strain to the Pope, to the Cardinal of Lorraine (a Guise, and Mary's uncle), to Philip II, and to the Nuncio at Paris. But not a particle of evidence exists, except a letter from the Nuncio, to show that they took him seriously, and even that letter is noncommittal. Darnley's character was by now very well known, as was his laxness in the practice of Catholicism. The bond which he subscribed for the murder of Rizzio, promising his Protestant accomplices that he "would stand by them to the uttermost, and religion should be established as they desired" hardly indicates that he was a tool of the "Jesuits."

The important consideration at the moment, however, is not

[8] Fantastic as this theory is, the General's books are well worth reading, as they contain a number of details about the terrain and technical information about the gunpowder available which are not easily found elsewhere.

whether Mary was actually guilty of planning the murder, or of knowing of it in advance; it was that the first shock of the news created an almost universal belief in her guilt. For instance, the Spanish Ambassador in England, Silva, wrote to his King on March 1, 1567: "The spirits of the Catholics are broken; should it turn out that she is guilty, her party in England is gone, and by her means there is no more chance of a restoration of religion." But this was only the immediate reaction: as time went on, people began to doubt more and more. The frantic efforts of Mary's enemies to fasten the crime upon her began to work in her favour, whereas in the beginning few had any doubts at all.

Mary's enemies lost no time in preparing a case against her. Elizabeth wrote to the Queen of Scots on April 8, urging her to see that the culprits were severely dealt with. The letter reached Maitland on the day before Bothwell's trial — and Maitland pocketed it. But even had Mary been allowed to see it — which she may have done, despite Lingard's statement — she still had her hands tied. Everybody about her wanted to let the matter drop: too much might have come out had the trial been pressed. As for Elizabeth, one wonders whether she was really as solicitous for Mary's reputation as she professed to be. The English government must have been well aware that nothing was going to be done, because nothing could be done. I suspect that Elizabeth merely wanted to place herself on record by writing a letter — which might afterwards be useful to her.

The fact that Bothwell got off scot free naturally did Mary no good; but it would not, by itself alone, have brought about her ruin; what followed effected that. On April 24 — two months after the Darnley murder and twelve days after Bothwell's trial — she was kidnapped by Bothwell and taken off to Dunbar. On May 15 she married him according to Protestant rites, the delay being necessary to allow him to secure an annulment of his existing marriage. To make sure of everything, he sought — and obtained — decrees in both Catholic and Protestant ecclesiastical courts.[8]

[8] The Catholic divorce was promulgated by that Archbishop of St. Andrews (a Hamilton), whose unclerical morals have already been referred to.

Now the whole world was utterly disgusted. For whether or not Mary was guilty of being an accomplice in Darnley's murder, she had married the man regarded as her husband's murderer. Her defence afterwards was that she had been forced, and it may well be that the ruffianly Bothwell did rape her. Leslie, the Bishop of Ross, could account for the marriage only on the supposition of "magical arts." Bothwell does seem to have thoroughly subdued his victim, yet his cynicism was so great that, according to Maitland, he wrote to his divorced Lady Jean to tell her that he still regarded her as his true wife and the Queen as no more than his concubine.

On one point Catholic and Protestant agreed — in condemning Mary. Knox, who did not care a particle about Darnley — who was, in his view, an idolater who got what he richly deserved — the same Knox who had called the murder of Cardinal Beaton a "godly act" and that of Rizzio "most just and worthy of all praise," now stormed against the "murdress and adultress," and the mobs he inflamed howled for her blood. But the English Catholics felt that Mary had by her own act confirmed all the suspicions against her, just when they were about to die down. As for the Pope, Pius V, he said that he could not see anything to choose between Elizabeth and Mary and wrote through his Secretary of State to the Nuncio in Paris, who had reported on "this last act, so dishonourable to God and herself," to say that he intended to have no further communication with the Queen of Scots, "unless, indeed, in times to come, he shall see some better sign of her life and religion than he has witnessed in the past." Had the case against Mary been allowed to rest on circumstantial evidence, she would have found it very difficult to make a convincing defence.

The Scotch nobles perceived that their hour had arrived. Probably few of them had failed to express the wish that Darnley might be assassinated, and some of them were no less justly suspected than was Bothwell himself. This was all the more reason for venting their anger upon the man who had stolen a march upon them and had married the Queen. Accordingly, they rose in arms, and on June 15, 1567, encountered

The Ruin of Mary

Mary and Bothwell at Carberry Hill. There those whose hands were stained with murder — Morton at their head — called for "justice." And Mary, yielding to force of numbers, arranged in a parley that she would go back to Edinburgh with the Lords on condition that Bothwell received their permission to leave the Kingdom. He left for Denmark, where he was imprisoned and died insane. His career suggests that he always had been unbalanced.

But what does the action of the Lords at Carberry Hill suggest? Why, having vastly superior forces, did they let Bothwell go? If he had not been brought to justice before, why did they not bring him to justice then? Surely there can be only one answer: they did not wish to have him tried, lest their own implication in Darnley's murder should come out. Some of these men had ridden with Bothwell only a couple of months previously in order to intimidate the Court. They were no more anxious now for an investigation. To drive Bothwell out could be made to look like the equivalent of a condemnation. And the person at whom they were really aiming was Mary: her they meant to destroy.

That night in Edinburgh a mob, incited by the Calvinist preachers, raged under the windows of the house where the Queen was imprisoned. Shouts of "Burn the whore! Burn the murdress of her husband!" came up to her as, distraught and half-naked, she screamed back, threatening to hang them all. But it was no good; she was in the power of merciless enemies. They hurried her, "for protection," to the castle in the middle of Lochleven, and there Lord Lindsay (a supporter of Rizzio's murder) threatened her with instant death unless she signed her abdication. After what she had gone through, she was in a state of collapse. But she still had enough spirit to vow that she would "have his head for this." To gain time, she signed.

She could not yet believe that her cause was lost; her heart was too brave to make any such admission. Besides, she still had friends in Scotland; she counted upon them, and upon being able to play the factions off against one another. Most of all, she relied on the pledge that had come to her from Elizabeth, who wrote on August 9, "If when you are at liberty, you think fit to proceed against your opponents, in that case I will not fail you." Elizabeth promised further, "Put yourself in my hands without reserve; I will listen to nothing which shall be said against you: your honour shall be safe, and you shall be restored to the throne." We know how that promise was fulfilled.

Moray, whom Knox would have preferred to see King, had been appointed Regent, and Mary's infant son was crowned. But Mary was still undaunted. She relied on her friends — and especially upon her cousin of England who "would not fail her." On May 2, 1568, after nearly a year's captivity, she escaped, whereupon Elizabeth wrote to congratulate her, and again promised help.

The Hamiltons and other lords hastened to join their Queen. She had some reason to distrust the Hamilton loyalty, for, from the old shifty Duke of Châtelherault down, they had called loudly for her execution after her capture, not so much from indignation as because they stood next in line to the throne. That failing, Châtelherault had tried to oust Moray as Regent and to get cutsody of the little King. But now as Mary was at large again, the Hamiltons thought it best to back her, though they would have betrayed her quickly enough had the tide turned.

Events followed too fast for that. At Langside the Marian army was routed. And instead of fleeing to the stronghold of Dumbarton, where she might have been safe, Mary decided to make for the South and to throw herself upon Elizabeth's protection. After a wild ride of sixty miles a day with a small band of troopers, in which she fared like a soldier and slept on the naked earth, she reached Solway Firth. On Sunday, May 16, she landed from a fishing boat at Workington in Cumberland, penniless and having only the soiled and tattered dress she wore. From that day, until her death nineteen years later, she was Elizabeth's prisoner.

11

∽∽∽∽∽∽∽∽∽∽∽∽∽∽∽∽∽∽∽∽∽∽∽∽∽∽∽

The Rising of the North

MARY of *Scotland* did not look much like a queen when she arrived at Workington; yet to this travel-worn, defeated woman there were at once accorded, quite spontaneously, royal honours. The nobles of the north, Northumberland among them, came with the lesser gentry; and for a few days she held Court at Carlisle.

English opinion toward her, especially Catholic opinion, had undergone a change. At the time of her greatest success — that is, in 1565 — these same men had looked at her askance. True, that since she had become only Queen Dowager of France she had also become less objectionable as a candidate for the English throne. In spite of this the Catholics had been cool because they had not trusted the genuineness of her religious convictions. Then there had followed the shock of the Darnley murder, and the still greater shock of the Bothwell marriage. During the past year, however, the world had witnessed the firmness with which Mary had refused to make peace with her foes by sacrificing her faith.[1] Everything would have been forgotten and forgiven if only she had apostatised: how well was that understood in England! How well, too, was grasped the fact that the use of the sponge of apostacy would have been a virtual admission that murder was written upon the slate. Her

---

[1] It should at the same time be remarked that there was a brief period (though not at the very beginning of her stay in England) when Mary tried to give the impression that she might be willing, after all, to accept Protestantism. At all events, Knollys derived such an impression, as probably enough she intended he should. But the constancy she had already shown — and still more the constancy she was to show — would indicate that she was merely trying to conciliate her captor so as to put him off his guard in case a chance should come to escape.

religious constancy was therefore not only admired for its own sake; it was taken as presumptive proof of her innocence of the crime of which she had been charged. The gallantry of Mary's bearing, the wrongs she had suffered, and the defamation of her character all drew out of these simplehearted North Country gentlemen, who were so far removed in every way from the intrigues of London, a generous sympathy. They divined at once that in her — Philip having so consistently failed them — they had their champion at last.

As soon as she reached England she let Elizabeth know of her arrival and asked for some clothes. Sir Francis Knollys brought her the wardrobe that had been sent: it consisted of a couple of torn shifts, two pieces of black velvet, and a couple of pairs of shoes. Sir Francis was extremely embarrassed when the package was opened before him in disdainful silence. He hastened to do what he could, explaining lamely that it must be that "her Highness' maid had mistaken, and had sent things necessary for such a maidservant as she was herself." Mary agreed that that was probably it. But there is no need for us to be so tactful: such meanness from a woman who was famed for the number of her dresses — at one time she is said to have had three thousand hanging in her closets — is astonishing. Or it would be if we did not remember that Elizabeth was almost equally famed for never giving any of her dresses away.

From the moment of her arrival at Workington, Mary was, though in rags, in some sense Queen of England, and in the minds of many Englishmen she remained their Queen until her death. Yet she was very careful to assert no claim to the crown. Her use, while Dauphiness and Queen of France, of the royal arms of England in her quarterings had been at the instance — we might say, insistence — of Henry II and Francis II. But though she still thought of herself as England's rightful Queen, the most she had asked while in Scotland — and it was the most she could expect to obtain — was the recognition of her right to succeed Elizabeth. That was all she asked now; she could ask no less.

The first thing she wanted, and naturally supposed she would

get — in view of Elizabeth's letters of invitation and promises of protection — was that Elizabeth should receive her. This,
however, was precisely what Elizabeth had no intention of doing, as it might have been taken as the equivalent to a formal
acknowledgement of Mary as her heiress. There was a convenient excuse to hand in the Darnley murder. Calumny had
so far been casual; because of the change in circumstances it
had now to be carried out with systematic thoroughness by
English and Scotch officialdom working in unison for a single
object.

Elizabeth wrote to Mary on June 8, 1568, promising "care
of life and honour," but saying, "Oh, Madam, there is not a
living creature who more longs to hear your justification than
myself. . . . But I cannot sacrifice my reputation on your account." Yet according to accounts that came through at the
time, she expressed her womanly cordiality in the Council and
would have liked to have given Mary some help. On May 22,
1568, Silva wrote to Philip: "The Queen has always shown herself favourable to Queen of Scots, and now takes her part." On
the same day the French Ambassador reported to his King:
"The Queen supports the Queen of Scots' cause with all her
power. She tells her ministers that she shall be entertained as
her rank and greatness deserve." Each time, however, she was
reminded that she was a Queen as well as a woman and had to
follow the line of political expediency. At the end of 1568
Guerau de Spes wrote to Philip, "The Council is sitting night
and day about the Queen of Scotland's affairs. Cecil and the
Chancellor [he means the Lord Keeper, Bacon] would like to
see her dead, as they have a king of their own choosing, one of
Hertford's children." Mary had created a problem; she was
being excluded from the presence of Elizabeth on account of
an accusation that had never been substantiated. Yet as the
humblest person has to be presumed innocent until proved
guilty, how could her admission be justly refused? There was
only one thing that could be done: Mary had to be persuaded
to submit to a trial, and she had somehow to be found guilty.

How this was to be done taxed even Cecil's ingenuity. Mary

would not hear of being tried by anybody, as nobody had the right to try a Queen. So the Secretary, as was his way, drew up a long paper setting forth all the reasons why Elizabeth should keep Mary a prisoner. The first step, he argued, was to find out whether or not the Queen of Scots was a falsely accused person. If she was innocent, why then, of course, she must be helped to the full measure of the power of England. She must be helped, too, to punish those who had slandered her, though this, he saw, was going to be no easy matter. It would involve forcing Mary upon the Scots, a people now specially bound to England by their common Reformation. Further he wrote, "She had openly made challenge, not as the second person after the Queen's Majesty, but before her." And she had failed to ratify the treaty of Edinburgh. If released she would be likely to "marry some foreign prince," for the marriage to Bothwell was of so questionable a validity that it presented no obstacle. In all this he kept harping upon the danger to Elizabeth herself: "All the old perils would be revived with the more extremity; her stomach kindled with ire and anger vindictive, and her boldness to attempt the more upon the opinion that she had a great party in England — some for religion, some for her title, others for discontent and love of change."

Yet he perceived some objections to keeping Mary a prisoner in England. "She would increase the boldness of evil subjects," and foreign powers might intervene if they saw her held in custody in a country to which she had come of her free will. (He neglected to mention that it was also on the pledge of Elizabeth's protection.) The logical inference, which he was too cautious to put in so many words, was that Mary should be put to death. That this is what he wished is certain; that he contrived to bring it about is also certain. As the time for that had not yet come, he went no further than arguing that Moray and the Scots Lords would not take her back until she had proved that she had had no part in the Darnley murder.

The last thing that he and Elizabeth wanted was that Mary's innocence be definitely established. To have done nothing would have been to have left her innocence in question; but they saw that it would be much better if doubt could be enlarged as a consequence of an ostensibly impartial enquiry. That this solution was in Elizabeth's mind is shown by the letter she wrote Philip II in August: "I am thinking of returning her to her kingdom with the title of Queen; and I think her acquittal should be so arranged that it should be left in doubt, for if her complete innocence were to be declared it would be dangerous to this kingdom, to my friends, and to myself." In other words, the verdict was determined upon before the enquiry began. Matters were "to be arranged."

The most that can be said in extenuation of Elizabeth was that Mary's presence in England had put its Queen in an exceedingly awkward position. If Elizabeth acceded to her "guest's" request that she be allowed to go to France, that might result in a French invasion of Scotland in her support. If Elizabeth herself invaded Scotland on Mary's behalf, that would cost money — and Elizabeth hated to spend money. If Elizabeth allowed Mary her liberty in England, she would become a centre of disaffection: the enthusiastic welcome accorded her by the Northern gentry made that much clear. In face of these considerations, honour and solemn promises had to be ignored.

Cecil managed to manoeuvre Mary into consenting to an enquiry. As she absolutely refused to submit to one into her own actions, he cleverly shifted his ground: he would never dream of enquiring into her conduct; what he wanted was an enquiry into the misdeeds of Moray. That would do just as well — in fact, better. He would be able to smirch Mary sufficiently for his purpose; he would be able to smirch her enemies at the same time. Already he knew enough about Moray and Maitland and Morton to hang them. An enquiry would be sure to bring out hints of hushed-up crimes. This would give him a golden opportunity for exercising blackmail upon those in office in Scotland. And if the word "blackmail" seem too strong, I do not know what other to use. It was not the first time that Cecil had employed the device, nor was it to be the last. But the main thing was to discredit Mary. Cecil was aware that her presence in Carlisle had sent a thrill through the Catholic North. Very well, she should be finally discredited in the eyes of all Catholics at home and abroad.

In this Cecil partially succeeded, though upon the whole he failed. Just-minded people, so far from being convinced by proceedings so flagrantly unfair, were indignant at her persecution. It was not that they looked upon the Queen of Scots as a saint; nor need we do so: it was left to that amusing and unsavoury eccentric, "Frederick, Baron Corvo," to canonize her in his character of Hadrian VII. But Cecil had taken the preliminary step in the judicial murder that was to be completed in 1587. The more rabid English Protestants who had persuaded themselves beforehand of Mary's guilt, after the new "revelations" clamoured for her execution. Mary ever afterwards lived under an unpronounced sentence of death.

The first enquiry was made at York. The English Commissioners were Norfolk, Sussex, and Sadler. Mary was defended by Leslie, the Bishop of Ross, and Lord Herries. The Scots sent Moray, Maitland, and Morton. The verdict, let me repeat, was prepared before the enquiry began.

When copies of what seemed to be highly incriminating documents — the Casket Letters — were produced, Mary demanded the right to appear in person: only in this way could she meet the charges.[2] When this was refused she wrote to her Commissioners, "Ye shall affirm in my name I never wrote anything concerning that matter to any creature; and if such writings there be, they are false and feigned, forged and invented by themselves." She countercharged that Morton and Maitland were implicated. And the "Black Douglas" was, as a matter of fact, beheaded for this very crime in 1581, as Maitland was arrested for it in 1569. As for Moray, though he too was probably "in the know" he had been careful to take no active part in getting rid of Darnley. The question of his guilt, however, is almost certainly merely one of degree.

---

[2] Cecil sneered that she made this demand only because she knew it would be refused. But why, if he really believed she would give herself away, when confronted by documentary proof, did he refuse?

POPE PIUS V
From the painting attributed to B. Passerotti —
Walters Art Gallery, Baltimore, Md.

The Rising of the North

He had been induced to accept an enquiry which, technically, was into his actions and not his sister's, only because he had been privately assured that, whatever the outcome, Mary would not be restored. Mary was similarly assured that, whatever the outcome, she would be put back on the Scottish throne. Yet while giving her this promise, Cecil wrote in cipher to Sussex: "It is not meant if the Queen of Scots shall be proved guilty of the murder to restore her to Scotland." He also intended that she *was* to be found guilty: not too guilty, just guilty enough. Similarly Maitland and Morton and Moray were to be put under a cloud. Everybody, in short, was to be double-crossed. Then when that happy end had been achieved, Elizabeth was to arrange a compromise under which she would have virtual suzerainty over Scotland.

The questioning of Moray turned into a trial of Mary — just as Cecil had planned. Herries protested in vain that the calumnies were invented by the Regent and his friends because they feared they would be deprived of the estates given them while Mary was still a minor. Equally in vain the Bishop of Ross charged Elizabeth with bad faith. Moray, slightly damaged, was confirmed in his regency.

It has been suggested that the Scots were disinclined to press the matter too far — though it is hard to see how much further they could have gone. And Froude expresses the opinion that Moray kept evidence back because of his beautiful affection for his father's daughter. He does not say what evidence. To give Moray an even wider latitude, and a packed court, the sittings were transferred from York, where they had begun on October 3, to Westminster at the end of November. The English Commissioners this time were the original three, to whom were added Nicholas Bacon, Leicester, Arundel, Clinton, and Cecil himself. In disgust at this new trick Mary's Commissioners refused to plead. The case was therefore made to appear to go against Mary by default.

Elizabeth now threatened to publish the findings unless Mary confirmed her abdication in favour of her son. She answered fiercely that she would live and die the Queen of Scotland, and appealed to her subjects to come to her aid against "the ancient and natural enemies" of their country. By way of asserting her right, she appointed Châtelherault Regent. It was an empty gesture of defiance: the old Duke could do nothing except act as the leader of the helpless Marian party in Scotland.

The verdict given out was that nothing — as yet — had been adduced against Moray and his associates that proved their lack of honour and allegiance. They were allowed to depart — with the implied threat that they had better behave toward England as England demanded of them. Which, to do them justice, they did.

As for Mary's guilt — though this was supposed not to be the matter under enquiry — Norfolk, Arundel, Clinton, and Sussex said they were unconvinced. Upon this, Bacon — supported by Sadler, Leicester, and Cecil — demanded an answer to the question: in face of the evidence was the Queen of Scots to be admitted to Queen Elizabeth's presence? For fear of incurring the Queen's displeasure — and a possible charge of high treason — they could only answer, no. Elizabeth had gained her point: she could refuse to recognize Mary's claim to the succession, and she could keep Mary in prison.

There were others who remained unconvinced beside the four dissenting English Commissioners. Catholics as a body — together with many who were not Catholics, but who had some remnants of honour left — were prepared to give Mary at least the benefit of the doubt. The enquiry had failed to have the desired effect either upon the aristocrats who wished to oust Cecil or upon those who hoped for a restoration of the "Old Religion." Mary more than ever had become the rallying point for both groups.

A word needs to be said about the Casket Letters. First, it should be explained that belief in Mary's innocence is in no sense part of the Catholic Faith. The only question under discussion is the authenticity of those letters. And though, in the absence of the documents themselves, which soon mysteriously disappeared, no final judgement can be offered, some considerations may be weighed.

The Rising of the North

The following is the case in brief: Bothwell is said to have left behind him in his flight a silver casket containing two written promises of marriage made him by Mary before Darnley's death, some other letters, and a few sonnets.

To take the sonnets first: It is hardly likely that anyone could have composed them under the conditions in which Mary found herself — riding about continuously, in ever present danger, and with no leisure. Any poet will smile at the suggestion. But even supposing the sonnets to have been composed by Mary, it is not impossible — in fact, it is far more likely — that she had written them to Darnley in 1565. If it should then be asked, how did it happen that Bothwell, in that event, had them in his keeping, the answer is that this would not have been the first time — nor was it to be the last — that a love poem addressed to one person was afterwards made to do service for a second lover. But here Brantôme makes a pertinent remark: he points out that Mary's Latin and French in her adolescence were much better than that of the letters. The style of the documents was simply not good enough for him to accept them as Mary's.

If they were forged, who forged them? That we do not know. The one generally suspected is Maitland, for the reason that his was the most acute and subtle mind among Mary's enemies. But others — notably Archibald Douglas, George Buchanan, and Thomas Crawford — are thought by some to have had a hand in the matter.[3] If the documents were available all this could be very readily settled, once for all, by modern experts in calligraphy. As it is, nobody can be completely sure that they were forgeries; and nobody can be sure that they were not.

What we can do, however, is to remember that Mary demanded to be confronted with these papers. That is hardly how a guilty woman would have acted. We can also remember that there is nothing to show to whom the Casket Letters were written, or when they were written. For all we can tell, they

[3] In view of Brantôme's criticism and Buchanan's ability as a Latin poet, we should perhaps rule him out — unless it was that he was cunning enough to write deliberately below his own level but was not quite expert enough to strike Mary's.

may have been written to several persons — and there is no positive proof that Bothwell was one of them. What is very suspicious is that in no single letter are Morton and Maitland so much as mentioned. The very absence of the names of these men says Lingard, "wears the appearance of fraud." It does, indeed, though, of course, it does not rule out the possibility that there were other Casket Letters — suppressed for good reason — in which their names did appear. The main difficulty, however, is that any impartial person will be reluctant to accept evidence offered in such circumstances and by such suborned witnesses. The production at York of only copies of the letters and translations (by the time of the Westminster enquiry "originals" could have been forged) and their disappearance afterwards creates a strong suspicion that Moray did not wish the documentary evidence to be examined too closely. Add to this the packing of the court of Commissioners and the refusal to hear Mary in person, and suspicion hardens into something more. The very completeness and neatness of the case is "fishy." When Henderson, who is often credited with having demonstrated the genuineness of the Casket Letters against the criticism of Andrew Lang, can only say of Letter II — the decisive one of the series — that *it,* at least, cannot be an "entire forgery," he makes an admission that ruins his whole case. My mind probably is very simple and naïve, but — using it to the best of my ability — I must confess that it seems to me that if Letter II (or any of the letters) have been tampered with, the whole series at once becomes inadmissible as evidence. Circumstantially, the case against Mary looks bad; by trying so hard to fasten the guilt on Mary — on Mary and Bothwell alone — by means of documentary evidence, Moray, Maitland, and Morton have compelled us to wonder whether, in the first place, even the circumstantial evidence had not been "arranged" and, in the second, whether the documents they produced had not been forged. So far from convicting Mary, they betrayed themselves.

So much for Mary's accusers: one more word is needed about her judges. When Mary demanded to see the letters, offering to show them to be forgeries — writing through her secretary,

The Rising of the North

"She shall be proved either innocent or culpable of the horrible crimes whereof she is yet accused" and conceding that "if by her answer she should not prove herself innocent, then of necessity the Queen's Majesty can never with her honour show her any favour" — all that Elizabeth offered was to allow her to see the letters, on condition that Mary should not afterwards complain that she was refused admission into Elizabeth's presence. What did this condition amount to? Simply this: that Mary should, in effect, renounce her claim to the English succession. But the whole enquiry was merely a means of securing such a renunciation. That was the end to be obtained; the means of obtaining it was the smirching of Mary's reputation. But Elizabeth would have very gladly given Mary a certificate of innocence, had Mary been willing, in exchange, to sign a quitclaim. That Mary indignantly refused must, I think, be taken as a psychological proof of a clear conscience. In face of such resoluteness against what amounts to blackmail, the court of enquiry, while exculpating Moray and his companions (with reservations) added that nothing had been "sufficiently proven or shown by them against the Queen their sovereign, whereby the Queen of England should conceive or take any evil opinion of her good sister for anything yet seen." It came to this: Mary had not been proved guilty, but neither had she been proved innocent. And though the *form* of the enquiry had been into Moray's, not Mary's conduct, and though Mary was admittedly not subject to any tribunal, nevertheless she could now be treated as a person suspected of murder. The judgement that history must deliver upon the judges accordingly is this: that whether or not Mary had any part in the murder of Darnley, they (including Elizabeth) were guilty of the betrayal of Mary. All promises of help and protection — made, it must be borne in mind, *after* Mary was supposed to be a murderess — had been broken; Elizabeth had tricked her (again with false promises) into consenting to an enquiry that was to be limited to Moray's actions; she had decided upon the outcome of that enquiry before it was begun; she had admitted as witnesses men believed to be murderers and had connived at their presenting their evidence in such a way as to make it seem that their Queen and not they were guilty; and then, without delivering any formal verdict (except a summation that was the equivalent of one), she decided to keep Mary in prison. The fact that the proceedings were not judicial, but merely political, was used to escape the embarrassment of a judicial sentence while reaping all the political advantages a judicial sentence would have given. There is no more monstrous miscarriage of justice in all secular history. And the responsibility for it must be laid directly upon Elizabeth herself.

In spite of — and also because of — all this, Mary was far from finished. Her presence in England, even as a prisoner, brought hope to the dispirited Catholics and, at the same time, seemed to give the old nobility a chance for shaking off the domination of the new men they hated and despised. Mary's presence did more: it precipitated action; it resulted in open rebellion.

But before telling the story of the rising of 1569, we should have before us some picture of the conditions under which English Catholics had languished for ten years.

They felt themselves to be deserted. In the beginning they had counted upon Philip's giving them aid; but it was Philip who had prevented the excommunication of Elizabeth which, had it been delivered while her religious establishment was still weak, might have been a fatal blow. Paul IV and Pius IV had in turn shown an excessive moderation, and now Pius V (elected at the beginning of 1566) was also withholding his hand. Meanwhile the Church in England had been dying for want of priests.

Other factors worked in favour of Protestantism. Though the government had not yet succeeded in making it positively treasonable to observe Catholic practices, it had already succeeded in making it appear "disloyal" not to accept the religion of the Queen. In those days of king worship this counted a great deal. We can understand it only by disabusing our minds of modern notions. Where democracy looks upon the state as hardly more than a function of government, the Tudors had come to regard themselves as embodying the state. Hegel merely stated the discarded doctrine of the divine right of kings in a new form. The fact that Catholics had so strong a tradition of obedience to established government robbed them of more than half their power to resist that government even in religious matters. They were, for the most part, bewildered and uncertain as to the proper application of their own principles.

Under these circumstances their numbers had already dwindled. How many there were in England at this time we do not know: possibly not so many as Catholic historians are accustomed to claim; but assuredly more than the official historians are prepared to admit. Yet although we lack statistics it seems safe to say that the bulk of the people were indifferent to religious issues, or not sufficiently interested to make any sacrifices for their faith. But the indifferent majority was upon the whole Catholic — in the sense of having a sentimental feeling for the "Old Religion." Those who, at all costs, not merely wanted the Mass but who declared themselves "Papists," were a relatively small number. Those who hated the Mass were also a relatively small number, but they had an effective leadership in those who had benefited by the spoliation of the Church. As for the Queen, she troubled her head very little about theology: her concern was to maintain an Erastian domination.

The government kept blandly explaining that it had absolutely no intention to persecute on the grounds of religious belief. A decree of the Star Chamber issued as late as June 15, 1570, said that "the Queen would not have any of their consciences unnecessarily sifted to know what affection they had to the old religion." And Elizabeth made her famous declaration that she did not wish "to make windows into men's souls." All that she sought was external conformity; people could believe what they pleased. It was such a little that was being asked of them, for as the Queen put it to Silva, "We differ from Catholics in things of small importance." Let Catholics, then, come to church, and no further questions would be asked. A premium was put upon hypocrisy.

Though laws had already been passed of a ferocious nature, it was hoped that they would have the desired effect if they remained merely a threat. Cecil believed that this would suffice: in process of time the few surviving Marian priests who had refused the settlement would die out, and with them Catholicism would painlessly expire. Even the laws that fined Catholics for nonattendance at the Anglican services were not, and could not be, rigidly enforced. To collect a shilling from everybody who stayed away from church on Sunday was hardly feasible; and when the fine for the gentry and nobility was later raised to the enormous sum of £20 a month on each adult recusant, the amount was much too large to extract from all except a few.

Yet despite the fact that all except the most stubborn "Papists" had been brought into a surface conformity, there were still means of hearing Mass. Indeed, this even contributed to that surface conformity. Many of the parish clergymen, who used the official Prayer Book in the church, would say in private a Mass for those who wished to attend. There were cases where Communion was administered to Catholics and Protestants together — the Catholics getting a consecrated Host, the Protestants plain bread. And where none of these expedients proved possible, Catholics — unless very resolute — not only attended the Anglican services but partook of the Anglican communion. They called it "bowing in the house of Rimmon." Some of these conformists would be punctilious about arriving late or leaving early by way of letting it be known that they attended under compulsion. At home they made up for their churchgoing by ridiculing the parson.

Quadra did his best, under instructions from Philip II, to persuade Rome to sanction these subterfuges. But though the Council of Trent severely condemned any association with heretics *in sacris,* Father Pollen points out that there was still a "probable opinion" of which Catholics could avail themselves which excused their practice from grave sin. Until 1565, and even afterwards, some form of external conformity was common. As late as 1575, Mary Queen of Scots told Pope Gregory XIII that the Catholic gentlemen of her household concealed their religion, in the belief that they could serve her better by doing so, and received the Protestant communion, getting absolution afterwards from her private chaplain.

It is easy to see how deplorable must have been the consequences of such compromise. Catholic morale weakened. Children who witnessed the outward acceptance of the state religion by their parents, not unnaturally thought Catholicism could not be worth fighting for. Protestant habits were insensibly formed, and disintegration set in. Consciences could not be sturdy which permitted deceit. When those who had attended Protestant services and received the Protestant communion confessed their sin — to priests who were equally craven in their own conformity — grave damage was inevitably done to the delicate organism of the soul. It called for the exercise of heroism to be a thoroughgoing Catholic, and few men are heroic. Even some of those who might have been willing to undergo a bloody death shrank from the slow torture inflicted on them. It was pleasantly explained to Aglionby in 1571, when he dared to make a protest in the House of Commons, that Papists were not obliged to suffer in conscience but only in goods.[4] That sort of bleeding was, however, something that might be harder to endure than the butchery of Tyburn. Catholics as a rule decided that it was better to bow in the house of Rimmon.

So things had drifted for ten years. Each year there were fewer opportunities for Catholics to practice their religion (even under the subterfuges described) and more inducements to abandon it. The midlands and the south had come to a tame conformity, submitting under pressure. And if Wales and the west were still overwhelmingly Catholic, being too far away to be reached from London, they were too far away to count for much; and they lacked leaders. There remained the north, the counties beyond the Humber. There the population was almost solidly Catholic, and its anger was rising. In those wild shires

---

[4] Grindal, then Bishop of London, and Cox of Ely, offered the suggestion in 1562, when Lady Carew's chaplain was arrested, that "if the priest were put to some kind of torment, and so driven to confess what he knoweth, he might gain the Queen's Majesty a good mass of money" — that is, he might give information that would lead to the fining of undetected recusants. The hint was not taken. The time was not ripe.

the feudal system, which was elsewhere becoming rapidly out-moded, was still firmly rooted. "There is no prince in North-umberland but a Percy" ran the proverb. The attachment of the people to the nobility was of an intimate sort that did not prevail elsewhere in England. The word had but to be spoken and they would rise in rebellion, as they had done so many times before in English history.

But the north was too sparsely inhabited to act alone. They were indeed united — these Percys and Nevilles and Dacres and Tempests and Nortons and Swinburnes and Markenfields — but they had to seek alliances elsewhere. Their plan was to act in concert with the disaffected nobles in other parts of the country; and they counted upon Spanish help.

The time seemed propitious. The Huguenots had been deci-sively routed on October 3, 1568 — a good augury. The Spanish were seeking redress for Elizabeth's seizure of their treasure ships the previous December. Don Guerau undertook that a force would be sent over to their assistance from the Nether-lands. And in the Council Cecil was believed to be tottering to his fall.

The causes of the rebellion, however, were by no means solely religious. The Duke of Norfolk, a Protestant, had prom-ised to lead those disaffected. Arundel, Lumley, and Pembroke were on their side; Derby, Cumberland, Worcester, Morley, Wharton, and Sussex were known to be sympathisers. Even Leicester was against Cecil — or was thought to be. He was, unluckily for the conspirators, in secret league with Cecil, or in Cecil's power.

Politically the object was the overthrow of the dominant Secretary, and the recognition of Mary Queen of Scots as Eliza-beth's successor. The intention was not to dethrone Elizabeth, but to force her hand. The Catholic tradition of loyalty to the reigning monarch forbade the taking of any stronger line.

The malcontents tried to avoid actual rebellion: other means less violent were first thought of. Three times a *coup d'état* was about to be attempted: Cecil was to be kidnapped and Eliza-beth freed from his influence. Each time the courage of the opposition members of the Council failed them; they did nothing. And Leicester, whom they were deluded into imagining was acting with them, went off to tell Elizabeth of their designs.

The threat against Cecil's ascendency was, nevertheless, sufficiently serious for him to make a show of accepting what had to be accepted. Those who resented his power were given a greater share in public business, while he discreetly retired into the background. The Council now felt strong enough to raise the question of Mary's being acknowledged as successor to the Crown — so little, after all, had the famous enquiry really damaged her reputation or her claim. That move, which would have undone Cecil had it succeeded, was cleverly countered by his publishing what purported to be Mary's cession of her English rights to the Duke of Anjou. It was a deliberate falsification: the cession had been made in favour of the dead Francis II, dead before she ever set foot in Scotland. But by the time the canard had been exposed, the danger had blown over.

Cecil had other cards to play. Knowing that the old aristocracy was meditating an appeal to arms, and that Norfolk, as the sole surviving Duke in England, was their natural leader, Cecil determined to detach him by putting him under an obligation to himself. It so happened that Lord Dacre had died in 1566, and that Norfolk had married his widow the following year.[5] Now Dacre's successor had suddenly died, and the old Lord's brother, Leonard Dacre, was claiming the title and estates; whereas Norfolk claimed those estates for his three wards, the nieces of Lord Thomas, whom he had betrothed to his sons. It was at this stage that Cecil quietly intervened, seeing to it that the law courts handed down a decision in Norfolk's favour. This, which happened on July 19, served the double purpose of placating Norfolk and of embittering Leonard Dacre who, when the rebellion occurred, would have nothing to do with it precisely because it was to be led by the man who had robbed him of his rights.

[5] She was not Duchess of Norfolk for long. Her death made Norfolk's subsequent adventures and tragic end possible.

Norfolk, however, hoped to marry Mary Queen of Scots. The project had been first mooted at the enquiry at York the previous year, and Mary had made a favourable response, though whether she ever intended to do more than use Norfolk for her purposes is open to question. The marriage had received the endorsement of Maitland, and even Moray pretended to be in its favour. To them it was represented that a Protestant husband for Mary would be the best guarantee of Scotland's Protestantism. The same argument prevailed in the English Council, and won Cecil's feigned assent. Mary Queen of Scots, it was held, would have to be accepted as Elizabeth's successor now that the negotiations for her marriage to the Archduke Charles had broken down.[6] But entangled with everything was the opposition of the aristocrats to Cecil.

Everything, in fact, was much too tangled. Norfolk and his friends on the Council were working for the Duke's marriage to Mary. They did not wish a restoration of the Catholic religion. But they did wish for Cecil's downfall unless he threw in his lot with them; in that event they were ready to work with him. The simple-minded Earls in the north were, on the other hand, immovably determined upon the elimination of Cecil, as they were upon the Catholic restoration they believed would flow from it. And the recognition, not the marriage, of Mary was what they were concerned to effect; if she did marry, they hoped it would be a Catholic prince — Don John of Austria for preference.

There was, therefore, little contact between two groups whose objects were so dissimilar and whose counsels were so divided. The one link between them was the Duke of Norfolk, whose conversion to Catholicism was expected, or rather, hoped for. For this reason, and because he could, it was thought, rally behind him the old aristocracy, they somewhat reluctantly ac-

---

[6] It might be remarked that the crisis of 1569 was almost entirely of Elizabeth's own making. The Hapsburg marriage would have satisfied nearly everybody, and would have eliminated Mary as a candidate — unless, of course, Elizabeth's marriage had been childless. The Queen must have understood this; so again we are forced to surmise that she threw away the political advantage she would have derived from marriage only because she was incapable of it.

cepted his leadership. Most unfortunately the Duke, though personally popular and amiable, was, as events were to show, weak and cowardly.

Everybody concerned wished to avoid open rebellion. And now that Cecil was favouring Norfolk's marriage to Mary, matters, it was supposed, could be amicably arranged. An English husband would remove the danger of Don John. In view of so satisfactory a solution, surely Elizabeth would not object.

Object, however, Elizabeth did. Having got wind of what was afoot, she slyly asked Norfolk whether there was "any talk of a marriage." In great alarm at discovering that the Queen was already posted, he attempted a joke. No, he told her, he valued his life too much to think of marrying Mary.

Elizabeth was still not satisfied. She invited the Duke to dinner, and, after it was over, gave him a playful nip and the advice that he "had better take good heed to his pillow." Her witticism sent him into a panic. On September 21 he was ordered to go to the Court at Windsor, and Pembroke, Arundel and Lumley were arrested about the same time. As Norfolk knew that he would be arrested too if he obeyed Elizabeth's summons, he pleaded that he was ill. On the 30th he sent a message to the Northern Earls advising them not to rise, and eight days later Sir Francis Knollys was instructed to convey the Duke to the Tower.

Cecil had chosen his moment carefully. On September 8 Maitland, who had been about to go to London to ask Elizabeth's consent to Mary's marriage to Norfolk, was arrested on a charge of complicity in Darnley's murder. Moray's approbation had, of course, been, like Cecil's, only a pretence. With Maitland in custody all possibility of Scotch intervention in Mary's behalf was removed. Cecil had the game in his hands. But this was only because of Norfolk's craven character: had the Duke been a man of a different stamp, had he gone on with what he had begun and joined the northern rebels, the whole face of England would have changed.

Now that Norfolk had withdrawn, Northumberland, "Simple Tom," an easygoing man with little stomach for a fight, would have liked to have withdrawn as well. Things, however, had gone too far for that. Westmoreland and his friends in Northumberland's own house at Topcliffe brandished pistols and shouted, "If ye will cast yourself away, ye shall not cast us!" And behind both the Earls stood valiant and fiery wives. Northumberland, still hoping to avoid taking up arms against the Queen, asked for what cause they were to fight and got the answer "For religion!" The plot had not begun quite like that, but that was how it ended.

Sussex, who was in command at York, sent several times to the Earls telling them to come to see him. He was himself listed among the members of the aristocratic party, but he was a soldier with his duties to perform. The Earls put him off, first with evasive answers, finally with a flat refusal. When his messenger left Topcliffe on November 4, he heard all the church bells ringing; it was the signal for the rising.

From all sides men poured in, wearing the red cross of the crusaders and carrying the banner of the Five Wounds. The Catholic north was on the march, and among them were many old men who had taken part in the Pilgrimage of Grace and were still, thirty-three years later, uncowed by the savage punishment Henry had inflicted. Old Richard Norton, a distant relative of Katherine Parr's, was one of these; he rode in with seven of his eleven sons. It was medieval England come to life or, as Professor Pollard puts it, "the last armed stand in England against the secular spirit."

For a while it looked as though the rebels might win, though actually they never had any chance. But Sussex had too small a force to oppose them, and his men were going over to the Earls. On November 15 the rebels entered Durham, and Mass was sung again in the cathedral — for the last time. There they issued a proclamation denying that they were rising against the Queen; it was only against "divers evil disposed persons" about her. It was these who by their "crafty dealing have overthrown the Catholic religion, abused the Queen, dishonoured the realm, and seek the destruction of the nobility." The proclamation ended with "God save the Queen!"

The Rising of the North

Past York they marched, leaving Sussex insecurely entrenched, through Richmond, Wetherby, Knaresborough, Tadcaster, Cawood, and Selby, which they reached on the 24th. Mary had already been removed from Wingfield to Tutbury to put her out of reach of possible rescue. A raid may have been attempted on Tutbury; if so, it was fruitless. Mary had been moved on the 25th to Coventry. The one chance of the Northern Earls was gone. Had Mary once been released, nearly all England would have risen for her — not to overthrow Elizabeth, but to assert Mary's right. As she was still in custody, the rebels could accomplish nothing.

From the south a huge royal army was now moving up to meet the Earls. And the help their foreign allies had promised to send failed to arrive. The Spanish Ambassador had given undertakings on his own authority; Alva declined to honour them, being sceptical about an enterprise so foolhardy. Let the Earls hold Hartlepool as a port, he argued; let them hold it for a month and prove their strength: not until then would he move.

With plans so badly coordinated, the Earls could hold nothing. They began to retreat slowly with Clinton and Warwick and Sussex in pursuit. On December 15 they were in full flight. Five days later the leaders crossed the Scottish border to safety. The mildest and most futile rebellion in history had lasted about a month. The rebels had not put a single man to death. They had, in fact, only issued a proclamation.

At the hour when his services might have meant all the difference between victory and defeat, Leonard Dacre had sulked like Achilles in his tent. He had even helped Lord Scrope to round up some of the rebels. Now he determined upon a rebellion of his own. In the middle of February, Lord Hunsdon, one of Elizabeth's numerous Boleyn cousins, was sent to take him at his stronghold at Naworth.

Hunsdon saw that a direct attack upon Naworth castle was too risky, and so pressed northwards to join forces with Scrope. Information had reached him that a body of Scots were already in England, on their way to reinforce Dacre. Had Hunsdon been allowed to pass, the royal army would have been trapped. Even at that last moment the Catholic cause might have been saved. For Moray had been assassinated on January 22 — an act of personal revenge but one that opened unlooked for possibilities to Mary's friends. The Scottish border was now unguarded, except by Marian troops. All, therefore, that Dacre had to do was to hold Naworth and cut off Hunsdon's line of retreat.

In his vanity he committed the crowning folly of a rebellion full of bad judgment. Disdaining sound and slow strategy, he intercepted Hunsdon at the Gelt. There he charged with all his three thousand rank riders, who were mown down by the steady fire of Hunsdon's disciplined arquebusiers. "They gave me the proudest charge that ever I saw," Hunsdon commented afterwards. But Dacre, the vain and unreliable, fled. The rebellion was over.

To Hunsdon, a forthright soldierly man, son of Anne Boleyn's sister, and a swearer almost as vigorous as the Queen herself, Elizabeth added in her own beautiful script a postscript to the official letter of congratulation: "I doubt much, my Harry, whether that the victory were given me more joyed me, or that you were by God appointed the instrument of my glory; and I assure you that for my country's good the first might suffice, but for the heart's contentation the second more pleases me." She might well have been pleased. As Hunsdon told her, a little more, a very little more, and her cause had been lost. He was more lucky than skilful.

From start to finish the affair had been bungled. Cecil had been allowed to select the moment to open hostilities. Alva had failed to come up. Norfolk had abandoned the undertaking at the last minute in fright. Leonard Dacre had hung back until too late. And the Pope's Bull of Excommunication was issued five days after Dacre had been defeated at the Gelt — on February 25.

Yet for this, Pius V cannot be blamed, though Mr. Belloc and others have blamed him. The truth is not so much that the Pope moved too late, as that the Earls moved too soon. But that they could not help; Cecil forced them into the open. His spies in Rome had sent him word that the Bull was about to be issued. Cecil knew very well that had it arrived in time many Catholics who hung back from the rebellion would have joined it.

This is no mere assumption. When the rebels consulted a priest as to the legitimacy of rising against the Queen, he answered that until her excommunication had been published, her subjects could not be absolved from allegiance. His opinion weighed with all, and some it restrained. Those who went on, even in the absence of the excommunication, did so because they had received private information that it was to be issued soon. This being the case, they ventured to anticipate it. Nevertheless, their position would have been immeasurably strengthened had the Bull been in their hands in the autumn of 1569.

In the appalling punishment that followed, Elizabeth took an active part. It should have been regarded as a reason for leniency that the Earls had done no more than demand the removal of some of the Queen's advisers. But if, until this year, there had been no executions for treason, the Queen made up for it now. She was not naturally cruel, as was her father, but she had had a bad fright, and fright is the spring of most cruelty. The insurrection having failed, exemplary mass hangings were carried out. As the lesson of the Pilgrimage of Grace had been apparently lost upon the north, Elizabeth would make sure that there was no third rising. On January 11, 1570, she wrote to say that she "somewhat marvelled that she had as yet heard nothing from Sussex of any execution done by martial law as was appointed." He was ordered to proceed to the work at once and to let her know what had been done. At the time of the rising he had been suspected of secret sympathy with it, for he was among the political opponents of Cecil. And there was the glaring fact that his brother, Egremont Radcliffe, had joined the Earls. Sussex was therefore required to prove his fidelity by his ferocity.

He hastened to do what was required of him, and wrote to the Queen, "I guess that it will not be under 6 or 7 hundred at the least that shall be executed of the common sort." Those who had any property were reserved to be dealt with under the law of treason: the thrifty Elizabeth wished to make the suppression of the rebellion pay for itself.

Actually, Sussex hanged about eight hundred of "the common sort" — men whose crime was a feudal faithfulness to their lords. In order that the maximum amount of terror should be struck in all hearts, it was arranged that if only one man from some wretched hamlet had answered the call, that one man should be hanged: every village green was to have its gallows. Further to emphasize the punishment, orders were given that the bodies were not to be removed but left until they rotted away. From Northumberland's house at Topcliffe there was no window from which one could look and not see a dangling man. As Sir Edward Horsey (a precious rascal who was deriving large profits from conniving at the depredations of the Channel pirates) wrote to Cecil, he was "eager to serve God" by a liberal use of the rope.

Working with Horsey was Cecil's eldest son, Thomas. As he had "adventured his carcase" in the Queen's service, he thought it no more than just that he should get all he could of the confiscated lands. And Topcliffe, the infamous torturer, seems to have smelled at this time the profits that lay in Protestantism. He began his career by securing part of the estate of "old Norton."

Norton himself got away safely to the Netherlands, where he lived what remained of his life in the English colony of Louvain. With him escaped Ladies Westmoreland and Northumberland, and Leonard Dacre. Westmoreland himself was attainted, but found a haven in Maestricht, where he was pensioned by Philip II. Ten years later he died in Rome.

Some of the gentry were spared, sometimes for rather singular reasons. John Markenfield was attainted but not executed, because, as the official report explains, "It was not meant that he should die, for he had no land" that is, nothing the Crown could confiscate. As for Astolph Cleisby, he was let off because Lord Hunsdon's son was a suitor for a girl who was one of his relatives; it was thought that young Cleisby "might assist if his life was spared in bringing about the match." Henry Johnson, a son-in-law of Norton's, was not hanged because he had made over his estate to his wife at the time of his marriage: "As by his life the Queen shall have his lands, and by his death his wife shall presently have them" — Elizabeth had an excellent inducement to be merciful.

Northumberland was not so fortunate, and his fate makes an interesting if dark story. He, like the other gentry who had got into Scotland, found a host. Only his host, Hector Armstrong, sold him to Morton, the moving spirit in the new regency of Lennox, and Morton, after keeping him a prisoner in Lochleven, waiting for a good price, sold him to Elizabeth. Armstrong, by the bye, had previously tried to do a little deal with Hunsdon on Westmoreland's account. He wrote, "Although it was a traitorous kind of service that he was wading in to trap them that trusted in him, as Judas did Christ" — he was nevertheless willing to perform it. To the soldierly credit of Hunsdon it must be recorded that he took no notice of the offer. Elizabeth was not so scrupulous.

Nor were those in power in Scotland — like their descendants who sold Charles I to Cromwell. Two years after the rebellion had fizzled out, Simple Tom was handed over to the English authorities. He had in the interval been attainted and his lands confiscated. Yet he could have obtained pardon had he apostatised: the adhesion of a Percy was well worth that price. In the early days of Elizabeth he and his brother had served on the royal Commission that exacted the oath of Supremacy from the clergy; but that was a lapse for which he had long since atoned. As he now stood firm, he was brought to York and beheaded, the crowd groaning with horror at seeing the sacred blood of this prince of the North. His fidelity to the Faith brought him beatification three hundred years later.

One more execution might be noticed: it is that of the priest who had sung Mass in Durham. As a special punishment devised to fit the crime, he was hanged in front of the open doors of the cathedral, where a vast congregation only a little while before had rejoiced in tears at what they took to be the first sign of a Catholic restoration. His executioners no doubt imagined that by choosing this place they were adding to the priest's pangs; it must have been his greatest consolation.

The failure of the rising established Elizabeth in a stronger position than ever. She had not only crushed insurrection at home; she now felt secure from foreign invasion. In 1568 stories had been circulated in England that the Guises intended a descent — stories that had been set in circulation by the King of Spain in order to keep Elizabeth apprehensive and so prevent her sending men into the Netherlands. It was now known that there had been some danger of a Spanish landing at Hartlepool — avoided only because of Alva's unwillingness to back an undertaking until it was assured of success. All those threats having passed away, the Queen could flaunt her triumph abroad as well as at home. The continental powers had believed her government weak; she had proved that it was not, though despite the poor organization of the rebels and the defection of Norfolk and Leonard Dacre, it had been touch and go. Now the English Catholics, who before had been accused of a general disloyalty because of their refusal to accept the Queen's religion, could at last have definite treason fastened upon them and therefore were discredited. Leicester as a new year's gift presented her Majesty in 1571 with an emblematic group of figures worked in gold. There she was shown seated on her throne, with the Queen of Scots crouching in chains, while Neptune, dashing his waves against France and Spain, lifted his trident in homage to Elizabeth.

It seemed to be the darkest of moments for the English Catholics. They had shot their bolt, and it had only revealed their impotence as well as their disaffection. The consequence was that many, who had so far declined to conform, hastened to accept the Elizabethan Settlement. The diminishing few who would not, had ahead of them a period of intensified persecution. For hardly was the rebellion over when the Bull *Regnans in Excelsis* was issued. It seemed to everybody the worst of all the Catholic blunders. While Elizabeth raged against the Pope, and against all Papists, even her excommunication, coming when it did, told to her advantage. With what sardonic smiles she and Cecil must have read the futile fulmination.

12

~~~~~~

The Fate of Norfolk

NOTHING," writes Meyer, the German Protestant historian of the Elizabethan Settlement, "not even the Gunpowder Plot, produced so deep and enduring an effect upon England's attitude to the Catholic Church as the bull of Pius V. Englishmen never forgot their queen's excommunication." The judgement is correct. Nor did Englishmen forget that the Bull failed.

It failed because it was issued a little too late — after and not before the Northern Rebellion of 1569. Even so, it might still have kept much of its force had France and Spain published it. The Most Catholic King and the Most Christian King, however, usually at loggerheads, agreed now. They did not like to see the Pope taking action against one of the sacred guild of monarchs; if such action had to be taken, they considered that they should have been consulted in advance; therefore they refused to act against Elizabeth, as was expected of them by Pius. She, angry and scornful, used the Bull as a pretext for persecuting her Catholic subjects.

Nevertheless, the promulgation of a sentence of excommunication had been dreaded. Though times had changed, and such a Bull could not have then quite the same effect as it would have had in the middle ages, it would have been a highly dangerous thing to encounter — except for the fact that the French and Spanish kings flatly refused to publish it in their dominions. Philip was especially furious, but not more so than the Emperor, who feared trouble from the German Protestant Princes. And without the cooperation of the Emperor and Philip and Charles IX, nothing could be done to make the

Regnans in Excelsis effective. Instead of being a bomb, it proved to be, politically speaking, a damp firecracker. As the Nuncio at Madrid wrote in October, 1574, "The Bull ought not to have been published until the army was on its way to conquer England. Men would have held the keys of Peter in one hand and in the other the sword of St. Paul." Which is all very well: only we must remember that Alva *could* have landed in England in November, 1569 and have had the Bull in his hand by the following March. The truth is that official Spain did not at all relish Elizabeth's excommunication.

To nobody did the Bull bring more consternation than to the English Catholics. They thought of themselves as having been deserted by the Church for twelve years. Now at last the Church had moved — only to blunder and to make their lot tenfold more difficult than ever.

For this reason many English Catholic historians of the period — including the two most prominent among them, Lingard and Belloc — have expressed the opinion that the excommunication was an enormous mistake. As Lingard expresses it, "The time had gone by when the thunders of the Vatican could shake the thrones of princes." And though Mr. Belloc asserts that, even in the late sixteenth century, such a sentence meant more than we are disposed to believe, he also considers it a tactical error.

The Dominican monk who had been nicknamed Brother Wooden-Shoes, and who since 1566 had occupied the Chair of St. Peter, did not pretend to be a politician. He was only a saint — though this he did not suspect. He had not consulted the Kings of France and Spain, or the Emperor, before issuing his Bull, because this was, after all, a purely spiritual matter. In later years he is said to have admitted that he made an error in judgment, and his successor, Urban VIII, explicitly cited the failure of the *Regnans in Excelsis* as a reason for his not excommunicating the Kings of Sweden and France.

The issuing of the Bull was, however, not in itself a mistake. The mistake (in so far as one was made) was that it was not issued either at the beginning of Elizabeth's reign — which would have been best — or early in 1569. But in fairness to Pius we must bear in mind two facts. One is that even in 1567 he was still considering representations offered by Sir Richard Shelley that England could be re-Catholicised by other means. The other is that, when hope for Shelley's plans had been abandoned, Nicholas Morton, who had been special preacher at Canterbury under Cardinal Pole, went to England on a secret mission and talked with some of the men who afterwards rebelled about the possibility of Elizabeth's excommunication. He went so far as to argue that Elizabeth was already, because of her actions, *ipso facto* excommunicated, and that it was therefore lawful to take up arms against her. On the other hand, Morton told Northumberland and Markenfield that they should not resort to rebellion until after the promulgation of the sentence. The opinions may be readily reconciled: the first was that theological "probability" was — in his view — sufficient to justify any rising; the second, that political wisdom, if nothing else, dictated their waiting until the Pope's pronouncement had put the matter beyond question. If the rebels acted too soon this was because Cecil had deliberately precipitated their challenge. Slowness of communication in those days made perfect synchronisation of effort something almost impossible to effect. Cecil took advantage of the fact, and made the Earls strike before the Bull had been issued.

Looking back upon the situation, I believe that Pius V was not nearly so much at fault as he himself came to think. What he did turned out to be in the end the right if not the most politic move. It is a pity that the Bull came after the suppression of the rising of the Northern Earls. It is better that it came late than never. Not human shrewdness but the wisdom of Divine Providence determines human destiny. The Bull saved Catholicism from utter extinction in England.

The English Catholics could, of course, have hardly been expected to see this at the time. Their sufferings were at once increased by a more stringent application of the existing laws and by the passing of others even more severe. The Bull, coming after rebellion, gave what was, in many eyes, complete confirmation of Cecil's contention that Catholicism was incompatible with loyalty to the sovereign. This won over thousands of wavering Catholics, as the ferocious punishment of the rebels cowed all but the most resolute. The Bull therefore had not only left Elizabeth politically unharmed, it damaged (or seemed to damage) the Catholic cause in England almost beyond repair.

How it actually saved Catholicism in England must be explained. The *Regnans in Excelsis* acted as an electric shock; it cleared the air as nothing else could have done. Though it reduced the number of Catholics, those who remained faithful were the best among them, and they now became still better. They perceived, more clearly than ever, that the practice of the Faith calls for heroism, and it is always bracing for Catholics to be made aware that theirs is a heroic religion, however much the form of heroism varies according to period and place. Though I cannot accept Professor Pollard's dictum that, as a consequence, "The catholicism of the English Romanists became less English and more Roman" (for the terms are misleading), English Catholics were brought sharply up against the fact that, if Catholicism was to endure, it must be *Roman* Catholicism and not an eclectic or insular preference. The Henrician compromise was shown to be untenable.

In spite of this, many English Catholics, who were quite sturdily "Roman," were inclined not to accept the Bull. They argued — and their argument was, in effect, sustained by the "explanation" of Gregory XIII — that the Bull was invalid until some means could be found for its enforcement. Until then their obligations of allegiance to Elizabeth would remain unimpaired. Loyalty to the Church could still be thoroughly compatible with loyalty to the Queen.

There was another line of argument available. Canonists could urge (and did urge) that the Bull was invalid because it did not observe all the technical requirements of canon law. A warning should have first been sent, and a year allowed to elapse before pronouncement of sentence. The Bull came too suddenly after the Papal toleration of twelve years. Whether this argument is sound, I must leave to others more competent to decide; it was one of the arguments used. In view of the "probable opinion," Catholics were not in conscience obliged to accept the Bull.

But if they did not, as a body, recognise its validity, Elizabeth and Cecil were perfectly willing to do so. The technicalities of canon law were of no more than academic interest to them: it was obviously to their political advantage to assume that the Bull was valid; then they could call it an instance of Papal aggression and hoist Pius with his own petard. Here, they said, was proof positive of the treason of Catholics. Cecil made much of the mention of the Queen's illegitimacy, though this was merely a minor and secondary point, one that was hardly more than implied by the Pope. The deposition was based not on Elizabeth's doubtful right but on her notorious heresy, as to which all the leading English Catholics in Rome had given detailed testimony during the hearings that preceeded the excommunication. This charge of heresy was therefore glossed over; Cecil made Pius V's action appear to be a deposition on account of bastardy. About the sentence of deposition there could of course be no question.

The first sufferer on account of the excommunication was John Felton, a young lawyer of means and social standing. Greatly daring, he nailed a copy of the Bull to the door of the Bishop of London's palace, selecting, as an appropriate day for doing so, the feast day of Gregory VII, the great Hildebrand who made the Emperor go to Canossa: May 25, 1570. He was arrested, put to the torture, and executed with the barbarous rites of hanging and disembowelling on August 8. With legal logic he refused to admit even on the scaffold that Elizabeth was rightfully Queen. Yet to express his personal good will he sent her a diamond ring, which the Bishop of London had expected to get as his perquisite; it was worth £400. As his wife had been a lady in waiting to the Queen, Elizabeth tried to soften the blow for her by giving her special permission to have Mass in her house until she died — an action kindly, but in its inconsistency, typical of the times.

Felton was soon followed to the scaffold by Dr. John Story,

also a layman. He had been a member of Parliament during Mary's reign and Chancellor to Bishop Bonner, as such having some part in the Marian prosecutions for heresy. When Elizabeth came to the throne he escaped to Antwerp, where he became a naturalized subject to Philip II and was employed in the Customs House in preventing the importation of Calvinist books to the Netherlands. An English ship now contrived to lure him on board, to kidnap him, and to take him to London. There he was condemned to the same death that Felton suffered on a charge of being a friend of some of the rebels of 1569, but really out of spite. Elizabeth's violation of international law was insolent; more nauseous were the trickery and hypocrisy of the proceedings against the victim. Felton's execution can perhaps be justified; Story's cannot.

The savage sentences served to show Catholics what they might expect. So also did a proclamation promising that those who gave information as to Papal Bulls or seditious — that is, Catholic — books "should be so richly rewarded, that during his or their lives they should have cause to think themselves well used." The informers were assured that they "should be preserved from the note of blaming or accusing, so far forth as might be by any ways devised." The system of spies and pursuivants had begun. From thenceforth Elizabeth's reign was to be one of terror.

Even so the Catholics did not give up all hope. Damaged as they had been by the Bull, some of them believed they might draw encouragement from it. Now that Elizabeth had been excommunicated, the Catholic powers had a justification for intervention. It also meant that Mary Queen of Scots' position was strengthened. For though her partizans had no intention of putting her at once upon the English throne, at least Mary now had a splendid bargaining point against Elizabeth. Men again began to work for her nomination as the Queen's successor.

In doing so they judged the political situation badly. No foreign aid was to be counted upon at that time. And Norfolk — who was again put forward as a possible husband for Mary — was the frailest reed upon which any cause could lean, his sole advantage being in his rank. The Northern Earls had accepted him merely as a *pis aller;* they would have much preferred a definite Catholic, and Norfolk was a Protestant, though one, it was supposed, with Catholic tendencies. Yet through him the malcontents still hoped to overthrow Cecil.

The Duke was released from the Tower on August 9, 1570, after undertaking to give up all idea of marrying Mary Queen of Scots. To make sure of him Cecil offered the needy aristocrat as his fourth wife his sister-in-law, the wealthy and often-married Lady Hoby, a sound Protestant.

Norfolk, however, was at once drawn into a new plot, the central figure of which was Roberto di Ridolfi, a Florentine banker doing a lucrative business lending money to the more extravagant members of the nobility. He also acted secretly, not precisely as a Papal agent, but as a factor for some of the Papal transactions. He had been arrested at the time of the northern rising but not detained long. It was Walsingham who had then stood as his guarantor — possibly because Walsingham, knowing his man, expected that by leaving him at large, and watching him closely, further evidence could be secured against the banker's clients. Ridolfi was, like Simon Tappertit, a very poor plotter.

But before coming to Ridolfi's conspiracy, it must be said that Elizabeth's government was still very nervous. Rebellion had indeed been crushed. But Mary was alive and, like Norfolk, dangerous. Though the Bull had failed in its immediate effects, nobody could be sure what the ultimate effects would be. Its promulgation was declared by the government to be the first stroke of the League for the extirpation of Protestants. The government's spies were accordingly set to work. Their task did not prove to be a difficult one.

Norfolk, despite his promise to Elizabeth, again entertained the idea of marrying Mary. It was never part of his plan to supplant Elizabeth; all he wanted was to secure the restored Scots throne for himself and Mary and their right to the English succession. But there can be little doubt that others in the plot were prepared, in certain contingencies, to go further than this.

The Fate of Norfolk

Ridolfi's ideas, which he did not reveal in full to his English associates, included the deposition — and perhaps the assassination — of Elizabeth. But what Norfolk did know — he could not have been spurred to action otherwise — was that it was proposed to bring over a Spanish army. He was kept in the dark about many things; about this he was informed — and it certainly made him technically guilty of treason.

Ridolfi was an able and active, but vain and consequential man, and he took it upon himself to make all the arrangements. He was well acquainted with some aspects of English conditions, though he saw them through the eyes of a foreigner. His mistake (so often laughed at) of not being aware that Harwich is a port in Essex was among the less serious of his errors. The worst were those of astonishingly bad judgment, which was all the worse because it considered itself so sound. He was with Alva early in April; the following month he was in Rome; and in late June in Madrid. Nobody can accuse him of lack of energy.

For the information of Rome and Madrid he drew up a list of sixty-four peers, forty of whom he claimed to be in sympathy with his scheme. Of the others, eighteen were marked "doubtful," and only six as belonging to the Cecilian group. The estimate may have been partly due to the sanguine nature of the man; it must, however, be suspected that he knew that nothing like forty nobles would support Norfolk, when it came to an issue, and that at least a tincture of deception crept in.

This list was shown to Alva. The taciturn soldier was not very favourably impressed by the banker, whom he described a *gran parlaquina* and *muy liberal en el hablar*. More specifically Alva wrote to Philip on August 29, 1571: "When the man that makes the discourse has no one to criticise the suppositions on which he argues, he will draw his conclusions most happily. It is like a judge passing sentence after hearing one side only. And it is a man like this, who is no soldier, and has never seen war in his life, who thinks one can pour armies out of the air, or keep them up one's sleeve, and effect with them what his fancy depicts. For to talk as though one might have one army to take the Queen of England, another to free the Queen of Scots, and at the same time to seize the Tower of London and capture the ships in the river — really, I think that even if your Majesty had agreed with the Queen of England to do all these things, you would not have enough to do it in an instant, as he proposes it should be done."

In spite of this, Alva did not immediately return a decided negative. After all, something might come of it. But he had no intention of himself initiating the rebellion by means of a Spanish invasion; for that, as he understood perfectly, would have been to have exposed himself to possible attack from the French or the German Protestants, or both. He committed himself therefore to only this much: if the English rose and proved able to maintain themselves in the field for six weeks, he would then see what he could do. By that time perhaps France would have declared for Mary, and so any danger to Spain of war from that quarter would have disappeared. If the scheme proved practicable, it might serve to prevent a marriage between Elizabeth and the Duke of Anjou, and so further Spain's advantage. All in all, however, Alva doubted its feasibilty.

To the Pope Ridolfi wrote on September 1. Alva, he said, was going to help. The English Catholics were going to revolt and put Mary on the throne and restore religion. Lord Derby was going to raise 12,000 men; Arundel and Lumley 15,000 more. At a stamp of the foot armies were to rise from the ground.

How far Norfolk was posted about the details of this absurd plan remains uncertain. He had listened to Ridolfi read over a paper, and he had given his general consent to what it contained. But he denied in his trial that he had designed any treason — which was true — or that he had declared himself ready to become a Catholic — which was not true. He was an indolent man who treated business with aristocratic hauteur. "Full well," he had remarked sarcastically, "does Ridolfi know our opinions!" Unluckily for Norfolk, he was as much in the dark about Ridolfi's.

The Fate of Norfolk

He could plead at his trial that he was in complete ignorance about any plot to assassinate Elizabeth. For this was not part of the original scheme as unfolded in England, but was discussed — no more than discussed — by the Council at Madrid when Ridolfi offered it as a second (and surer) method of attack. The Spanish Council did not actually sanction murder; they merely debated how far they should go in intervening in England in the event of the murder occurring.

Further, even Ridolfi had at the back of his mind in what was called "the enterprise of the person of Elizabeth" no more than killing her if there was any attempt at rescue after she had been captured. He no doubt thought that such an attempt would probably be made, and he had no compunction about assassination. But killing was something to be reserved as a last resource. Such was Ridolfi's idea; it was not Norfolk's, or any Englishman's.

What is more important is the often-repeated story that Pius V approved Elizabeth's murder, to which even Lord Acton, the Catholic historian, has given the authority of his great name. Father Pollen, however, has proved in a long footnote on page 125 of his *English Catholics in the Reign of Elizabeth* that the misunderstanding has arisen from a mistranslation. The Latin Life of Pius V in the *Acta Sanctorum* can, it is true, be made to read "Pius thought of making away with her who was the cesspool of all iniquities." But if the original Italian from which the Latin version was made be consulted we find only the harmless: "Pius, thinking on the one hand of helping the Queen of Scotland, and on the other of clearing away the cesspool of so many evils, deputed certain persons among the Catholics to give him information." Pollen's reference is to the *Vita del Glorioso Papa Pio V* by Girolamo Catena, published in Mantua in 1587.

To return to England: it was, as usual, Leicester who played false, even if he did not act in the affair as an *agent provocateur*. It was he who had gone to Norfolk with the suggestion that he try again to marry Mary. It was he who promised to talk over Elizabeth, whom he professed to believe he could persuade. It was he who joined Cecil against the Duke.

Queen Elizabeth

The documentary evidence needed for conviction was obtained by Cecil. He had been waiting for just such a chance. Norfolk, the leader of the party that had long threatened his downfall, had withdrawn from the northern rebellion just in time and could show that he had tried to prevent it. On that score it had been impossible to charge him with treason. The case was quite different now. Cecil perfectly understood that this was a duel to the death. For should Mary ever become Queen of England her first act would be to behead him. Therefore he determined to exterminate Norfolk and all that Norfolk stood for — the aristocratic tradition of an earlier England.

Dispatches were intercepted. These indicated that something was going on — it was not clear precisely what. But in May, 1571, a messenger named Charles Baily with letters from Ridolfi was arrested at Dover. They were addressed to the Bishop of Ross, Mary's Ambassador, and were marked "Trente" and "Quarante." Under the threat of torture the Bishop broke down and said that these numbers stood for Norfolk and Lumley.

Cecil now employed the services of one Herle as a stool pigeon. The man was confined in the Marshalsea along with the Bishop and Baily, and made friends with each, to worm out what he could. By way of covering up Herle's character, he was called before the Council, severely examined, and having been pronounced contumacious, was sent back to prison loaded with irons. The part he was playing was that of a recusant.

Ridolfi's messenger knew no more than he had already revealed. The Bishop of Ross, however, again theatened with torture, again broke down: on his new information Norfolk's secretaries were arrested. Higford, one of them, when put on the rack, told about some letters which his employer kept hidden under a tile on the roof of his house. A few weeks previously another letter, and some money that Norfolk was sending for the use of Mary's party in Scotland, were taken. With these documents in their hands the government had a case against the Duke sufficient for a charge of high treason.

The Fate of Norfolk

The Duke was brought to trail before a panel of twenty-six peers on January 16, 1572. Most of his judges were his friends; many of their names had been on Ridolfi's list of his supporters. But they dared not find Norfolk innocent, and on the evidence presented to them they could hardly have done so. There was the usual unfairness: the prisoner was allowed no counsel, or even allowed time to prepare his own defence; and the prosecuting lawyers read out in court only such parts of the documents or confessions as told against the accused. The eight-hour trial ended with Norfolk's being led away with the edge of the axe turned toward him.

Yet he did not believe that the Queen would sign his death warrant. And it must be said that she showed extreme reluctance to do so, in part due to the fact that the Duke was her second cousin, in part also because it seemed a shocking thing to take the life of the one remaining Duke in England. Perhaps another deterrent was the fact that Elizabeth needed a counterweight to Cecil. She could not tell what unforeseen conditions might appear in which Norfolk would be useful to her as a "leader of the opposition" in the Council.

In the end, nevertheless, she yielded. Cecil had command of Parliament and arranged matters in such a way that apparently spontaneous petitions came from both Houses calling for the execution of the Duke and Mary Queen of Scots. It was not hard to get these petitions: feeling was strong in some quarters; about all that Cecil had to do was to provide an outlet. The Bishops presented a memorial whose title is enough: "Reasons presented to the Queen's Majesty by the Bishops to prove that she may lawfully put to death the Scottish Queen by the word of God." Knox wrote to Cecil: "If ye strike not at the root, the branches that appear to be broken will bud again, and that more quickly than men can believe. . . . Yours to command, John Knox, with one foot in the grave."

Notwithstanding the dying Knox and the "word of God," Elizabeth steadfastly refused to kill Mary. "Can I put to death," she asked, "the bird that, to escape the pursuit of the hawk, has flown to my feet for protection?" It may have been that Cecil got Parliament to demand both lives because he was sure that Elizabeth would spare one. It left a margin for compromise. Mary could wait for the present. What Cecil was immediately concerned with was that his political enemy should die.

It was not that he had any personal ill feeling against the Duke — or the Duke against him. To Cecil's custody Norfolk, in a last letter, committed his children. But then, nobody disliked the Duke. Only, in those days, the block was the best means for extinguishing political rivals.

Time after time Elizabeth signed a warrant for the Duke's execution; time after time she recalled it. One of the countermanding orders — as we know from Cecil's notation upon it — reached him at two in the morning. Another the Queen signed at dawn after a sleepless night. Yet in the end, with Parliament pressing, Elizabeth felt she had to give it a victim. On June 2, 1572, Norfolk was led out to die on Tower Hill.

He died bravely and with aristocratic calm; his defect in courage was moral not physical. At his execution he was attended by Foxe, the Martyrologist, the tutor who had been provided for him after the execution of his father, Surrey the poet. It is rather ironical that the man whom the Catholics had looked to as their hope should have had his last moments consoled by the ministrations of the fiercest enemy the Catholics had. But it may have been that by making this demonstration of Protestantism Norfolk hoped that a reprieve would be given him at the scaffold; in so far as he had any religion at all, he was a Protestant. His son was to be beatified as a Catholic martyr.

We need shed no tears over his personal tragedy. He had inherited his father's charm without his father's genius. Weak and unstable he had always shown himself to be. What may be deplored is that with his passing at the age of thirty-six all hope of an aristocratic reaction against the Cecilian domination died too. The Earl of Northumberland was to follow him to the block three months later. Pembroke and Northampton and Winchester had descended to the tomb within the past two years. Though Arundel was to live on until 1580, the power of the old nobility was already broken; Norfolk's execution was a sign for all to read that England was captained by the new men. Sir William Cecil had been created Baron Burghley on February 25, 1571. He took his title from the abbey of nuns which was part of his share of the loot of the Reformation.

13

"And Christ Their Capitain"

FOR the English Catholics everything now seemed to be lost. The coming of Mary Queen of Scots to England had sent up their spirits — and these had not been greatly dampened by the fact that she had been vilified and was a prisoner, for she remained their rightful Queen. But when in 1569, and again in 1571, efforts had been made to enforce only so much as her right to the succession, these had failed. The Northern Earls had been crushed, and Norfolk had died on the scaffold. Now the Pope's Bull *Regnans in Excelsis* was used as a pretext for further persecution. Cecil was seated more firmly than ever in the saddle. It could only be a matter of time when the few survivors of the nonconforming Marian clergy died out.[1] Those who remained were too dispirited to attempt active missionary work: they, like the diminishing Catholic laity, were waiting for the end.

Every day was demonstrating the powerlessness or the unwillingness of the Catholic powers to give them aid. France and Spain were too jealous of one another to permit either to interfere in English affairs. Yet both had to submit to English interference in their own. The sea dogs were harrying with impunity the Channel and the Spanish Main. Drake raided Nombre de Dios in 1572, and Venta Cruz the following year. The national arrogance was mounting. And among the new men coming into power was Sir Francis Walsingham, who was to be the most ruthless of the Catholics' enemies. The most that they could do

---

[1] "This was a cause for the great decay of religion, as there was no one to teach it, and none professed it, except those who had special grace given them." (Mendoza to Philip.)

was to endure and to die and to go to God. For England they
no longer had any hope.

Even their professed friends often turned out to be traitors.
Sir Thomas Stukeley's is a case in point. This engaging scoundrel, a cousin to Hawkins and a reputed natural son of Henry
VIII, had served under Somerset and had been used in 1552
by Henry II in connexion with the capture of Calais, after
which he promptly betrayed Henry, and was in turn betrayed
by Cecil and imprisoned in the Tower. Later we find him arrested for piracy, but upon being pardoned he proceeded to
Ireland where, because he managed to ingratiate himself among
its people, he was suspected of treason. In 1570 he escaped to
Spain to receive a pension from Philip II and to profess himself
a Catholic: he gave out that he would lead an expedition to
Ireland. In Rome his plausibility took in the Pope, who conferred upon him the title of Marquis of Leinster and agreed
to send him with James Fitzmaurice Fitzgerald to raise a rebellion. Some believe that Stukeley's real intention was to seize the
ship with which he had been provided, to hand over his ecclesiastical passengers to Elizabeth, and then proceed to further
piracy. Be this as it may, he was persuaded upon reaching Portugal to join its King Sebastian in an invasion of Morocco.
There he fell fighting in 1578 in the battle of Alcacerquiber (or
Alcazar). He was typical of his time in his courage and his
shameless treachery. Yet so low had fallen Catholic hopes, that
the services of such adventurers were desperately grasped at as
drowning men grasp at straws.

In spite of the darkness of the hour, the English Catholics,
though greatly diminished, stood firm. For those who remained
faithful had been strengthened in their faith and recalled by
the Bull of 1570 from temporizing with the Anglican Establishment. However extreme their humiliation and suffering, at
least there was no longer any compromise with conscience. But
they were holding on only with a desolate and dogged loyalty,
believing their cause to be doomed. Or they would have believed it to have been doomed had it not been for their naked
trust in God.

Suddenly help arrived. It did not come from Rome, which in their eyes had done nothing except to make their position almost intolerable with the *Regnans in Excelsis*. It came instead with the arrival from abroad of a new generation of young missionaries of absolute fearlessness and devotion. Had they not come, a few more years would have sufficed to suppress even the most resolute of recusants, and England would have been another Scandinavia. That they were supplied was mainly the work of one man — William Allen.

This great man, who had been Principal of St. Mary's Hall, Oxford, in the previous reign, conceived the idea of founding a Catholic college at Douay in the Low Countries. This was established in 1568, with very meagre funds — mainly from the founder's own pocket — when Allen was thirty-six. His intention, in the beginning, was merely to provide an institution for the education of young Catholic students — a kind of little Oxford abroad. Only gradually did the thought take shape in his mind of sending some of these students — many of them converts, and some of them of noble, as most were of gentle blood — back to England as missionaries. In doing so he provided a working model; so that in 1575 the English College at Rome was founded, followed by the establishment of the seminaries of Valladolid in 1589, and Seville in 1592, as well as by the colleges founded still later for English Benedictines and Franciscans and Scotch Jesuits and Franciscans. It was to Allen, too, that we owe the publication in 1582, of the Rheims New Testament, as well as the complete English Catholic translation of the Scriptures known as the Douay Bible.

About Allen's political activities nothing need to be said at this stage, except that he always kept his work as head of the seminary and his association with the "Spanish Party" in strictly watertight compartments. His main function was to train priests to work in England.

We may go even further: Allen and the heads of the seminaries afterwards founded set out to train martyrs. So far from making any attempt to conceal from the seminarians the almost certain fate that awaited them when they became missionaries, no grisly horror was spared them. On the walls of the lecture rooms and the refectory hung pictures that showed in realistic detail all that was involved in an execution at Tyburn. When Allen's students signed the oath, soon after their admission, "I swear before Almighty God that I am ready and always shall be ready to receive holy orders in His own good time, and I shall return to England for the salvation of souls whenever it shall seem good to the superior of this college to order me to do so," they were fully aware that they were signing their own death warrants. The saying of Mass or the reconciling of any lapsed Catholics to the Church was an offence punishable with a traitor's death; but so, for that matter, became their own reception of ordination abroad. If the first of these offences might be difficult to prove, the second was always easy: the government, through its spies, was kept supplied with a list of all the students at Douay and elsewhere. Well, therefore, might St. Philip Neri when he encountered the students of the English College at Rome on the streets, salute them with a beaming face and reverence and the cry, *Salvete, flores martyrum!* It is said that all the young missionaries before leaving for England went to St. Philip to receive his blessing. All who did so suffered martyrdom; the one man who failed to ask the Saint's blessing also failed to obtain the martyr's palm. Authentic or not, the story reveals the spirit that animated the priests of the English mission.

The first of them to suffer was Cuthbert Mayne. He was charged in 1577 with having said Mass, with upholding the Pope's authority, and with having brought an Agnus Dei into England. The last charge was quite ridiculous; it is like making a priest guilty of treason for having given away a rosary or a scapular medal. It was, for all that, the most securely established point in his indictment.

Even so, the jury would not convict Mayne until Sir Richard Grenville (the hero of Tennyson's poem) had forced his way into their presence and threatened them. This Grenville was the sheriff of Cornwall, a violent ruffian who used to assuage his rages by chewing glass. Before such a man the jury were terrified and brought in the demanded verdict. Yet we may doubt whether Grenville's concern was primarily for the "Gospel." He was acting for Sir George Carey, one of Elizabeth's Boleyn cousins, who coveted the lands of Francis Tregian, who had harboured Mayne; and Tregian's dispossession could not be effected unless Mayne were convicted.[2]

A word might be said about this Tregian. He was a collateral descendant of Elizabeth Woodville, the Queen's great-grandmother. He had been a courtier but, according to his contemporary biographer, had incurred Elizabeth's displeasure by repulsing her amatory advances. His sister was the mother of the martyr, Thomas Sherwood. If he himself escaped martyrdom, he was imprisoned twenty-five years. During his early days in jail he wrote a touching poem to his wife, from which I quote a few lines:

> "For lack of ink the candle coal,
> For pen a pin I use,
> The which also I may allege
> In part of my excuse.

> "Bless in my name my little babes,
> God send them all good hap,
> And bless with all that little babe
> That lieth in your lap."

Not very polished verse, no doubt — much better poetry was to be produced by some of the other recusants — but it has at least a simple pathos, and in its conclusion an epigramatic turn:

> "Farewell again, thou lamp of light,
> Vicegerent of my heart;
> He that takes leave so oft, I think,
> He likes not to depart."

The main blot upon Elizabeth's fame is that she, a latitudinarian in religion, if not an actual atheist (as she is sometimes accused of being), should have persecuted members of a Church

---

[2] Mayne's execution was soon followed by that of other Douay priests.

to which she had once readily conformed, and to which she was prepared, if occasion demanded it, to conform again. Yet in justice to her and to her advisers we must admit that there were extenuating circumstances. The rising in the north had frightened them. So, too, had Norfolk, futile as his conspiracy had been from start to finish. But most of all we should remember the effect of the Massacre on St. Bartholomew's Day. This, coming after the Bull of 1570, seemed to the excited imagination of Protestants the first stroke of that suppositious Catholic League for their extirpation. Anything they did in their turn was, as Froude puts it, in a "rage that yet failed to satisfy the cravings of justice." Their own terror in no small degree accounts for the torture to which they subjected others. However unfounded was their fear, we must allow for it.

So, too, we must allow for fear in the government's knowing that the massacre represented a Guisan victory. When Philip II heard of what had taken place, he is said to have laughed — for the first time in the memory of man. It was not in sadistic satisfaction, nor even because his fanaticism was gratified: he perceived that Catherine de' Medici had played into his hands. With the likelihood of Spain and France now drawing together, England set herself all the more savagely to deal with the Catholics at home. That the Church herself had no connection with the Bartholomew's Day Massacre did not enter into her consideration.

Finally we must allow for fear in the dastardly plan to have Mary judicially murdered by handing her over to the new Scots Regent, Mar, who promised that she would not be alive four hours after she was in his hands. It would have been a convenient way for Elizabeth to have got rid of the troublesome captive whom "honour and conscience" forbade her to put to death herself. If nothing came of the pleasant project, that was because Mar died a few days after he had discussed it with Killigrew, the English agent who had been sent to Scotland to make the arrangements. In all this we must bear in mind that Elizabeth had by now a Parliament largely Puritan, and though Parliament was not as yet anything like so powerful as it was to become, its wishes were having increasing weight. While in the beginning the Puritans were comparatively quiet, later on Elizabeth persecuted Catholics largely to placate the Puritans.

If Elizabeth had only realised it, however, she had now a wonderful opportunity of a totally different sort: she could very easily have made sure of the grateful loyalty of her Catholic subjects: she could have made sure of it by the simple process of recognising it. They had already found ingenious reasons for denying that they were bound by the Bull of 1570, and the Papacy, having seen that the excommunication had missed fire, would have been glad enough to have come to terms. As a matter of fact, the next Pope, Gregory XIII, did issue an "explanation" that put the Bull into abeyance. A few slight concessions to Catholics would have permanently secured their adhesion to the Crown. But a judgment affected by fear is always clouded: Elizabeth decided upon severe repression. As the coming of seminary priests showed that Catholicism was not going to die out after all, it had to be stamped out.

With the arrival of the first Jesuits in 1580, the Protestant fury redoubled. Their arrival coincided with an event that was, to say the least, unfortunate: the Pope sent Nicholas Sanders — "Dr. Slanders" — as his envoy, not his Legate, to Ireland. And with him were conveyed a contingent of Papal troops to what was claimed as a Papal fief. The coincidence was capable of the worst possible construction, though there was no connexion between it and the mission of the English Jesuits who, of all men, were most alive as to how much it would hamper their work. It was nevertheless at once seized upon by the government as a proof that priests generally, and Jesuits in particular, were political agents.

In face of the Irish expedition, even the instructions given by the General of the Jesuits and the *explanatio* issued by the Pope in 1580, could be twisted from their true meaning. The Jesuit General wrote: "Let them not entangle themselves in matters of state or write hither political news." So far, so good: it was in this way that his instructions had been originally

drawn. But there was added a clause capable of sinister interpretation: "Except perhaps in the company of those whom they
know to be exceptionally faithful, and who have been tried a
long while; and even then not without serious cause." What the
General wished was a complete avoidance of political discussion, but knowing that this would perhaps not be humanly possible, he drew his instructions accordingly. Later, as this clause
created misunderstanding, not on the part of the Jesuits themselves but of their persecutors, he made the prohibition absolute, and the next General Chapter of the Society settled the
matter once for all by prohibiting all interference in politics
on the part of Jesuits. But by then the damage had been done:
Cecil could say that the absolute prohibition was only a wily
Jesuit trick and continue to persecute them without remorse as
traitors. Every Jesuit, and for that matter every priest, was
branded.[3]

So also with Gregory's explanation of his predecessor's Bull.
It was this: that Bull, while it bound Elizabeth and the English
heretics, did not bind the English Catholics in any way. But the
Pope added — as he was obliged to add, unless he was prepared
to formally rescind the *Regnans in Excelsis* entirely — that it
would bind Catholics when it could be executed. Until then
their allegiance was to the reigning Queen.

As the Papal explanation may be considered disingenuous, it
should be added that the experts in canon law went much
further in a liberal interpretation. Father Pollen quotes the
opinion of one of them — probably the Jesuit Antonio Posse-
vino — to the effect that, as the Bull had been issued for a particular occasion (the rising of 1569), changed circumstances
made it no longer in force. And, indeed, what the Pope's explanation amounted to was that the condemnation and deposition
of Elizabeth would be quietly allowed to drop — for there was
no expectation that the Bull ever could be executed.

[3] We have a conclusive answer to the charges of priestly political activity in
Mendoza's letter to Philip of April 26, 1582: "They, though ardently zealous as
regards religion, cannot be trusted with matters of state unless they are taught
word for word what they have to say." It is his admission — and a regretful one
— that the priests were not politicians but merely missionaries.

This did not suit Cecil's book. He unduly emphasized the phrase: "As for the Catholics [the Bull] obliges them in no way, while affairs stand as they do; but will only do so in future, when the public execution of the Bull can be made." He argued, plausibly enough, that if the Queen's Catholic subjects professed loyalty, it could be only a loyalty of a conditional sort; that they would rebel the instant they got the chance. But however plausible such a point was, it was Cecil and not the Pope who was really disingenuous. An understanding with Rome was readily procurable — which was just what Cecil did not want. He preferred to find in the *explanatio* a justification for charging Catholics with treason. It was manifestly impossible, he maintained, for them to be faithful to Elizabeth as England's monarch while they acknowledged the Papal Supremacy. And this argument is still advanced by some historians — by Bishop Creighton, for example.

Such were the difficulties with which the Jesuits were confronted. When they had cited against them what Gregory had written, they answered — perfectly sincerely, perfectly correctly — that it raised a subtle question open to debate in the schools and that they took no sides, only to have quoted against them the instructions given by their own General. Oh yes, their judges could observe, they were told not to talk politics — but there was an exception: *they might do so with those whose fidelity was certain.* What did this mean but that they had to be careful of their company? What did it mean but that they were fomenters of conspiracy?

Yet the first two Jesuits who came to England in 1580, Robert Persons and Edmund Campion (two converts), made every effort, as did those who followed them, to confine themselves to purely spiritual functions. Persons' subsequent political activities were outside of his original purpose and arose out of a change of mind after he had left England. He made in this, I believe, a serious error of judgment, though a very natural one. So far from being politically minded, his first desire, after having become a Catholic, was to bury himself in an Alpine monastery and to devote himself to a life of prayer. And his first ambition, after he had joined the Jesuits, was to go as a missionary to America. When he went to England it was under orders from his superiors — orders which forbade even talking about politics, orders which Persons scrupulously observed. As for his loyalty, he published in the year of his arrival a pamphlet dedicated to Elizabeth. Mistaken as he may have been in some of his later activities, he was characterised by a passionate love for his native land. That was his tragedy. He never suffered, as Campion did, at Tyburn; but as Ribadeneira said of him, "He was not the martyr of a moment but of a life-time."

The work he undertook, with Edmund Campion, was that of ministering to the Catholics and of meeting Protestants in controversy. For such controversy, both men were equipped with a fine sense of style. The difference between them was that where Campion loved the ornate magnificence of Elizabethan prose, Persons — the supposedly crafty politician — was a master of a direct lucidity that foreshadowed Bunyan and Swift and Cobbett. Isaac D'Israeli, the father of the famous Prime Minister, ranked him among the masters of a vigorous vernacular, saying that "in clear conceptions and natural expressions, no one was his superior."

Campion's *Ten Reasons* was written in Latin and designed for the consumption of the learned. The congregation at St. Mary's, Oxford, was very much surprised one morning to find copies of the little book lying on their seats. It is still well worth reading. More interesting, however, to a modern reader is the famous "Brag" dashed off at top speed and addressed to the Privy Council. "Touching our Society," a passage runs, "be it known unto you that we have made a league — all the Jesuits in the world . . . cheerfully to carry the cross you shall lay upon us, and never to despair of your recovery, while we have a man left to enjoy your Tyburn, or to be racked with your torments, and consumed with your prisons. The expense is reckoned, the enterprise is begun; it is of God, it cannot be withstood. So the Faith was planted: so it must be restored."
To Elizabeth he wrote in Latin: "Make thyself worthy of thy ancestors, worthy of thy genius, worthy of thy praises, worthy

of thy fortune. . . . There will come, Elizabeth, the day which will show thee clearly which have loved thee, the Society of Jesus or the offspring of Luther."

In these works there is reference to his expectation of martyrdom. Never did he pass Tyburn, so Persons tells us in his *Memoirs*, "But Campion would always pass bareheaded, and making a deep bow, both because of the sign of the Cross, and in honour of those martyrs who had suffered there, and also because he used to say that he would have his own combat there." When that day at last came and he stood beneath the gallows praying for the Queen, the mob yelled at him, "Which Queen?" and he made answer, "For Elizabeth, your Queen and mine."

This beautiful and romantic spirit had an astonishing knack for saying at all times just the right thing. When sentence was passed upon him and six other priests in Westminster Hall — which witnessed that day one of the most memorable scenes enacted even under its roof — Campion began to chant the *Te Deum*. He could hardly stand during his trial, so terribly had he been racked, and he could not raise his hands; but he found strength to make a speech which concluded: "The only thing that we have now to say is that, if our religion do make us traitors, then we are worthy to be condemned, but otherwise are and have been as true subjects as ever the Queen had. In condemning us you condemn all your own ancestors, all the ancient priests, bishops and kings — all that was once the glory of England, the island of saints and the most devoted child of the See of Peter. For what have we taught, however you may qualify with the odious name of treason, that they did not uniformly teach? To be condemned with these old lights not of England only but of the world by their degenerate descendants is both glory and gladness to us. God lives; posterity will live; their judgment is not so liable to corruption as that of you who are now going to torture us to death."

Yet even after that he might have escaped. Now and then it happened that one of a batch of martyrs who had seen the ghastly butcher's work done upon those who had gone just before into the hangman's hands, broke down at the last minute and abjured to save his life. Campion could have escaped, not with humiliation, but with glory of a kind. He was given the special privilege of a private interview with Elizabeth in Leicester's house, when it is said that the Queen offered him the Archbishopric of Canterbury if only he would recant. This is, on the face of it, unlikely. But it is probable enough that she offered him high preferment. It would have been worth a great deal to the English Reformers to have secured the adhesion of so distinguished a man. Instead he refused, "Come rack, come rope," and went so blithely to his death that the crowd gasped to see men being drawn on hurdles laugh and, on ascending the ladder, kiss the executioner's bloody hands.

Cecil stood beside the scaffold on which Campion and his fellow priests died. So did a young man of fashion named Henry Walpole. A drop of the martyr's blood splashed on his fine clothes, and he went away meditating.[4] Not many years afterwards he died, a Jesuit himself now, at Tyburn.

I am not wishing to write a Catholic Book of Martyrs. But these things must be recorded if we wish to understand the spirit of the Jesuits and the other missionary priests. If there is not a great deal in the conduct of the clergy at the time of Elizabeth's accession which is particularly heroic — for heroism, after all, is a quality of which not all men are capable — nothing can surpass the courage and faith of the Elizabethan martyrs, clerical and lay, men, women, and children. Thus when Richard Gwynn, who had kept a school at Overton and was executed on that sole account, was sentenced, his wife called out in court to ask why she was not sentenced too: all they needed, she said, was that they give a few bribes and they would find enough suborned witnesses to send her to the gallows with her husband. Margaret Clithero submitted to the penalty of *peine forte et dure* rather than plead, so was pressed, a pregnant woman, to death. Young Thomas Sherwood, for only planning to enter Douay, endured the quartering knife. In all, about a hun-

---

[4] The executioners turned a pretty penny in selling relics of the martyrs to Catholics.

dred and fifty priests and fifty lay people were put to death, and between fifty and a hundred more died in prison. Each case has its distinctive features; any case might serve for all the others.

The means employed for effecting these judicial murders may not have been any worse than those in vogue in the modern dictatorships, but we have to go to the Ogpu and the Gestapo to find parallels in history. The government relied upon spies, whom it introduced sometimes into the seminaries, where several of them actually took orders. No Catholic was ever safe from delation, even from relatives or supposed friends. Campion, for instance, was betrayed by a man who had served his Mass on the day he was taken. The priests, therefore, had always to go in disguise — as doctors, or soldiers, or hunters, or fashionable men of the world. Cecil, of course, sneered at them for discarding the clerical garb — laid aside because of him.

From house to house they were passed along, at each saying Mass and hearing confessions and reconciling the lapsed. Of "conversions" in the ordinary sense, there were no doubt few: the priests rarely came into sufficiently intimate contact with Protestants for that. Their mission was to the neglected Catholics who were in danger of falling away. The "converts," then, must be understood to be people who had, in a time of stress or weakness, conformed to Anglicanism, but who had remained Catholics at heart, as were many who were never reached by the missionaries.

Now and then the priests found shelter with friendly Protestants, men who retained a vague sympathy for the "Old Religion" or who acted as they did out of human decency. But it was dangerous for such men to harbour "seditious Jesuits" — all priests were often lumped together under that designation — as it was still more dangerous for the priests to accept their hospitality.

Even with their own people they could not always be safe. Too great an enthusiasm or some other indiscretion might betray their secret. Spies and pursuivants, hungry for reward, were constantly on their trail. But hiding-holes, many of which

PHILIP II OF SPAIN
From the painting by Titian in the
Gallery in Florence.

"And Christ Their Capitain"

are still in existence and show with what elaborate cunning they were made, proved at times a refuge when a suspected house was searched. These, however, were looked for, and often discovered.

Once captured, the lot of the missionaries was hard indeed. Almost invariably they were put to hideous tortures, the rack being the most effectual instrument. Its use was, strictly speaking, illegal, for it was considered a royal prerogative to be employed only on occasions of extreme need. This was waived in the case of priests; it was always hoped that the sufferer would in his torment give information implicating other Catholics. Few were the men who could bear the pangs without saying anything: even Campion had some matter dragged out of him by this means.

Of the priest hunters, Richard Topcliffe was the most infamous. He commenced his career, as we have seen, by getting hold of "Old Norton's" lands, and he continued to find persecution profitable. In addition to his fees he got rich pickings. Thus we hear of him wrangling with Sir Christopher Wray, the Lord Chief Justice who sentenced Campion, for a stall in Lincoln cathedral. It was only fair that the Elizabethan Establishment should suffer depredations to provide for priest hunters.

Perhaps the incident that throws the worst light upon Topcliffe, was his suing a certain Fitzherbert for £5,000, a sum that he alleged Fitzherbert had promised to pay him on condition that Topcliffe got hold of Fitzherbert's father and uncle and a Mr. Bassett and torture them to death. The arrangement was not denied by Fitzherbert — only he made what he considered the conclusive objection that Mr. Bassett was still alive, and contended that, though the other two victims were dead, they had died from jail fever and not from the effects of Topcliffe's racking. In the end, it is consoling to reflect, Topcliffe obtained the reward of virtue — and Fitzherbert's estate.

There does not seem to have been in this man, a person of culture and a Member of Parliament, anything of that implacable hatred of Catholicism which may be offered as a partial excuse for Walsingham — a hatred which may have been increased by his own cousin's joining the Jesuits. It was rather that Topcliffe enjoyed inflicting torment for its own sweet sake. Yet — and this is a very Elizabethan touch — he was a connoisseur of belles-lettres, reminding us of Anthony Munday, the poet, who found that the "taking of priests" paid better than the making of plays. As an example of Topcliffe's disinterested appreciation for literature, we have the following letter written by Francis Bacon to his brother Anthony:[5] "I send you the *Supplication*[6] which Mr. Topcliffe lent me. It is curiously written, and worth the writing out for the art; though the argument be bad. But it is lent me but for two or three days. So God keep you." I, too, am tempted to copy out a passage from this book here. But surely praise from so eminent an authority as Bacon — to say nothing of Topcliffe — will suffice. It is — like Southwell's style — curious to reflect upon what the exquisite relations between the torturer and the tortured must have been in that inner room in Topcliffe's house.

As a tribute to the confidence in which he was held — and to his proficiency in his profession — Topcliffe had special permission to keep a private rack at home to which the official rack in the Tower was reputed to be a mere tickling. Though we need not believe that he had the Queen's favour to the extent of which he boasted, it is evident that he had her approval.[7] Yet Elizabeth had the effrontery to tell Mendoza: "I have never castigated the Catholics except when they would not acknowledge me as their Queen; in spiritual matters I believe as they do."

Conditions being what they were, it was almost impossible for a priest not to be captured before long. The dark, morose Walsingham had his spies everywhere, and many a missionary landed only to be arrested, notice of his coming having been sent to England in advance. Some of the "correspondents" were

---

[5] The letter may be found in Spedding's *Life of Bacon*, Vol. III, p. 308.

[6] *A Humble Supplication to Her Majesty* (Douay), 1595.

[7] One of the seminary priests racked by Topcliffe in 1592 reported some very lewd conversation from his tormentor about the Queen. In saying what he did, Topcliffe was surely a liar. I record the fact only because his obscene talk further reveals his character.

no doubt engaged in more reputable work than giving information about priests, and among these must be included most of the men Walsingham had posted in thirteen different parts of France, with seven in Holland, nine in Germany, five in Spain, and three even in Turkey. Many, too, of the Catholic exiles on the continent, in the hope of keeping in the good graces of the government, acted as its "correspondents" — though not to the detriment of their coreligionists. Walsingham is said to have actually had a cardinal in Rome who posted him on affairs.

Ordinary secret service, however, is one thing; spying upon priests, quite another. This, as may be imagined, was undertaken only by the basest sort of men — men of the type of the ex-priest, Tyrrell, and of the seminarian, Gifford. Another of Walsingham's agents entered the college at Douay in order to attempt to murder everybody there including — and especially hoping for — Dr. Allen himself. A typical letter of one of these spies, written some time in the early eighties, and signed Samuel Pittingat, is headed "Jesus" and tells of "such manner dealings as the Papists do use towards protestants for to make them deny their Lord & Master and so revolt from their faith." The pious spy goes on: "We learnt works without faith to be sufficient for salvation. . . . Of purgatory also there was somewhat to be seen, and how in the Sacrament we did eat and drink the body and blood of Christ really and substantially with an infinite company more of such devilish doctrines amongst Christians not to be named." After much more of the same stuff, the Elizabethan Uriah Heep got down to business at last and sent — what Walsingham was paying him for — a list of the students in the seminary. No wonder that Cecil, who was a man of rather finer grain than the head of his secret service, would write upon some of these documents, "I know this man to be a liar," or notations to the same effect. There was no reason why the government should treat agents of such a stamp with any consideration. Once they undertook this employment they could never leave it, nor was there any assurance that a spy would preserve a whole skin. There is good reason to believe that toward the end of the reign men who had been used as *agents provacateurs* were sacrificed as soon as their usefulness, except for adorning a scaffold, had ceased.

Elizabeth had a strong dislike for Walsingham, which was to her credit — as was perhaps even the fact that she several times threw her slippers at his head; but she found him indispensable in the dirtier sort of matters of state. She once told him "The only thing you are good for is a protector of heretics." (She meant "Puritans"; she might have said "a persecutor of Catholics.") All the same, she understood well enough that she had to have available somebody who would do the kind of work that Cecil shrank from. Walsingham was destined to perform the foulest of all her jobs for her — the snaring of Babington and the sending of Mary Queen of Scots to her death.

Cecil, however, cannot be acquitted from all responsibility for the hunting down and execution of priests. The policy was his, though he relegated the details to others. But in a really important case he would himself interrogate a man stretched on the rack. And persecution was defended by him in his pamphlet, *The Execution of Justice*. It was he who devised the "bloody question" which had nothing to do with fact, but with the accused's private opinions: not with what had actually been done, but with what a man might do in some purely hypothetical situation. For example, if the Catholic prisoner answered that he *did* acknowledge Elizabeth as his lawful Queen, he was at once faced with, "But do you acknowledge her supremacy in all cases as well spiritual as temporal?" To that there was only one answer a Catholic could honestly give — and it sent him to Tyburn, although it is obvious that the falling back upon such questions was an admission on the part of the prosecution that it lacked definite evidence.

There were questions on which a Catholic could hedge, but there was no dodging the dreaded "bloody question," introduced in 1588: "In the event of a Catholic invasion, which side would you take, the Queen's or the Pope's?" It was no use for the wretched man to say that the question was unfair, that it implied simplifications which did not exist, or that he would decide when the moment arrived — if it ever did — or that it depended upon whether the invasion was for a secular or a spiritual reason. No fine scholastic distinctions were permitted at these tribunals. The accused was lost, whatever answer he gave. Here we touch the very core of cruelty. The tortures of the rack and the knife at the gibbet were hardly worse than the choice forced upon all who remained under the Roman obedience: for it was a choice between a beloved country and a God who was loved still more — or rather between Elizabeth and God. The only way out was the acceptance of the official religion.

To show how hopeless was the predicament of a Catholic — especially one who was a priest — I might cite as an example the examination of Father James Bell, which Father Pollen includes in his *Unpublished Documents relating to the English Martyrs.* He got the usual short shrift. When the court demanded whether or not he was reconciled to the Catholic Church, and he admitted that he was, the judge exclaimed, "Oh, that is high treason!" Nothing more was necessary.

Yet the laws against Catholics were too ferocious to be uniformly enforced; had they been, the whole Catholic population of England and Wales would soon have been wiped out. Even the £20 a month fine for recusancy brought in, on an average, no more than £6,000 a year — which is what twenty-five recusants would have had to pay, if they paid in full. But the laws were there, ready to be enforced at any time. It was high treason to go abroad without the government's permission; it was high treason to stay abroad when summoned home; it was high treason to say Mass; it was high treason to harbour a priest; it was high treason for a priest to reconcile anyone to the Catholic Church (and also high treason to be reconciled); it was high treason to be ordained abroad; it was high treason to admit the Supremacy of the Pope; it was even high treason (as Cuthbert Mayne found to his cost) to bring an Agnus Dei into England. Everything was high treason that the government chose to make high treason. There was not a single Catholic in England who could not have been prosecuted and executed under laws so comprehensive.

Such laws could only be enforced by massacre. Therefore, the government took credit to itself for mildness in their application. Priests were not always hanged; some were even allowed to go abroad, on condition that they remained there. It may have been that the gorge of Elizabeth and Cecil rose at the thought of a strict enforcement of their penal legislation; they certainly shrank from the odium that a strict enforcement would have brought upon their heads. They must be condemned, not because of the number of Catholics they put to death — these were an insignificant few when compared with the hundreds hanged every year for felony — but for the fact that they put men to death for their religious beliefs — and then labelled it treason. Well might Milner, in his *Letters to a Prebendary,* call Elizabeth's persecution meaner than her father's; he at least made no attempt to misrepresent the attitude of More and Fisher. Mary, too, had been honest in the matter; Elizabeth and Cecil never were. They gave themselves away completely by providing a standing offer of pardon to such of the condemned as would apostatise.

Yet this is not to deny that there was some sort of a Protestant case. There was no very clear differentiation drawn in those days between politics and religion. An unqualified allegiance was considered necessary for the safety of the Crown. And though such an attitude is incomprehensible today, it was taken as axiomatic then. Whatever force the prevalent theory may have had (which was a great deal) there was also the impulsion of what was thought of as practical politics. Rome had made an enormous blunder by sending an expedition to Ireland at the same moment that the General of the Jesuits sent Persons and Campion to England. Though nobody deplored the Papal intervention in Ireland more than the two Jesuits — for nobody realised more keenly than they what complications this would create for missionaries working in England — it was inevitable that in the popular mind the two efforts, while entirely unconnected, should have been regarded as two factors in the same general scheme. And to make matters worse, the Pope sent to

Ireland as his agent the "Dr. Slanders" who had proposed Elizabeth's excommunication at the Council of Trent and who had written a book attacking her. To have urged that the Pope was acting as he did because Ireland was a Papal fief, forfeited by Elizabeth because of her heresy, would have only further infuriated the English government.

Therefore, everything united to put the English Catholics into what Professor Black calls a "tragic dilemma." No men were more patriotic than the missionaries who were ready to lay down their lives for their country's good; no men could be more easily convicted, under the existing laws, of high treason. Yet had the government been satisfied with a protestation of full temporal allegiance on the part of Catholic subjects the difficulty would have vanished. Unfortunately Elizabeth did not wish it removed: rather she seized upon it as a weapon. She and her advisers were determined to admit no compromise; she would revenge herself in England for the affront of Papal intervention in Ireland. The political concepts of the time were her justification. Bishop David Mathew explains: "As the old idea of the Church was weakened, [the] Tudor theory of kingship increasingly filled the place and borrowed the phrase of religion, working through the still Christian trend of the de-Catholicised mind of that century." In other words, nothing less than an absolute submission in matters of religion was required. Queen Elizabeth had virtually become Pope Joan.

All the same, one would hardly wish the story — stained though it be with infamy — to be told in any other terms, since it is also the story of so much moral splendour. If the Catholic mission in England ultimately failed, or seemed to fail, the martyrs won their palms, and gave an enduring inspiration — to Catholic and Protestant alike. Desperate remedies were afterwards sought by some Catholics, decisions so wrong as to be all but fatal were taken by men who, brought to believe that nothing could be accomplished except by invasion, came to associate themselves with the "Spanish Party." Yet even these men had another ideal at the bottom of their hearts: the general

tone of the period was most fully expressed in one of the poems
written about the execution of Campion:

> "God knows it is not force or might,
>   Nor war nor warlike band,
> Nor shield and spear, nor dint of sword,
>   That must convert the land;
> It is the blood of martyrs shed,
>   It is the noble train
> That fight with word and not with sword —
> And Christ their Capitain!"

14

"The Faith of a Monkey"

WHEN Campion and the priests condemned with him lay in prison awaiting execution, an appeal was made on their behalf to Francis, Duke of Anjou, who was in London at the time. It was supposed that if anybody could move Elizabeth to mercy it was the man who appeared to have at last obtained her definite promise of marriage, and that, as a Catholic, he could not refuse such an appeal. He was found playing tennis. In courteous silence he listened to what was said. Then he stood rubbing his chin for a few minutes, still silent. At last he swung round to his opponent and called "Play!"

The last of Elizabeth's courtships has been called the masterpiece of diplomacy and was certainly among the great exhibitions of her dissimulating finesse. It was, however, a good deal else. The long-drawn-out wooing — it lasted for ten years — had about it something genuine and pathetic, especially in its later stages. The more quaint, grotesque, and even ridiculous, it became, the more evident it also became that the heart of the Queen was really touched.

I do not propose to enter here at any length into the political aspects of the affair, except to say that there always was a political aspect — and that the most important one — to everything Elizabeth did. She would never have entertained her lover's suit except for the political advantage to be extracted from it; nor would he have laid seige to her except for the same reason. Whether or not she ever wished to marry the Duke, she wished to keep him in play because of his ambitions in the Netherlands: these she could restrain most effectively by holding out the prospect of marriage. He, for his part, was able to further his ambitions by being known as Elizabeth's prospective husband. Moreover, though niggardly with regard to money, she kept him in funds. She was good for that, if for nothing else.

Before coming to the career of this young man, it might be as well to say something about his name. At the baptismal font he was christened — of all things in the world! — "Hercules," a name which, upon the death of his brother, the husband of the Queen of Scots, he quickly and understandably changed to Francis. When he was first put forward as a possible husband for the English Queen, shortly before the Massacre of St. Bartholomew's Day, he was fifteen — twenty-four years younger than his prospective bride. At that time he was the Duke of Alençon, and is often called Alençon to the end of his life by historians who wish to distinguish him from his brother Henry, Duke of Anjou, to whose title he succeeded when Henry ascended the throne of France.

There is a further confusion. When Henry became King of Poland in 1573 Francis was called "Monsieur" in his place, the designation by which the heir presumptive was known. He did not become Monsieur *and* Anjou until three years later. These explanations should be borne in mind, because we first hear of him as "Alençon," then as "Monsieur,"and finally as "Anjou." Let us for the sake of convenience stick to the "Alençon."

He was an unprepossessing little fellow, pockmarked and with an extraordinary nose. His enemies in the Low Countries seized, so to speak, upon this feature, and made up a song which I will render as:

"Flemings, what would you suppose
From Francis of the double-nose:
For reason shows it but well-placed —
The double-nose for one two-faced!"

Elizabeth used to address him by the endearment of "little Frog." She must, however, have found his vivacity as amusing as his youth was appealing. It is clear that in some strange way she was really fond of him.

If he was dropped after the massacre in 1572 he was taken up again in 1576. The reason for this was, in part, that he was expected to be more amenable than his brother Henry had been about religion. In 1575 he had gone over to the Huguenot side, though this may have been largely by way of making a political diversion against his brother the King. It seemed to be a standing rule in France that the heir presumptive led the opposition to the royal policies. So embarrassing a move made Catherine de' Medici entertain a suggestion made by the Walloon nobles that Alençon marry one of Philip's daughters and be appointed viceroy of the Catholic provinces of the Netherlands. Alençon, in order to aid this plan, switched to the League for support, though he was careful at the same time not to give up all pretensions to Elizabeth's hand. She was to be held in reserve. Besides, he needed her backing in Flanders. Therefore, to free himself from the new Guise threat, Henry was obliged, in his turn, to give some sort of sanction to Alençon's adventures. He did not want his brother to be established and dominated by Spain. It was preferable to allow him to play his own hand, at the same time disclaiming that he was given any official support. From Elizabeth's point of view Alençon could be used in two capacities: that of strengthening England's ties with France as against Spain, and that of wrecking the Catholic designs of the Guises.

Yet Elizabeth, however much she might waver from day to day, never wished to involve herself in so open a connexion with Alençon's Flemish affairs as to bring upon herself a war with Spain. It was not part of her scheme that Philip should be actually ousted from the Low Countries — least of all by France. She merely wished to weaken the Spanish administration, and for this Alençon served well enough. Therefore to the end of his life the hope of marriage was kept dangling before him — a hope which was at once a spur and a bridle. As in the case of Alençon's brother before him, Elizabeth wanted a French alliance rather than a French marriage.

This was, at all events, true of Elizabeth as Queen; as a woman she got a good deal of fun out of the courtship and also some sly enjoyment of her own cleverness in throwing dust in the eyes of foreigners and her English subjects. Even in 1579, when Alençon was about to make his first visit to England, she told her Council that she "would give them her word she would not marry." But they, knowing how rarely she kept her word, of course took that promise as meaning the opposite. In spite of everything — Elizabeth's age and the extreme unlikeliness of her bearing a child, and their past experience with her marriage projects — they debated it as a serious possibility, the Council being about evenly divided in its favour and in opposition. Cecil said it met with his approval, but took care to keep out of the way most of the time Alençon was in England.

What happened was, indeed, not very edifying. In June, 1579, the Duke sent over to England his friend Jehan de Simier, Baron de St. Marc, his Master of the Wardrobe and his dearest friend. And Simier at once began to make violent love to Elizabeth, which she relished enormously — all the more because her situation was so piquant.

This Simier was what many people think of as a "typical Frenchman." The fact that he had had a great tragedy in his life, when he caught his brother and his wife in an intrigue — it ended in a stabbing for the one and the poison cup for the other — had not turned him into a misogynist. So far from that, it actually increased his address with women and perhaps even made him all the more attractive in their eyes. At all events, it seemed to do so in Elizabeth's. We hear of him being very much at home in the Queen's bedroom, stealing her nightcap and sending it (along with one of her handkerchiefs) as a tender token to his master. Elizabeth liked it that he stood on no ceremony with her. Once when she called on him early in the morning, before he was dressed, he appeared, perfectly at his ease, in naked legs. She had no objection to such free familiarities.

An elaborate pretence was kept up on both sides that the ardent love making was really between Elizabeth and Alençon; but it naturally aroused a good deal of comment. Leicester and Hatton grew so furious that they threatened to murder Simier, with the result that, to protect him, Elizabeth lodged him in a bedroom beside her own — thus making them more furious still. Though Dudley had long abandoned all hope of marrying the Queen — and was now (this was something Elizabeth did not know) married again — he still claimed prior rights in her affections. About Sir Christopher Hatton — who was also reputed to be her lover — a word needs to be said.

Everybody has heard how Elizabeth had singled him out for her favour because his graceful dancing had caught her eye: it is about all most people do know of the man. But having caught her fancy, Hatton was made Captain of the bodyguard in 1572, and Vice-Chamberlain and a knight in 1578. As a favourite, his pickings were good. To him went part of the Bishop of Ely's London estate, the Bishop retaining little beyond the right of gathering a strictly limited number of roses every year. The names of the London Streets, Ely Place and Hatton Garden, commemorate this transaction. Elizabeth ended by creating him, in 1587, her Lord Chancellor, though all the lawyers wondered what his legal qualifications could be. However, he seems to have been an amiable fellow and was probably not so much of a fool as is often supposed — any more than Leicester was a fool — even if he did owe his rise, as Leicester owed his, rather to the Queen's caprice than to his own ability.

As to the charge that Hatton was Elizabeth's lover, this rests on a letter by Mary Queen of Scots, and on one of Hatton's own. The latter, dated June 5, 1573, reads in part: "Would God I were with you for but one hour! My wits are overwrought with thoughts. I find myself amazed. Bear with me, my most sweet dear Lady; passion overcometh me. I can write no more. Love me; for I love you. . . . Shall I utter this most familiar term 'farewell'? Yes, ten thousand thousand farewells. He speaketh it that most dearly loveth you." That would seem conclusive; yet we need not, I think, take it quite at its face value. Elizabeth's courtiers were expected to use the language of hyperbole. It did no one any harm to declare himself in love with the Queen.

Whether Leicester and Hatton were Elizabeth's lovers or not, they had been sufficiently favoured to feel pangs of jealousy when they saw how she was treating the smirking Frenchman. She admitted him to the intimacy of her private menagerie. Where Hatton was her "Sheep," and Cecil her "Spirit," and Walsingham her "Moon," and the Master of Gray her "Hare," and Leicester her "Eyes," and Alençon (when he appeared in England) her "Frog," Simier received the affectionate title of her "Monkey." And Leicester and Hatton did not like it at all.

But Simier was not without a good card to play. As Leicester had tried to murder him, Simier "told on" Leicester, who had not long before secretly married Lettice, the widow of Walter Devereux, Earl of Essex, by whom he had had two children while Essex was in Ireland. Rumour even whispered that Leicester had poisoned the husband. But Elizabeth (though she must have heard something about the liason) had so far been kept in ignorance about the marriage. So Simier's talebearing effectually spiked Leicester's guns. The Queen flew into one of her grand rages and the Earl was, for the time being, obliged to retire in disgrace, leaving a clear field to Simier.

On August 17, 1579, Alençon arrived at the palace at Greenwich to pay court in person, and remained about a fortnight. He, too, wooed in whirlwind fashion, while his understudy withdrew to the background. Though Elizabeth must have got a shock when she saw the French Prince's double nose, Gallic ardour proved an almost sufficient compensation. He made such rapid progress that, upon returning to the Low Countries, he felt the game was as good as won.

Others were not so sure: they knew Elizabeth better. When Hatton asked her how she proposed to get out of the marriage, she answered, "With words, the coin most current with the French." There were so many words — compliments, evasions, vows, and ambiguities — and action dragged so slowly that in 1581 the by-this-time disillusioned Simier said that he would believe the marriage had taken place only when he knew the curtains to be drawn, the candle out, and Monsieur in bed with the Queen. Nevertheless, so as to leave nothing undone, he wrote to Elizabeth, "Be assured on the faith of a monkey that your frog lives in hope."

"The Faith of a Monkey"

The quaintness of the courtship was exceeded only by its dilatoriness — a dilatoriness not all on one side. It would be absurd to suppose that young Alençon ever loved the aging Elizabeth, in spite of all his fine fantastic speeches. How could he be expected to marry one whom his brother so many years ago had ungallantly described as an old hag with an ulcer on her leg? But since it was as necessary, for the furtherance of his ambitions, that it should be believed he was going to marry her as it was for Elizabeth's own schemes, a marriage treaty was signed on November 24, 1579. The Queen thereafter wrote fervent love letters to Alençon — and kept denying to her English intimates that she had any intention of marrying at all. On the one hand we have her words to Alençon: "Now all the world will see whether I, as was pretended, have made you a prisoner, or you have made me a prisoner." On the other hand, this captive of love told her Council, "I would not marry Alençon to be empress of the world."

It was about this time that we first hear of Elizabeth's carrying around a volume of polyglot prayers, two of which were in English, with one each in French, Italian, Latin, and Greek. This precious compilation, written in her own hand, is still preserved, and translations of the prayers may be found in Mr. Chamberlin's *Private Life of Queen Elizabeth*. If some of the devotions may be dismissed as mere literary exercises, there is among them at least one brokenhearted cry of apparently genuine religious feeling. For the Greek prayer has "Thou didst not drive from Thee the sinful woman who approached Thee with tears, nor didst Thou reject the publican who repented, nor banished the thief who acknowledged Thy kingdom." Can it be that, even so late in her life, Elizabeth was prepared, in the event of marrying Alençon, to become a Catholic, if somehow she could break her fetters? That we do not know; at any rate love — for there *was* love here, mixed with the baser elements of politics — having been experienced, induced a spasm of piety.

Perhaps it was that Elizabeth had never really known her own mind. Cecil had complained in 1579 that she blazed in anger at anyone who argued against the marriage, though she would not say definitely whether or not she wanted it. "She looked," he said, "from their hands that they should with one accord have made a special suit to her for the same": the pleading of the Council was to relieve her of responsibility if she did marry; whether she married or not it would be flattering that they should ask her to do so. In 1581 she took up the same attitude, telling the Council that she expected them to beseech her to "marry and have a child of her body." She resented any doubt as to her capacity to bear children, and considered that such a doubt was implied in the Council's failure to urge the marriage with sufficient eagerness. Yet at no time could she have really intended to marry Alençon.

There were moments, however, during this courtship when it would seem that as a consequence of having made a lifelong practice of deceiving others she lost all sense of realities — and only succeeded in deceiving herself. Thus, she informed the Swedish Ambassador that she meant to marry for the sake of an heir; on another occasion she said, "In marrying I hope to have children, to which I see no obstacle." People, with their tongues in their cheek, brought her tall yarns of a woman they had seen with their own eyes: she was fifty-six and eight months gone with child. (We hear no more of that wonder a month later.) Elizabeth's doctors were consulted; they agreed that childbearing was still possible in her case. Despite this, she sighed in Alençon's ear, "My doctors warn me that if I have a child I shall die in childbed." It is impossible to say how much of all this was play acting; it appears, however, that at fleeting moments Elizabeth was willing to accept marriage — and even to run the rather remote risk of motherhood — at forty-eight. But only at fleeting moments.

On November 1, 1581, Alençon came again to England, and this time he stayed three months. On November 22 a remarkable scene took place in Greenwich palace. To Mauvissière, the French Ambassador, the Queen suddenly turned and told him, "Write this to your master: the Duke will be my husband." Then, as though by a sudden impulse, she kissed Alençon on the lips in front of everybody there and, that not being sufficient, she sent for the absent courtiers and presented the Duke as their future King. On his hand they saw the ring Elizabeth had just given him. At last the business was settled. Cecil was informed, upon which he murmured, "Blessed be God! Her Majesty has done her part; the realm must complete the rest."

Yet even after that it was still not all plain sailing by any means. Protestant feeling against the Queen's marrying a Catholic (with whatever safeguards on paper) ran high. Cecil's approbation was in all likelihood given merely because he knew that nothing was going to happen. Others, who were not so deep in Elizabeth's confidence, could not feel so sure. As an instance of Puritan sentiment we have what happened, in September of 1579, to John Stubbs. He had been a Member of Parliament and had written pamphlets for the government and had officiated at the racking of Dr. Story. These services did not save him when he ventured to publish his *Discovery of a Gaping Gulf, wherein England is like to be swallowed up by another French Marriage, if the Lord forbid not the Banns by letting her see the Sin and Punishment thereof.* With the same explicitness shown by his title he wrote that if the Duke's Mass were brought to England it "would be as a wild fire that no seas could quench." Bluntly he told the Queen that the Valois were rotten with disease, and that this was a French trick to kill her by leading her into marriage at a time of life when childbearing would probably prove fatal. Elizabeth was furious at these remarks about her age; but the people in general, wrote Mendoza — of course he was in a position to observe only the noisy London Puritans — "threaten rebellion about it."

The Queen had Stubbs and his publisher, Page, tried and sentenced to have their right hands cut off. "God save the Queen!" shouted Stubbs, waving his hat with his left hand; he then fainted. Page instead lifted his bloody stump and remarked, "I have left there a true Englishman's hand." Elizabeth's anger increased when she heard of it; for she heard as well that the crowd had not cheered her name when Stubbs had so dramatically expressed his loyalty. Very well, since he had caused the trouble, he should go to jail. And in the Tower he stayed for eighteen months to expiate his additional tactlessness.

Meanwhile official England went through the make-believe that the Queen's marriage to Alençon was going to take place. To celebrate the approaching betrothal, the French Commissioners who came over to arrange the details were entertained not only with the grosser delights of bear- and bull-baiting but a charming symbolical spectacle in the tilting yard at Whitehall. Sir Philip Sidney, Fulke Greville, the Earl of Arundel, and Lord Windsor — called for the occasion the Four Children of Desire — set out to capture the Fortress of Perfect Beauty. They issued their formal challenge to the Queen as she left her chapel on Sunday morning. Then the heroic Four, appearing in all their magnificence, sang songs, made ornate speeches, and threw roses at the Fortress. Its defenders, among whom were Adam and Eve, of course beat off the attackers. As if that were not enough, the Four champions came again the next day in a chariot, this time with a lady named Desire. Again they failed, despite their valour, and at sunset sent a herald to make their surrender. Desire, they had to admit, was impotent against a citadel armed by Virtue. It was a subtle way of telling the French Commissioners that they were wasting their time.

In prosaic fact, as against the poetic pageant, it is not quite so certain that Elizabeth's virtue was invulnerable. Mauvissière, it is true, wrote in his *Mémoires:* "If some persons have wished to tax her falsely with having amorous attachments . . . these are inventions forged by the malevolent, and from the cabinets of Ambassadors, to prevent those to whom it would have been most useful from making an alliance with her." It may be so. But all that Henry IV would commit himself to was that "Among the things most inscrutable to intelligence was whether Queen Elizabeth was a maid or no."

It is still inscrutable. One of the minor poets of her time wrote in celebration of

> "A most renowned Virgin Queen,
> Whose like on earth was never seen."

"The Faith of a Monkey"

He did so with no ironical intention; but Elizabeth's virginity was, according to most accounts, of an unusual order indeed: the like on earth was never seen. Even Miss Strickland, who admires Elizabeth and is careful to veil her improprieties under early Victorian reticence, is frequently obliged to admit sadly that the Queen did not always behave as a "gentlewoman" should. And the sober Lingard wrote that "Dudley, though the most favoured, was not considered her only lover; among his rivals were Hatton, and Raleigh, and Oxford, and Blount, and Simier, and Anjou; and it was afterwards believed that her licentious habits survived, even when the fires of wantonness had been quenched by the chill of age." I cannot feel so sure. If the Queen was, in fact, licentious, it is questionable whether she ever had a "lover" in the ordinary sense. However, I need not repeat what I have already said about this.

What is exceedingly pathetic is to find Elizabeth ensnared during these late years in what looks very much like love — as much love as she was capable of giving. Some "wantonness" there may have been in it; but this last love sprang, I cannot help feeling, from loneliness and a desperate determination to defy old age. One day when Alençon was talking to her wildly — "laying it on" for her benefit — she begged him "not to threaten a poor old woman in her kingdom." One cannot forebear a smile; one is at the same time touched. In June, after he had left her never to see her again, she wrote — about a hundred such letters passed between the couple — "Monsieur, my dearest, grant pardon to the poor old woman who honoured you (I dare say it) as much as any young wench you will ever find." That, too, may be pondered; whatever it meant, it is a genuine *cri de coeur*.

But whatever Elizabeth's secret purposes — or her secret desires — may have been, when it came to the inescapable issue, she tried to bind her little Hercules to Protestantism, as she had tried to bind her previous suitors. He proved almost embarrassingly complaisant to the new conditions she imposed when negotiations began again in 1581. He even said he would abjure his faith for her sake. But he probably agreed to that condition

243

only because he knew that the other conditions in the contract would prove impossible. It was he who artfully suggested that she demand Calais and Havre as security for the carrying out of the French King's promises, and he could have made such a suggestion only because he knew that his brother would never accept it. In the end his insistence on religious privileges brought the marriage project to nothing. On the essential point he was firm. In any event what he sought was not to marry Elizabeth but to be known to be going to marry her.

An undated letter, written just after the breakdown of the negotiations, makes Alençon's stand about religion clear. Elizabeth writes to him: "I beg you to believe that I am not such a bad Christian, and that my love for you is not so small, that I should refuse to agree, and that you should have your own religion for yourself, free and without let, though under such conditions that it would offend our people as little as possible. But seeing that you insist on the articles, while I perceive such dissatisfaction as I do, I must consider myself as most unfortunate that I was [not] born for that great hour which God seemed lately to be preparing for me. . . . And notwithstanding that I cannot be yours, as you desire, yet grant me at least this grace — that a friendship be accorded me the most close that ever was between princes." She, like Alençon, found religion a good excuse for avoiding marriage.

The Queen, having to get rid of him, promised to lend him £60,000 — allowing for the £10,000 she had paid at the beginning of the year. It was really damages for breach of promise or what Americans call (with a mixture of cynicism and sentimentality) "heart balm." It was just like her that she did not pay the full sum she had promised.

But she accompanied Alençon as far as Canterbury, where in parting she avowed that she already held herself to be his wife. Then the impatient courtiers took him to Dover and put him on board. Leicester, who was glad to see the last of a rival, saw him safely to Flanders and wrote to Elizabeth to say that he had left the Duke stranded like an old hulk on a sandbank. Elizabeth was not amused. She sat day after day silent and brooding.

"The Faith of a Monkey"

Her recorded comment is "I would give a million to have my Frog swimming in the Thames instead of the stagnant waters of the Netherlands."

To ease her melancholy she wrote a poem, the best that she produced. It runs:

> "I grieve, yet dare not show my discontent;
> I love, and yet am forced to seem to hate;
> I dote, but dare not what I ever meant;
> I seem stark mute, yet inwardly do prate;
> I am, and am not; freeze, and yet I burn;
> Since from myself the other self I turn.

> "My care is like my shadow in the sun —
> Follows me flying; flies when I pursue it;
> Stands and lives by me; does what I have done;
> This too familiar care doth make me rue it.
> No means I find to rid him from my breast,
> Till by the end of things it be suppressed.

> "Some gentler passion steal into my mind —
> For I am soft, and made of melting snow:
> Or be more cruel, love, or be more kind;
> Or let me float or sink, be high or low;
> Or let me live with some more sweet content;
> Or die, and so forget what love e'er meant."

Yet having unbosomed herself in poetry, she confided to the Spanish Ambassador, "An old woman like me has something else to think about beside marriage. The hopes I gave that I would marry Alençon were given for the purpose of getting him out of the Netherland States: I never wished to see them in the hands of the French." Which is no doubt true, though not the whole truth. Elizabeth never told that.

Alençon in spite of everything continued to hope — or to profess hope — and Elizabeth continued to encourage his hope. He had been offered the title of "Defender of the Liberties of the Netherlands" in October, 1578, and this was followed three years later (on the part of the Catholic provinces) with the offer of their sovereignty. Elizabeth had been shrewd enough in 1576 to refuse a still better offer, and again in 1583 she would not accept a sovereignty that was Philip's. There are reasons to believe that she secretly — and using Simier as her agent — worked against Alençon's ambitions. She certainly was annoyed that Alençon had snatched a new honorific, and it may be that Parma's victories the following year were due to Elizabeth's subterranean intrigues. Lacking her support, the Duke could accomplish little. His Dutch allies chased him away in 1583 and on June 10, 1584, he died, his last gesture being one of adoration to the Blessed Sacrament while Mass was being celebrated by his bed.

When the news of Alençon's death reached her, Elizabeth wrote to Catherine de' Medici expressing "The fellowship of regret that I afford you, which cannot exceed mine; for although you were his mother, yet there remain to you several children. But for myself, I find no consolation if it be not death, which I hope will make us soon to meet." The most tough-fibred cannot fail to be moved by such words; the most simple-minded cannot but recall words of Elizabeth's in a very different strain.

This one love, however, grotesque as it may seem, was yet surely real love, whatever may have been its imperfections, whatever the contradictions and duplicities, and even treacheries, with which it was entwined. Whether it was that Elizabeth drew back because she knew Alençon's disillusionment would follow, or because marriage was impossible to her, or because she had achieved her political object without marriage and her cool head told her to refrain, her heart nevertheless hungered. She would not have been Elizabeth had she not indulged herself in a thousand vacillations and inconsistencies. All we can do, in this matter as in others, is to balance her actions and professions one against the other — not trusting either too much — and hope that perhaps we have reached something not too far from the truth.

15

The Netherlands

TO ATTEMPT to trace the relations between the Elizabethan government and the Netherlands would call for the writing of a substantial book. And then it could be no more than an *attempt* — so complex, so constantly wavering was the whole of Elizabeth's diplomacy, so shrouded in mystery were many of its details. As this belongs rather to a history of the times than to a biography of the Queen, I shall permit myself to deal with it very briefly. In so far as it concerns this study its main features can be fairly clearly traced.

At the outset certain things must be remembered. These are the strategic importance of the Low Countries, the traditional friendship between England and the House of Burgundy, the fact that the chief gateway for English exports was the mouth of the Scheldt and, finally, religion.

As the last has generally been given an undue prominence, let me take it first.

The rebellion against the rule of Philip II did not have a motive primarily religious; it was rather that religion was made a pretext for rebellion. The majority of the inhabitants even of the two Northern provinces were Catholics;[1] elsewhere they were overwhelmingly and stoutly Catholic, as they still are. The rich merchants of Antwerp and Amsterdam, however, were largely Calvinist, so that when the rigid fiscal policy of the Spanish administration proved hampering to trade, they were able to discover in their Protestantism the sanctions they needed.

[1] Even today two fifths of the population of Holland — though it is usually thought of as a Protestant country — are Catholic.

247

Further, Elizabeth was not greatly concerned about giving help to Protestants as such; she would have helped any rebels. Her views were put in offhand style to the Spanish Ambassador: "What does it matter to his Majesty if they go to the devil in their own way?" As Professor Black has justly written, "Her one thought was how she could use their respective idealisms for the furtherance of her secular aims." The Dutch Calvinists, though they, too, used religion to serve other ends, bitterly criticised the English on the ground that they "do put on religion, piety, and justice for a cloak, to serve humours withal and please the time, while policy is made both justice, religion, and God."

The second thing to bear in mind is that England was tied to Spain by Philip's having inherited from his grandfather, Philip of Burgundy, the sovereignty of the Low Countries. Elizabeth, as we have seen, was also indebted to Philip for his services in holding off the Pope's excommunication as long as he did and for keeping France in check. But after the signing of the treaty of Blois in 1572 Elizabeth had a French alliance and the previous year Pius had shot the ineffective bolt of the *Regnans in Excelsis*. The change in the situation amounted to a diplomatic revolution.

As for trade, after Alva's embargo at the beginning of 1569, in retaliation for Elizabeth's seizure of the Spanish treasure ships, England, though cut off from the Scheldt, found an outlet for her commerce in German ports, so that it became to the advantage of Spain to patch up an agreement on August 28, 1574 (the convention of Bristol), under which the claims on both sides were assessed and settled. The arrangement aided the Dutch merchants more than it did the English, but it gave Elizabeth a right of re-entry which did not prove to the political benefit of Spain. The Prince of Orange, it is true, rather regretted this — with characteristic selfishness — as the blockade of Scheldt was, upon the whole, to his profit, since his strength lay in Holland and Zeeland. But Elizabeth saw no reason why she should suffer on his behalf, and the Scheldt was reopened.

All through Elizabeth played off Orange and Philip and

The Netherlands

France against one another with a cynical disregard for anything except what she might get out of the troubled conditions. Very early in her reign, when she was on her friendliest terms with Spain, she deliberately fomented local uprisings against Cardinal Granvelle's administration. Pamphlets written and printed in England were smuggled in, along with paid agitators, stressing religious and other grievances. Yet then, as always, she protested that she was not responsible for what was being done, and that nobody was more devoted to Philip's interests than herself.

Her position in the matter was roughly this: while respecting Philip's theoretical sovereignty, she wished to weaken it, without weakening it so much that it would be overthrown. Any open assistance to rebels against their rightful monarch was contrary to her principles; to this extent she was sincere. She was only defending — abroad — the local liberties and the religious freedom she refused at home. She did not wish to have Spain completely subjugate the Netherlands — when it might become a menace to herself; all she was aiming at was to keep Philip so fully occupied with suppressing insurrection that he would have no time or men or money to spare for other designs. But the overthrow of Spanish rule, she feared, would mean the entrance of France into the Netherlands, and that would have been much worse for her than Spain's being there. Accordingly she backed Orange just sufficiently — just barely sufficiently — as to enable him to worry Philip. In the same way she later backed the independent effort of Alençon, on condition that it remain a private enterprise and not be pushed too far. She wished neither adventurer to obtain too much success.

So elaborate a piece of diplomacy — or dissimulation — was never anything but difficult to execute. It called for the utmost finesse. The hotter heads in England — the members of the so-called "war party" — were for stronger measures. "Better not deal at all than not go roundly to work," wrote Thomas Wilson, the Ambassador to the Netherlands. "Valiant working never wanted good fortune." But that was not Elizabeth's way, and she was supported by the temperamental caution of Cecil. It was so much safer to let others do the rebelling, with her secret connivance, even though she gave, by such encouragement, a dangerous precedent to her own subjects. Everything had to be held in exquisite balance.

Some historians are still irritated with her for not accepting the sovereignty of the Low Countries when it was offered her. Thus Creighton complains, "She was eager for small gains, but she refused great opportunities. She would not embark on enterprises of which she could not foresee the end. She possessed no great ideals." The fact is, however, that she did foresee the end only too plainly — a war with Spain, and with a France that would never have allowed England to become entrenched on her northern border. Had Elizabeth been as bold as tradition makes her, she might have accepted the risks — probably with disastrous results to herself. So her fixed policy remained to curb the daring of more ardent spirits, or to give them countenance only so long as they snatched — and fled. It was not heroic; it was not morally defensible; it was merely shrewd.

It is noteworthy that just prior to the signing of the treaty of Blois (on April 21, 1572) Elizabeth decided to refuse Count La Marck, the Dutch pirate, the use of Dover as his base. The result was that he swooped upon Brille and held it as his centre of operations. It was the signal for a general rebellion. One cannot help but believe that Elizabeth calculated upon such an outcome.

Philip II was no man to cope with such a situation. Dull, honest, plodding, and unimaginative, he would make no concessions to his provincial subjects, especially none regarding religion, which he held as a sacred trust.[2] That, indeed it was; but he used Spanish methods of repression quite unsuited to his northern dominions. His pedantic rigidity denied the few concessions of local autonomy that might have made all the difference. It must, however, in fairness to Philip be said that Orange

---

[2] Nor did he make concessions about religion even with regard to England. He was misinformed about conditions there, and probably honestly believed that a conciliatory policy would be better, in the long run, than aggression. His two capital errors in judgment were in not acting when he might have acted, and then acting when it was too late.

was not a person with whom it was easy to effect any compromise. He was fully as stubborn as the King.

The governors, Granvelle, Alva, Requesens, Don John of Austria, and Parma were all able men. But though some of them won notable victories in the field, little real headway was made in reducing the provinces. On January 23, 1579, those belonging to the northern group signed the Union of Utrecht, thereby breaking off from the Catholic provinces of the south. By doing so they passed under the control of the Calvinist oligarchy headed by Orange, and eventually developed into what we now know as Holland.

Projects of invasion to help the English Catholics had been mooted in 1569 and in 1571 but came to nothing because Alva refused to commit himself unless the English, who were to rise first, proved themselves to be strong enough to maintain themselves alone for a reasonable period. But in 1576 it began to appear that such an invasion was at last likely to take place. Philip had appointed, with some reluctance, his half brother Don John of Austria, the famous victor of Lepanto, to the governorship. Such a man could be counted upon to act with daring and resolution. A project was formed — one which did not arouse Philip to enthusiasm — for marrying him to Mary Queen of Scots, and putting him with her upon the English throne. He had several years previously been mentioned as a possible husband for Mary; now within striking distance of England, he thought he could hardly fail.

No scheme could have been more harebrained: Don John had few soldiers in Spain, and these were needed for garrison service. Had he landed he might, it is true, have defeated — in initial engagements — such forces as Elizabeth could have brought against him; and the English Catholics might at that time have risen. But his eventual success was out of the question: the sober Alva had steadily refused to have anything to do with schemes such as this.

In any event, Don John soon found that his hands were tied. To be accepted as Governor, he saw that he must accept the Pacification of Ghent, under which it was stipulated that he remove his Spanish garrisons. Yet if he sent them away, how could he invade England? In the end he bowed to the inevitable and undertook to respect the ancient liberties of the Catholic provinces and remove his soldiers overland to Italy. Only then was he received in Brussels with the shout, "There was a man sent from God whose name was John!" But the compromise was the shattering of his hopes; eighteen months later the young hero was dead, Walsingham writing the pious epitaph, "God dealeth most lovingly with her Majesty in taking away her enemies."

Don John was succeeded by Alexander Farnese, the great soldier better known as the Duke of Parma. Under his administration Spain gradually consolidated her power in the Netherlands, until in 1584 two deaths occurred which removed her chief obstacles. On June 10 Alençon died; exactly a month later Orange was assassinated by Baltasar at Ghent. The Prince had been put beyond the ban by Philip's edict, after which any man might take his life. Baltasar dared, and having achieved his object, was torn to pieces with pincers, consoling himself with what he had accomplished and with the iron fortitude he showed in enduring his torments. Now all that remained to be done was to complete the subjugation of the Netherlands and to turn Spanish arms against England.

Elizabeth's danger was extreme. Never had Spanish power been at a greater height. For recently the Crown of Portugal had fallen to Philip, and with it the Portuguese possessions in America and the East Indies, and — a dire threat to England — the fine Portuguese navy. Now added to the possibility of invasion there was the possibility of Elizabeth's being assassinated. Moray had fallen in 1570 under the bullet of a Hamilton. Now Orange had met the same fate, as Henry III was to be stabbed five years later. And though the Pope's Bull of 1570 absolving Elizabeth's subjects from their allegiance had been "explained" by Gregory XIII, it was not at all unlikely that some wild man might act as Baltasar had acted. The age was one of political assassination.[3]

---

[3] Elizabeth had no scruples about using the same weapon. She meditated

The Netherlands

It must be admitted that there seems to have been some sort of approbation given by Rome for a plan for so disposing of Elizabeth. Early in 1583 the Cardinal Secretary of State, Tolomeo Galli, had been asked by the Nuncio at Paris whether he would lay this before His Holiness, the Nuncio writing, "Although I believe everything would be lawful to the Pope by which God might chastise His enemy, still it would be unseemly that His earthly representative should do it by such means as these." The Cardinal Secretary opened the matter to Gregory and then sent the reply: "His Holiness can only feel pleased that that kingdom should be set free from oppression by whatever means and restored to God and our holy religion." If the words sound far from seemly, it must be borne in mind that this was not an ordinary case of "removing" an obnoxious person, but that Elizabeth was — or so it could be argued — still under the ban. The Cardinal wrote explicitly, and we must presume with the Pope's sanction — though it would be well to note that we do not know the precise terms in which such sanction was given: "Since that guilty woman of England usurps two such noble kingdoms of Christendom and is the cause of so much injury to the Catholic faith, and the loss of so many millions of souls, there is no doubt that whoever sends her out of the world with the pious intention of doing God service, not only does not sin, but gains merit, especially having regard to the sentence pronounced against her by Pius V of holy memory. And so, if those English nobles decide actually to undertake so glorious a work, your Lordship can assure them that they do not commit any sin."[4]

having both the Pope and the King of Spain murdered in 1581. Before that, a plan to assassinate Don John of Austria had been discussed, according to Mendoza's letter to Philip, dated May, 1578, at Leicester's house — and this with the approbation of the Queen. If Elizabeth was no worse than others in this respect, she was certainly no better.

[4] Pastor (Vol. XIX, p. 441 of the English translation) gives the Italian text. The letter was first published by Meyer (pp. 427–8 of the English translation). He renders "usurps," however, as "rules over" — thereby missing the essential point. Elizabeth's right to the throne of England had never been acknowledged by Rome. But who, it might be asked, were "those English nobles" referred to in the letters?

We may as well candidly acknowledge this letter to be anything but edifying. But let us follow that admission with another: however much we may disapprove of political assassination, few would in our day be greatly shocked if someone among the people savagely afflicted by him should dispose in this way of Hitler. Elizabeth's was a case of equal extremity — that of a usurping tyrant maintained in power by terror. And, as the Cardinal Secretary pointed out, she was already deposed by the Bull of 1570.[5] By deposition she had been put under the ban.

Such being Elizabeth's difficulties, she at last decided, in 1585, upon active intervention in the Netherlands, though still without any declaration of war. For that matter, there was no declaration of war even in 1588, and at the very hour that the Armada sailed, English and Spanish Commissioners in Flanders were discussing possible terms of peace. Leicester was therefore appointed to the high command and arrived at Flushing at the end of 1585. Why he was appointed has always been something of a mystery, so incompetent did he prove himself to be. The apologists for Elizabeth say that he was sent because the States had asked for him, with the secondary argument that the appointment was approved by Cecil. But the Dutch request was made mainly because it was known that no noble stood so high in Elizabeth's favour; and Cecil's consent — it must be recalled that he was of the more cautious "peace party" — may have been given because, knowing Leicester, he could feel sure that nothing too aggressive would be done. Elizabeth's choice, in so far as it was not dictated by mere personal whim — the kind of whim that made Hatton Lord Chancellor — also may have been determined by the fact that she did not want to send too energetic a general to the Low Countries. As a figurehead Leicester would serve perfectly.

Mr. Chamberlin has recently tried to prove that Leicester, almost more than any other man, was the architect of Eliza-

---

[5] The argument, however, was not quite disingenuous, so it seems to me. For Gregory's explanation of Pius V's Bull was that it remained inoperative (so far as Elizabeth's Catholic subjects were concerned) until it could be executed. This demanded a public promulgation that had not yet been made. However, the matter is something to be decided by canon lawyers not by myself.

bethan greatness. The contention is not likely to find much acceptance, though I think Leicester was abler than is generally supposed. In his own curious fashion he had already made himself useful to the Queen and her ministers. Now in the Netherlands he began to take himself a little too seriously, accepting from the Dutch the title of "Governor and Captain-General."

Elizabeth was furious. A minor point, of which altogether too much has been made is that Lady Leicester, the detested Lettice (Knollys' daughter and a Boleyn connexion), was receiving semiroyal honours. This unquestionably annoyed Elizabeth; but what she was mainly concerned about was that Leicester's "governorship" implied her own sovereignty over the Netherlands — and this she had long ago definitely declined, with a recent repetition of her refusal. She wished to keep up the fiction that she had entered the country merely in order to preserve Spanish territory from the French — an action of disinterested generosity on her part toward Philip, though one that he somehow failed to appreciate. On February, 1586, she therefore wrote the "Governor" a stinging letter: "Our express pleasure and commandment is, that all delays and excuses laid apart, you do presently, upon the duty of your allegience, obey and fulfil whatsoever the bearer hereof shall direct you to do in our name: whereof fail you not, as you will answer the contrary to your uttermost peril." As so often happened with her, she did not commit all the details of the instructions to paper. But their general purport may be inferred: Leicester was to cease to be Governor and consider himself merely in command of the English garrisons. These he was told to hold; he was not to prosecute a too active war. Indeed, for its prosecution he was hamstrung by being stinted of supplies. And Sir Christopher Blount, a Catholic of sorts, was sent over to keep an eye upon his behaviour.

Under such circumstances the campaign was one of the least glorious in the history of English arms, and the Dutch soon grew disgusted with an ally who did so little. The few English successes that occurred were due not to Leicester but to the brilliant bravery of some of his subordinates. What Englishmen can reflect on with most pride is the gallant death of Sir Philip Sidney at Zutphen.

One enormous act of apparent treachery must also be recorded — not so much because of its intrinsic importance but because of its political and other consequences. After Leicester had been recalled to England, following the execution of Mary Queen of Scots, Sir William Stanley surrendered Deventer to the Spaniards and Roland York, Zutphen, both going over to the Spanish side.

Whatever may be said in their defence — Cardinal Allen defended them on the ground that they held their commissions from Leicester and that the Dutch towns they were garrisoning belonged to the Spanish administration — their treason had, understandably enough, a disastrous effect upon the Catholic cause in England, some English Catholics giving up the practice of their religion on this very account, and all being hard put to explain away what had happened.

The facts, briefly are these: Sir William Stanley was not, at any rate at this period of his life, a particularly zealous Catholic. His action was dictated mainly by personal grievances, for he considered himself inadequately rewarded for his services in Ireland. On top of this he had been left in the Netherlands with grossly insufficient supplies, and some members of his command (mostly recruited in Ireland) had been in communication with the "Papists" of Deventer. Thomas Wilkes wrote to warn him on December 17, "I pray you have a careful eye to the Irish people."

Already he was not beyond suspicion, so that Leicester had been exceedingly careless in leaving him in charge. Presumably the Earl thought that, in view of the English ships outside Flushing, he could do no serious harm. Stanley, however, was fearful for himself, for in a disgruntled mood he had been in some sort of communication with the Babington conspirators and could not know how much had been discovered. It was not that he was guilty in that matter, but he knew how severely "treasons" that reposed on much slighter evidence than could be adduced against himself had been punished. With York at

WILLIAM CECIL, LORD BURGHLEY
Engraved from the original by Marc Gheeraedts, in the
collection of the Marquis of Exeter.

his elbow, he became convinced that his sole chance of escaping arrest was to act as he now did. But he probably did not consider his surrender of Deventer as treachery. Had not the Queen said over and over again that she was only holding the Seven Provinces for Spain? What harm could there be in giving up to Parma towns that it was in any event impossible to hold much longer?

Bishop David Mathew argues that Stanley and York did not think that they were finally cutting themselves off from their country. This I do not think can be maintained; they must have known that, unless Spain invaded and conquered England, the breach would be permanent. But he offers the interesting suggestion that "the seventeenth century example of the Fronde provides a clue to the outlook of many of the politically minded Catholics abroad in the years between the Queen's accession and the final outbreak of the war." This is an explanation probably not far from the truth: we cannot regard Stanley and York as traitors in the strict sense; they were merely in opposition — according to their own point of view — to the Cecilian administration.

Any other defence of the two English captains may as well be given up. It can only be on the technical grounds I have mentioned, but which I do not accept as quite satisfactory. While their defection did only slight harm to England, it did vast harm to the English Catholics, for it could be pointed to as a proof of how thoroughly infected Papists were with disloyalty. Coming when it did — just after the execution of Mary Queen of Scots, and at the very time that Spain was known to be preparing her Armada — the deed could be painted in even darker colours than it deserved.

All that was left for Stanley and York was to accept service with Spain, which was further damnatory. York was appointed to the command of a troop of lancers, but died soon afterwards. Stanley, who lived to be over eighty, not dying until 1630, confirmed his treason by advising the invasion of England through Ireland and announced himself ready to go with Parma's expeditionary force in 1588. He ended his days as Spanish Governor of Mechlin. Though we may credit him — as we may credit the other exiles — with the higher patriotism which recognised that the best good that could befall their country was its return to the Catholic Faith, his judgment as to the means of effecting this was, like theirs, ill-founded. He and all the members of the Spanish Party, did unwittingly a grave disservice to the cause of Catholicism.

16

‹‹‹

Plots Real and Bogus

FROM what has already been said it must be evident that I make no attempt to deny that there was a certain amount of disloyalty among individual Catholics at this time. The wonder, however, is that there was not a great deal more. Under extreme provocation the overwhelming mass of English Catholics remained firm in their allegiance to Elizabeth, and nothing more clearly demonstrates this than their spontaneous association with Protestant Englishmen to repel the threat of the Armada.

Nevertheless, there was from 1583 on a series of plots against the life of the Queen, though most of them bear all the marks of having been hatched by Walsingham, as the culminating plot — that of Babington — was certainly carefully nursed and brought to a head (even if it was not actually initiated) by the government's spy service.[1] All of these plots were used to justify the decision to bring Mary to her death; all that was being waited for was a sufficient pretext.

It must, nevertheless, be granted that the government always looked upon Mary as a tiger whom they held only by the tail; at any moment she was likely to rend them. Nor can it be denied that, though the conspiracies of 1569 and 1571 had as their object the freeing of Mary (in the one case) and (in the other) the marrying of her to the Duke of Norfolk and (in both) the recognition of her right to succeed Elizabeth, it is not at all unlikely that, had either plot succeeded, the conspirators might have been pushed further than they intended to go, and would

---

[1] He had succeeded Cecil as Secretary of State in 1573, after Cecil had been made Lord Treasurer, in which office he was more and not less powerful than before.

259

have dethroned the Queen. In both cases there was, therefore, incontestable treason — if only in the project to bring in Spanish assistance for the design.

Further there had been a series of political assassinations. Moray's murder has been mentioned; it was not political in motive, though it could be represented as such. Morton, as already indicated, had been beheaded in 1581, and though he confessed having known in advance that Darnley was to be killed, so almost certainly had several of the judges who condemned him: his can accordingly be described as a case of judicial murder whose motive was political. On top of this came the assassination of Orange. And while the English government could hardly have been informed of the general approbation that Gregory XIII has been quoted as giving to such a plan, it must have been well known to Walsingham's spies that the removal of Elizabeth had been discussed in the Council at Madrid. In later years the Queen told de Maisse, the French Ambassador, that Philip's attempts were due "to the force of love which made the King of Spain behave so" — a piece of highly modern psychology!

We must therefore allow for the fact that Elizabeth stood in real danger, even if she was careless of it — though perhaps her famous "indifference" was due to her confidence that the all-seeing Walsingham was quite competent to catch any conspirators. But a still more important fact to bear in mind is that Walsingham, alarmed by the royal carelessness, wished to bring home to the Queen the danger in which she stood. Cecil had early in the reign discovered an infallible method for inducing Elizabeth to do what he thought she ought to do: it was that of frightening her. As the government could not always lay their hands upon perpetrators of genuine plots, Walsingham was instructed to provide the bogus plots that would serve just as well. For the main purpose of these inventions was not to induce Elizabeth to be on guard for her life — the government could see to that even if she neglected the ordinary precautions; it was to inflame public opinion against Mary and to overcome Elizabeth's reluctance to execute her prisoner.

Plots Real and Bogus

In this the government was eminently successful. The chief blame for Mary's beheading — to which all these plots were intended to lead — must be laid at the door of the Council, especially at that of Cecil and Leicester and Walsingham and Knollys. Yet Elizabeth cannot wholly escape blame. She perfectly understood that a group of men around her wished the death of Mary and that she was herself consenting to a policy which was sooner or later going to result in that death. That is why in one of her spasms of compunction she tried again, as late as 1584, to escape from the dilemma by making a new effort to have the Queen of Scots restored — under certain conditions — to her throne. If this effort came to nothing, it was largely the fault of James VI, an unpleasant and precocious "old young man" who was destined to be King of England. When it failed, Elizabeth fell back upon the Cecilian policy; so clear sighted a woman could not but have perceived what its outcome was going to be.

It is, however, uncertain (as it is nearly always uncertain with Elizabeth) just how resolved she was in her intentions. She may have already resigned herself to the situation and made her move in 1584 only by way of a gesture that could afterwards be used to show that she wished to save Mary, as no doubt she did. All that one can say is that her actions were inconsistent: in 1571 she stood between her prisoner and Parliament; but the following year she was ready to hand her over to Mar to be put to death. She wriggled and squirmed to get out of her difficulties; she never would take the decisive action that honour dictated.

How much she swayed from side to side according to what seemed to be, for the moment, expedient, is rather amusingly indicated by the events of 1582. Hearing that there was a plan on foot to marry James of Scotland to a Spanish Infanta, the oft-betrothed maiden of forty-nine put herself forward as a bride for the sixteen-year-old King. It was, of course, merely a device for gaining time. She soon substituted a proposal that James marry either Anne of Denmark (whom he did eventually marry) or some English lady of high birth to be selected for him by herself. When Leicester heard of it he thought he saw a chance for one of his stepdaughters (who was of Boleyn blood). Elizabeth stopped this at once. Swearing her most lurid theological oaths, she protested that she would sooner take the crown off her own head and give it to James than allow him to take any "whelp of the she-wolf" — Lettice Knollys. To intimidate Leicester she vowed that she would publish his "horns" to the world unless he at once desisted. For though she had taken him back into favour after the period of his disgrace when Simier had revealed his secret marriage to the widow of Walter Devereux, Lettice herself was never forgiven. Not even when her son Robert, the more famous Earl of Essex, had become the apple of Elizabeth's eye, would she have anything to do with his mother. Her objection to James's marriage was therefore not on the grounds of policy — on the contrary, a Boleyn should have been regarded as eminently eligible; it was nothing but a flaring up of feminine spite. Just this sort of thing, alternating with the most cold-blooded political considerations, generally stifled the Queen's decent impulses.

But to return to the attempts on her life.

According to Mr. Waldman, "Without exception every plot for Elizabeth's assassination could be traced to one of the Jesuit missionaries." That the government did its best to fix responsibility in that quarter is true enough, but I do not know of a single case where it succeeded in doing so. The nearest approach to Jesuit implication was that of Father Henry Walpole's connexion with the absurd attempt made in 1598 by Edward Squire; and that has been thoroughly exploded, if anything so nonsensical ever needed to be taken seriously. Even Mr. Waldman is kind enough to admit that the man named Appletree, who was arrested for firing a shot that hit one of the rowers of Elizabeth's barge about the time of the series of plots with which we are now concerned, was not a Jesuit. The man was arrested and condemned to death, the entire Council going on their knees to beseech the Queen "that this slave might not suffer this death [that is hanging, disembowelling, and the rest] but a hundred thousand deaths (if it were possible so to do) for his most vile and fearful offence." On this occasion Elizabeth showed more sense than her "jittery" Council. It was proved that the gun had gone off by accident, so Appletree was released. The incident is worth mentioning only because it reveals the prevalent nervousness, the disposition to see a spy or (like Mr. Waldman) a Jesuit under every bed.

Actually very little came out as a consequence of all these prosecutions for treason, though a number of men were sent to horrible deaths. Upon the rack this or that captured "seminary"[2] would tell what he knew — the gossip heard in the colleges about the boasts of renegade soldiers such as Stanley, or the threats of embittered *emigrés*. They had nothing else to tell. Even in the reports of Walsingham's spies, as Major Hume remarks in his by no means pro-Catholic *Treason and Plot,* rarely was there anything of importance. "The names of Englishmen ostensibly in the Spanish service; their movements, salaries, and conversations are given *ad nauseam;* but as many of these men were actually in Burghley's pay, and sent him regular advices, we can imagine the grim smile of the aged Lord Treasurer as he read this vague tittle-tattle of the dangerous places."

It was, however, the business of a spy to unearth conspiracies; when they did not exist he was obliged to manufacture them himself to obtain credit with his employers. The tiniest mole hills were magnified into mountains. Or, as this method was unsafe to use continuously (for Walsingham was too clever a man to be hoodwinked), the spy turned *agent provocateur* and so set the wheels of conspiracy in motion.

Three typical plots will suffice. They came successively in the years 1583, 1584, and 1585.

In Warwickshire there lived a weak-minded man of twenty-three named John Somerville. He and his father-in-law, Edward Arden, the High Sheriff of the county, and a priest named Hall, whom Arden, a man of some means, kept as a private chaplain disguised as a gardener, were arrested for designs against the life of the Queen. Arden may have been a relation of Shakespeare's mother, though this is denied by the *Diction-*

---

[2] A current expression for priests trained in the continental seminaries.

ary of National Biography. Be that as it may, Somerville had indulged in some wild talk, flourishing a pistol with which he declared he was going to shoot Elizabeth — or so it was said. If he had ever vented anything of the kind, or had "hoped to see her head on a pole, for she was a serpent and a viper," he must have been insane. Insane or not, Walsingham needed to produce a conspirator. Hall on the rack admitted that Somerville had once remarked that he "wished the Queen were in heaven." On such evidence the men were sentenced to death. The poor half-wit who had caused all the trouble escaped by strangling himself in his cell in the Tower. Arden was executed. Hall was allowed to leave the country.

Let us note what even the annalist Camden — who was very much on the official side — had to say about the affair. Arden's woeful end, he comments, "was generally imputed to Leicester's malice. Certain it is that he had incurred Leicester's heavy displeasure, for he had rashly opposed him in all he could, reproaching him as an adulterer and defaming him as a new upstart." Arden had also been so unwise as to refuse to sell Leicester some land. This, it is consoling to reflect, passed to the Earl as a reward for his services in unravelling the plot. But as not everybody was so well informed as Camden, the condemnation of the "traitors" was skilfully used to rouse the country against Papists.

The second plot, that of Francis Throckmorton, had rather more substance to it. This, too, was one of Leicester's discoveries. Cecil kept out of it because young Throckmorton was a nephew of the Ambassador, Sir Nicholas, who had been his friend at one time but with whom he had quarrelled. Leicester did not have the same degree of delicacy, which is perhaps not surprising in view of the fact that Nicholas Throckmorton was regarded by many people as among his numerous victims by poison.

What we know is this: Francis Throckmorton had been in Paris, where he had been in touch with Morgan, Mary Queen of Scots' agent. He had also written to Mendoza and, when he was arrested, he was in the act of composing a letter to Mary

FATHER ROBERT PERSONS, S.J.
From the engraving in Vol. VI of *Galerie Illustrée de la Compagnie de Jésus,* comp. by Hamy.

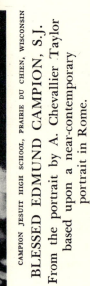

BLESSED EDMUND CAMPION, S.J.
From the portrait by A. Chevallier Taylor based upon a near-contemporary portrait in Rome.

Plots Real and Bogus

herself. Among his papers turned up a list of prominent Catholics, and some geographical information which appeared to indicate that he was suggesting suitable places for a Guise landing. Under the torment of the rack he made a confession, but when he was removed he murmured, "Faith broken, honour lost!" On the scaffold he repudiated his confession and protested his innocence. He was probably guilty enough, as such things went in those days, but still more probably he was merely a romantic young fool with no very clear idea as to just what it was he meant to do. The government, however, took — or pretended to take — a grave view of the matter, as is shown by their ordering Mendoza to leave the country within fifteen days. They had long wanted a pretext for expelling a too-outspoken Ambassador.

As an offshoot of the Throckmorton plot there occurred the tragedy of Henry Percy, who had succeeded to his brother's title of Northumberland.[3] He had taken no part in the rebellion of 1569 but had been arrested in 1571 for communicating with the Queen of Scots, then released, as nothing could be proved against him. More correctly, he had been left in a dubious position: he was fined five thousand marks, which would indicate belief in his guilt; but the fine was never exacted, and he was allowed to take his executed brother's earldom, which would indicate belief in his innocence. Now, thirteen years later, the government thought they could convict him. A Percy would be a convincing victim.

But they still had no definite proofs, so failed to bring him to trial. On June 20, 1585, he was found in his cell in the Tower shot through the heart, whereupon it came out that on the night of his death the Lieutenant of the Tower had received orders to remove the usual jailor and to put in his place a man named Bailiff, a servant of Sir Christopher Hatton's. Though a verdict of suicide was brought in at the inquest — mainly on the testimony of a witness that the Earl had been heard to swear

[3] It was characteristic of the times that he should have been a connexion by marriage of Cecil's. The ramifications of the governing classes of the time are bewildering. This fact may have accounted for this Percy's having kept out of the 1569 rising.

that "that bitch" (meaning Queen Elizabeth) should never get his lands by convicting him of treason — from that day to this it has never been satisfactorily explained how it happened that a prisoner in the Tower should have been allowed to bolt his cell from the inside. Those inner bolts, produced (along with the pistol) as proofs of suicide are, to say the least, decidedly suspicious. For though it might have been possible for Percy to have smuggled in a loaded gun, the door bolted from the inside has every appearance of having been contrived *after* the event. A ladder, of course, would have served to get Bailiff out of the window. The government that had been afraid to try Percy, fastened his guilt upon him by making him out a suicide.

The third case, that of Dr. William Parry, is the most mysterious and, at the same time, the most instructive of them all. In it, as in the other cases, Leicester was, significantly enough, the leading figure. Concerning Parry himself we know that he had married two rich wives and had run through their money, that he had tried to murder his chief creditor, and that — perhaps by way of paying for protection from punishment — he became one of Walsingham's spies on the continent. There, somewhere around 1579, he professed conversion to Catholicism, but was never trusted very far by his coreligionists, who were by now acquiring a keen scent for Judases.

Going back to England, Parry was rewarded by Burghley with a seat in Parliament, which he apparently did not think sufficient compensation for his distinguished services. By way of bringing pressure to bear on his employers, he took a pro-Catholic line in a speech, and was in consequence arrested. He asked to be brought before the Queen and, when his request was granted, presumably explained to her that his speech was merely a bit of character acting, and certainly opened his bag of horrors. Among its contents was a letter which purported to come from the Cardinal Secretary of State which gave a guarded approval to an unspecified "undertaking" of his.[4] This under-

---

[4] Mendoza declared the letter a forgery, though, as he could not have examined the letter, he dismissed it on general principles only. But the letter may have been genuine; we have already seen that the Cardinal Secretary wrote a far

Plots Real and Bogus

taking, according to Parry, was the murder of Elizabeth, though Mendoza pointed out that it did not necessarily refer to anything of the kind. Parry was promised immunity and released, but when he began again to make extravagant demands for further reward, the government determined to get rid of him. There is some reason for suspecting that the speech in Parliament was made at the instigation of Leicester, who wished to lure him to his doom.

Arrested once more, and this time racked, he made the confession demanded of him, though he afterwards vehemently asserted that, to the positive knowledge of Cecil and Walsingham and the Queen herself, he was innocent — which is more than probable. This, however, did not save him from Tyburn.

We need not waste any tears over his fate, however indignant and disgusted we must feel with those who betrayed him. He had made himself a nuisance; his usefulness was at an end; the government was looking for a traitor to execute. The pro-Catholic speech in Parliament and the confession on the rack marked him out as the appropriate victim.

It would be going too far to say definitely that the fellow was an *agent provocateur*. But he patently looks like one, and was, in any event, a government spy — one of those many spies who pretended conversion the better to gain the confidence of Catholics. All such spies, then as now, as I have previously said, found it virtually impossible to escape from their profession once they had ended it. In Elizabethan times there was a specially effective way of making sure that they would be assiduous. They were well paid, but had to prove their usefulness; otherwise another use could always be contrived for their services. It was exceedingly easy to "frame" such scoundrels. A government that had executed a Campion would have no compunction over a Parry.

These executions had a powerful psychological effect. The

more explicit letter along these lines to the Nuncio at Paris. Pastor thinks that Parry must have extracted the letter from the Cardinal by a species of fraud, by inducing him to write something that might be twisted into approval of murder but which was really about something quite different (Vol. XIX, Eng. ed., p. 452).

people in those days had no means of discovering the real facts about anything, for all the sources of information were controlled by the administration. We have seen much the same system operating in Germany and Russia in our own time where propaganda and strict censorship create the atmosphere in which hysterical trials and preposterous public confessions are swallowed as genuine. When the Elizabethan crowds that gathered around the gibbet at Tyburn saw a barbarous sentence carried out with fierce solemnity, what else could they conclude but that the offence (whatever it was) must have been terrible to have deserved so terrible a punishment? By fixing upon Catholics — even upon Catholics of the type of Parry — the stigma of treason, waverers could be drawn to conformity, while those who had already conformed discovered an additional reason for loyalty to the Crown and hatred for the Papacy. Nobody stopped to reflect that confessions extorted upon the rack were without any value; that few men, however innocent, but confessed at least *something* in their torment. People like Parry, of course, piled it on, for they had no conviction or character to sustain them; they hoped that by "coming out strong" they might be pardoned. Yet in none of these cases — except perhaps that of Throckmorton — was there any "proof" except the confessions gasped out under torture. The confessions had to be obtained, and the traitors executed, in order to whip up patriotic frenzy, to smirch the "Jesuits," and to show what an admirable custodian of the national safety was Walsingham. Above all, these trials were each a calculated step in the road whose goal was to be the killing of Mary Queen of Scots.

Two curious circumstances that escaped the notice of the men of that period — and that usually escape the notice of men of our own — should have attention drawn to them here. One was that, despite all the talk about plots, nobody ever made any actual attempt on Elizabeth's life. The other is that Philip of Spain — whom a fevered public imagination supposed to be at the bottom of all the plots — was precisely the man who would have been most embarrassed politically had Elizabeth been murdered while Mary Queen of Scots was alive in England

and ready at a moment's notice to ascend the English throne. As against Mary the King of Spain had no claim to advance in favour of the Infanta: it was Mary's death, not Elizabeth's, that would have best suited his convenience. This does not, of course, apply to the years following 1587; it certainly bore heavily prior to Mary's execution.

Nor was it, for that matter, in the English Catholic interest to remove Elizabeth, though it is perhaps not surprising that some Catholic hotheads failed to see so obvious a point. An assassination while Mary was alive could have resulted only in a bloody civil war, at the end of which — had the anti-Marians won (as with their control of the machinery of government they almost certainly would have done) — a violently anti-Catholic party would have come into power, with no Elizabeth to act as a restraining influence. Therefore what even the last of the plots on Mary's behalf had as its object — at any rate in its inception — was no more than her release from prison and her recognition as Elizabeth's successor. That was the sole safe and prudent plan. It was because it was a possibility that might at any time be realised that the administration was obliged to fasten upon Mary personally a complicity in all the plots, whether genuine or bogus, craftily presented to the befooled public. The Queen of Scots was for this reason always loudly proclaimed — after the hosannahs for Elizabeth's preservation had gone up — to be the "bosom serpent," "the monstrous and huge dragon" who had to be destroyed if the realm were to have any peace. Not even Herr Göbbels was a more consummate master of the arts of propaganda than were Cecil and Leicester and Walsingham.

17

The Killing of Mary

"CAN I put to death," asked Elizabeth in 1572, "the bird that, to escape the pursuit of the hawk, has fled to my feet for protection?" The answer is that she could and that she did. How gradually but how remorselessly the killing was prepared for by the manufacture of plots we have already seen. We shall now see how Elizabeth — while clinging desperately to the end, with one part of her mind, to the intention of somehow saving her cousin — came to acquiesce in what she must have known from the beginning was made inevitable by the policy she permitted. Like most people who systematically practise deception upon others, Elizabeth came eventually to practise it upon herself. There is no escape from the fact of Elizabeth's responsibility, however plausibly it be argued that, in signing Mary's death warrant at last, she never wished it to be executed.

I will permit myself a personal explanation at the outset. I am not concerned with trying to prove Mary innocent. Whether or not she was implicated in the Darnley murder is beside the point: it was not for that that she was tried at Fotheringay. And she may have been guilty in the Babington conspiracy. All I reserve is a doubt. My objection is to the way the evidence against her was obtained and presented; and I deny altogether that Elizabeth had any right to try a sister queen. It would, in fact, have been less of a crime had Elizabeth had Mary murdered in prison, for that would not have touched the sacredness of the royal office. What Elizabeth did was, under the show of a judicial trial, to shake the whole principle upon which monarchy reposed.

Any questioning of Mary's guilt — and here there is only a question raised, no affirmation of innocence — is in some quarters regarded as sentimental and romantic. To that I reply that it is not necessary to be in love with the nearly four-hundred-years-dead Queen of Scots to have a prepossession in favour of justice and decency. This is the point that is so commonly missed: whether Mary was guilty or not, Elizabeth was guilty. If it was an outrage that Mary should have been accused at York and Westminster by men known — let us put it at the mildest and say men who were reputed to be — Darnley's murderers, it was no less of an outrage to have as one of her judges the very man, Walsingham, who had devised the Babington plot, and to allow her to be condemned on the evidence he produced. This would be no less true even had those judges the clearest title to sit in judgement upon her. I hope I shall never be so "impartial" a historian as not to feel indignation when I encounter so unspeakable an injustice, or so unpatriotic an Englishman as not to feel horror at so foul a blot upon England's fame. Having now unburdened my soul, I shall make an attempt to state the facts of the case dispassionately.

Though John Knox died at the end of 1572, Mary's cause was finally lost (though this she refused to admit) on May 29, 1573, when Edinburgh castle, the last Marian stronghold fell. Kirkaldy was executed at the market cross, and Maitland (who had become a Marian once more) would have shared Kirkaldy's fate had he not died in prison. Twice about this time there was talk of handing Mary over to her enemies in Scotland for execution, and if nothing came of the 1572 plan it was mainly because the English and the Scots did not trust one another, though I think we may perhaps safely credit Elizabeth with the intention of vetoing it had it ever got beyond the stage of negotiation. That she had consented to the proposed action did not mean that she would have consented to that action being carried out.

On the whole Mary received good treatment in England: that is, she was made comfortable, treated with the externals of royal deference, allowed to maintain a large retinue of servants, and was given as much freedom as was consonant with a close watch upon her. She went hunting; she corresponded indefatigably with her friends, appealing to them (as was natural) for help; and she maintained ambassadors both at Elizabeth's Court and abroad. For this purpose she used the income of £12,000 which was her portion as Dowager of France. Her maintenance in England cost Elizabeth £52 a week, a sum reduced in 1575 to £30. She did a good deal of artistic embroidery to pass the time, often sending presents of her handiwork to Elizabeth — rather to Elizabeth's embarrassment. And she amused herself with a menagerie of small animals and birds. Though her health was not always very good, she remained to the end vigorous and active, so that in her last year she was able to write, "I thank God that he hath not yet set me so low, but that I am able to handle my crossbow for killing of a deer, and to gallop after hounds on horseback." Elizabeth was justly able to claim in her letter of February 23, 1570, to Sir Henry Norris, Ambassador to France, "She for the most part when she lived in Scotland, had no better entertainment or diet, but many times worse and baser." Mary, of course, complained vociferously whenever she could, writing, for example, from Tutbury to say that the privies were under her window and stank noisomely. But that state of affairs was presumably remedied. Elizabeth wanted Mary to have all the comforts of prison.

The captive even made a friend of the Earl of Shrewsbury, her jailor — too much of a friend for the liking of his Countess, the shrewish "Bess of Hardwick." Despite this, Mary did not get along too badly with Bess herself. At the end of 1574 Lady Shrewsbury's daughter by a former marriage married the younger brother of Darnley, Lord Charles Stuart, an alliance which served to cement the Shrewsbury friendship. From that union was born Lady Arbella Stuart (she was not known at that time as "Arabella") whom Elizabeth at one time thought of as her successor.

With Bess of Hardwick Mary enjoyed the delights of malicious gossip. It was from Bess that she got all the details about Elizabeth's love affairs and sexual incapacity. This she set down in the famous letter first printed by Murdin, a letter which may or may not be authentic but which unquestionably indicates the kind of thing the two women talked about. The captivity, for this and other reasons, was not altogether unpleasant. It was, however, captivity, and as such Mary raged against it.

She was upheld by the thought that her friends in England, or her friends abroad, would eventually secure her release. And there was always the strong possibility that she would outlive the ailing Elizabeth and peacefully ascend the English throne. To further her immediate release she worked for a marriage — to Don John of Austria, to Norfolk, to anyone who would get her out of prison. The Pope had annulled her marriage to Bothwell on the ground that she had been forced into it. The thought of these possibilities induced Cecil and Leicester and Walsingham to intrigue steadily to have her removed: they understood perfectly well that her accession would mean their ruin, indeed their probable execution.

By way of insuring their future, however — so far as that was possible — many of the courtiers, even those who were Mary's bitterest enemies, made courteous advances. Leicester — of all people! — sent her potent charms against poison: a stone in a gold box, a silver box with Mithridate, and the horn of an exotic beast; and Elizabeth was once angry with him for going to Buxton for the waters at a time when Mary was also taking the cure.[1] Hatton, too, sent a private messenger to say that, in the event of Elizabeth's death, he would himself come to her support with the royal guard of which he was then the Captain. Even Cecil was suspected by Elizabeth of having private communications with her prisoner. He, like the rest, wanted to be prepared for all eventualities.

These men did every now and then think that they had reason to congratulate themselves upon their precautions. For instance, in 1581 an overpowering Marian reaction set in in Scotland with the arrival of Esmé Stuart, Sieur d'Aubigny, who was made Duke of Lennox, and whose domination over the young King became, for a year, complete. The Jesuit Fathers Holt and Crichton arrived to convert James, and a Guisan

---

[1] His pretence in 1577 that he would help her to marry Don John of Austria was treated by Mary with the contempt it deserved.

effort against England from the Scotch border was expected. With this reaction was associated James Stewart (who usurped the Hamilton title of Earl of Arran) the commander of the royal bodyguard. It is amusing to recall that he was a son of the Lord Ochiltree whose seventeen-year old daughter John Knox had married in 1564 at the age of fifty-five.[2] For a time it actually looked as though Scotland would become Catholic again. Unfortunately Esmé Stuart was an unprincipled adventurer — with a foot in both the Catholic and Protestant camps[3] — and was concerned mainly with his own advancement, while the King was merely playing with Catholicism in the delusive hope of securing Spanish backing. He had no wish to see his mother back in Scotland. When he was abducted by the raid carried out by Ruthven (the son of Rizzio's murderer), which was executed, as one would expect, with Elizabeth's secret connivance, he came once again under Protestant control, and Esmé Stuart fled to France.

But in 1584, as has already been mentioned, Elizabeth considered the possibility of restoring Mary to Scotland and giving her joint sovereignty with James. This time it was the son — though by now he had succeeded in shaking off the domination of his Protestant nobles and was even broadly hinting to the Pope that he might become a Catholic — who raised obstacles. As he wanted the throne alone it suited him better that his mother be kept in custody. As Mr. Henderson remarks: "It was one of Mary's bitterest experiences gradually to realise that she had no hold on her son's affections, but that his political aims and intentions were quite at variance with her own." When the crisis of 1587 occurred he made no serious effort — not even then — to save his mother. He was kept quiet by having the hope of the English succession held out to him, subject to his good behaviour, and by a pension.

Almost the only thing one can say in extenuation of the King's base conduct is that he had been irritated by his mother's

[2] This made Knox, though dead, a kind of distant connexion by marriage to Mary Queen of Scots — greatly to her disgust.

[3] He professed himself at this time to be a Protestant.

The Killing of Mary

having in 1577 bequeathed her right to the succession in both England and Scotland to Philip of Spain unless he himself became a Catholic. This was clearly *ultra vires* on Mary's part, and was a bad political move besides, for it only alienated James without winning over Philip. So far from being an inducement to the King of Spain to come to her assistance, it was really a reason for his leaving matters alone. Mary, though an inveterate politician, never knew how to play her political cards.

Her strength — but also her weakness — lay in the fact that, after her imprisonment and the failure of the enquiries of York and Westminster to convince the world of her complicity in Darnley's murder, she became the hope of English Catholics. She was even more than that: her sufferings made her a symbol of the stricken Church. There was little wonder that ardent youth regarded her with such enthusiasm. Nor is there any wonder that the Elizabethan government discovered in the same circumstances a necessity for the execution of one so dangerous to Protestantism and to themselves.

In 1584, when the scare of Elizabeth's assassination was at its height, Leicester devised the scheme of an "Association," whose members pledged themselves to pursue to the death anyone who made a plot against the Queen's life — or even anyone in whose interest such a plot was made. It was nothing less than the affirmation of lynch law, and though Parliament could hardly approve the private murder of Mary (for this was the true object of the bond of the Association) it nevertheless declared that the person — and who else could it be but Mary? — who might benefit by such a plot would be forever incapable of the succession. Such an enactment was preposterously unjust, for it was to punish the Queen of Scots for deeds perpetrated by others, deeds of which she might be in complete ignorance. Despite which Mary, when the bond of Association was read to her, offered to subscribe it — an offer which was refused.

She was no doubt clever enough to realise that laws of this kind could not be other than invalid. The government realising that too, it set about the discovery of a conspiracy against

275

Elizabeth which should inescapably implicate Mary. Otherwise a conspiracy would place merely a piece of parchment between Mary and the throne, something which would count for nothing at the instant of Elizabeth's death. The only solution was the fabrication of a plot in which the Queen of Scots could be proved to have been a prime mover. With that object in mind Walsingham proceeded to his last move. It had as its object the killing of Mary.

We cannot positively affirm that Walsingham initiated the Babington conspiracy, though that was the opinion of Robert Persons. But it is quite certain that he nursed it and through his *agents provacateurs* encouraged the plotters to go much further than they had intended. In Anthony Babington, a young Derbyshire gentleman of means, romantic, foolhardy, and indiscreet, he found the perfect victim.

This Babington had known Mary in the days when he had been a page in Shrewsbury's household. Now through her Paris agent, Thomas Morgan, he managed to get in touch with her, hoping to liberate her, but with no other purpose than that. He soon gathered a group of friends about him, among whom were John Ballard, a priest (though not, as is sometimes said, a Jesuit), and John Savage, a soldier of fortune who had served under Parma.

Ballard I suspect of having been an *agent provacateur*. The fact that he was executed for his part in the conspiracy means nothing. At all events he was not living the life of a missionary priest in England — which in itself is suspicious — and he made it his function to egg Babington on. But the other priest involved in the matter was admittedly a spy. This was Anthony Tyrrell. He supplied the government with information and, after a public recantation at Paul's Cross, was rewarded with a benefice. He died in Belgium in 1610 a Catholic, wavering until the very end. It would seem that he was forced into his profession by weakness rather than that he went into it out of determined wickedness. It was while he was imprisoned in 1585 that he had offered his services to Cecil. Not all the missionaries were able to face the thought of Tyburn.

The Killing of Mary

The main villain of the piece was Gilbert Gifford, who had been in the colleges at Rheims and Rome, from both of which places he was expelled, but who succeeded in obtaining deacon's orders. Even while in the seminary he became one of Walsingham's paid spies. Why he did so is not quite clear: he was of a staunch Catholic family and must be supposed to have had at one time a sincere desire to work and give his life as a priest in England. He fell into the depths of infamy, it would seem, because of ordinary moral frailty. The suggestion has sometimes been offered that he played his rôle of a Judas as a means of obtaining money for his debauches: we know that he was once found in a bawdy house. It is more likely, however, that his depraved manner of life was a method of stifling conscience. Bishop Mathew thinks that he was actuated by vanity and injured feelings and that "he succumbed to that Levantine pleasure in the continuous and unravelling skill of an undiscovered deception." If so, he now had a unique opportunity for the exercise of his perverse talents. With a letter from Morgan to the Queen of Scots he arrived in England in December, 1585, and at once set to work with Thomas Phillips, Walsingham's expert forger and reader of cipher letters, with whom he lodged.

This Phillips was in his way a genius. He was a shortsighted, ugly little fellow with sandy hair and a pock-marked face, an excellent linguist, and one from whom no cryptogram long withheld its secrets. With him was associated as assistant a man named Arthur Gregory, whose speciality it was to open letters and reseal them again so skilfully that nobody could tell that the wax had been broken. Both posed as Catholics, and with them worked another supposititious Catholic, one Poley, who was in the entourage of Sir Philip Sidney's widow, Walsingham's daughter.[4] It was Poley's office — as it was also Ballard's — to keep up Babington's nerve. This was very important, because poor Babington had moods in which he was inclined to throw the whole project up — which would never have done. It was essential to Walsingham that the conspirators fully commit themselves, and, by so doing, commit Mary.

[4] She afterwards married Elizabeth's favourite, the Earl of Essex.

Queen Elizabeth

The Queen of Scots had by this time been removed from Tutbury to the young Earl of Essex's country house at Chartley. Her complaints about the discomforts of her former prison were met by sending her to a pleasanter place — which was incidently more convenient for Walsingham's purposes. There she was given Sir Amias Paulet as her jailor. He was a sour Puritan; Shrewsbury would never have undertaken the dirty work that was about to be performed.

Paulet, Gifford, Phillips, and Gregory between them arranged a very ingenious device by means of which Mary might safely correspond with her friends. In the weekly barrel of beer conveyed to the Scots Queen an airtight leaden box was let down, and in this letters could be passed in and out, the brewer, who figures in the correspondence as the "honest man," being paid extra for his beer by Mary and for his services by Paulet.

These letters were read and copied by Phillips, who added whatever he thought advisable, after consultation with Walsingham. They were then neatly resealed by Gregory and sent on their way. All this took time, for Walsingham did not want to strike too soon. He could at any moment have arrested Babington and his friends. But he was not aiming at them; he had to entangle Mary in the toils first. As Lingard points out, there were two plots: one for the freeing of the prisoner, and perhaps for the assassination of Elizabeth; the other was for the destruction of Mary. They coexisted, running along side by side.

In April, 1586, Gifford was sent over to Paris to see Morgan again. When he returned Ballard also came to England. He urged assassination upon Babington, while Gifford pressed the same project upon Savage. It would have been too bad if they had withdrawn just then. Even so, Babington was for dropping the scheme and going abroad. In order to get a passport he applied to Poley, who through his Walsingham contacts undertook to see that one was obtained. But — as this was so much better — he managed to persuade Babington to defer his trip and to live with him. He would then have at hand — when Walsingham was ready — that dear friend with whom he had had so many beautiful conversations about spiritual matters.

The Killing of Mary

So things went on until Walsingham had completed his case. Then Babington and fourteen other men were arrested. Put to the rack, they made the confessions demanded of them and on September 20 and 21, they were hanged, drawn, and quartered in two batches in St. Giles-in-the-Fields. It should be noted that the government did not allow much more than a month to elapse between their apprehension and execution. They were hurried out of the world before Mary's trial, at which they were definitely not wanted as witnesses.

Elizabeth had asked that some new method of execution be specially invented for them, and when Cecil told her that the customary method was as painful as could be imagined, the Queen demanded that it be "protracted to the extremity of pain." It was therefore carried out with such lingering gentleness of cruelty that, as Mendoza records, Babington was distinctly heard to cry "Jesus!" three times while his heart was in the hangman's hands. Those executed the following day were rather more fortunate. Even an Elizabethan crowd had had its fill of barbarities and so shouted to the executioners to let the condemned hang until they were dead.

Babington and his friends were now silenced. That they were at least technically traitors need not be disputed, though it is at least questionable whether they were fully resolved to go further than release Mary and perhaps kidnap Elizabeth. Nor is there anything intrinsically improbable in the charge against Mary herself. She admitted freely enough that she had plotted escape, but claimed that she had a perfect right to make such an attempt — a claim that must be granted. It might even be argued that, as she was a sovereign imprisoned without cause, she would have been justified in using force to secure her release. At all events the code of the time would have admitted the cogency of such a contention. The more important question at issue is the legality of her trial and the authenticity of the documents produced as evidence.

At first the Queen of Scots refused to plead at all, because she rejected the authority of the court of forty-six peers appointed to try her; she changed her stand only because she was told that a refusal would be taken as an admission of guilt. But she was correct: the trial was invalid, the court had no authority over a Queen; she would have been well advised not to plead. They allowed her no counsel — though as this was the invariable procedure at treason trials, she perhaps could not complain, as she had agreed to accept the court's jurisdiction. If it set her at a grave disadvantage, this she largely offset by making a spirited defence in which time after time she scored heavily.

The case for the Crown rested mainly upon a letter, of which only a copy was produced, as the original had, of course, been sent on after being transcribed by Phillips. The decisive passage reads: "As no certain day can be appointed for the performance of the said gentlemen's enterprise, I desire them to have always near them, or at least at Court, four brave men well horsed to advertise speedily the success of their design, as soon as it is done, to those appointed to get me away from thence, so as to be able to get here before my keeper is informed of the said execution." Of course that could be easily interpreted as meaning that Elizabeth was to be killed, but the "execution" could just as well be only the execution of the plan — to hold the person of Elizabeth until Mary was set free. Mary insisted that the notes of her secretaries — Nau and Curle — which had been seized by the government, be produced. She averred that they would prove beyond all doubt that there was no mention of a murder project. She also demanded that Curle and Nau appear in Court so that she might question them. She was refused.

Now it must be obvious that, had the notes taken by her secretaries been incriminating, Mary would never have ventured to ask for them to be shown at Fotheringay. It is equally obvious that, even without her asking for them, Walsingham would have flourished them in triumph had they corresponded to the copy of the letter. Walsingham's handling of the situation was what one might expect: he got up in court and said that he "wished to God they might be found." Surely we cannot be asked to believe that he had lost the secretaries' notes — his essential evidence: he would have been as likely to mislay the apple of his eye!

MARY QUEEN OF SCOTS
From the painting by an unknown artist in the
National Portrait Gallery.

The Killing of Mary

Further, we have in Walsingham's own handwriting the admission that the postscript to this letter was forged by Phillips to his own instructions. I submit that this puts him completely out of court as a witness — even if he were not put out of court by sitting there as a judge upon the evidence he himself supplied. If no more than a single sentence can be shown to be forged or interpolated how can we rely upon anything in the letter? But the forgery was, in this instance, clumsy, for as Lingard has pointed out, Phillips, usually so clever, overlooked something in the body of the letter and allowed the project of *escape* to stand in it, while the postscript indicated *murder*.[5]

Another point that has, so far as I know, always been passed over is this: there was no urgent need for Walsingham to strike in August, 1586; he could have afforded to have waited a little longer. Had he been sure of his case this is just what he would have done. A man as astute as he was would have preferred to have in his hands documents about which no questions could be raised instead of resorting to forgery, which is always liable to detection. Yet we know that he *did* resort to forgery, at least in the matter of the postscript. If he did so it could have been for only one of two reasons: either because of a sudden spasm of impatience (which was not like Walsingham) or because he had come to see that he was never going to get out of Mary what he was looking for. I submit that it was for the second of these reasons that he decided to allow Phillips to fabricate the evidence.

What is the argument on the other side? The one advanced as though it were conclusive is that Mendoza wrote to Philip on September 10: "The Queen of Scotland must be well acquainted with the whole affair, to judge from the contents of a letter she has written to me." The letter of Mary's to which he refers is clearly the one written the previous July. The passage in it that is supposed to settle the question of her complicity 'n the Babington conspiracy is this: "What I have again

---

[5] It must be remembered that these letters were written in numerical cipher, a fact which explains the ease with which alterations or variations could be made.

heard of the good intentions of the King toward this particular quarter, I have again written fully to the principals of the said Catholics on the design which I have sent them with my advice on every point." The words, however, are noncommittal. All we can definitely extract from them is that Mary had passed on to Babington what Philip had written to her, adding some advice of her own. But nobody doubts that there was a "design": everything turns on whether that design was for Mary's escape (as she maintained) or for Elizabeth's assassination (as the prosecution maintained). The matter could have been determined beyond dispute in only one way — by the production of the secretaries' notes; and these were suppressed or "lost" by Walsingham. Under threats of the rack the secretaries did, it is true, admit that the copies of Mary's letters they were shown "seemed" to be the ones she had written: and there is no dispute that these letters were — in the main — identical with those that had actually been sent to Babington. But in 1605 Nau insisted that the murder charge against his dead mistress had been "false, calumnious, and supposititious." Not even Babington's admission on the scaffold that he had received letters from Mary that referred to Elizabeth's assassination can be taken as finally fixing complicity on the Queen of Scots. He may well have read into Mary's letters — which used general rather than specific terms — more than she ever intended. And there were the bits which, unknown to him, had been added by Phillips. If he was pushed on by the *agents provacateurs* to a purpose of assassination, in addition to his original one of abduction, he accepted it with extreme reluctance and probably continued to hope to the end that it need never be carried out. As for his own letters, ignorant of the world and sanguine though he was, they did not tell Mary more — there was no need that they should — than that he and his associates were planning her release.

What may be granted, however, is that Mary, though too experienced a politician to commit herself too definitely, probably guessed that Babington had more in his mind than he wrote down, or that he might be hurried on, in spite of himself, to a killing. She could, however, truthfully declare before her judges that she had no knowledge of any plot of murder; she was not obliged to declare that she had any suspicions as to what Babington might do. And it is at least as likely as not that she had none, or that she deliberately shut her mind against hypothetical possibilities. After all, she could not justly be condemned to death for what she may have thought, but for nothing less than conclusive proof of complicity in a settled design of assassination. If it comes to that, she could not justly be condemned to death even then, for though the court at Fotheringay might have proved her guilty at the bar of history, they had no jurisdiction over her.

There is finally the farewell letter that Mary wrote to Mendoza in which she says: "They have not been able to get anything out of me, except that I am a free Catholic princess and an obedient daughter of the Church, and that I am in duty bound to seek my deliverance, and since I tried fair means unsuccessfully, was obliged to listen to other proposals made to me with the same object." Professor Pollard expresses the opinion that there she "practically admits that she had encouraged attempts on Elizabeth's life." It does not seem to me to make any such admission, though that of course can be read into it. If the "fair means" refer to Mary's appeals to Elizabeth, to her son, and to the continental powers, cannot the "other proposals" be understood as meaning merely an escape from prison? Does "seeking deliverance" necessarily mean Elizabeth's assassination? I do no more than raise these legitimate doubts; I do not affirm that Mary was guiltless. All that I maintain is that nobody can be justly convicted on documentary evidence that was at least in part forged, even granting for the sake of the argument that the court set up to try her had any authority to do so.

What follows is the question of Elizabeth's responsibility for the carrying out of the sentence.

Paulet at once strode into Mary's room and tore down her insignia of royalty, after which he put on his hat and sat down in her presence. Mary in place of the canopy and the coat of arms hung up a crucifix. This Paulet allowed to remain, as he had been rebuked by Elizabeth for his boorishness.

It was still very far from certain whether the Queen would ever allow the death penalty to be exacted. Indeed she several times let it be known that it would be left suspended except in the event of an invasion for the purpose of rescue. Such a suspended sentence was common enough. For instance, Philip, Earl of Arundel, the Catholic son of the Protestant Duke of Norfolk who had been beheaded in 1572, was condemned to death in 1589 and lived in the Tower, expecting every day to be his last until 1595.[6] In Mary's case pressure from various quarters was brought to bear upon Elizabeth to spare her, especially from France. The matter was left undecided.

From Scotland there came Patrick, the Master of Gray, as James's envoy. As in decency bound, he protested against the sentence; in private he whispered into Elizabeth's ear that "the dead do not bite." He was a protégé of the Jesuits. But they cannot be blamed for him, any more than they can be blamed for their pupil, Herr Göbbels. He was merely typical of the conscienceless politics of the age. His method was to use strong language in public, to save his face, and to avoid strong action. "If she die, I shall be blamed," he said; "and if she live I shall be ruined." He preferred not to be ruined.

To another ambassador who pleaded that Mary be kept alive so that negotiations might continue, Elizabeth stormed, "Not for an hour!" and swept out of the room. Yet despite her bluster she hesitated, as well she might, for the execution of a monarch was without precedent in Christendom. And it was still debatable whether it would not be better to hold Mary as a hostage against Spain. While she lived Philip had no claim upon the English throne.

At this stage the Council, whose inner circle had long been working steadily for Mary's death as the solution of all their problems, invented a French plot, in which the Ambassador, Châteauneuf, was supposed to be implicated. This gave a pre-

[6] Executions ran in the family. His father and grandfather were beheaded; his great-grandfather escaped merely because Henry VIII died before he signed the death warrant. His grandson was the Lord Stafford who was executed, without a shadow of justification, at the time of the Titus Oates "revelations."

text for making him a prisoner in his own house and so preventing negotiations with France. After everything was over Elizabeth had the incredible effrontery to jest publicly with him on the subject. Taking his arm, she said to her courtiers, "Here is the man who would get me murdered!" By then the dead had ceased to bite.

To help Elizabeth to make up her mind — and also to relieve her of some part of the responsibility — Parliament was summoned to meet on October 29. The Tudors were great sticklers for legal sanction for their crimes. The Queen knew beforehand what it would advise; yet upon getting the expected petition for Mary's execution she sent them the following characteristically ambiguous reply: "If I should say unto you that I do not mean to grant your petition, by my faith I should say unto you more than perhaps I mean. And if I should say unto you that I mean to grant your petition, I should tell you more than is fit for you to know." What Elizabeth was going to do nobody, not even herself — perhaps least of all herself — could be sure.

Leicester made a recommendation of "the slow and efficacious operation of poison." Did he remember that he was once — in fact, twice — proposed as Mary's husband? Did he even remember the charms he had sent her against poison? But poison was his panacea. Elizabeth, taking the hint, approached Paulet, who very properly refused.

His refusal, though he based it on moral grounds and expressed it with all the unction of his kind, was really due to the fact that he knew Elizabeth. She would have promptly taken his head had he ventured to carry out her wishes. When his refusal was carried to her she raged against "the daintiness and perjury of Paulet and others who, contrary to their oath of association [it will be recalled that this included lynching], do cast the burden on myself! The niceness of these precise fellows who, in words, would do great things for my safety, but, indeed, perform nothing!" Elizabeth, in short, wanted Mary killed — so long as she could get somebody else to see to it.

This was precisely what everybody was determined not to do.

Queen Elizabeth

If Mary was to be killed, Elizabeth was to do the killing. The difficulty now was to jockey her into signing the death warrant. A very pretty piece of work came out of this.

Davison, the new Secretary, had drawn up the warrant, and one day when Elizabeth was in a good mood, she asked him casually what it was he had for her to sign. He told her and she signed it, but threw the paper to the floor, as though she were absent minded. A day or two later she told Davison of a terrible dream she had had of Mary's being beheaded. Rather frightened at this, the Secretary enquired whether she really wished the warrant executed. "By God I do!" she screamed at him, but then fell to muttering something about "another way of doing it." She still hoped she would be able to arrange for a nice quiet little murder at Fotheringay.

The Council now determined to act. They had the warrant, which had been signed on February 1; they decided to send it off without telling the Queen. It was a despicable action, for Cecil had already decided to repudiate Davison after the event. Some scapegoat had to be found, and as Davison was a new man — appointed only the previous July — he could be most easily sacrificed. Moreover, Cecil had his eye on Davison's position for his son Robert — a position which Robert duly obtained. Davison was therefore fined heavily (though the fine was never collected) and sent to the Tower. While there he managed to protect his fame with a full account of what actually happened. He even records Elizabeth's light jest as she signed the warrant. She told him to show it to Walsingham, who was ill in bed, saying, "The news is like to kill him outright!" It is impossible to doubt in face of Davison's dossier, either that Elizabeth was personally responsible for Mary's execution or that she meanly tried to shift the responsibility.

On February 7 the Queen of Scots was informed that she must prepare to die the following morning. She went to her death with the noblest courage and a final affirmation of her Catholic Faith. They had refused her the ministrations of her private chaplains, and sent an ill-mannered fellow, Fletcher, the Dean of Peterborough, to pray with her and to preach at her. She

286

declined to hear him and said her own prayers in a loud voice until he desisted. With a firm step she ascended the scaffold in the great hall of the castle, dressed all in black, confronting the silent and malevolent faces of those who had come to see her die. Her women wept, but she remained calm.

When the executioners divested her of her dress she made a wry joke about not being accustomed to being disrobed by such grooms. Underneath she was dressed from head to foot in scarlet. Holding up her crucifix she cried, "As Thy arms, O God, were stretched upon the cross, so receive me into the arms of Thy mercy, and forgive me my sins." Roughly the Earl of Kent bade her "leave such Popish trumperies, and hold Him in your heart." She fronted him: "I cannot hold in my hand the representation of His sufferings, but I must at the same time bear Him in my heart." There was never a more valiant or a more Catholic end.

Had Mary consented to become a Protestant she could not only have regained the Scots throne but made sure of the English succession. Yet this proud and ambitious woman unhesitatingly accepted the ruin of her pride and ambition rather than renounce her faith. No Pope is likely to canonise her, for all but the most uncritical of her admirers must admit that there are blots upon her character; but if not much like the usual saint, she was of the metal of the martyrs. With her died all hope of a Catholic restoration in England.

After the execution Elizabeth wrote to James (on February 14, 1587): "My dear Brother — I would you knew (though not felt) the extreme dolour that overwhelms my mind for that miserable accident, which, far contrary to my meaning, hath befallen." To the French Ambassador she expatiated on "the misfortunes and vexations that have befallen me." Warming to her hypocrisy she went on, "The members of my Council have played me a trick which I can never forgive, and by God! but for their long services, and for the supposition that they acted out of consideration for the welfare and safety of my person and state, every one of them would lose his head!"

James made a pretence of preparing war against England. He

had to do that much: Scotland considered its honour touched. But it all got no further than talk. The canny James was extremely careful not to do anything that might endanger his succession. Elizabeth cracked the whip when in the following August she sent for the twelve-year-old Lady Arabella Stuart, and kept her at Court as though she were about to declare the child her heiress. Accordingly, as Lingard says of James: "His indignation gradually evaporated; the cry of vengeance was subdued by the suggestions of prudence; and his mouth was stopped by a present of £4,000."

On Mary's funeral Elizabeth spent £40,000, laying her to rest in Peterborough cathedral beside Katherine of Aragon. Such unwonted generosity speaks volumes as to Elizabeth's compunction. But if she felt ashamed, she would undoubtedly have done the whole thing over again had it been necessary.

In its political effects the execution was completely successful — upon which the government had all along counted. The back of Catholic resistance was now broken. Just at the moment when the Papal sentence of 1570 was at long last about to be enforced, the legitimate and Catholic candidate to the throne was obliterated. Nothing was left to politically minded Catholics except to support the shadowy Plantagenet claims advanced in favour of Philip's daughter. Professor Pollard misjudges the matter when he writes, "Mary herself [had been] regarded less as the rightful Queen of England than as the forerunner destined to make straight the path of Philip or the Infanta." If the Infanta was now put forward it was merely because there was no other Catholic candidate available. Even so, she was never supported by more than a small group, most of them living their desolate lives abroad and out of touch with English sentiment. These were the members of the "Spanish Party." Previously to Mary's death, though Cecil could argue plausibly that Catholics were not "loyal," he and they shared the knowledge that Mary and not Elizabeth was their rightful Queen. Now there was nobody left for Catholics to back except the Infanta, a foreigner. Their allegiance to Elizabeth acquired the strength of despair.

The Killing of Mary

Yet in spite of the immediate and vast political gains there was an ultimate political loss even more stupendous. The institution of monarchy had been shaken. Never again would kings be what they had once been, for sacred blood had been shed on the scaffold. When Elizabeth signed Mary's death warrant she signed at the same time the death warrant of Mary's grandson, Charles I. Successful as the two mightiest of the Tudors appeared to the outward eye, they united to defeat their dearest purposes. Henry, Defender of the Faith, had opened the door to Protestantism and had permitted the emergence of the new rich who were to subdue the monarchy. Elizabeth might nevertheless have maintained the reverence with which the monarchy was regarded, though not even she could have prevented the growth of the oligarchy. Lacking true vision and insight, she perceived merely a chance to get rid of a nuisance in Mary. To that consideration she sacrificed her honour; to that she sacrificed the royal line of kings.

18

The Armada

WE LEARN from Gray's *Memorial* for January 12, 1587, that when Leicester was induced to act as the spokesman for a group who wished to transfer Mary's rights to the English Crown to James — she had willed them ten years before to Philip, contingent upon her son's not becoming a Catholic — Elizabeth swung round on him fiercely. "Is that so?" her harsh voice rasped. "Get rid of one and have a worse one in her place! By God's passion! that were to cut my own throat." Then for the benefit of Leicester himself she thrust, "And for a duchy or earldom to yourself, you, or such as you, would cause some of your desperate knaves to kill me. No, by God! He shall never be in that place."

In spite of this outburst, James was now the only serious claimant in the way of Philip. He was, however, far too serious a claimant to the throne of the aging Queen to permit Philip to delay any longer. The King of Spain had once somewhat callously remarked that the English would be sure to put the Queen of Scots to death as soon as he attempted invasion; he now drew from her execution a new determination, because a new incentive, to attack. He would execute the Pope's Bull,[1] restore the Faith — and make his daughter Queen of England, basing her claim, however, primarily not on Mary's will but on his own descent from John of Gaunt. France, he hoped, might support him: that country was ringing with denunciations of the English Jezebel. At the very least the French would remain

---

[1] We must note that there was no new Bull issued. An undated proclamation *in English* was printed, reaffirming the excommunication, but, as Meyer points out, this was, precisely on that account, not a new excommunication. Sixtus had no wish to exhibit a second time the impotence of the Papacy.

friendly neutrals. His road to conquest was at last clear.

As to whether he would have actually deposed Elizabeth had he been successful in defeating her is open to question. Probably to foist his daughter on the country would have seemed, when the time came, more than was feasible. He had always had a weakness for Elizabeth personally as well as politically; indeed, we have heard her say that if he tried to murder her it was because he loved her so much. It is likely that had he found the English throne at his disposal he would have been more than willing that Elizabeth remain on it — on condition that she submit to the Roman jurisdiction. And we must remember that the Papal arrangement of July 29, 1587, gave Philip the right of nomination — subject to the Pope's approval; so far from the Papacy's being committed to the enthronement of the Infanta, Sixtus V made little attempt to conceal his distrust of Philip. There are reasons for believing that Elizabeth would have agreed to re-establish Catholicism and perhaps, after thirty years' experience of Protestant domination, she would have done so with a sense of relief.

Philip's problem, in fact, was by no means a simple one, nor were his aims unconfused. He regarded himself, quite sincerely, as the champion of the Catholic cause in Europe. Yet he would no doubt gladly have made peace — for the war which we think of as beginning in 1588 had actually begun some years previously — had Elizabeth withdrawn from the Netherlands and ceased to harrass his possessions in the New World. It was for this reason that Sixtus V, whose motives were purely religious, while undertaking to contribute a million gold scudi to Philip's war chest, stipulated that the first half million was to be paid only after a Spanish army had landed in England. It was the Pope's method of reserving some control; to all of Philip's pleadings that the money be paid over at once, Sixtus remained immovable.

Only a long series of provocations patiently endured for thirty years had at last brought Philip to his decision. His forebearance — though in the beginning it was largely due to his belief that a country so weak as England could do him no great harm, and so might be disdainfully ignored — was also largely due to his strange infatuation for his tormentor. His attitude disgusted those who had been trying to egg him on. Nicholas Sanders in 1577 wrote bitterly, "The King of Spain is as fearful of war as a child of fire," and in Spain they grumbled, "The King thinks and plans while the Queen of England acts." He tried to console himself with the reflection that Elizabeth's perfidy sullied English honour far more than it sullied Spain's, and when he caught pirates he hanged them.[2] It was a very long time before he was brought to see that he must do something more drastic.

His tolerance had, however, certain things to be said for it. Piracy — at least in the Channel — was nothing new. Chaucer's fourteenth-century Shipman

"Of nice conscience took he no keep.
If that he faught, and hadde the hyer hond,
By water he sente hem hoom by every lond."

Before and since that time it had been the practice of some sea captains, when legitimate business was poor and a good opportunity offered itself, to turn temporary pirates, though of course, the vast majority of captains never went outside the bounds of honest commerce. Moreover, the offence could not be fastened exclusively upon Elizabeth: it was the Huguenots and Dutch who had led the way. Indeed, Elizabeth made some attempt to suppress the freebooters, but could not accomplish much because of the connivance of the vice-admirals and other officials. A list exists of 960 names of men indicted for piracy between 1568 and 1600, and we have records of 106 of them being hanged between 1561 and 1580, including 28 in 1573, and 14 in 1579. At least the Queen could profess that she was doing her best, even if the records indicate that the majority of those brought to trial escaped the gallows, to return to their trade.

Such, I say, were Elizabeth's professions. It unfortunately

[2] Thus John Noble was executed in 1574, Andrew Barker in 1576, and John Oxenham in 1580.

grew by degrees all too apparent that her performance did not quite correspond. Froude has described Hawkins as "not a virtuous man — in the clerical sense." Neither was Elizabeth virtuous in that sense. It became more and more notorious that she was in partnership with her "sea dogs," acting as a kind of receiver of stolen goods. If she could hang them for their misdeeds, they, by getting her to take shares in their ventures, or valuable presents afterwards, compromised her and made their own position safe.

The case of Drake is one very much in point. When he returned in the *Golden Hind* in 1581, after his celebrated voyage, his shareholders got over four thousand per cent profit on their investment. Among the investors was Elizabeth, and she openly showed her approval by going down to Deptford and knighting Drake on board his ship, quite indifferent to the fact that this was an insult to Spain. She even added to her offence by making a humorous pretence, while giving the accolade, of cutting Drake's head off, saying that she would send it to Philip. But of course by 1581 there was very little attempt made to conceal the fact that such raids had official sanction. Drake had become a national hero.

In his own queer way this strange genius was a religious man — if hatred of Catholicism may be considered religious. Yet his genius, like his religion, was not far removed from insanity. Two instances must suffice. When he executed Doughty (who perhaps had been sent out by Cecil as a spy upon him, Cecil not liking piracy) he charged him with "witchcraft," then sentenced him to death, which was quite beyond his commission, then took the communion with him, and finally himself acted as the executioner. And when the ship's chaplain ventured to disagree with him upon some small point of sea-dog divinity, Drake made himself a Pope and — half solemnly, half humourously — excommunicated him. His religion, derived from his father, who had been a naval chaplain under our old friend Admiral Seymour, found its most natural expression in cutting the throats of Catholics. It was Drake who was mainly responsible for fixing in the minds of English seamen that piracy was not merely a profitable, but, when directed against Spain, a "godly action."

The pirates of Elizabeth's first period did not avow themselves to be such. Most of them went through the legal formality of obtaining letters of marque before proceeding to plunder. This meant — technically — that they were merely making reprisals by seizing goods of nations against whom English merchants said they had a claim. What they did, therefore, was looked upon as a form of distraint. From this they went on, by degrees, to fabricate claims or to put them far in excess of their real value. And as relations between England and Spain got worse — principally as a consequence of piracy itself — the pirates dropped all pretence of acting under legal authority. A virtual state of war existed by the beginning of the ninth decade of the sixteenth century. By then any Spanish ship was fair game.[3]

Two facts should be remembered: facts that are usually forgotten. The first is that piracy benefitted only the pirates themselves and the Queen and the courtiers who got their "rake-off." So far from being a help to English commerce, it created so much dislocation of normal trade that the London merchants continually complained. The second fact is that theft and murder were exalted into something heroic. That these pirates were brave and skilful seamen is of course true. It is also true that the crews they trained and inured to danger provided a personnel that would otherwise have been lacking in 1588. But they did not contribute to the founding of the British Empire, except in the sense that they were perforce explorers. Even these opportunities, however, were usually neglected, as when

[3] The pirates were not always scrupulous, however, about confining their attentions to Spanish ships. So in February, 1591, a proclamation was issued against "Some of the Queen's subjects who have been this last summer under cover of recovering recompense on the Spaniard for the notable injuries by arrests and barbarous cruelties practised in Spain and Portugal, and have taken ships and goods of other princes and states." This meant that English piracy was to be restricted to Spanish and Portuguese shipping. At the same time, as officially there was no war, the fiction was kept up that loot seized from Spain was taken only by way of reprisal. No letters of marque were necessary any longer: the Spanish "arrests and barbarous cruelties" were a sufficient excuse for anything an English pirate chose to do.

The Armada

Drake, after sailing up the California coast, made no effort to discover the Northwest passage to China. Off Vancouver Island, according to himself, he ran into arctic conditions which made it impossible to proceed further! It is to my mind astonishing that such men should still be held up to the youth of England for admiration. Upon the whole they must be considered as no better than vulgar and commonplace thieves, adorned with a few eccentricities. They shed no lustre upon their country. I confess that so far from swelling with pride at the thought of their exploits, I am ashamed of them — just as a German who understands the true genius of his people is ashamed of the brigandage of Hitler.

However, now that the crisis with Spain was at hand, the services of these desperadoes could be put to more honourable use. The parsimonious Queen had never spent much money on building up a navy and hence was forced to rely on Drake and Hawkins and the like, now giving them commissions as officers.[4] Without them, the Armada must inevitably have triumphed.

If Philip had delayed so long before attacking England this was because, though his armies were invincible, he possessed practically nothing in the shape of a navy until he ascended the throne of Portugal and, in so doing, secured that country's ships. Even with them at his disposal, much had to be done before he was ready; and then he found it difficult to decide upon a plan of campaign.

Two plans, both quite different from — and either better than — the one eventually adopted were suggested. Santa Cruz, who had defeated Strozzi at Terceira in 1582, advocated an invasion directly from Spain. This would have given unity of command, but was laid aside as too costly. Philip thought it would be better to use the Armada chiefly to hold the seas open for Parma's forces in the Netherlands and to convoy reinforcements.

---

[4] John Hawkins, who had started in life as a businessman, was appointed Treasurer of the Navy in 1578 and served honestly — unlike Sir William Winter, who was a notorious grafter. But Hawkins, like Drake, turned pirate again in 1595.

Mendoza in December, 1586, proposed another method. He advised the King to send a relatively small army to Scotland, where the Scotch Catholics could be raised in Mary's defence and from there join hands with the Catholics in England. Mendoza, though he was now a diplomat, and was to die a monk, was essentially a soldier. His suggestion was overruled.

To Philip's bad judgment was added bad luck. And prodigious worker though he was, he always procrastinated. This was not altogether because of his sluggish temperament; he could never catch up with his work, as he insisted upon personally supervising every administrative detail. In the two capital matters under consideration he accepted the wrong advice.

The first of these errors of judgment was that of deciding to effect a juncture with Parma, and *then* invading England. The fatal flaw here was that the only harbour of the Low Countries capable of holding the Armada was in the enemy's hands. His ships, therefore, were obliged to anchor off shore, where, as events proved, they were at the mercy of the English.

His other error of judgment was scarcely less disastrous, though this may not appear at first sight. Philip had been assured for years by those who were reckoned authorities in English affairs — and he prided himself upon his knowledge of them, though he had not been in England for over thirty years — that, as soon as Parma landed, the Catholics would rise, if they did not rise as soon as they knew that the Armada was on its way.

This opinion had been expressed by Persons: "All Catholics without a single exception regarded the invasion with approval. Nay, they even burn with longing for this undertaking." It had the defect of being the view of a man who had been many years out of England and who did not know what public opinion was in his own country. He had in him that mixture of the sanguine and the soured so often generated by exile. But not only Persons — Cardinal Allen, the Duchess of Feria, Nicholas Morton, all of them united to mislead the King.

They firmly believed what they told him. There seemed to be solid ground for it. In 1569 there *had* been a rising; another had been prepared two years later; and perhaps if Parma had landed in 1588 a few Catholics would have joined him. That, however, is doubtful, so completely had the situation changed since the execution of Mary Queen of Scots. Now Catholics as a body were no less eager than Protestants to repel the Spaniards, as Philip's success would mean (or was likely to mean) the Infanta on the English throne. Rather than have a foreigner, the English Catholic preferred to suffer persecution. Even had Parma defeated all the English forces in the field it is improbable that the Infanta would have been able to maintain herself for long — that is, assuming that she had been crowned.

The English Catholics may have been wrong in taking this attitude. Had I been alive at the time I think I should have felt otherwise, and have acted accordingly. But that is not the point: right or wrong, this was the Catholic attitude. And about it Philip and his English advisers were egregiously mistaken. The only correct element in the calculation was that it would hardly be possible to conquer England unless the Catholics rose. On everything else the *emigrés* were wide of the mark.

What should have been done, of course, was to have announced that the Spaniards were coming, not to depose Elizabeth, but to restore religion. They would probably have had to leave her on the throne in any event; they should have guaranteed this from the outset. Then many others besides Catholics would have seized this opportunity to fling out Cecil and his associates.

Instead, Cardinal Allen unleashed a personal attack on Elizabeth. He, like most of the exiles, had up to this moment concentrated his fire on Leicester and Walsingham and Cecil and Knollys as the men responsible for the establishment of Protestantism. Now he boldly accused the Queen herself. It was a grave tactical mistake.

The controversial style of the time demanded that he take a very strong line, with what we should now consider unjustifiable abuse. But even allowing for this, it is rather painful to read his *Admonition to the Nobility and People of England and Ireland.* According to Allen, Elizabeth was an "incestuous bastard, begotten and born in sin of an infamous courtezan, Anne Boleyn, afterwards executed for adultery, treason, heresy, and incest, among others with her natural brother." Another passage runs: "She hath exalted one special extortioner — Leicester — whom she took up first of a traitor and worse than naught, only to serve her filthy lust. . . . With the aforesaid person and divers others she hath abused her body . . . by unspeakable and incredible variety of lust, which modesty suffereth not to be remembered." Lingard might well comment that the author of the *Admonition* (whom some believed to be Persons but is now generally admitted to have been Allen himself) must have studied the works and acquired the style of the Genevan exiles during Mary's reign. The obvious rejoinder was: why, if Elizabeth was as bad as all that, had she been so far treated so gently by the Catholic controversialists?

Allen had been made a Cardinal and appointed Legate in 1585 in anticipation of the Spanish invasion and England's reconciliation to the Church. Such a provision was wise: Allen would have treated his erring countrymen with sympathy and discretion. The tone of the *Admonition,* however, made the country doubtful about this. It was one thing to denounce Leicester as a man who had "caused his own wife cruelly to be murthered, as afterwards for the accomplishment of his own brutish pleasures with another dame it is openly known that he made away with her husband" — for many did believe precisely that of the Earl. It was something else again to attack Elizabeth in the same way. Though there is little in the *Admonition* that is not now accepted as fact, or at least as highly probable, its publication was a blunder. Too late the book was suppressed — after the failure of the Armada. But of course Cecil contrived to get hold of a copy and made the use of it one would expect. The gouty old man with the delicate face and silvery hair had not yet lost his wits — or his capacity for vengeance.

Nor had England's navy lost its striking power. Philip had been warned that he was no match for Elizabeth on the sea, but he would not listen, thinking only of the weak English armies he had seen in the war of 1557. Even Drake's raid in

The Armada

April, 1587, did not convince him. Now that he had accepted his mission he meant to see it through.

Drake's celebrated raid demands a word here. I pass over the burning and sinking of the ships in Cadiz harbour, except to remark that in naval circles the blow is still held up as a model of its kind. What is more to my purpose is that Elizabeth, as soon as Drake had sailed, sent a message after him ordering him *not* to do the very things that he did. England was still officially at peace with Spain, and the Queen did not wish to appear as the aggressor. Her instructions to Drake were, almost certainly, intended to be flourished afterwards to prove that the raid was unauthorised. She was still hoping that it would be possible to avoid war at the last minute; it was sure to be expensive, and she hated spending money; besides, the outcome of the war might, after all, mean her downfall. At the same time she did not wish to lose so magnificent a chance of crippling the Armada before it sailed.

The result was that the invasion had to be put off for a year, and in the meanwhile Santa Cruz, the Spanish Admiral, died. The Duke of Medina Sidonia, a landsman, was put in his place, mainly because he was a Duke. Even he had many misgivings about the undertaking.

His appointment was not so foolish at it may seem. The Armada, in so far as it was a force for fighting at sea, was looked upon as a kind of naval cavalry that charged the enemy, grappled, and boarded. These were the classical tactics that had won the great battle of Lepanto, where soldiers, not sailors, fought. And such tactics would have won again in 1588 if the English had allowed the Spaniards to use them. For the Armada carried thirty thousand men — two thirds of them soldiers.

The popular idea still prevails that a small English fleet defeated a large and powerful Spanish one. This is not at all the case. Sir Julian Corbett has gone into the matter in detail and with expert knowledge in his *Drake and the Tudor Navy*, the standard work on the subject. There he points out that "Though Howard had but five of the 'great sort,' that is of 800 tons and upwards, against Sidonia's eight, of the 'middle sort'

299

he had eleven to Sidonia's seven or eight, and of the 'lesser sort' six to Sidonia's three." The majority of the Spanish ships were small and poorly armed.[5] The Armada must be thought of as a fleet of transports convoyed by battleships. These were either galleons, which were not very well suited for northern waters, or rowing galleys which, while excellent for chasing corsairs in the Mediterranean, were useless for a long voyage.

To oppose Medina Sidonia's fleet of a hundred and thirty sail the English had mustered about two hundred ships, most of which were also small — smaller on the average than those of the Spaniards — but much more heavily armed, and with guns of a longer range. The total tonnage of the two fleets was roughly equal.

The English advantages lay in their ships being more seaworthy, better adapted for a fight in the Channel, and manned by extremely skilful seamen. To their gunners the stately — and clumsy — galleons presented easy targets, while they could keep safely out of range because, being close hauled, they could manoeuvre more quickly.

Yet with all those English advantages Medina Sidonia would have achieved his purpose except for making an irreparable mistake. Nobody could have asked for better luck than to surprise Drake's fleet while it was bottled up in Plymouth. All the Spaniards had to do was to blockade it and destroy it; then three quarters of the battle would have been won. This Medina Sidonia's experienced captains begged him to do. Instead he insisted on keeping to his instructions of pressing on to the point of the Flemish coast where Parma was waiting for him. With that he threw his opportunity away — and so decided the fate of Europe.

Drake's squadron managed to get out and, securing the wind gauge, peppered the Spaniards at will. There was no coming up with the agile English ships and, therefore, no chance of boarding them. Drake ran in and out inflicting great damage while he himself was hardly touched. His tactics were something

---

[5] Laughton estimates that only about fifty — and probably fewer — of the Spanish ships could be called men of war.

new to the Spaniards; all that they could do was to bear east-wards on their stately way.[6]

But not even the full force of the English fleet — gained when Drake joined his nominal superior, Lord Howard of Effingham — was able to stop the Spaniards or to break their formation. Camden describes this as a half-moon, and so no doubt it appeared from a distance. But Corbett, who gives a plan of how the Spanish ships were drawn up, calls it, more correctly, that of a spread eagle. In the centre was the vanguard of galleons followed by the main battle line, which in turn was followed by twenty caravels, riding in a column five abreast. Between the double wings of the eagle were guarded the smaller vessels. Not all the skill and daring of Drake could impede that progress. A few Spanish ships were sunk or captured, but the fleet, as such, remained intact — a spread eagle still. The results of the battle in the Channel were disappointing to the English, for they had as yet done nothing to prevent Medina Sidonia from joining Parma and convoying his flat-bottomed boats across the straits. It looked as though that objective were going to be achieved. So long as they kept their formation unbroken, the Spaniards could afford to lose a few ships.

The individualistic character of the English attack is made evident by the fact that Drake, having disabled the ship captained by Pedro de Valdes, stood by it all night off the Isle of Wight to capture it, when he should have been pursuing the Armada.[7] Sir Julian Corbett tries to excuse Drake for this, but admits that "to many it seemed the act of an incorrigible pirate." It seems so to me. It was not merely a question of "plucking the enemy feather by feather"; it was that the taking of a prize was to Drake more important than victory itself.

So far the Armada had proved a success. It had discovered

---

[6] Naval authorities tell us that there were, strictly speaking, no naval tactics employed. The English ships kept no formation. Their method was a kind of guerilla warfare. Howard described it as "plucking the Spaniards' feathers one by one."

[7] Its captain was kept a prisoner in England until March, 1593, when "after being taken to Court by orders of the Queen," as a contemporary tells us, "and treated very handsomely, being visited by the Council, the nobles and the captains of the ships," he was allowed to go home to Spain.

that it could take — and disregard — heavy blows. Steadily and slowly it came up the Channel in a calm sea under a light breeze and on the evening of July 28 dropped anchor off Griz Nez. Only a few miles up the shore Parma and his army were waiting at Dunkirk to be carried to England. Medina Sidonia could regard the campaign as virtually won, for the English infantry was thought to be no match for that of Spain; and the Catholics were expected to rise. On the previous day Howard had written of the Armada, "This is the greatest and strongest combination, to my understanding, that ever was in Christendom." And other English reports indicated disappointment and alarm. After the issue had been determined there was, of course, a great deal of boasting. But it is clear that the English had found the Spaniards far more formidable than they had dreamed.

Drake, however, still had a trick up his sleeve. He was about to justify the name of *El Draque*. Of the English vessels eight hulks that were of little use for fighting were taken and filled with gunpowder and pitch and other combustibles. These, having had square sails set upon them, were sent on the wind and tide toward the anchored Armada.

Down the blazing ships came toward the sleeping Spaniards, who awoke in a panic, cut their cables in a general *sauve qui peut,* and got out in confusion from the path of the fire ships that meant their destruction. It was two in the morning. By the time the Spaniards had scrambled away from the shore the dawn had broken.

Then the whole English fleet fell upon them. All the grand formation the Armada had maintained as it rode proudly up the Channel was gone, and Medina Sidonia found this something impossible to regain. The next day in a raging gale the English raked his ships with their long-range guns, getting among them at last, and tacking so swiftly as to present poor targets themselves while they hammered the high hulls of the galleons. It was the decisive battle of Gravelines.

Upon the medal struck by Elizabeth to commemorate the famous triumph was inscribed *Flavit Deus et dissipati sunt.* Yet

it was not the weather that undid the Spaniards but the confusion caused by the fire ships — that and the deadly English
gunnery. Indeed, only by the luck of the weather was the
Armada saved from total destruction, for the fleet flying northwards, was almost on the shoals of Zeeland when, on the 30th,
as though by a miracle, the wind shifted and Medina Sidonia
was able to make for the safety of the open seas.

Even so, the English might have destroyed the Spaniards had
it not been for the niggardliness of the Queen who had provided
an insufficiency of stores and munitions and so robbed them of
"the famousest victory that ever our navy might have had at
sea." So ignorant was Elizabeth of naval matters that she complained that no Spanish ships had been boarded and so few
ships and such little treasure taken. Had the Spaniards at that
moment been able to turn upon their enemies the verdict of
history would have been that Elizabeth had plucked defeat out
of the very jaws of victory.

Ten days later — that is, when the crisis was safely past, and
not before the defeat of the Armada — Elizabeth went down
to Tilbury to review the army under Leicester. (The other English force, commanded by Hunsdon, hardly existed except on
paper.) Even Leicester's men were for the most part raw levies
not at all capable of meeting the eighteen thousand trained soldiers Sidonia had on board and Parma's seasoned army; and
they were under the command of a fat and incompetent general, who had perhaps been appointed by Elizabeth because he
could be relied on to make terms with the invaders if they
seemed to be winning. But now, as the Armada had been scat-
tered, the Queen could dramatise the situation; she was always
at her best at such things. Wearing a steel breastplate and a
preposterous farthingale, bareheaded, and with a truncheon in
her hand, she rode "like some Amazonian empress through all
her army."

The report of her speech has come down to us, and although
it may not have been word for word what she said, it was no
doubt in substance as follows: "Let tyrants fear. I have always
so behaved myself that, under God, I have placed my chiefest

strength and safeguard in the loyal hearts and good will of my subjects; and therefore I am come amongst you, as you see, at this time, not for my recreation and disport, but being resolved, in the midst and heat of the battle [!] to live or die amongst you all, to lay down for God, and for my kingdom, and for my people, my honour and my blood, even in the dust. I know I have but the body of a weak and feeble woman, but I have the heart and stomach of a king, and of a king of England too, and think foul scorn that Parma and Spain, or any prince of Europe should dare to invade the borders of my realm; to which, rather than any dishonour shall grow by me, I myself will take up arms."

It was splendid rhetoric; yet perhaps the most appropriate comment upon it is the verse of Lewis Carroll:

> "When the sands are all dry, he's as gay as a lark,
> And will talk in contemptuous tones of the shark;
> But when the tide rises and sharks are around,
> His voice has a timid and tremulous sound."

By which I do not mean to suggest that Elizabeth was wanting in courage; it was rather that she was a cynical opportunist who was always perfectly ready to accept realities and to make a virtue of necessity. Had the Spaniards won, she would have come to a compromise with them: as it was, she could afford a magnificent boast.

Meanwhile the Armada ploughed its way heavily up the coast of Scotland, rounded the Orkneys, and came down by the Hebrides to the coast of western Ireland. All the way along vessels were lost; but the worst awaited them in Ireland. There, when they put in for water, the savage kerns massacred those who had escaped the less savage seas. Sir Geoffrey Fenton, the Irish Secretary, wrote to Cecil on October 28: "When I was at Sligo I numbered on one strand of less than five miles in length eleven hundred dead bodies of men which the sea had driven on shore. The country people told me the like was in other places, though not to the same number." Sir Richard Bingham, the Governor of Connaught, relates that when Don Pedro de

The Armada

Mendoza landed forespent on Clare Island, Dowdany O'Malley, chief of the island, coveting his treasure chests and the fine armour of his officers, slaughtered them to the last man. Sir George Carew makes a similar report to Walsingham on September 18; the Spaniards, he says, were "so miserably distressed coming to land, that one man, named Melaghlin M'Cabbe, killed eighty with his gallowglass axe." Complacently he adds, "The blood which the Irish have drawn upon them doth assure her Majesty of better obedience to come, for that friendship being broken, they have no other stranger to trust to." But indeed the Spaniards, even before this, had often expressed a low opinion of the Irish. If they ever helped them against England, it was not out of love but for political reasons.

At Rome the defeat of the Armada was received with perfunctory grief. Sixtus had neither liked nor trusted Philip, and had openly expressed his admiration of Elizabeth. A pleasant but unlikely story has it that he permitted himself to make the jest that it was a pity that he and she could not marry, "as they would have produced children who would have mastered the world."

The disaster was humiliating to Spanish pride but did not quench Spanish courage. Though only half the ships of the Armada reached Spain, Philip believed, with some justice, that he might have better luck next time. Medina Sidonia had, after all, come near to succeeding; now with the lessons of the naval war learned, the King determined to try again.

19

Gloriana

IT IS not necessary to say much here about the subsequent Armada projects. If I mention them at all it is mainly because most people seem to be unaware that they were ever entertained. But so far from the battle of Gravelines having permanently crippled Philip, he set to work in his slow, dogged way to build up his fleet anew. To England he remained a perpetual threat, and almost every year the rumour arose that the Spaniards were coming. Despite the English boasting, and the confidence they felt in the discovery of their sea power, they were aware that luck had been on their side, and that a better planned invasion might still succeed. They had, indeed, thrown their enemy back; they had proved themselves; they had some right to exult. They also had some cause to dread the unbroken might of Spain.

To disentangle the more important facts from a welter of details, we must fasten upon two things, which appear to be contrary. One is that the English pirates continued to capture ships, between 1590 and 1593 taking no less than eight hundred, among which was the "great carrack" the *Madre de Dios,* a prize of 1,600 tons with a cargo worth £150,000, while during the same period no ship of the royal navy was lost — of course, there were some merchantmen — with the exception of the *Revenge;* and that was lost mainly because of Sir Richard Grenville's bravado. The other thing is that the undeclared war that lasted until 1604 was by no means all to the English advantage. The treasure ships from the Indies — which were the main English objective — were never caught, though in 1597 a *flota* loaded with bullion from the mines of Peru escaped the fleet watching for it by only a few hours. Had this or any other of the treasure *flotas* fallen to England, Spain would at once have been obliged to yield for lack of money to fight any war. "El Draque" and "Achines" and their fellows made their depredations — as they had made them long before 1588 — but accomplished little else.

The reason for this is twofold. Elizabeth was mortally afraid to allow her ships to venture far afield, lest England be left defenceless. Therefore she could not cut Philip's life line to the Indies. And Philip, having learned by experience, built up Spain's naval defences at home and in the New World. His galleons were now constructed on English and Flemish lines and were often armed with the bronze cannon cast in England and smuggled to Spain by Scotch or German ships. Four years after the Armada of 1588 Philip was more powerful at sea than before. His newly devised convoy system, though it could not be extended to ordinary traders, at least served to save the indispensably important treasure pouring across the Atlantic. The English raids on merchantmen continued, and were a nuisance, but nothing of decisive military value was achieved.

There was during these years only one serious assault upon the Indies, when Hawkins, who was growing old and cautious, and Drake, who had for several years been under a cloud, were beaten off from Porto Rico and dislodged from the Isthmus of Panama. These valiants had performed wonders in the past, when they had defenceless towns to sack. They were not so successful now when they reverted to type as pirates, for their early raids had put Spain on guard. They wilted before the determined fire of the Spaniards and, dispirited by failure, prowled about the Mexique Bay until Hawkins died on November 12, 1595, and Drake at the end of the following January; whereupon what was left of the expedition crawled back to England.

Nor were English arms victorious elsewhere during this period. The expedition to France to help Henry IV obtain his crown as a Huguenot obtained no solid results. And the force sent with the Portuguese pretender, Don Antonio, in 1589 was, like the "Islands Voyage" of 1597, a showy failure. Corunna was taken by a fleet of two hundred sail that carried an army of 20,000 men — a great effort. But the march overland did not raise the Portuguese in Don Antonio's support, and Lisbon, which might well have fallen had it been the direct object of attack, locked itself up securely against the invaders. Young Essex thrust his spear into one of the gates of the city "demanding aloud if any Spaniard mewed therein durst adventure forth in favour of his mistress to break a lance." As apparently no Spaniard durst, the English returned home. Even from Cadiz, taken in 1597, Essex and Raleigh brought back little except the library of Bishop Osorius, and a couple of galleons. The expedition merely balanced the Spanish raid on the coast of Cornwall and the Spanish capture of Calais in the spring of 1596.

Philip's Armada designs, however, also failed. That of 1596 directed, not against the Isle of Wight, as is often said, but Ireland, was driven back by the weather to Ferrol with twenty of its ninety-eight ships wrecked. Had it landed in Ireland, Tyrone would assuredly have ejected the English, and England itself would have been in peril. As for the still stronger Armada of October, 1597, that sailed side by side with the English fleet returning from the Azores, neither English nor Spanish suspecting how close they were to one another. But again a storm sent the Spaniards home. If Philip had at last been roused to resolute and desperate action, his commanders could not forget what had happened in 1588. On September 13, 1598, the King died, with his great dream unfulfilled. There was no further attempt to conquer England and to bring it back to the Church by force of arms.

Though it is a somewhat futile exercise to try to rearrange history in the light of what might have happened, we may say that Philip might have had a good chance had he decided upon a landing in Scotland — which was Mendoza's old plan — as the Scots in 1588 would have been glad to take their revenge on England for the execution of Mary. But as Philip's claim on behalf of his daughter was tenable only if James was ruled out as a heretic, he had no wish to have that shifty young theologian turn Catholic — which is what he promptly would have done under such circumstances. To have seized Ireland would have been a still sounder plan; at least that country could have been held, and from that vantage ground England attacked. But Philip ruled that out until it was too late.

It is virtually certain that England itself could never have been permanently reduced — not without the help of the English Catholics. And though these had strikingly demonstrated their loyalty to Elizabeth, the exiles who made up the "Spanish Party" — men who firmly believed that they could best serve the Church by backing Philip — hampered the Catholicism for which they would gladly have laid down their lives. Afterwards even Robert Persons, the leader of the *emigrés,* and the most vehement of politicians if also the most selfless of priests, said with acrid candour, "God had destroyed the Armada to preserve the English Catholics, who had already suffered so much from the heretics, from suffering still worse things at the hands of the Spaniards." No Catholic need mourn that there was no Spanish conquest of England.

If all could rejoice that England had been spared invasion, all could also rejoice over English sea power. Yet to brag about the "licking" of Philip — in so far as he can be said to have been "licked" — is rather schoolboyish. England's Elizabethan glory ought to be regarded as reposing on something more substantial than the miscalculation that determined the fate of the Armada. Especially should it be thought of as finding its noblest expression in the intellectual and literary life of the age, and in the first small beginnings of the British Empire. The last item, however, I include with some dubiousness: England might have been more truly great had she never acquired her vast possessions.

Let me touch briefly on these two matters. In an age when a poet had to secure a patron to live at all, Elizabeth was nobody's patron. Writers fulsomely flattered her — generally, it is to be feared, in the hope of reward — and she complacently pocketed their compliments; they did not pocket her gold. Poor Spenser, though the least unhandsomely treated of them all, wrote of his lingering "at prince's court and expectation vain," and had to turn at last, in writing his "Prothalamion," to Essex, "Great England's glory, and the world's wide wonder." It was in vain that he apotheosized Elizabeth as "Gloriana." As for Lyly, who surely spread his flattery thick enough to satisfy even Elizabeth, he had to write to the Queen, "After ten years' tempest I must at the Court suffer shipwreck of my times, my hopes, and my wits." Little enough was done for either of them. As Professor Cheney remarks, "Elizabeth had few generous impulses. No one of the great men of her time, in literature, learning, civil, military, or naval life was fully recognised or adequately rewarded by her. She was occasionally liberal to her favourites, but never lavish, except for her own personal adornment or gratification." When she did enrich a man it was either, as in the case of Hatton, at the expense of other men, or, as in the case of Leicester and Essex, at the expense of the country. The literary splendours of the age owe practically nothing to her.

Nor can those who set such store in colonial expansion credit the Queen with its encouragement. Not a quarter of the possibilities were exploited. It is useless to say that Spain was the dog in the manger of the New World; the northern continent was open, and so was Africa. The most that one can say is that the boundless opportunities had been completely ignored before Elizabeth's time, and now England was one of the last countries to enter upon a career of exploration and extension of commerce. When a few adventurous individuals went to Russia and the far East, it was merely as traders; even as such they were not nearly so successful at this time as the Portuguese.

Such efforts at colonization as were attempted were dismal failures. Sir Humphrey Gilbert took a hundred Catholics to plant them in Maine — and so get rid of them. But he and all his passengers were drowned off the coast of Nova Scotia. And Sir Walter Raleigh's Virginian settlement, though it was made, did not flourish. Grenville went out with them and amused himself for a while with hunting the Indians and rounding them up for his gold-seeking schemes. Yet except for the few survivors who were later taken off by Drake, the colonists were either massacred by the savages or were themselves assimilated into savagery.

There were, of course, grave difficulties in the way of establishing any permanent colony. Those difficulties, however, were mainly created by the very men who conceived the colonial designs. For on the slightest pretext they reverted to their trade of piracy. So much was this so, that even as late as 1603 Maffeo Michiel, Governor of Zante, wrote to the Doge to unburden his soul on the subject of Englishmen, saying, "I am convinced that there is not a sailor of that nation who is not a pirate." It was at all events near enough the truth to justify the Spaniards' hanging any Englishman they caught in the New World. The English were hardly more than robber wasps preying upon the industrious bees that made the honey, when they plundered Spanish and Portuguese ships that were bringing home cargoes from East or West. Such a state of affairs was anything but conducive to the expansion or security of trade, or the establishment of peaceful and prosperous colonies.

Sir Martin Frobisher was perhaps the most notable of the explorers proper, but even his adventures ended in a fiasco, after which he turned to the more profitable occupation of piracy. He went out three times from 1576 to 1578 with the object of discovering the Northwest Passage. His first voyage resulted in some useful geographical information, an encounter with the Esquimaux, and the bringing back of samples of ore which the assayers pronounced to contain gold. This induced Elizabeth to invest £500 for his second voyage and £1,000 for his third — Cecil and the Lord Admiral and Walsingham and Sir Thomas Gresham and even the alchemist, Dr. Dee, also subscribing capital. The cargo of "gold" Frobisher produced this time was, however, declared worthless — and was used to mend a road at Deptford. These arctic voyages gave Englishmen some notion of the coast line of northeast America, kept alive hope of the eventual discovery of a passage to China, and made colonization an ideal for a few enthusiastic minds. But for all that, in both exploration and colonization England lagged far behind the other maritime powers. The glow of anticipation is to be found in Drayton's magnificent ode "To the Virginian Voyage"; but it was no more than a poet's fantasy of what might be. Any steady effort for founding colonies had to wait until the Stuarts were on the throne. Elizabeth was much more interested in plundering Spaniards.

She was now growing old and lonely, and a little more preposterous each year, though her brilliance and vivacity were quite undimmed. But the very fact that she refused to accept her invalidism or her age added to her pathos and her spiritual solitude. Her friends were dying, Hatton passing in 1591 — according to one account of chagrin at being ordered to refund some money to the Crown, according to another of "a flux in his urine" — and Leicester had preceded him shortly after the defeat of the Armada. There may still be seen what Elizabeth inscribed with her own hand "His last letter"; yet her grief at Leicester's death did not deter her from making a distraint upon his goods for a debt he owed the Crown. It was a means of getting even with his detested widow.

The Queen's loneliness and restlessness are shown by her moving about from place to place according to sudden whim. Greenwich, Whitehall, Nonesuch, Oatlands, and Richmond — to say nothing of the smaller royal manors — saw her descend unexpectedly and leave as unexpectedly. She could be at rest nowhere, and she was always changing her mind about where she wanted to be.

About this an entertaining story has come down to us. The movings always involved a good deal of trouble for the household, for every time about a hundred carts had to be used to transfer the clothes and baggage of Elizabeth and her courtiers. One of the carters who had received orders to assist in the move, and then had heard the order countermanded only to be issued again, grumbled humourously under the royal window, "Now I see the Queen is a woman as well as my wife!" Delighted by the comment, Elizabeth sent him a couple of gold pieces, in an unusual fit of generosity. This was a jest in her own rough vein. It was in a similar spirit that she greeted a deputation of eighteen tailors with "Good morning, gentlemen both!" And when she told a celibate clergyman, "Whitehead, I like thee better because thou livest unmarried" she laughed boisterously when he ventured upon the retort, "In troth, Madam, I like you the worse for the same cause!"

It was probably due to the combination of her dread of isolation and her relish for badinage that accounted for her fancy for surrounding herself as she grew old with young men. These she permitted a breezy familiarity that she would never have tolerated in her ministers. Her patronage of Essex, in which many historians have seen a sinister significance, may have really been akin to the indulgence shown by a maiden aunt to a high-spirited nephew. The same thing would apply to her relations with her godson, John Harington. While he was still a boy she wrote him one of the most charming of her letters, with which she enclosed a copy of her speech to Parliament: "Boy Jack: I have made a clerk write fair my poor words for thine use, as it cannot be such striplings have entrance into Parliament as yet. Ponder them in thy hours of leisure, and play with them, till they enter thy understanding; so shalt thou hereafter, perchance, find some good fruits thereof, when thy godmother is out of remembrance; and I do this because thy father was ready to serve and love us in trouble and thrall."[1] Some years later, when he was grown up, he wrote to celebrate his invention of the water closet his scabrous *Metamorphoses of Ajax*, at which the royal godmother affected to be shocked. But she soon hung up a copy of the book in her own *cabinet*. Young men, especially if they managed to blend a display of sychophantic respect and a profession of uncontrollable love with their free and rowdy humour, could always endear themselves to the old Queen. In their company she found the illusion of keeping age at arm's length.

Those, on the other hand, who reminded her that she was

[1] We do not often hear of Elizabeth troubling herself with young women or children. However, there is the pretty incident of her pinning up the dress of the child, Lady Talbot, whom she kissed and took with her in the state barge. There was, after all, a heart beneath the humbug. In other circumstances the Queen might have been a good and beloved woman.

growing old felt her sharp displeasure. Thus, when the Bishop of St. David's preached before her on the text, "Lord teach us to number our days that we may apply our hearts to wisdom" — and quoted in his sermon the passage from Ecclesiastes about "the grinders being few," using some elaborate symbolical arithmetic to enforce his point — she sent for him afterwards and told him she perceived that "the greatest clerks were not always the wisest men." In truth the Bishop might have been more tactful in the presence of a lady who had lost most of her teeth.

What Elizabeth demanded from old and young alike was flattery. This they ladled out so lavishly that one is sickened to read over the things they wrote and said. Disraeli was three hundred years later to express the opinion that in the case of royalty one should lay the flattery on with a trowel. No men ever used the trowel with so extravagant a flourish as the Elizabethan courtiers and poets.

Let us look at some of the stuff contemporary poets published about Elizabeth. To them she was "Judith" and "Deborah" and, as time wore on and the note had to be pitched still higher, "Diana" and "Cynthia," the "Lady of the Sea," and "Gloriana," and "Belphoebe." To Sir Walter Raleigh she was "Virtue's perfect image cast" — to that same Raleigh who made the devastating remark about her minions not being so happy as was commonly supposed, because of their being ordered to uncomely employments. But he knew his Elizabeth, and when he was sent to the Tower because of an affair with Elizabeth Throckmorton (the cousin of the executed traitor, whom he afterwards married) he begged his keeper to be allowed to go out on the river in disguise when the royal barge was passing, "to ease his mind with but a sight of the Queen, or else his heart would break." His request being refused, as he knew it would be, he threatened to stab himself and feigned madness — in the expectation that all this would be passed on to Elizabeth. In a letter to Robert Cecil he wrote, "I that was wont to behold her riding like Alexander, hunting like Diana, walking like Venus, the gentle air blowing her fair hair" — which was a wig! —

Gloriana

"about her pure cheeks, like a nymph; sometimes sitting in the shade like a goddess; sometimes singing like an angel; sometimes playing like Orpheus. Behold the sorrows of the world! Once amiss hath bereaved me of all."

Spenser, of course, has reams in celebration of Elizabeth's chastity. But one passage will suffice: in it he expresses his belief in the immaculate conception of Anne Boleyn's daughter!

> "Her birth was of the womb of morning dew,
> And her conception of the joyous prime,
> And all her whole creation did her shew
> Pure and unspotted from all loathly crime
> That is ingenerate in earthly slime.
> So was this virgin born, so was she bred,
> So was she trainèd up from time to time
> In all true virtue and true bountyhead,
> Till to her due perfection she was ripenèd."

Let us pass to Ben Jonson. To him Elizabeth was "the bright mirror of true Chastity" and the "Goddess excellently bright" — though to do him justice he draws the line at Spenser's theological imagery. Yet Jonson was the very man who, sitting at his ease with Drummond of Hawthornden, talked with such cynical frankness of Elizabeth's sexual impediment and sexual perversion. One can only conclude that there was a complete divorce in his mind between the formal and public praise he addressed to the Queen and his private conviction. Shakespeare, though he, too, has a few "Elizabethan" references, is offhand and perfunctory in comparison with his fellow poets.

Even the Catholic Constable wrote poems about Elizabeth, but his is merely the Petrarchan hyperbole of the time. He does not assert, as a rule, her resplendent virtue. Instead he ingeniously contrives to accuse her (but it is needless to say, flatteringly) of having made him sin:

> "Thus sin thou caused — envy I mean, and pride —
> Thus fire and darkness do proceed from thee.
> The very pains which men in hell abide:

Queen Elizabeth

> Oh no; not hell but purgatorie this,
> Whose souls some say by angels punished be,
> For thou art she from whom this torment is."

And Robert Persons, the Jesuit, dedicating his *Brief Discourse* to her in 1580, refers to "her noble and merciful disposition known and renowned throughout the world." At that time he was hoping that she would mitigate the lot of Catholics; afterwards his attitude toward her changed.

If flattery in the form of literary exercises were all, one could stand it; what is really shocking is the blasphemous attempt to put Elizabeth, whom Mr. E. M. Forster has wittily called a "public virgin," in the place occupied in Catholic England by Our Lady. "The living God is only the English God" wrote Lyly with Elizabethan arrogance. And a poem in Dowland's *Second Book of Songs or Airs* contains this stanza:

> "When others sing *Venite exultemus!*
> Stand by, and turn to *Noli emulari!*
> For *Quare fremuerunt* use *Oremus!*
> *Vivat Eliza!* for an *Ave Mary!*"

Nobody will seriously object to the association of Elizabeth with the mediaeval myth of the fierce unicorn that could be captured only by a chaste maiden acting as a decoy, though one may perhaps wonder how many unicorns this virgin captured. The sort of thing that does arouse indignation is the publication of books to look exactly like Catholic manuals of devotion, in which terms hallowed to the use of the Blessed Virgin are bestowed upon Elizabeth. In disgust, but to exhibit a sample of what was actually printed, I quote the first paragraph on page 307 of Thomas Bentley's *Monument of Matrones,* which appeared in 1582. It goes: "Elizabeth, thou virgin mine, the King's daughter and fairest among women; most full of beauty and majesty, attend a little to my hest, and mark what I shall say. Thou art my daughter indeed, this day have I begotten thee, and espoused thee to the King Christ, my Son, crowned thee with my gifts, and appointed thee Queen to reign over my holy mount Zion." The rest of the book is in the same abomin-

Gloriana

able strain, and if perhaps an extreme instance, by no means stands alone.

The only extenuation one can offer is that the whole period was preposterous, and that Gloriana was its fitting symbol. Never in the world's history has the human body been so disguised and distorted. To splendour was sacrificed all sense of beauty, by men and women alike. It is not surprising that the literature of the age should have been so often fantastically remote from truth and reason. When Shane O'Neill arrived in London in 1562, just in time for the Twelfth Night festivities, his gallowglasses with their matted hair and their saffron robes appeared laughably outlandish in the eyes of the English courtiers. But what did O'Neill think of *them?* No African savages have more disfigured themselves than these same Elizabethans.

The sixteenth century, especially in England, was one of glaring contrasts — heroism and the basest treachery, exquisite sensibility and a brutal insensitiveness, utter selflessness and a crude greed: these qualities existed side by side, and not infrequently the most extraordinary contradictions existed in the same person. Certainly few more inconsistent Elizabethans were found than Elizabeth herself. In one respect, however, she was always the same. In avarice she grew — so to speak — more like herself as she grew older. It was not enough that poets should hymn her praises and that courtiers should frame elaborate compliments: she had to have tangible proofs of the estimation in which she was held. She expected (and received) every New Year's Day valuable presents, and the ones that pleased her best were those in hard cash.[2] We have a record of what she got at the opening of 1578 — it was £993.13.4, close on to $30,000 in modern values. The third volume of Nichols' *Progresses* tells us that she got only £750 in 1600, which is perhaps an index to her waning popularity. She had so little longer to live that it was hardly worth while to purchase her favour.

[2] The ladies of the Court usually gave clothes. Men gave gold and silver. But, of course, this giving of presents was by no means limited to New Year's Day. At any time a favour was sought it was advisable to pave the way with a handsome gift.

Queen Elizabeth

Her indubitable splendours were, in truth, increasingly tinged with the farcical. She was Gloriana, full of sprightliness, kicking her heels in old age, but angular now and so toothless that it was not always easy to understand what she said. She had had, according to common repute, an endless series of lovers, and was still supposed to have lovers. Yet in spite of this she was the "mirror of chastity" and the "Virgin Queen." The absurdity of the situation was not lost upon those who praised her to her face and snickered behind her back. They had to revenge themselves somehow.

Astonishing pictures have been drawn for us by the Ambassadors at her Court. Thus de Maisse notes that she "talked of her foolishness and ugliness to provoke compliments, which she swallowed; she apologised for her dowdiness when she was clothed in silver tissue and loaded with jewels. She was coquettish, gay, frivolous, and indelicate." He relates going to see her one day when "She had a petticoat of white damask, girdled and open in front, as was also her chemise, in such a manner that she often opened this dress and one could see her belly, and even to the navel." On another page he remarks that this exhibition was clearly quite deliberate, for it was several times repeated. Mr. Lytton Strachey mildly surmises that "Perhaps the unaccountable woman had merely been feeling a little vague and fantastic that morning when she put on her clothes."

De Maisse has a number of other observations to offer on Gloriana. "When a man speaks to her," he writes, "and especially when he says something displeasing, she interrupts not seldom; and by reason of her interruptions very often she misunderstands what is said to her and misreports it to her Council. Hence comes the custom of delivering to the Council in writing what has been said to her. She is a haughty woman, falling easily into rebuke." Elsewhere in his books he says, "As for her face, it is and appears to be very aged. It is long and thin, and her teeth are very yellow and unequal, compared with what they were formerly, so they say, and on the left side less than the right. Many of them are missing so that one cannot understand her when she speaks quickly." Yet he is fair enough to add, "It is not possible to see a woman of so fine and vigorous a disposition both in mind and body," shading in his portrait with "When anyone speaks of her beauty she says she was never beautiful, although she had that reputation thirty years ago. Nevertheless she speaks of her beauty as often as she can." One can almost hear the guffaws ringing yet of the young gallants who regaled each other later with the titbits of flattery they had offered the Queen and that she had gobbled down.

Abroad, too, her weakness was well known and systematically traded upon. Thus when Unton, the English Ambassador, showed Henry IV a miniature of Elizabeth while he was walking in his garden with his mistress, Gabrielle d'Estrées, the King had immediately to snatch away the picture and cover it with kisses, vowing that he had never in all his life seen anything so lovely. He knew that Unton could be relied on to send Elizabeth a full report of what had happened. Nor did it lose anything in the telling: Unton was careful to assure his Queen that she completely outshone the beauteous Gabrielle. Elizabeth was a connoisseur of such dramatic settings.

There was at times a touch of the macabre about her. We have an account of her in her sixty-fourth year receiving a German visitor and wearing upon her breast, which he noticed was otherwise bare, a filigree lace shawl on which sat a hideous black spider that appeared to be alive. But the foreigner did not fail to notice at the same time the vigour of the old lady. She kept him standing, while she herself stood, for a full hour.[3]

In every way, indeed, she was robust, not least of all in her taste in pleasures, for though she delighted in dancing and music — playing excellently on the virginals, having for instructor William Byrd — she turned with equal zest to cock-fighting and bull-baiting, sometimes varying the noble sport by setting an ape on a mule's back and sending mastiffs after them. But in this respect she must be admitted to have been no more Elizabethan than a good many other people of her times. Philip Stubbes might well ask in his *Anatomie of Abuses* (1583): "What Christian heart can take pleasure to see one poor beast

---

[3] Von Klarwill's *Queen Elizabeth and Some Foreigners*, p. 394.

rend, tear, and kill another for his foolish pleasure?" The answer is that the Christian heart of the Virgin Queen enjoyed the spectacle mightily.

She was in fact a virago as well as a virgo. Gloriana had a glorious temper; she spat and swore and shied her slippers at Walsingham, and slapped her maids of honour, and had violent tantrums and fits of hysterics; and her biographers politely cough behind their hands and murmur, "Nerves, just nerves!"

Often enough it was just bad manners. Thus when Sir Roger Williams appeared before her to present a petition she refused to notice him except to scream, "Pho, Williams, how your boots stink!" (He had on boots of untanned leather, and perhaps they were a trifle "high.") He drily retorted, "Tut, Madam, it is my suit that stinks, not my boots!" That we may excuse; it was redeemed by Sir Roger's wit. But what excuse can we find when, having taken an odd dislike to the fringe on a courtier's dress, the Queen spat on it! Her coarseness was at any moment all too likely to manifest itself in such ways. Yet with it all — and partly because of it — she was a great personality.

Eccentric, ill-natured, vulgar — and all the same a genius, an "original," a "character." To such the English always extend their admiration. The state she kept was gorgeous even if her manner of life was gross. De Maisse notes: "When the Queen is served, a great table is set in the Presence Chamber near the Queen's throne. The cloth being laid, a gentleman and a lady come in, walking from the end of the room with the cover, and make three reverences, the one by the door, the next in the middle of the chamber, the third by the table." But he also notes that "her service is neither very sumptuous nor delicate." One shudders still at the thought of her hideous breakfast of beer and mutton broth. Even the delicious airs played by the musicians can hardly reconcile us to that.

The ceremonial deference with which she was treated was characteristic of Gloriana's demands upon her subjects. When she visited a country house — as she often did, since the expense had to be borne by her entertainers — her host and hostess received her upon their knees. This, however, did not always get

SIR FRANCIS WALSINGHAM
From the painting by an unknown artist in the
National Portrait Gallery.

them gracious words of thanks at their guest's departure. " 'Madam,' I may not: 'mistress' I must not call you," said Elizabeth to Archbishop Parker's wife in good-bye. As for Edward Rookwood of Euston, a Catholic who in 1578 entertained the Queen and her entourage for several days, he was arrested for having ventured into her "Real Presence." A handsome way of saying farewell!

It was in an attitude of abasement that the House of Commons was expected to listen to the speeches from the throne, and when the courtiers addressed the Queen they, too, dropped on their knees. At the service in the royal chapel Dr. Bull and the other members of the choir on entering and departing had to make a low obeisance to Elizabeth's chair — if she happened to be absent. We even hear of how Dr. Dawson of Trinity College, Cambridge, when preaching at Paul's Cross on November 2, 1602, kept on his velvet cap while praying, or when in his sermon he mentioned God, but raised it obsequiously at the name of the Queen.[4]

So much for Gloriana herself; something must now be said about Gloriana's England. It can be only a few words, for the subject of social conditions in the sixteenth century fills many books. Such works as those by Thorold Rogers and R. H. Tawney present a very different picture than that which dazzles the popular imagination. Hubert Hall puts the matter succinctly when he says, "With good reason we may call the Elizabethan a 'golden' age, for gold was the national divinity," and concludes that "The state of society was the worst that had ever before been in the land." The best men of the time were nearly all *laudatores tempori acti* and considered their age one of degeneration. Shakespeare is full of this. But the line of the minor poet, Thomas Bastard, may be taken as representative of the widespread idea. "The first and riper world of men," he wrote,

[4] Some rather comical things occurred as a result of England's transition from Catholicism to Protestantism. The members of Parliament still keep up the quaint tradition of wearing their hats inside the House, but have to raise them while passing the Speaker. Few of them know that this is a deformed survival from Catholic times — when there was a chapel to be passed. Then the Members doffed their caps to the Blessed Sacrament.

in a nostalgic feeling for the past. It was the sentiment of all except the vulgar money grubbers.

The Elizabethan was, in short, the period when, as never before, a few men made fortunes and the mass of the people became more and more impoverished. The "prosperity" which both Cecil and Elizabeth herself[5] advanced as a token of Heaven's favour and a proof of the truth of the new religion — so anticipating the popularisation of the argument by Macaulay — was merely that of the wealth of the wealthy, upon which was founded the capitalist system that still plagues us. Magnificent buildings were being put up everywhere — that in Hertfordshire which Cecil took sixteen years to build and Hatton's Holderby House in Northamptonshire are examples that occur immediately to the mind — but at the same time there was griping destitution for rapidly increasing numbers. The courtiers, the yeomen, the pirates, and some of the merchants were getting rich — a few disgustingly so — but the enactment of poor laws tell their tale. The regulations governing "masterless men" (or the unemployed) and the stringent conditions binding employers not to pay more than a certain sum, or the employed to accept more, and forbidding them to leave their employment, indicate that the only kind of social security was along somewhat fascist lines. It certainly was far removed from either mediaeval or modern concepts of liberty.

So severe were these laws that vagrants and the unemployed, unless they found work or entered a workhouse, often ended by travelling in a cart to the gallows — this, except at Halifax, which went in for the axe instead, and so was carefully avoided by all rogues and vagabonds. Many an old soldier, broken in the wars and unable to work, called to the bystanders as the rope was being fastened round his neck that this was a shameful way to be treated by the country for which he had fought. Over

[5] "It is clear as daylight to the world," Elizabeth wrote, "that God's blessing rests upon us, upon our people and realm, with all the plainest signs of prosperity, peace, obedience, riches, and power and increase of our subjects." A finer and more profound mind than Elizabeth's or Cecil's — Francis Bacon's — observed that prosperity is the blessing of the Old Testament, adversity of the New. I deny, however, that there was any prosperity — except of the kind of which society should be ashamed.

eight hundred people, men and women, were hanged every year on a charge of "vagabondage," and quite half of those so condemned were sentenced by magistrates at Quarter Sessions at which no juries were called. All this was in an England that even at the end of the reign had a population of hardly more than four million.

Because of the widespread distress petty thieves and pickpockets abounded. Greene was their contemporary historian and gives expert information: the good pickpocket or "Exquisite Foist" (to distinguish him from the crude cutpurse) must have, he says, three properties that a good surgeon should command — an eagle's eye, a lady's hand, and a lion's heart. The vast increase of beggars and bandits and bawds is very far from bearing out the claims of prosperity. The best one can say for Elizabeth is that the dispossession of the poor was begun not by her but by her father and the gang that ruled England in her brother's time; she merely inherited their havoc. And though she had no compassion for the poor — unlike her sister Mary, who used to vist them *incognita* — she must be credited with so careful a management of her estate that the incidence of taxes was relatively light.

Then, too, years occurred when trade was good, and there was something like a boom to cover up the fact that the majority of Englishmen were desperately poor. During 1576 and 1587 the merchants reaped a rich harvest. Afterwards the wool trade declined, for many reasons — among which must be mentioned the insecurity brought about by piracy and the competition of the Dutch; and during the same period, because England had largely ceased to be a grain raising country, food prices skyrocketed. On the other hand, as rents steadily rose, the landowners were able to recoup themselves for their other losses by bearing down on their tenants. The poor could always be invited to console themselves for their hard lot by remembering Gloriana their Virgin Queen and the wickedness of the Catholics and the machinations of Spain.

Because of these circumstances there was something artificial about the extravagant talk of the poets who lived on the courtiers' patronage. Their note was too forced to be convincing. It was all the more feverishly forced because the fact was every year becoming more clear that a victory over the Spaniards did not altogether compensate for a lack of bread. The official adulation waxed perfervid as the popularity of Elizabeth declined — as decline it did at the end of her reign. Not all the adulation in the world could quite conceal that the years 1594 to 1596 especially were "years of dearth." We hear of people having sometimes to travel as far as sixty miles to buy corn; that was what the Dean of Durham reported. And the letters of the time show that prices of wheat doubled and sometimes quadrupled themselves. Even the rich were getting a little nervous over the situation. From them, too, we catch the note of a desire for a change. The horizon was being scanned for the Queen's successor. Parliament was growing restive. The death of Elizabeth — which had once been dreaded as a calamity that would set the Queen of Scots upon the English throne — was now awaited with impatience. Perhaps when England got a King — even if he did come from Scotland — things would in some way improve.

But Gloriana lived doughty to the last, and never failed to stage a striking performance when it was called for. Her ministers humoured her; her courtiers continued to flatter her: all of them knew that, however ridiculous she might be, she was, nevertheless, a remarkable old lady, not only a great personage but a great personality. She could still give her exhibitions; she still retained all her arts of showmanship. Thus when Paulus Jaline, the Ambassador of Sigismund, King of Poland, came for an audience in July, 1597, and instead of dishing out the customary flattery read off a list of complaints, the aged lioness roused herself and at once shot back a fierce reply in abusive Latin — much to the Ambassador's astonishment. When he had bowed his dumbfounded self out, the Queen turned with a flushed face and cackled, "God's death, my lords! I have been enforced this day to scour up my old Latin."

No other monarch in Christendom could have done it. Elizabeth was, after all, still Gloriana.

20

20

Martin Marprelate

AFTER the defeat of the Armada the English Catholics looked for some relaxation of persecution. There were, they thought, good grounds for this relief: the danger from Spain was now removed, and they themselves had proved their loyalty to the Queen. This was all the more something that deserved a reward because both Philip and the leaders of the exiles, Allen and Persons, had counted upon the Catholics rising as soon as it was known that the Armada had sailed. The English government had indeed been so apprehensive at the time that it had suggested a general massacre of the "Papists" — and though Elizabeth, to do her justice, had vetoed this, they did clap the leading recusants into jail. Surely now it had been shown that, even if the Armada had among its objects the promulgation of the Bull of 1570 releasing Catholics from their allegiance, the Catholics did not wish to be released. As their persecution had been on ostensibly political grounds — a distrust of their adhesion to the Queen and not on account of their religion — some degree of toleration was to be expected.

Instead of getting toleration, their persecution was intensified. On a single day in August — that is, immediately after the defeat of the Armada — six laymen and thirteen priests suffered as traitors. And the Earl of Arundel, the Catholic son of the Duke of Norfolk, who was already in the Tower, was sentenced to death on a charge of having had a priest named Bennett say Mass for the success of the Spanish invasion. In vain he produced a letter from Bennett saying that he had made his confession only under the threat of torture; the government, desiring a highly placed victim, preferred to accept the confession.

All the mercy that Arundel got was that he was allowed to live under the shadow of the axe until 1595. He was beatified as a martyr in 1929 who for six years had died daily.

Such treatment was anything but generous or even fair. But the English, though they are usually good losers, are not always such good winners. Inflamed with national pride and hatred of Spain, they made the unfortunate Catholics suffer. The only pretext the government could offer was that Persons and Allen had declared for Philip and had, in anticipation of Parma's landing, furiously (and we must admit scurrilously) attacked Elizabeth. That these two men were only individuals who were woefully out of touch with Catholic opinion at home, was ignored. The Puritans, who had provided so many of the naval officers, were hungry to flesh their fangs. Their belligerent and vociferous zeal was about to lead to their own persecution: yet this they seemed willing to endure so long as Tyburn had its holocaust of Papists.

It is, however, curious to note that in several respects the extremes of Rome and Geneva touched. The tone of Elizabethan society — apart from the Catholics and Puritans — was very largely secular. If we must discount Miss J. M. Stone's contention about the prevalence of speculative atheism — for the chief instances that she and those who follow this line are able to adduce are those of Sir Walter Raleigh and Christopher Marlowe — there was no doubt a good deal of what we must call practical atheism. That is, a large number and perhaps the majority of the upholders of official Protestantism — including the Queen herself — supported it merely because it *was* the official religion: to religion itself they were indifferent. Catholic and Puritan were at one at least in regarding religion as something not of this world. Each might have taken as his motto the inscription *Non sufficit orbis* that so scandalised the raiders who found it on a Spanish *residencia* in the New World. This, properly understood, expressed not so much the arrogance of Spanish imperialism as the passion of Christian hope.

Of course, there were important differences between the

theories of Catholics and Puritans. Where Catholics acknowledged that both God and Caesar had their claims, the puritan theocracy, in practice, tended to give all to God, and to lay the people under a domination of the presbytery far more rigorous than that of the Papacy. But they agreed that the Anglican Establishment gave God's due to Caesar. Each being convinced of the paramount claims of the divine revelation, Catholic and Puritan could not but concur in rejecting Erastianism. Though their religion remained patriotic — patriotic in the highest sense — Cecil's patriotism was, by contrast, religious: the only real religion he had.

As against this Catholic and Puritan affirmed, as all deeply religious people must, that there is an authority higher than that of the state. They were not disloyal but were faced with conflicting claims. In the case of the Catholic, however, the alternative was particularly cruel. The Puritan, broadly speaking, did no more than assert that the Reformation had not been carried far enough; the Catholic was obliged to reject it altogether. Submission was therefore possible to the conscience of the one and impossible to that of the other. In the official view the Puritans were men who went too far — but who were, after all, going in the right direction. As Archbishop Whitgift is reported to have said of them, "They were servants of God but dangerous to the state." But however obstructive to good order they might be, they could not be represented as being in league with the Spaniards. And it was with precisely this that Catholics, despite the service they had rendered in the war, were branded. Yet they were the very people who were seeking to preserve the ancient traditions of England; they were the true conservatives, whereas the Protestants — and especially the Puritans — were, in sober fact, revolutionaries who were determined to create a new order of society.

It was for this reason that the Puritans were not content that Cecil pursue a policy of suppressing Catholicism gradually; they called for its immediate extermination by fire and sword. It was according to their fierce fanaticism equally meritorious to slit a Spaniard's throat on the high seas or to drag a "Massmonger" to Tyburn. To placate them over sixty priests and fifty lay people (including two women) were condemned to die for their faith in the years following the Armada.

The government soon found, however, that nothing could really placate the Puritans. Overexcited by their zeal, they had begun their attack just before the sailing of the Armada with the publication of the first of the Martin Marprelate tracts. Elizabeth was accordingly soon obliged to conduct a campaign of persecution on two fronts.

That on the Puritans had been simmering for some time, so that in 1583 Whitgift, Elizabeth's "little black husband" — a Calvinist in theology though a strong upholder of the episcopal system — began to demand from every minister adhesion to Anglican orthodoxy thereby arousing complaints from Cecil that "The inquisitions of Spain use not so many questions to comprehend and entrap their preys." The reply of the Puritans now took the form of anonymous and secretly printed pamphlets, written in vigorous and racy English and packed with broad humour — excellent popular journalism. The central idea of the author of these works — who was possibly the Welshman, John Penry, assisted by Job Throckmorton, cousin of the Francis executed in 1585 — was that the most effectual means of strengthening Protestantism was to strike at the Elizabethan prelates and to sweep away, if possible, everything in the Anglican ceremonial that savoured of the "Old Religion." The Prayer Book, to them, was "culled and picked out of that Romish dunghill, the Mass-book, full of abomination."

As the very name "Martin Marprelate" was intended to make clear, the Bishops of the Establishment were the targets aimed at. Many men considered episcopacy obnoxious simply because it had been taken over from the Catholic Church. And of those who accepted it, relatively few subscribed with any enthusiasm to the doctrine of the Apostolic Succession. This was true of Cecil himself, and even of some of the bishops. They believed episcopacy to be a useful form of church government; they were by no means so strongly persuaded that it was in accordance with the Scriptures. There were, of course, a certain num-

ber of "high Churchmen," who held the Church of England
to be still part of the universal Catholic Church; the majority
accepted the settlement for no better reason than that it was the
law, and that, as such, it had obvious advantages. In the view of
"low churchmen" today, as in the view of all those Protestants — the overwhelming majority — who are outside Anglicanism: episcopacy is no integral part of Christianity. Even
American Methodism, with its episcopalianism, regards its bishops as no more than supervisors of denominational activities.

The Puritans, therefore, were not at all disposed to make the
respectful allowances Catholics are always prepared to give even
bishops whose personal conduct is not all that it should be.
What the Puritans saw were "proud prelates" who, despite
the spoliation suffered by the Church, were often immensely
rich, and often so grasping that they were pluralists. Hughes of
St. Asaph, for example, adorned a richly endowed archdeaconry
and ten other benefices. And when he sold livings to the highest bidder and leased manors for long terms to his wife and
children — and even his sisters and his cousins and his aunts —
there was some justification for indignation. In fact, the majority of Elizabethan bishops could hardly be described as ornaments to their order. It was quite a common procedure for a
new incumbent to begin his jurisdiction with a legal action
against his predecessor for spoliation — a favourite device of
which was stripping the lead off the roofs of cathedrals and
churches and selling the plate — before he himself proceeded to
much the same sort of spoliation in his own turn. One cannot
but feel a good deal of sympathy with the Puritans who looked
upon such dignitaries as rapacious parasites. Nor can one help
chuckling at Martin Marprelate's humourous list of *errata* in
his first tract: "Whenever the Prelates are called 'My Lords'
. . . take that for a fault," "There is nothing spoken at all of
that hypocrite Scambler, Bishop of Norwich. Take it for a great
fault."

The government answered with pamphlets of its own and
by searching in vain for Martin Marprelate's secret printing
press. All other methods having proved futile, it proceeded to

prosecute some of the leading Puritans on a charge of high treason, using for this purpose the Act of 1581 that had been designed to suppress Catholicism.

It must be noted that these prosecutions were differently based than those against the Anabaptists. *They* were openly and honestly charged with heresy, and two of them were burnt at Smithfield in 1575, with others in the years 1578 and 1589. The statute *De Heretico Comburendo* was still in force, and it would be as well to remember that Elizabeth burned heretics — as every one of the Tudors did.[1] It is an error to imagine that it aroused any special horror. Neither, alas, did the official hypocrisy that sentenced men — Puritans as well as Catholics — to death for their opinions and then pretended that it was for treason.

Thomas Cartwright, the distinguished theologian, who was the leader of the English Prebyterians, took refuge for a while abroad, but was imprisoned in England, only the fact that he had powerful friends saving him from a worse fate.[2] Job Throckmorton also had powerful friends and was acquitted, though it is practically certain that the Martin Marprelate tracts were printed in his house, if not partly written by him. John Udal, however, was condemned in 1591 but pardoned later, dying a few days after his release. And Barrow and Greenwood, the moving spirits in what was to develop into Congregationalism, suffered as traitors in April, 1593, as, in the same year, did Penry, who was reputed to be Martin Marprelate himself. On the other hand, Robert Browne, the founder of the sect which bore his name, found it prudent to conform and was rewarded — perhaps because he was related to Burghley — with an Anglican living, which he held until 1631. If he died in jail

---

[1] Burning was also the legal punishment for women who murdered their husbands, and was sometimes enforced as late as the eighteenth century. In Elizabeth's time we hear of Anne Brewen being burnt for this reason in June, 1592, her paramour and assistant in the murder, John Parker, being only hanged "in front of her eyes."

[2] Leicester appointed him Master of the hospital at Warwick. Cecil made similar provision for Lever and Sampson when they were deprived. Catholics, of course, had no such good fortune.

in the end, he was there because of an assault he had committed in his ungovernable bad temper.

All these men would today be considered harmless enough people. Their opinions — apart from their rigid Calvinism, which is now virtually extinct — are much the same as those now generally accepted by all Protestants, except those of the "high church" persuasion. But being in opposition to the Elizabethan Establishment, they could not be tolerated. Under such pressure the Puritans — though they had the support of Knollys and Walsingham and that very queer partizan of theirs, Leicester — bent to the storm. They relished persecuting Catholics; they by no means relished persecution when it was applied to themselves. A few irreconcilables sought a refuge in the Low Countries; the rest decided that it was useless to resist the government. What they thought about things was inscribed upon the coffin of one of their number who died in prison at the end of February, 1593: "This is the corpse of Roger Rippon, a servant of Christ and her Majesty's faithful subject, who is the last of sixteen or seventeen which that great enemy of God, the Archbishop of Canterbury, with his High Commissioners, have murthered in Newgate within these five years, manifestly for the testimony of Jesus Christ. His soul is now with the Lord; and his blood crieth for speedy vengeance against that great enemy of the saints and against Mr. Richard Young, who in this, and many the like points, hath abused his power, for the upholding of the Popish Antichrist, Prelacy, and priesthood."

These men were at least normal Puritans whose views, however erroneous in many ways, could be logically urged against the Elizabethan Establishment which professed to be Protestant while it attempted to retain some of the outward forms of the proscribed Catholicism. There was one notorious case of men who, though clearly unbalanced, were sent to their death.

Three lunatics named Hacket, Arthington, and Coppinger, began to preach in the London streets in the summer of 1591, Coppinger crying out in a stentorian voice, "Repent, England, repent!" after which he and Arthington — who described themselves as "two prophets, the one of Mercy, the other of Judgment, sent and extraordinarly called by God" — announced to the astonished crowds that Hacket was "Christ's representative on earth by partaking of His glorified body, by His spirit, which had been conferred upon him, of separating the good from the bad." This Hacket had, up to this transformation, lived so wildly that once in a tavern brawl with one Freckington he had bitten off the man's nose, and "though both Freckington and a surgeon who chanced to be present begged him to restore the nose, so that it might be stitched on again while the wound was still green, he not only refused to part with it, but showed it exultingly to all who cared to look; some even say that he ate it up."[3] Such a man should obviously have been confined in Bedlam; instead he was charged with treason.

Arthington managed to escape death, but Hacket and Coppinger suffered at the cross in Cheapside. And the following account has come down to us of the end of the self-appointed Pope's career. When he was exhorted to beg God and the Queen for pardon, he bellowed, "O God of heaven, mighty Jehovah, Alpha and Omega, Lord of Lords, King of Kings, and God everlasting, thou knowest me to be the true Jehovah whom Thou hast sent, send some miracle out of a cloud to convert these infidels and deliver me from mine enemies. If not, I will fire the heavens and tear Thee from Thy throne with my hands." At the executioner he screamed, "Ah, thou bastard's child, wilt thou hang William Hacket, thy king?" To the last he struggled, now whimpering, "O what do you do, what do you do? Have I for this my kingdom bestowed upon me?" But he got no sympathy from the mob; they only shouted that "he should be cut down at once, being very angry with the officers for not showing more haste. As soon as he was taken down, almost in a trice, his heart was cut out and shown openly to the people."

It was a scene highly typical of Elizabethan barbarity. As a companion piece I present the execution of a young Catholic layman named James Bird who was hanged on March 27,

---

[3] I have followed here Richard Cosin's *Conspiracy for Pretended Reformation by Hacket*, published in 1592. It forms the basis of the accounts given by Camden and Stow.

1593, at Winchester. As he was mounting the ladder of the gallows he said, "I beg you, Mr. Sheriff, seeing that I am a native to this city, that you grant me one favour before I die." When the Sheriff asked, "What favour?" Bird answered, "Tell me what I die for." The Sheriff of course said that Bird already knew that perfectly well, but added kindly, "Come now, confess your crime, promise to go to church, and the Queen's pardon will be begged for you." It was what Bird wanted to get out of him. "Right heartily I thank thee," he called out for all to hear. "If by my going to church I can save my life, surely all the world will see this, that I am executed solely for faith and religion, and for nothing else. It was just this that I wished to elicit from you. Now I will die gladly."

The same thing was true of every one of the Catholic martyrs — or, for that matter, of those of the Puritans who were put to death for "treason." Even on the steps of the gallows they could escape by recanting. The Catholics merely had to undertake to "go to Church." With very few exceptions all refused. Now and then, it is true, a man who had witnessed what a "traitor" who had just preceded him had suffered, broke down at the last moment and apostatised. The rest, after having suffered the rack repeatedly — like the Jesuits Henry Walpole and Robert Southwell — faced the disembowelling knife with composure. Yet all these "traitors" could have not only got off but have been rewarded with a comfortable Anglican benefice.

The Puritans contrived to make a grievance of this, and Cecil supported their plea that it was a shame that "in a land where no Papist was ever put to death for religion theirs should . . . be the first blood shed." On this ground he managed to get a respite for Barrow and Greenwood; it was the bishops who set their faces against clemency. Yet the Puritan argument was disingenuous: Catholics would — like the James Bird just mentioned — have been greatly consoled had their execution been admittedly on account of religion. Their complaint was that the government pretended not to interfere with consciences, and yet put them to death for what they believed, at the same time branding them with treason.

There were, however, Catholic as well as Puritan lunatics. For instance, there was the case of Edward Squire, who confessed to having attempted to murder Elizabeth by rubbing poison on the pommel of her saddle. Perhaps he really believed it was possible to kill her in this way, though it is altogether too much to ask us to accept the confession he made on the rack that it was the Jesuit, Walpole, who recommended this absurd method. King Philip, too, was alleged to have had a hand in the affair, but we now know that on the day Squire professed to have seen him, the King was ill at the Escorial and unable to see anybody. For all that, Sir Edward Coke, the attorney general and the celebrated writer on law, made a great histrionic pretence of being so overcome with horror as to be unable to proceed with his speech.[4] Squire was, of course, duly executed.

This man, however, may have been an imposter rather than a lunatic. In any event he does not fall into the group of the martyrs; he was merely one of those the government liked to get hold of from time to time to give some colour of justice to its persecution. A more representative case is that of the Jesuit, Edmund Jennings, who on December 10, 1591, together with Swithin Wells, the layman who had sheltered him, endured the rope and the quartering knife on a scaffold specially erected for the occasion in front of Wells's house in Holborn.[5] When Jennings was invited to confess and ask pardon of the Queen he answered, "I know not ever to have offended her. If Mass be treason, I confess I have done it and glory in it." This so enraged Topcliffe, who was present, that he ordered the executioner to cut the rope at once. We read in the contemporary record that "In this agony Jennings began to call on St. Gregory to the great astonishment of the hangman who cried out with a loud voice, 'God's wounds! his heart is in my hand and yet Gregory is in his mouth.'" Similary Father Barkworth, a

---

[4] Here is another instance of the intertwining marriages of the Cecil clique. Coke married Cecil's granddaughter.

[5] On the same day three other Jesuits — White, Plassden, and Lacy — and two laymen were executed at Tyburn.

Benedictine, when admonished by a minister at the gibbet to remember that Christ died for him, replied, "And so do I for Christ."

Yet we need not suppose that the members of the government, because they countenanced such atrocities, were therefore exceptionally cruel. It was rather that they were men of their age and took these things for granted. Though Elizabeth personally asked that the torture of the Babington conspirators be "protracted to the furthest extremity of pain," this was because she sincerely believed the crime to be so exceptional as to call for exceptional punishment; on other occasions she managed to get convicted priests off and either imprisoned or sent abroad. But it simply never occurred to her to question the morality of torture, or the use of paid *agents provacateurs*. Disagreeable duties had to be carried out. The officials looked upon them as does the head of a modern state who — though he may have a private objection to capital punishment — nevertheless signs as a matter of course the death warrants laid before him. It is not the barbarity of these executions that was their worst feature but the intellectual dishonesty of saying (as Cecil did in Elizabeth's behalf) that she condemned to death only those "who profess themselves by obedience to the Pope to be no subjects to the Queen; and through their outward pretence to be sent from the seminaries to convert people to their religion, yet without reconciling them from their obedience to the Queen they never give them absolution." Both Elizabeth and Cecil must positively have known that this was untrue. Whatever they might publish to the world as propaganda, they were as well aware as we are now that not one of these priests — Jesuits or seculars — was other than a missionary confining himself to spiritual duties. On the contrary, it was precisely the "converting people to their religion" which was the capital offence. As for the renewal and intensification of persecution after the Armada, that was for the purpose of showing a fanatically Puritan Parliament that the Establishment, though episcopal in constitution, was no less anti-Catholic than themselves. Hypocrisy rather than cruelty was therefore what the government was guilty of: cruelty was no more than a consequence of hypocrisy and of genuine fear.

To the existing anti-Catholic laws were added new laws. The last of these, passed in 1593, placed recusants under a quarantine, forbidding them to approach any corporate town without special permission, and even depriving them, in some instances, of the right to educate their own children. And this was merely supplementary to the statute which could, whenever the government chose to enforce it, make treason out of the bare profession of Catholicism.

Yet even during the worst years of the persecution, the laws against the recusants were enforced only spasmodically; otherwise there would have been a complete extermination of all Catholics in the country. A good deal of open Catholicism existed in remote parts, especially in the North and West. So that in 1592 we find the Council taking steps to deal with Wales where "many, both men and women, in the night season and the day, repair to certain places where in times past were pilgrimages, images or offerings; they assemble sometimes in great numbers, a thing intolerable to be permitted after so long a preaching of the gospel. These superstitious and idolatrous monuments are to be pulled down, broken and quite defaced so that no remnant, token, or memory may remain. Should any hereafter repair to those places they shall be apprehended and severely punished for their lewd behaviour that others may be warned by their examples to take heed of such intolerable abuses." It seems rather late in the day to have tried to suppress this popular manifestation of Catholicism. Clearly local officials sometimes winked at a good deal.

Indeed, in spite of persecution and proscription and quarantine, Catholics were often met at Court itself, and they were prominent in several of the professions. This was the case in those of law and medicine; still more was it true in that of music. Of the old composers, Tye, White, and Tallis were Catholics, as were — among the younger men — Byrd, Bull, and Peter Philips, almost the only Anglican composer of equal rank being Orlando Gibbons. But of course artists, whatever their religious beliefs, had to be encouraged, and they were never regarded as likely to be a political danger; and good doctors were still too few to be killed off. As for the lawyers, they could usually circumvent the law. The Catholic courtiers existed by royal caprice and, for the most part, took care not to parade their religion.

It was the ebb and flow of the government's sense of its own danger that explains a state of affairs so full of apparent inconsistencies. For example, during 1596–7, when England and France were allies against Spain, the number of executions dropped to a half and then a quarter of what it had been, jumping up again in 1598 as soon as Henry IV made the treaty of Vervins with Philip. All of which indicates that the persecution arose from fear, mounting with that fear and diminishing with it. Not only the persecution of recusants but the scares that resulted in the hanging of such men as Squire and Lopez reveal how conscious the government was of its own instability. We are accustomed to think of Elizabeth reigning securely — apart from the solitary threat of the Armada; actually there was always a possibility (or so it was believed) of her being overthrown. Nor did the struggle, in fact, really end until a hundred years later, when James II was expelled and foreign Kings — whose sole merit was their Protestantism — were brought in to occupy the English throne.

Yet after the Armada even the most bitter of the exiles showed an inclination to come to terms with the Elizabethan government. Between 1581, when Gregory XIII had issued his explanation of Pius V's Bull — only to see it misinterpreted and lead to further persecution — up to 1588 there had been an advocacy abroad of invasion as the last desperate remedy for the ills of the English Church. Subsequently to 1588 the leading exiles — with the exception of Persons, who stood stoutly to his guns — modified their tone. But I think we must admit that the irreconcilable attitude of Persons did the Catholics in England a great deal of harm. His absolute sincerity and selflessness are not in question: it was his judgment that was at fault. His publication in 1594 of *A Conference about the Next Succession* —

which Cardinal Gasquet has called a "pernicious book" — was, to say the least, unfortunate. There he openly argued in favour of the claims of the Infanta Isabella, Philip's daughter, a fact that the government could use (and did use) as an excuse for not relaxing the persecution. Cardinal Allen, however, reverted to the moderation more natural to him.

His work was now done. If his hopes in the Armada had been disappointed, he had begun the establishment of the seminaries which saved the Faith in the country he loved so well. He retired to Rome, not a very old man, but worn out with his labours, and there passed his last years in peace. Thomas Heywood, in his edition of 1851 of Allen's *Defence of Stanley,* has a charming picture of the Cardinal "In the chariot to which his infirmities obliged him to have recourse, gazing from the Janiculum on the broken and singular outline of the Eternal City; the Tiber beneath his feet — the seven hills, each except the Viminal, clearly defined — the desolate Campagna, with its aqueducts from the Alban hills to Soracte, bathed in the splendour of a southern sun; yet his inclinations, and his fancy, even then bearing him to the Abbot's Walk at Rossall, where against sand hills covered with star grass, the waves of the ocean beat, — where through a dull and misty Lancashire sky, are sought, at rare intervals, views of the Black Coomb in Cumberland, or the Ormes Head, and Snowden range, and on some fortunate mid-summer evening are seen in high relief, before the setting sun, the mountains of Wales."

Allen was now Librarian of the Vatican, and was at work upon a critical edition of the works of St. Augustine. Yet we do not think of him as primarily a scholar but as a man of action, all of whose acts were animated by a profound love of England. In these last years he constituted himself the protector of such Englishmen at Rome as were in danger of imprisonment by the Inquisition. It was the final service he could render his country. He had seen too much of persecution to countenance it, even in its milder forms. He had seen too much of the futility of force and political effort not to regret some of his own activities. John Mush, a secular priest, said that he had often heard the Cardinal say that his friend Persons was "a man of too violent and hard a nature." His own former association with the "Spanish Party" was now completely severed. What he could look back to with deep satisfaction was his sending of priests to England and securing the cooperation of the Jesuits. All those men had been trained by him for martyrdom. It was they who had saved Catholicism from utterly dying out in his dear country. This was a nobler triumph than any the Armada could have won.

21

"Till Birds Sing in the Morning"

R OBERT DEVEREUX, Earl of Essex, was Leicester's step-
son, and soon came to be regarded as his political heir. He
had, indeed, advantages of birth that Dudley lacked, and so
could hope to be a more effective leader of the old aristocracy
against the dominant Cecils. In addition he had personal brilliance — though hardly solid ability — and boundless courage.
If his high spirits had a guilelessness that laid him open to
attack, they were extremely attractive to the aging Queen. She
liked to have good-looking and dashing young men about her;
none of them did she find more to her taste than Essex.

His rise was meteoric. He was Master of the Horse at the age
of twenty-one, a Knight of the Garter a year later, a Privy
Councillor at twenty-seven, and in command of the expedition
to Cadiz at thirty. The Cecils might have regarded him as a
dangerous antagonist had they not perfectly measured the rash-
ness of his character. Even so, his favour with the Queen, and
his ambition, marked him out as a man to be destroyed.

It was soon noted, however, that though he seemed to have
great influence, he generally failed whenever he intervened to
use that influence on behalf of a client. It was in vain that he
tried in 1591 to have Davison restored to office. It was in vain
that he tried to help Sir John Perrot, whose son had married
his sister. It was in vain that he sought the Attorney Generalship for Francis Bacon. The Cecils blocked him at every turn.
His solitary success was that of getting the Queen's Jewish physi-
cian, Dr. Lopez, tried and executed for high treason — a crime
of which the ill-fated doctor is now generally conceded to have
been innocent.

Essex did nevertheless make great personal headway. Elizabeth gave him the monopoly for sweet wines — an extremely lucrative thing — and now and then added other handsome emoluments. For instance, when a cargo of cochineal arrived from the Indies, he was allowed to buy it all for £50,000, about half its true value, and was given an amount worth £7,000 free. In modern values this meant that Essex might hope to clear well over a million dollars on the transaction. Even a young man of his extravagant mode of life could hardly complain of niggardly treatment.

His escapades themselves were condoned as proper to the hot blood of youth. He had one affair after another with ladies of the Court, and the Queen pardoned him every time. She did not even mind a great deal — such was her indulgence toward him — when he married Sir Philip Sidney's widow, Walsingham's daughter, though she was usually very angry over her favourites' marriages. His period of disfavour on this account was brief, the disfavour, perfunctory. And when he fought a duel with Charles Blount, Lord Mountjoy, Elizabeth gave both young men a mild scolding and nothing worse; after all, it was rather flattering to hear that the duel was on her account. So complete was the reconciliation that Mountjoy became Essex's friend and follower, and entered into a *liason* with Essex's sister, Lady Rich, the "Stella" of Sir Philip Sidney's poems. As for the younger brother, Sir Christopher Blount, he married Leicester's widow, Essex's mother. Yet the Earl stood in the popular mind as a leader of political Puritanism — that is, he was for the vigorous prosecution of the war with Spain.

Elizabeth, however, did not treat the Earl seriously as a politician. She found him amusing, and wanted to have him near her; but some of his keen-sighted friends — particularly Francis Bacon — advised him to limit himself as much as possible to the purely personal relationship. This was the road that Leicester had found so safe and profitable. Anthony Bagot, writing to his father, notes: "When she is abroad nobody is near her but my Lord of Essex, and at night my Lord is at cards, or at one game or another with her, that he cometh not to his own lodging till birds sing in the morning." It was reputed that he was now her lover, though he was thirty-three years younger than the Queen. That there was a curious devouring senile passion on her part would seem to be true; he, for his part, was merely using her for his advancement.

But he was much too ambitious to be content with the rôle of the Queen's *gigolo*. He thirsted for glory, though as Mr. Strachey puts it, he "had never shown any military genius — only a military taste." He went off on expeditions to France and Portugal — sometimes without the Queen's consent — and while showing no real capacity for generalship, succeeded in gaining a reputation for bravery. De Maisse wrote of him in 1597, "I believe that, so far as an Englishman can, he covets glory." It made him vastly popular, but Elizabeth was not impressed. She was not inclined to accord him "domestical greatness" on this account; only too clearly she saw what he was aiming at — to establish himself as a national hero and by means of this to overthrow the cautious Cecils who were working for peace.

He played his cards badly. In the Council one day when he had been heatedly arguing against the Cecils — whom she was supporting — in his anger he turned his back on her, and received a stinging box on the ears and a "Go to the Devil!" Instantly he swung round with an oath and his hand on his sword. He shouted in her face, "This is an outrage that I will not put up with! I would not have borne it from your father's hands." The outburst would have cost any other man his head. But Elizabeth forgave him — and appointed him to the Governor Generalship of Ireland. Everybody was glad to see him go: the Queen to get rid of him, the people at large because they believed that if any man could subdue Ireland it was Essex, the politicians to ruin him.

Ireland had long been considered the grave of reputations. Its administrators had been able men, but they had been handicapped by a policy impossible of execution. Henry VIII had had the sagacity to make the greater chieftains Earls, and the lesser, knights, and to leave them in the main free to carry on the government themselves in accordance with Irish customs and Irish laws. Elizabeth insisted that these laws conform to England's, and especially that the Irish accept the Protestant settlement of religion.

Her policy proved a fatal error. The Irish Earls had accepted willingly enough, as a technicality, Henry's claim to ecclesiastical supremacy. They had accepted, more than willingly, their share of ecclesiastical spoliation. But now they were asked to agree to the suppression of the Mass. And the extirpation of Catholicism was avowedly made a part of that general Anglicisation of the country which included the abolition of the Irish system of land tenure and the right of the clans to elect their own chiefs.

In Shane O'Neill the English found in 1566 a determined and capable opponent. The weakness of the English army of occupation is indicated by the alarm shown by Sir Henry Sidney at the fact that this chieftain, as he wrote, could put a 1,000 cavalry and 4,000 foot into the field. It would not have taken much to have driven the English out at that time. Shane had been sustained by Elizabeth in 1562 in his claim to be Earl of Tyrone. He dismissed the claim of his half brother jauntily: "Being a gentleman, my father never refused no child that any woman named to be his." Under the Irish system he had been elected The O'Neill. This made him a man to be reckoned with. Had he lived the story of Ireland might have been different.

On the other hand, his Catholicism was dubious enough, and there was no doubt at all about the morals of a man who dragged around in chains his mistress, the so-called Countess of Argyle. And Ireland was so torn by the rivalries of its chieftains — who were continually entering into temporary alliance with the English against this or that clan or faction — that a small garrison managed to hold the country for the Crown. But Shane O'Neill was dangerous enough to be got rid of in the usual way. On June 2, 1567, he was stabbed in a drunken brawl, while he had taken refuge with the Scotch MacDonnells in their settlement in Ulster.

Queen Elizabeth

Wild as the tribal life was outside the English "Pale," it offered more security to life and property than was given within it, for the clans, however much they might quarrel among themselves, acted as units. Within the radius of the Crown's control there was confusion except within the towns, for no basis of law, recognised by all, prevailed. The government's administrators were completely unable to cope with the situation created by the policy that English law, English customs, English religion, and even English dress be forced upon a people who furiously refused them all. Elizabeth had therefore to maintain a costly military establishment in a country from which she received nothing but a total annual revenue of £5,000. Many a time she wished Ireland, with its priests and chieftains, its rhymers and gallowglasses and kerns at the bottom of the sea. The one thing she dared not do was evacuate it, lest it fall into the hands of Spain. What she need not have done was to persist in a policy that was to breed hatred for centuries and is still the darkest blot upon England's record.

The immediate trouble was mainly caused by the confiscation of Irish lands and the farming of them out to Englishmen. The worst type of adventurer was attracted to the unhappy country. Goldwin Smith has put it, "The eagles of enterprise spread their wings for the Spanish Main; the vultures swooped upon Ireland." Perhaps it was that they were all really vultures, but only looked like eagles at a distance. At all events there was no mistaking, near at hand, the devastation they inflicted. Spenser's account has often been quoted, but may be quoted again: "The miserable poor were brought to such wretchedness that any stony heart would have rued the same. Out of every corner of the woods and glens they came creeping forth on their hands, for their legs would not bear them; they looked like anatomies of death; they spoke like ghosts crying out of their graves; they did eat the dead carrion, happy where they could find them; yea, they did eat one another soon after, insomuch as the very carcases they spared not to scrape out of their graves; and if they found a plot of watercresses or shamrocks, there they flocked as to a feast for a time. . . . Yet were they not all long to continue therewithal, so that in a short time there were none almost left, and a populous and plentiful country was suddenly left void of man and beast; yet surely in all that war there perished not many by the sword, but all by the extremity of famine which they themselves had wrought." Nothing need be added to that terrible description except to say that it was written, not by an Irish partizan, but by an English official — Lord Grey de Wilton's secretary.

Massacres occurred on both sides — though mostly on the side of the English — and one chieftain after another was got rid of, as were Sir Brian Phelim O'Neill and the O'Mores, by inviting them to a banquet with their followers and then slaughtering them as they sat at table. It was a record of cruelty and treachery that no Englishman can look back upon except with shame. If an administrator tried to deal fairly with the natives, he was soon recalled at the instance of the settlers. This was the fate of the bluff, foul-mouthed soldier, Sir John Perrot — who is said to have been one of Henry VIII's bastards and who unquestionably looked and talked very much like the old King. He was ordered back to London in 1588 in disgrace, and tried in 1592 on a charge of having spoken disrespectfully of the Queen. (It was rather more than disrespectfully if his words were correctly reported.) He was condemned to death but not executed — perhaps because he really was Elizabeth's half brother — but died in the Tower a few months later.

All through this period Spain and Rome were counted upon to help the Irish but did little except keep alive their disaffection. The great Gaelic poem of the seventeenth century cries out in passionate exultation:

> "There's wine from the royal Pope
>   Upon the ocean green;
> And Spanish ale shall give you hope,
>   My dark Rosaleen."

Unfortunately the Pope's wine was never sent in sufficient quantities, nor was the Spanish ale strong enough.

In 1580, however, the Papacy did act. It claimed Ireland as its fief, for though it had made Philip and Mary joint sovereigns, the sovereignty — according to its theory — lapsed with Elizabeth's heresy. It was therefore well within its rights in sending a small force to the country. Yet these rights — of temporal sovereignty as well as spiritual jurisdiction — Elizabeth of course would not admit, and it must be confessed that the time for asserting them was badly chosen. It was when James Fitzmaurice Fitzgerald and Nicholas Sanders arrived simultaneously with the arrival in England of the first Jesuits.

Feeble as the Papal invasion was, it seemed for a while likely to succeed. Lord Baltinglas rose in rebellion and defeated an English force on August 25, 1580, at Glendalough. But Fitzgerald was slain by Theobald Burke, a cousin of his, in a skirmish, and Sanders was hunted into the bogs where, some time in the spring of 1581, he died. Meanwhile Lord Grey de Wilton marched against Smerwick, where the Hispanic-Papal force of 600 men had established themselves, and when they surrendered they were all put to the sword under the direction of Sir Walter Raleigh, the gentle Spenser looking on. As they could not show any commission from Philip, and as England would not recognise that Ireland was a Papal fief, it was possible to treat them as pirates having no legal standing. Nobody at the time thought there was anything shocking about the massacre; at least it had a show of justification not attaching to some of the other English brutalities.

The only excuse usually offered for killing the Irish at sight was that they were savages of whom the world was well rid. And this contemptuous view was by no means limited to the English: the Catholic Feria described them "a sort of beggarly people, great traitors to one another, and of no force." Their deficiency was really that of clinging to the tribal organization in a world where it had long been out of date.[1] They had their own culture, as is amply attested by their abundant and extraordinarily elaborate verse, which is now vastly admired. Its very conventions indicate a high civilization, so that one would

[1] The "wild" or "mere" Irish is what Fynes Moryson calls them — to distinguish them from the Anglo-Irish.

"Till Birds Sing in the Morning"

almost infer from it that Ireland was decadent did we not know it to have been "primitive." But "efficiency" is always too prone to think it has a heaven-given duty to grind the inefficient beneath its heel.

The "efficient" English showed themselves extremely unintelligent. Nothing would have been easier than to have won the Irish at that time by a conciliatory policy tolerating their religion and their native customs. It was because they would not be pressed into the English mould, that they had to be exterminated like vermin. The Irish, for their part, had they only been willing to drop their feuds for a while and unite against the English, could have overwhelmed them. But they had, as yet, no conception of a larger unit than the clan.[2] So the crafty administrators could overcome the weight of their numbers by fostering tribal jealousies, and rule by dividing.

It was just at this point that the English government was guilty of its most egregious blunder. Cecil had largely succeeded by identifying Protestantism and national feeling in England; by trying to force the Irish into Protestantism, he made the Catholic Church the centre of unity through which by degrees Irish nationality emerged into being. That nationality had not yet discovered itself; the bickerings of the clans continued; but though the Irish would not yet act together, they were certain that they did not want to be turned into Englishmen. The government virtually offered them a choice between Anglicisation and extermination.

It was at this stage that Essex was jockeyed into accepting the Governor Generalship of Ireland. Matters had reached a desperate pass. Hugh O'Neill, Earl of Tyrone, and nephew of the ill-fated Shane, patched up the traditional feud with Hugh Roe O'Donnell, and carried on sporadic war against the English, always awaiting the Spanish help that never came. The Armadas of 1596 and 1597 were beaten back by storms and in 1597 Tyrone made an ostensible submission. This was not for long: in 1598 he rose again and defeated a force under Sir

---

[2] All terms such as "chieftain" or "tribe" or "clan" are no more than approximations. It might be more accurate to speak of magnates and autonomous principalities, and more accurate still, to think of cantons.

Henry Bagenal (who was his brother-in-law), and this and other successes set the country on fire. The *sugane* (or "straw-rope") Earl of Desmond was set up against the "Queen's Earl" in Munster, and it began to look as though this time the English would be driven into the sea. It was to win fame by defeating the Irish rebels that Essex agreed to take over the Irish command. As he wrote to John Harington (soon to be knighted by him), "By God, I will beat Tyrone in the field; for nothing worthy her Majesty's honour hath yet been achieved." Supremely confident that he would accomplish what nobody else had been able to do, he entered Dublin on April 14, 1599, accompanied by Lords Southampton and Rutland and Mountjoy and such a train of fine gentlemen, all dressed in the height of preposterous fashion, as Ireland had never seen before.

He was supplied with an army that should have been ample for his task — a larger and better equipped force than had been put at the disposal of any previous head of the Irish administration. It consisted of sixteen thousand infantry and fifteen hundred cavalry. Previous English armies had been small and wretchedly appointed, and so hard had it been to obtain recruits that men said they would rather go to the gallows than to Ireland. And so inefficient and corrupt were the officers that they had got into the habit of hiring Irish kerns to fill their depleted ranks when an inspection had to be made. These kerns as a rule decamped with their weapons afterwards — while the officers, having used them to complete their musters, pocketed the pay of nonexistent men. Now all was to be changed. Elizabeth was going to give her favourite every chance to distinguish himself.

His enemies on the Council, however, had let him go as the surest means of discrediting him; they guessed that he would seek military glory rather than a conquest which needed patient pressure. And Elizabeth, having spent money so lavishly upon his adventure, demanded to see results. When these were not forthcoming, her comments grew acid. Always at her shoulder there was Sir Robert Cecil dropping hints about Essex's incompetence, which every day was becoming more patent. When he wrote complaining that he was being thwarted by the Council, they sent him reinforcements; they sent him money: he should never be able to say that he had failed for lack of support. They knew he would fail.

Fail he did. After marching about the country — going on procession at a thousand pounds a day was how Elizabeth described it — he found that his effectives had dwindled to 4,000, and began to think of returning to England to make his appeal — precisely for what? — in person. When at last he struck it was in a little skirmish that ended in his meeting Tyrone — both on horseback — in a ford, out of earshot, and concluding with him a six weeks' truce, indefinitely renewable. After that the enemies of Essex in England were able to say that at this meeting he made a secret bargain for securing Tyrone's backing of James of Scotland for the succession, offering as a reward a prince's autonomy to Tyrone. Be that as it may — and it is as likely, as it was certainly not proved — the campaign from which so much had been hoped, and which had cost so much money, had resulted in the accomplishment of precisely nothing. Not even a defeat could have been more ignominious.

Now Essex decided to go back and explain the situation to Elizabeth. Such a decision was in itself upon the whole wise, though by going back without permission he gave his enemies a handle against him. The error was not so much that he returned to England, but that he was uncertain in his mind as to what he was going to do when he got there. His first plan was to take his whole army with him and march on London. This was discarded as meaning civil war. Eventually he took only a couple of hundred picked men — sufficient, he thought, for a *coup d'état*. Neither plan accorded with that of making quietly reasonable explanations to the Queen — if such a method had been possible to one so hotheaded as Essex. All he knew was that he must somehow get rid of the cabal against him in the Council.

He galloped to the palace of Nonesuch on the morning of September 28, 1599, and at once unceremoniously pushed his way into Elizabeth's bedroom while she was dressing. Though caught without her wig and her jewels and her paint, she ap-

349

peared to be delighted to see him; she appeared to be even delighted at his audacity in coming before her all bespattered with mud and at such an hour. That same day Roland Whyte wrote from Nonesuch to Sir Robert Sidney that Essex "was very pleasant and thanked God, though he had suffered much trouble and storms abroad he found such a sweet calm at home."

Whyte spoke a little too soon. Before the day was out Elizabeth's mood had changed. She was demanding answers to searching and disagreeable questions. Why had he dared to return? And why had he had his private and friendly interview with Tyrone, the enemy he had been sent to Ireland to crush? That night he was ordered not to leave his room until his case had been investigated.

The Queen was very angry, and she was afraid. Gradually rumours leaked in of secret communications with the King of Scots, and the truce with Tyrone began to wear a worse look than ever. Elizabeth had previously sworn after one of her lover's quarrels with the Earl, "I shall break him of his will and pull down his great heart!" To Sir John Harington she now stormed, "By God's death, I am no Queen! That man is above me!" Yet nothing was done to Essex except to keep him kneeling for hours at the Council table while his conduct was enquired into, after which he was subjected to a mild form of imprisonment in his own house. Elizabeth was prepared to re-admit him eventually to favour; but first she meant to humiliate him.

She therefore refused to see him, often as he begged for an interview. She refused to melt even when he wrote in the sugared strain she loved: "Haste, paper, to that happy presence, whence only unhappy I am banished! Kiss that fair correcting hand which now lays plasters to my lighter hurts but to my greatest wound applieth nothing. Say thou comest from shaming, languishing, despairing Essex." He made the mistake of introducing into one of his letters to her a request for a renewal of his monopoly of sweet wines which, having just run out, left him almost penniless. Upon this the Queen commented sourly to Francis Bacon: "Essex has written me some dutiful letters, which moved me; but after taking them to flow from the abundance of his heart, I find them but a preparation to a suit for renewing his farm of sweet wines." To another she explained: "When horses become unmanageable it is necessary to tame them by abating them in the quantity of their provender." If there was no other way, Essex was to be starved into an absolute submission.

Such a submission his unruly heart would never give. He pleaded and sulked and raged in turn, then tried to get Lady Warwick, who was an old friend of his mother's, to arrange matters so that he could throw himself at the Queen's feet while she was walking in her garden. It was imperative that he see her again, if only to forestall the intrigues against himself he was sure were going on. And there was still that question of the sweet wines. But nothing came of it all: Elizabeth would not yield, nor would Essex — not abjectly enough to satisfy the Queen.

In anger he burst out one day, when somebody made a remark about "Her Majesty's conditions," or her state of mind. He snarled, "Her conditions! Her conditions are as crooked as her carcase!" That speech of course was carried to her.

By now he was not quite sane. He began to say — and apparently to believe — that Raleigh was trying to murder him. Robert Cecil he was convinced was in a plot to put the Infanta on the throne when Elizabeth died. That he had enemies was true enough; but he was seeing enemies everywhere. His last move was that of an entirely unbalanced man.

When a summons came for him on February 8, 1601 — nearly a year and a half after his unauthorised return to England — to appear before the Council, he made up his mind to raise the city of London and then march back to Whitehall. He would show the Queen how beloved he was; he would eject those who were poisoning her mind against him. Distraught as he was, he had no intention of rebellion. Yet rebellion, of course, it was.

Not a man in the city rose on his behalf. With his devoted followers he strode along the Strand calling out that his life was threatened and that Cecil was about to make the Infanta Queen. His hysterical shouts were received in silence. He had counted upon his popularity — and this *was* great. But the citizens of London had no hankering to be involved in treason. The same night Essex surrendered.

He had made of Essex House a centre for all the disaffected. Rabid Puritans gathered there, as they looked upon the Earl as the leader of the anti-Spanish party. Yet many of his closest friends were Catholics, or Catholic sympathisers. The Blounts, the Earl of Southampton, Sir Charles Danvers, and finally, Francis Tresham, Robert Catesby and his brother John, and Christopher Wright — who survived this rising to be implicated in the "Gunpowder Plot" of 1605 — were all of his entourage, as all of them, it might be noted, were strongly anti-Spanish, like the majority of English Catholics.

With a little luck Essex might have escaped. Perhaps it was because of his confidence that the sentence would never be carried out that Francis Bacon consented to be Crown counsel against his former patron: let us hope it was that. The prisoner bore himself proudly, accusing Robert Cecil to his face. And when Walter Raleigh appeared as a witness, the prisoner cried, "What boots it to swear this fox?" It all made a brave showing; there could be no question about his technical guilt.

Nor can there be any question about the reality of Elizabeth's anger. When Bacon, during the period of Essex's disgrace, had suggested that he be sent back to Ireland, the Queen retorted, "Essex! When I send Essex back into Ireland, I will marry you. Claim it of me." And later, when Bacon was drawing up the indictment and styled him "My Lord of Essex," Elizabeth interrupted with "Write 'Essex.' " And so it appeared.

Cecil had made up his mind that Essex should die. He was an unruly subject, a perpetual threat to the government — Norfolk all over again, an aristocratic leader with more than Norfolk's ability, and far more than Norfolk's courage. There could be, in those days, only one end to such a career. Elizabeth had long been suspicious of him; he had deeply offended her; now she was afraid of him.

ROBERT DEVEREUX, EARL OF ESSEX
Engraved from the painting by Hilliard in the collection
of the Earl of Verulam.

"Till Birds Sing in the Morning"

Her suspicions and her fears had been fanned even by so trivial a matter as John Hayward's dedicating his Life of Henry IV to Essex; it was enough that Henry IV had been a usurper. Summoning Bacon, she demanded if there were not in this book grounds for a charge of treason. Bacon looked it over and made reply, "Not, I think, for treason, Madam, but for felony." When she asked what he meant he explained, "He has stolen so many passages from Tacitus." But now there was something not to be passed over with a witticism. With singularly little hesitation she signed Essex's death warrant.

On this Lytton Strachey has a characteristic passage of romantic psychology. "In all that had happened there was a dark inevitability, a ghastly satisfaction; her father's destiny, by some intimate dispensation, was repeated in hers; it was supremely fitting that Robert Devereux should follow Anne Boleyn to the block. Her father! . . . but in a still remoter depth there were still stranger stirrings. There was a difference as well as a likeness; after all, she was no man, but a woman; and was this, perhaps, not a repetition but a revenge? After all the long years of her lifetime, and in this appalling consummation, was it her murdered mother who had fully emerged? The wheel had come full circle. Manhood — the fascinating, detestable entity, which had come upon her concealed in yellow magnificence in her father's lap — manhood was overthrown at last, and in the person of that traitor it should be rooted out. Literally, perhaps . . . she knew well enough the punishment for high treason. But no! she smiled sardonically. She would not deprive him of the privilege of his rank. It would be enough if he suffered as so many others — the Lord Admiral Seymour among the rest — had suffered before him; it would be enough if she cut off his head."

That is, I think, altogether too subtle and rarified. Elizabeth was scared. She knew that she held the throne precariously, in spite of her seeming security. This ridiculous rising had failed, it is true, but an example had to be made by the younger Cecil, now in his father's place. To make sure that Elizabeth was kept afraid long enough to kill Essex, Cecil caught a soldier of the

353

name of Lee who was lurking about the royal kitchens, and at once manufactured a plot — of course with the usual confessions extorted on the rack. It was his dead father's favourite trick in such emergencies; he now played it himself with complete success. Lee was duly executed; he had to be: his execution was a means of making certain that the sentence on Essex would be carried out.

Yet it may be too simple to account for it all on the grounds of Elizabeth's fear. With that passion were entwined the others of love and rage. It was this man, whom she had spoiled and pampered, who had lifted his hand against her! It was this man who, after writing her love letters, had sneered at her crooked carcase! She had herself said that King Philip had tried so often to murder her because he loved her so much. She knew that the two wives her father had sent to the block — her mother and Katherine Howard — were the very two he had loved most. With Shakespeare's Shylock she might have asked, "Do men kill the thing they love?" Her emotions demanded satisfaction. She took no blame, as she should have done, for the disaster. She had allowed Essex to believe that he could do what he pleased, and then be forgiven everything in the deliciousness that came after a lover's quarrel. She had indulged him — and herself — in these emotional outbursts. Now, unfairly, she sent him to death for what it would have been quite possible to have treated as an escapade.

Possibly she could no longer trust herself. She loved Essex too much to dare to become reconciled with him now. If she spared him, she would live hagridden by a fear more desperate than that for her life — which was indeed safe enough in his keeping; she was afraid that his mastery over her would be absolute. She could not leave him in permanent disgrace; her weakness would make her yield; and yield she would not. Outraged love would not let her.

On February 25, less than three weks after his march through London, the Earl was beheaded on Tower Hill, his personal enemy, Raleigh, having the bad taste to be present. The news was immediately carried to Elizabeth. They found her playing at the virginals. And she went on playing — such was her self-control — even when told that the axe had fallen.

But with it darkness fell upon her. Later in the day she was caught in tears. And in the months that followed how many were the days of morose gloom, how many the nights of sleepless remorse! Essex was dead.

James of Scotland, when told of it, remarked, "My martyr!" But no one knew better how unnecessary the martyrdom was. His envoys to England had had quiet talks with Cecil and Bishop Bancroft and were now sure of the succession. They, no less than Essex, had been working for James. Only they did what had to be done discreetly. They did not have a fatal candour. Even the truce with Tyrone was renewed, though in Mountjoy the English government found at last a general who would act with decision and promptitude. To that extent Essex was justified.

To that extent also his splendid futility is further emphasized. In history the Essex affair has been given an exaggerated political importance. The main importance it had was in the life of Elizabeth herself. It was the crisis of her last years.

Essex's career has been often described as typical of the English Renaissance. It was actually, however, a flaring up of the mediaeval spirit. He was the last of the barons who dreamed that he could dominate the throne. In his vanity he imagined he could do what he liked with the Queen, and that through her he could eject the Cecilian government and make himself supreme in the state. Actually all that he did was to fascinate Elizabeth for a while; but she was a woman too cold to allow her feelings to exercise any permanent control over her cautious judgment. He had pitted himself against the Cecils, and had boasted that he "would make the old fox cringe and cower." And old Burghley had answered with what proved to be a prophecy. Drawing a Prayer Book from his pocket at the Council Board — this he used to display as he did his rosary in Queen Mary's days — he had pointed to the verse: "Bloody and deceitful men shall not live out half their days." He himself had not lived to see that prophecy fulfilled. The undoing of

355

Essex was the work of Burghley's hunchbacked son.

Robert Devereux was one born out of due time. It was much too late in the day for anyone to play the role of Norfolk. In so far as Essex stood for anything it was for vigorous and truculent youth, seeking the recovery of a heroic past, as against the pedantic bureaucracy of dry, timid old men. Hence his popularity; hence, too, his fall.

22

The Last Years

THE war with Spain dragged on — still undeclared — a war that was no war, the kind of war that Elizabeth preferred to any other, since it cost few lives and little money. It had settled down to the routine of piracy, which now could be called privateering. But the world had begun to recognise the importance of sea power, and England herself to perceive that it might be used for more solid purposes than that of raiding. When James Lancaster took three ships past the Cape of Good Hope to Ceylon and Sumatra, he led to the founding of the East India Company in 1599. That may be more properly considered the beginning of the British Empire than the adventures of Drake, or even Raleigh.

Of greater ultimate significance than the war with Spain were three other developments: the conquest of Ireland, the emergence of something like a spirit of independence in Parliament, and the Appellant controversy. This last made it look for a moment as though after all there was going to be the complete triumph of Protestantism; it was in such a conviction that Elizabeth died. I must touch upon these matters briefly here, taking them in order.

Lord Mountjoy, though his appointment to the head of the Irish administration, when suggested in 1598, had been opposed by Essex on the ground that he was a scholar rather than a general, proved himself, when he succeeded Essex, to be an excellent commander. He committed atrocities, to be sure, as had all his predecessors, but his *schrecklichkeit* had some military value. The Queen, therefore, shut her eyes to what she knew of his correspondence with King James and confirmed him in office.

He had under him the energetic Sir George Carew and Sir Henry Docwra, and with them moved steadily forward, seizing and fortifying strategic points, from which they ravaged the territory in Irish hands. When at last Juan dell' Aguilla arrived in the south with thirty-three Spanish ships and three thousand men, the Irish were already half subdued. Though Tyrone and Tyrconnell and Desmond now rose again, the English fleet blockaded Kinsale, thus cutting off the Spaniards from receiving reinforcements and supplies, and Mountjoy invested the town with an army of eight thousand.

The Irish Earls marched to lift the siege; but Tyrone arrived only to be driven back, and on January 2, 1602, the Spaniards were obliged to surrender, a relieving fleet having already been destroyed by Sir Richard Leveson at Castlehaven. Tyrconnell eventually escaped to Spain; Desmond was captured and taken to England, where he died insane in the Tower in 1608; and Tyrone gave in his adhesion upon getting a promise of pardon and the restoration of his estates. It was at the end of March, 1603, that Tyrone yielded. He was ignorant of the fact that Elizabeth had just died.

Ireland's conquest was now apparently complete. It was, however, to plague England for centuries. By achieving their immediate object — the destruction of the clans — the English government lost their ultimate one. The rivalries of the chieftains — though the existence of the clans was obstructive to English rule — had prevented the union of the country. Therefore by destroying the Irish tribal system, the English unwittingly created the Irish nation.

Further, by attempting to force Protestantism upon the Irish as part of the process of Anglicisation, the English ensured the Irish attachment to the Catholic Faith. Even those who had no better reason for rejecting the official religion, rejected it simply because it was English. In any event the tribes would have disappeared as an anachronism in the modern world, but their disappearance need not have coincided with the emergence of so fierce a national feeling. It might have come about that Protestantism woud have prevailed in Ireland — at any rate to a much greater extent than it did — had it not found here a force strong enough to repel it. In this respect the Elizabethan conquest of Ireland was the greatest of Elizabethan failures.

When we turn to Parliament we must avoid the common error of regarding it as the instrument of democracy. That it was potentially such may be admitted, though it may also be questioned whether Parliament, even now, is more than potentially such. At that time it was a convocation of landowners who were thinking mainly of the interests of their class; and those interests — because of the spoliation of the monasteries — called for the proscription of Catholicism. But whereas Parliament at the beginning of the reign was fairly docile in carrying out the orders given it by the Queen and the Council, as time went on it did, without becoming definitely refractious, show some signs of restiveness. An open struggle with the Crown was still far off, but already we may discern, however dimly, Parliament's consciousness of its increasing strength and a disposition to assert it.

We must remember that the Queen still had the right to suspend any existing statute or to issue a proclamation which would possess the force of law. When she summoned her first Parliament, Bacon, the Lord Keeper, was careful to explain to its members that she was not *obliged* to consult them at all but did so only in order that her laws might have their sanction and derive additional weight from the fact. Actually Elizabeth consulted Parliament as rarely as possible, and practically never except when she needed additional money.

As Green puts its, her famous thrift "was dictated not so much by economy as by the desire to avoid summoning fresh Parliaments." By managing her estate prudently, she could keep her hands free. In those days it was expected of the Crown that it should use its own revenues for the ordinary business of government and call for Parliamentary subsidies only under grave necessity. Professor Neale has said that "for all its drabness and difficulty, finance is the essence of Elizabeth's story." Caution and hard bargaining rather than dash and daring mark her age; the parsimonious paring down of accounts was the secret of her success. Her legend is heroic; her true history is not. Gloriana was more in her element as an accountant than as an Amazon. Normally she managed to carry on the work of administration on an income of £250,000. Had Ireland not so drained her she would have managed very well.

The provision she made for her favourites, however — in the form of granting them monopolies — caused dissatisfaction to fester and come to a head. When the unrest had passed a certain point, she promptly yielded. The quality that made her so consummate a showman served also to make her instinctively understand when popular demands had to be satisfied.

Yet on the principle of her royal prerogative she remained firm. For instance, when Parliament petitioned in 1592 for liberty of speech — by which was meant the right to free debate in its chambers without the danger of arrest — she answered, "Your liberty of speech extends no further than 'ay' or 'no': and if any idle heads hazard their estates by meddling with the Church or State, the Speaker will not receive their bills." She promised freedom of arrest and the right of Parliament to send her delegations with the conditional "It is not to cover any man's ill-doings. As for your access to my person, that is wholly to depend on the importance of the occasion and my leisure." She was an adept at using ambiguous phrases that conceded precisely nothing.

But she perceived that the monopolies had better be withdrawn; they were creating too much discontent. The only possible defence for them is that they represented a farming out of taxes, bearing much the same relation to the present civil service that privateering has to the royal navy. But they were bad for the country, and the Queen received no profit — except that she was relieved of the necessity of handing out money to her favourites. Some monopolies were, of course, what we should now consider patents, but it was not of these that Parliament complained. It was when starch, which had been imported at eighteen shillings a hundredweight went up to fifty-six shillings and salt from sixteen pence to fifteen shillings a bushel that it became clear that the monopolist was a mere extortioner.

Therefore when in Elizabeth's last Parliament a long list was read out of the monopolies, a member named Hakewill rose and asked sarcastically, "Is not bread there?" When some other members more innocent, or stupid, than Hakewill, murmured bewilderdly, "Bread? bread?" Hakewill rose again to say, "If order be not taken for these, bread will be there by the next Parliament."[1]

The time had come, Elizabeth saw, to call a halt. Sir Robert Cecil was accordingly put up to denounce those who ground the faces of the poor, and a few days later the Queen herself made a speech. She told Parliament that she did not so much rejoice that God made her a queen as that He had made her a queen over a thankful people. Grandly she assumed all the credit to herself: "That my grants should be grievous to my people, and oppressions privileged under our patents, our kingly dignity shall not suffer it; yea, when I heard it, I could give no rest unto my thoughts until I had reformed it." One would almost think that this was the first time she had ever heard of the monopolies! "To be a king and wear a crown is a thing more glorious to them that see it than it is pleasing to them that bear it. For myself, I was never so much enticed with the glorious name of a king or royal authority of a queen, as delighted that God had made me His instrument to maintain His truth and glory, and to defend His kingdom from peril, dishonour, tyranny, and oppression." Consoled by oratory, everybody went home happy. The Queen had dodged a perilous situation.

These matters, however, are usually adequately dealt with in the histories of the time; so I need spend no more space upon them. What the histories usually say little about is the Appellant controversy which in the last years of Elizabeth came close to resulting in the submission of Catholics — or at any rate close enough to enable us to see how acute the danger was. The fining and imprisonment of recusants, and the execution of

[1] Among the monopolies were such strange commodities as ox shinbones, ashes, bags, aniseed, currants, and salted pilchards! The process, had it not been checked, would have eventually made everything a monopoly.

both priests and laymen as traitors went on to the end of her reign, and beyond it; and these the Catholics heroically accepted as their lot. Their greater danger was what now arose from their internal dissensions.

I shall treat this question as briefly as possible, and only because it can hardly be avoided. No complete account of it has yet been published. My account must, therefore, be taken as a mere sketch of the issues involved.

It is commonly said that the dissensions among the missionaries made their first appearance with the arrival of the Jesuits among them. That this is not the case is proved by the fact that the signs of disunion may be noted as early as 1577. And the charge made by some of the secular priests that it was the activities of the Jesuits that brought the persecution on their heads is again not true; priests had been executed long before 1580. If the persecution was intensified after that date it was rather due to the error of judgment in sending a papal force into Ireland. Nobody was more aghast at that than the Jesuits themselves.

The real source of the trouble was the absence of any ecclesiastical jurisdiction. The Marian Bishops — such of them as were alive — were in prison and unable to exercise control. And though the Pope is Bishop in all lands as well as in Rome, he was too far away to attend to details. William Allen, the future Cardinal, was indeed recognized as the leader of the English Catholics, as he was the trainer of the first missionaries, but he had no formal authority. He himself, in a letter written on August 10, 1577, complained that there was no head, "no one who governeth the rest."

What happened was that by degrees discord arose between the disciplined body of the Jesuits and the other missionaries, who had grown accustomed to independence. Persons shrugged his shoulders over the matter, dismissing it as the immemorial quarrel between religious and seculars. Unfortunately it went a good deal deeper than that.

There was, of course, bound to be a certain amount of jealousy of the Jesuits, especially on the part of the older priests. The Jesuits were much more efficiently trained men, and efficiency is always resented by the less efficient. The cry was raised that the Society did not understand the English temperament, and sneers were directed against the Jesuits' "trade of syllogising." Possibly some tactless Jesuits made some seculars conscious of their intellectual and spiritual superiority to them. It is certain that some seculars believed that the Jesuits, because of having their headquarters in Rome, could pull wires with the *curia* in order to obtain special privileges.

But we still have not come to the heart of the matter. It has been stated by such men as T. G. Law that the essence of the quarrel lay in the too close association of Persons — and it was thought, all Jesuits — with the Spanish Party. Recent research has brought to light the fact that the conflict actually originated in the English College at Rome, where dissatisfaction arose in regard to matters of food, quarters, and discipline for which the Jesuits were unjustly blamed, since the funds supplied them were insufficient. But Persons' political manoeuvres, so the malcontents held, fixed upon them the stigma of disloyalty and treason. After the death of Mary Queen of Scots — which left the Catholics broken and bewildered — Persons supported the Spanish claim to the English throne. And to most Englishmen such a claim was intolerable. Besides, it made all Catholics liable to be charged with working in the Spanish interest.

Yet Allen himself had supported this claim and had collaborated with Persons in proving Philip's Lancastrian descent. After the Armada, however, the Cardinal had withdrawn from politics, for which he had no natural inclination. It would have been well had Persons stuck to what he wrote in 1584: "Dr. Allen and I . . . had resolved to leave cogitation of these matters and follow only a spiritual course, whereupon all dependeth, though in longer time." Instead he reverted to politics, and though no actual breach of friendship occurred between him and Allen, there was no longer the former close association.

In the year of Allen's death (1594) Persons provoked a stupendous storm by publishing his *Conference on the Next Succession*. He did not, it is true, advocate the union of England

and Spain under a single crown. He professed himself ready to back *any* thoroughly Catholic claimant who had a good case.[2] He argued very dispassionately, weighing the pros and cons with regard to all the candidates in the field. But his conclusion was inescapable: the Infanta should be the next Queen, not because of her Spanish blood but because of her genuine Catholicism. It is hardly surprising that many English Catholics agreed that Persons' book was "the most pestilential work ever written," and that the somewhat absurd Father Watson should pray in his *Quodlibets: "A machinationibus Parsoni, libera nos, Domine!"*

It is not to be supposed that the majority of the English secular priests shared the antagonism of Watson and the other Appellants to the Jesuits. But most of them heartily disapproved of the *Conference,* and many, in their anxiety to prove their loyalty to Elizabeth and in their hope of getting some degree of toleration, were prepared to throw the Jesuits into the raging waters, like so many Jonahs, that they might have calm themselves.

Conditions were made worse among the Catholic clergy by the appointment in 1598 of George Blackwell as "archpriest" — that is, a supervisor with some of a bishop's authority but without the powers conferred by consecration. Blackwell proved to be unsuited for the position, which because of his ill-health he accepted reluctantly. He gave the impression of officiousness and was even accused of resorting to sharp practice.[3] What obviously infuriated the Appellant party most was that he was given instructions to confer with Father Garnet, the Superior

[2] For that matter, Philip III later gave the English Catholics to understand that he had no political interests of his own to serve, and that he was prepared to cede his rights to any candidate the English Catholics could agree upon.

[3] For example, when the appeal against him was made to Rome and he was told — while being confirmed in his office — that he must use it "for the edification and not the destruction of souls," he was also ordered to see that there was no more publication of controversial matter. But as the Jesuit, Thomas Lister, had a book already in the press, he held back the brief for several months, until the book was safely out. It should, however, in justice to Blackwell be said that he, in his turn, was sometimes tricked: the government now and then sent him letters, which he accepted as though they had come from Rome, and so believed himself to have sanctions when he did not have them at all.

of the Jesuits in England, on all important questions. As one of them wrote: "All Catholics must hereafter depend upon Blackwell, and he upon Garnet, and Garnet upon Persons, and Persons upon the Devil." The appointment was regarded as a move to further the aims of the Spanish Party. As such it was fiercely resented.[4]

An appeal was now made to Rome — hence the name "Appellants" — against Blackwell; and the government, seeing a chance to sow further dissensions, took a hand in the affair. At Wisbeach castle a number of priests were imprisoned, living there a kind of collegiate life under the unofficial direction of William Weston, a Jesuit. They were treated fairly well, and were sometimes even allowed to make visits in the town. One of these priests, who had shown himself active in the "stirs" against the Jesuits and the Archpriest, an ex-parson of the name of Bluet, was sent for by Bancroft, the Bishop of London, and examined also by the Council and even by the Queen herself. He was told that he might go with several of his friends to Rome to lay their complaints against Blackwell before the Pope. It would seem that he promised Elizabeth that he would bring about the recall of the Jesuits and to have received in return her promise of toleration for the seculars.[5]

The Appellants were, of course, perfectly within their rights in making their appeal. They should have known, however, that the government was merely using them for its own purposes, and that no promises would be kept.[6] That they had some

---

[4] Even Lingard writes: "It is plain, from the subsequent conduct of Clement, that the pontiff sought only to put an end to the dissensions among the missionaries: but the projectors of the measure had in view a great political object. They had persuaded themselves, that by subjecting all the secular priests to the government of a single superior attached to their party, they should be able, at the death of the queen, to employ the influence of the whole body in support of a favourite candidate to the throne."

[5] An amusing scheme was set on foot while Bluet was on his way to Rome. In Belgium he had some conversations with Frangipani, the Nuncio there, who wrote to Cardinal Aldobrandini, the Pope's nephew, in August, 1602, suggesting that he allow himself to be captured by an English ship and carried before Elizabeth so as to be able to discuss Catholic affairs with her. Upon the margin of the letter the Cardinal Nephew wrote, "The idea is charming!"

[6] The persecution was, in fact, renewed after the government had achieved its object.

grounds for complaint against the Archpriest is shown by the decree they eventually secured against Blackwell, in which he was reproved, ordered not to exceed his authority, forbidden further consultation with the Jesuits and told to admit three Appellants among his assistants. At the same time Blackwell was, in general, sustained.

But the unhappy differences were still not over. The patriotic zeal of the Appellants so carried them away that on January 31, 1603, thirteen of them signed a declaration of loyalty to Elizabeth which came very near to committing them to disobedience toward the Holy See. That no disciplinary action was taken by the Church was due mainly to the circumstance that the Queen died the following month; it was therefore considered inadvisable to do anything that might awaken the anger of her successor. Rome as well as the English Catholic body hoped that the accession of James of Scotland would bring some relief.

The signing of this declaration — only thirteen priests out of the three hundred working in England signed it, and Bluet was not one of them — was a technical victory for Elizabeth, though as she was now dying she probably never heard of it. A still greater victory might have followed had she lived and the controversy been permitted to continue. Blackwell himself was deposed for taking in 1608 the oath of allegiance formulated two years previously. He was a pious, well-meaning man, but he never had much political acumen and, as his later action shows, no very clear perception as to what were the real issues involved in the Appellant controversy.

To sum up the unhappy affair, I should say that the Jesuits, though entirely right on the main point, were wrong on the incidental one of the succession — in so far as this can be considered a "Jesuit" project. What they stood for so resolutely was an undeviating loyalty to the Church, even when this looked like a deficiency in patriotism. They never lost sight of the principle that far above our natural affections for our country, and the natural duty we owe duly constituted secular authority, is our obligation to God. It is to be feared that the

Appellants, out of dislike for all things Spanish, had come under French influences to such an extent that they were tinged with Gallicanism. That spirit was to hamper English Catholicism — or rather a certain group of English Catholics — for another couple of centuries.

As for Persons, upon whom I may be thought severe, the counter opinion of a scholarly secular priest should prove worth citing. "The only English Catholic churchman of the time" he writes, "who had the necessary courage, and with all his faults, the ability, to reorganize the shattered House of God in England, was Father Robert Persons, the Jesuit. . . . Father Persons understood the religious situation of his country more cogently than any living Catholic at that period; and it is to be regretted that jealousy and political intrigue failed him in his gallant attempt to save the realm to the Church."[7]

As for the Queen, her "Proclamation against Jesuits and Secular Priests" issued on November 5, 1602, only a few months before her death, reveals how set her face was against any modification of the anti-Catholic laws. The Seculars, she indicates, are only a shade less guilty than the Jesuits; so she denies "that we have some purpose to grant toleration of two religions within our Realm, where God (we thank Him for it, who seeth into the secret corners of all hearts) doth only know our innocency from such imagination, but how far it hath been from any about us, once to offer to ears the persuasion of such a course, as would not only disturb the peace of the Church but bring this our State into Confusion." So her conferences, and those of Bancroft, with Bluet, and the sending of the Appellants to Rome had from the beginning no other object than that of fomenting internal strife among Catholics!

I end this chapter with sadness of mind, because in it I have to record a belated weakening which should never have occurred. But these things do happen in an imperfect world inhabited by imperfect Christians. The story of the Elizabethan Church, taken as a whole, can be thought of with pride; and we can be thankful that dissensions did not develop into an actual

[7] Peter Guilday, *The Life and Times of John Carroll*, Vol. I, pp. 135, 136.

schism. It is the German Protestant historian Meyer who calls the steadfastness of the Elizabethan Church "the most glorious page in the bloody annals of the counter-reformation." Poor Watson was so disgruntled that he mixed himself up in the "Bye Plot" early in James's reign, and, though he tried to implicate his old enemies the Jesuits, was himself executed in the end for high treason. His angry and misguided career does nothing to tarnish the lustre of Campion and Southwell, or of a host of others — seculars and Jesuits — who laid down their lives that the Faith might live in England.

DEATH MASK OF QUEEN ELIZABETH
From the reproduction in the *London Illustrated News*.

23

Into the Darkness

A T THE end of 1602 the Queen's coronation ring had to be filed from her finger, so embedded was it now in the flesh. The superstitious mind of the sceptic must have regarded it as a bad omen.

It had long been apparent that Elizabeth was drawing near her end. The wonder to all was that she had lasted so long with such poor health. Almost every year she had been expected to die; yet she had reached what was for those days a great age. But now even her superb vitality, her fierce holding off of death, could do no more. She was very weary. She no longer gave much attention to state affairs. Instead, she retired, as the old do, into things loved in youth, and spent hours over the *Canterbury Tales*. Raleigh found the phrase for her: she was "a lady whom time had surprised." Often she was heard to mutter *"Mortua, non sepulta! mortua, non sepulta!"*

She had never really been herself since the execution of Essex. Her last two years were lived in mourning for him. And her resentment was quickly aroused, never to be appeased, against anyone who had had any share in his death. Thus Barlow, who had preached the official sermon in St. Paul's justifying the execution — a sermon seen beforehand and approved by Elizabeth herself — was not admitted again into her presence. The Prebendary was used as a whipping boy.

There were whole days when the Queen sat silent and, in her melancholy, refused to eat. Her familiars preferred such days to the ones when she gave way to violent and capricious rages. Sir John Harington, her godson, tells how she kept a sword always by her, and how she relieved herself in her fits of fury by thrusting it into the arras. Then she would retire to a darkened room and give herself up to hysterical tears.

But Harington was one of her favourites, a man who brought back memories of happier years. So though she would sometimes send him away, she would now and then consent to see him. He did his best to cheer her up with his stories and epigrams, but as he told his wife, he "found her in most pitiable state." Her memory appeared to be failing, he noticed. She once asked him whether he had ever seen Tyrone, completely forgetting all he had previously related. As for his clever rhymes, they now brought only a wan smile and the remark, "When thou dost feel creeping time at thy gate, these fooleries will please thee less. I am past relish for such matters." It was all very depressing to the kindhearted and vivacious poet. To Henry IV, Elizabeth wrote a month before her death, "All the fabric of my reign, little by little, is beginning to fail." She was full of a vague remorseless sense of failure. Her councillors, she guessed, were ignoring her and working behind her back.

Nevertheless she had too much vitality to relapse into consistent gloom. Her low spirits and her bad temper would suddenly pass, and those around her would be astonished at the change. She then refused to accept her invalidism and would insist on doing things quite beyond her strength. She would put her bony frame upon a horse and ride out to see the hunt. And even in her last years she went on her annual "progress." By way of consoling herself she would acidly remark that her new statesmen were not the equal of their predecessors. She would not admit that it was she who was failing.

We hear of her dancing before the Scottish Ambassador — who was permitted to peep from behind a screen — on July 1, 1602. But that was intended to impress him; he could pass the news back to King James, as a way of letting him know that she was not yet ready for the grave. It was perhaps less impressive than she supposed. The dances in vogue called for little more than the ability to walk. He saw on old woman in a wig and with a few black fangs in otherwise toothless gums tottering around a room. Still, it was remarkable that she was able to dance at all.

Her humour sometimes flared up. It had often been of a

somewhat spiteful sort, as when she had objected in Essex's time, to the diminutive Lady Mary Howard's grand dress. To humiliate her the Queen had put it on herself and then demanded of her ladies how they liked it. When even Lady Mary had to admit that it was too short, Elizabeth had snapped, "Then if it becomes not me, as being too short, I am minded that it shall not become thee, as being too fine; so it fitteth neither well." The dress was therefore put with the other three thousand in her Majesty's wardrobes. They were all soon to be cut up by Anne of Denmark's scissors to provide costumes for a court masque.

But more often Elizabeth's humour was merely broad, vigorous, and indelicate. She loved to play practical jokes, as she loved to bestow nicknames. When she wrote to Lord Mountjoy on December 3, 1600, addressing him as "Mistress Kitchenmaid" he was expected to take it as a sign of the royal favour. Her rough boisterousness was a relaxation from her tangled emotions and the tortuous subtlety of her political manoeuvering.

Under all the now rather forced gayety there was an immense loneliness. Since Katherine Ashley had died, early in her reign, she had perhaps never had a real friend — certainly no woman friend. There were men who flattered her; men who admired her; men who conspired against her. Was there among them all one who had loved her? Of course they had, most of them, protested love — but they had protested it too extravagantly to be convincing. She had nursed Leicester when he was ill, and the dying Burghley she had fed, in his weakness, with her own hands. But Leicester was merely a cynical adventurer out to get what he could out of the Queen; and old Cecil, though she was grateful to him, was as cold and cautious as herself. There could have been no more than an intellectual friendship between them, one without tenderness. She had loved the Admiral perhaps, and it cannot be doubted that she had loved in turn Leicester and Alençon and Essex. But they had not returned her love; and Alençon and Essex had said of her contemptuous and devastating things. Even from her father and mother she had received no affection. And now she was dying, with the sycophantic courtiers waiting with ill-concealed impatience for her death.

Nor had she found, as many a lonely heart does, a friend in God. His name had been useful for oratorical purposes or for the garnishing of her oaths; that was all, or very nearly all. Her mind was thoroughly secular. Though there were moments when she feared God — as the moving cry for mercy in her book of prayers shows — it was never with a fear so steadfast as to keep her faithful to any principles. She had guided herself by the Machiavellian maxims. Her spasms of religiosity came only when she felt low spirited or when the Shadow fell upon her. In her was nothing of the new Protestant spirituality that was so different from the negative fanaticism of the early years of her reign. John Donne was already wrestling with God. Hooker had produced his famous book. Lawrence Andrewes was shining, and Jeremy Taylor was to shine before long. In a more commonplace way the diary of the much-married Lady Hoby lets us see that, busy as she was among her preserves and her distilling and her famous housekeeping, even the rich sometimes turned their thoughts to heaven. But in Elizabeth there was hardly a trace of religious sentiment. In desolate isolation she travelled her road to the end, shuddering at death now marching to meet her. Except for a pagan stoicism she had no armour against it.

In writing these words I know that no human soul can do more than pass a tentative judgement on another. The facts of Elizabeth's life, however, seem to admit only one conclusion. A good death, such as that of the rake Charles II, reveals a lifetime of secret hunger for God; and many men and women show what they are only in their last hours. The deathbed of Elizabeth is one of the most dreadful in history.

Those who saw her dying had little thought for anything except the succession. It had been shelved time after time by Elizabeth; now it had to be settled. There were, indeed, many claimants, though most of them had no chance, so the field narrowed down to Lady Arbella (or Arabella) Stuart, the Infanta,

Into the Darkness

James of Scotland, and Lord Beauchamp, the son of Hertford and Lady Catherine Grey. This last candidature was the best under statutory law, which was why Elizabeth had taken pains to see that some doubt should be cast upon the legitimacy of Beauchamp's birth. When his name was mentioned to the dying Queen, she roused herself to snarl, "I will have no rascal's son in my seat!"

But the enquiry was a mere matter of form. Sir Robert Cecil and Bishop Bancroft had already decided that James was to be the next King. He had also the support of the Catholics as a whole, for they had deluded themselves into thinking that from him they would obtain toleration. Such a belief was useful in keeping the Infanta out.[1]

Cecil had devised another means of dishing her. She had been told that if she became Queen of England she would have to surrender the Belgian provinces to Philip III, and the Secretary was well aware that she would never renounce a certainty for a possibility, something that in any event she would have to fight for. A subtle smile must have flickered over the pale, gentle face of the hunchback when he thought of this brilliant stroke of policy.

Even Arabella Stuart, though she had the advantage of English birth, could be considered out of the running. The English Jesuits had assured the King of Spain that she was secretly a Catholic, but she was too prudent to avow herself one. Cecil had found it convenient to keep her in play; he had never had the slightest intention of letting her ascend the throne. She was so eccentric as to be considered insane by many people. She had now served her purpose of keeping James upon what the English government considered his good behaviour.

James had played his difficult hand well, even to the extent of making no serious fuss about his mother's execution. For some time past he had been receiving clandestine letters from Cecil, which had been sent, for safety, through Mountjoy by way of Ireland. Cecil's habit of going behind Elizabeth's back

---

[1] James had, of course, given what amounted to "campaign promises" to Catholic, Anglican, and Puritan alike.

is damagingly apparent in one of his covering letters to Mount-joy: "If, therefore, you will, for accidents unlooked for, return this letter, I will thank you; your warrants for that which you must do, or can do, remaining under your own hand." He did not even trust Mountjoy to burn the letter. The Lord-deputy was to show publicly the formal instructions from the Queen — acting upon them at his discretion — meanwhile keeping secret the private instructions of a very different character he had received from the Secretary of State. Of course Cecil most solemnly denied that he was having any sort of communication with James — an asseveration Elizabeth was too shrewd to believe.

The accession of James was therefore a foregone conclusion. The Queen's last illness was just long enough to enable Cecil to put the finishing touches to his scheme. Eight large ships of the royal navy, each with five hundred men on board, lay in the river. The city of London had been made sure of. In the North, Sir Robert's elder brother, the second Lord Burghley, was in command, holding the door open for the Scots King. And any prominent Catholics known to be of the Spanish Party had been put into precautionary confinement. Even the proclamation that James was to issue had already been drawn up and sent to Scotland for his approval. Cecil, like the King elect, was waiting for Elizabeth to die.

One thing alone was lacking — a nomination from the Queen. She had always refused to give it, but they hoped that at the last minute it could be dragged out of her. Though Cecil was prepared to act without it, he wanted to be able to say afterwards that Elizabeth had accepted James as her successor. Now that she was dying and, being speechless, was incapable of contradicting him, he interpreted the sign she made in answer to his question in the sense he wished. It was given out that there had been a gesture of assent.[2]

Perhaps she did make one, but it did not matter a great deal

[2] This is the version of the affair which is generally accepted. The account given in Carey's *Memoirs*, which indicates that Elizabeth nominated James of her own accord, has every appearance of being a fabrication. Had that really happened, Cecil would have been the first person to have published the fact.

either way. The dying woman knew that the battle was over, and she had always been, after her own strange fashion, a realist. James was going to succeed her; that much she knew to be beyond her power to prevent. All this asking for her nomination was merely a piece of play acting. As it had to be gone through, she might as well take her part in it. But every time before when the question had been brought up she had said, "The name of a successor is like the tolling of my own death-bell." Whatever confirmation was given was withheld until the last possible moment.

All that remains to be told is the horror of Elizabeth's end.

In January, 1603, she had a cold, but was moved on the last day of the month, a wild wet day, from Westminster to Richmond. There she stayed, growing weaker and more depressed, until in March she collapsed. Yet she refused to see a doctor, but sat huddled in a low chair. When at last she stood up, she found she could not walk, and so was rooted for hours in the middle of the floor — it is said for fifteen hours. When she dropped from exhaustion she would not permit her attendants to carry her to bed, but stayed where she was, propped up on pillows, silent, staring fixedly, her finger in her mouth.

Lady Scrope, a relative as well as a maid of honour, tried to persuade her to go to bed, only to get the fierce answer, "I saw one night my own body, exceedingly lean and fearful, in a light of fire." Then clutching at hope, she asked wildly, "Do *you* see sights in the night?" When Howard, the Lord Admiral, tried what he could do, he was told, "If you were in the habit of seeing such things in your bed as I do in mine, you would not persuade me to go there." He persisted and she moaned, "My lord, I am tied with a chain of fire about my neck. I am tied, I am tied, and the case is altered with me!"

People around her were whispering that she was demented, and her illness has sometimes been diagnosed as the general paralysis of the insane which is usually due to syphilis. She caught the whispered words and said to the Secretary, "Cecil, I know I am not mad. You must not think to make Queen Jane of me." It was an allusion to the mother of Charles V.

Queen Elizabeth

Some of the contemporary accounts say that she lay on the floor for fourteen days and nights; others say only four. In either case it was long enough. But at last she yielded and they got her to bed. I do not think we see here an insane woman but a lost soul.

Despair held her fast. When Archbishop Whitgift, her "little black husband," came to bring her the consolations of religion, she sent him packing. All that was too late for her now. Nevertheless she eventually let him come and pray by her bedside. He was over seventy, as old as she was, and he could not long endure the kneeling posture. After half an hour of this he wanted to stop; she would not permit it. He had to continue praying — another half hour, and another again — his voice growing louder and louder every minute, proclaiming his physical pain, until she fell asleep. The next morning — it was that of March 24th — she was found dead.

A Catholic tradition has it that in these last hours Elizabeth called for a priest, but the story rests on no sound historical basis. All that we can say is that she may have asked for one — but if so, it was impossible for her councillors to grant such a request. It would account for her absolute and overwhelming despair; in so far as any religious feeling lingered in that heart of icy stone it was for the ancient faith of England, the faith she had spent forty-five years in trying to extirpate. Wild-eyed, desperate, and afraid she went out into the darkness. The mask she wore in all her portraits was now dropped. Her true self appears only in the death mask.

Bibliography

This does not pretend to be anything but a practical select bibliography. Far more complete lists will be found in Conyers Read, Pollard, Black, and Wernham and Walker. And Fathers Pollen and Code provide valuable Catholic bibliographies.

Acts of the Privy Council of England. New Series. Edited by J. R. Dasent, London, Stationery Office, 1890–1907.

Aikin, Lucy, *Memoirs of the Court of Queen Elizabeth,* London, 1822.

Annals of Loch Cé. Edited by William M. Hennessy, 2 vols., London, 1871.

Annals of the Kingdom of Ireland, by The Four Masters. Edited by John O'Donovan, 2nd ed., 7 vols., Dublin, 1856.

Anstey, Thomas C., *A Guide to the Laws of England Affecting Roman Catholics,* London, 1842.

Anthony, Katherine, *Queen Elizabeth,* New York, 1929.

Armada Papers (see Laughton, Sir John Knox).

Arundel, Charles, *Leicester's Commonwealth,* London, 1904.

Ascham, Roger, *The Scholemaster.* Edited by D. C. Whimster, London, 1934.

Ashley, Sir William James, *The Economic Organisation of England,* London and New York, 1935.

——— *An Introduction to English Economic History and Theory,* 2 vols. London, 1888–92.

Attridge, A. H., *The Elizabethan Persecution: Did its Victims Suffer for the Old Faith of England or for Treason?,* London, 1928.

Aubrey, John, *Brief Lives.* Edited by Andrew Clark, London, 1898.

Aydelotte, Frank, *Elizabethan Rogues and Vagabonds,* Oxford, 1913.

Bagwell, Richard, *Ireland Under the Tudors, with a Succinct Account of the Earlier History,* 3 vols., London, 1885–90.

Bayne, C. G., *Anglo-Roman Relations, 1558–65* (Vol. II of *Oxford Historical and Literary Studies*), Oxford, 1913.

Bedingfield Papers (see Manning, Canon C. R.).

Beesly, Edward Spencer, *Queen Elizabeth,* London, 1892.

Belloc, Hilaire, *A History of England,* Vol. IV, London, 1931.

——— *How the Reformation Happened,* London, 1928.

——— *Characters of the Reformation,* New York, 1936.

Bibliography

Bellesheim, Alphons, *History of the Catholic Church of Scotland.* Translated by D. Oswald Hunter Blair, O.S.B., 4 vols., Edinburgh, 1887–90.

—— *Geschichte der Katholischen Kirche in Irland von der Einführung des Christenthums bis auf die Gegenwart,* 3 vols., Mainz, 1890–1.

Besant, Sir Walter, *London in the Time of the Tudors,* London, 1904.

Birch, Thomas, *Memoirs of the Reign of Queen Elizabeth,* 2 vols., London, 1754.

Birt, H. N., O.S.B., *The Elizabethan Religious Settlement,* London, 1907.

Black, John B., *The Reign of Elizabeth, 1558–1603,* Oxford, 1936.

Brewer, J. S., *English Studies,* London, 1881.

Bridgett, Thomas E., *The True Story of the Catholic Hierarchy Deposed by Queen Elizabeth,* London, 1889.

Bruce, John (see James VI, King of Scotland).

—— (see Hayward, John).

Buckley, George T., *Atheism in the English Renaissance,* Chicago, 1932.

Burton, E. H. (see *Douay College Diaries*).

—— (see Pollen, J. H.).

Calendar of State Papers, Domestic, of the Reign of Elizabeth.

Calendar of State Papers, Foreign, of the Reign of Elizabeth.

Calendar of State Papers, Foreign, of the Reigns of Edward VI and Mary.

Calendar of State Papers, Ireland.

Calendar of State Papers, Foreign and Domestic, of the Reign of Henry VIII.

Calendar of State Papers, Roman.

Calendar of State Papers, Scottish.

Calendar of State Papers, Spanish.

Calendar of State Papers, Venetian.

Camden, William, *The History of the Most Renowned and Victorious Princess Elizabeth, Late Queen of England.* Edited by Richard Norton, 3rd ed., London, 1630.

Camm, Bede, O.S.B., *Lives of the English Martyrs,* First Series, 2 vols., London, 1904.

Castelnau, Michel de, Sieur de Mauvissière, *Mémoires.* Edited by Jean Godefroy, Paris, 1731.

Catholic Encyclopaedia.

Cecil, Lord Algernon, *A Life of Robert Cecil, First Earl of Salisbury,* London, 1915.

Cecil, Sir Robert (see James VI, King of Scotland).

Cecil, Sir William (Lord Burghley), *The Execution of Justice in England for maintenaunce of publique and Christian peace, against certaine stirrers of sedition,* London, 1583.

Bibliography

Challoner, Richard, *Memoirs of Missionary Priests*. Edited by J. H. Pollen, S.J., London, 1924.

Chamberlin, Frederick Carleton, *Elizabeth and Leycester*, New York, 1939.

—— *The Private Character of Queen Elizabeth*, London, 1921.

—— *The Private Character of Henry VIII*, London, 1932.

—— *The Sayings of Queen Elizabeth*, London, 1923.

Cheyney, E. P., *A History of England, from the Defeat of the Armada to the Death of Elizabeth*, 2 vols., New York, 1914–26.

—— *Social Changes in England in the Sixteenth Century as reflected in contemporary literature*, Boston, 1895.

Cobbett, William, and Howell, Thomas Bayly, *A Complete Collection of State Trials and Proceedings for High Treason*, 42 vols., London, 1816–98.

Code, J. B., *Queen Elizabeth and the English Catholic Historians*, Louvain, 1935.

Corbett, Sir Julian, *Drake and the Tudor Navy*, 2 vols., London, 1898–99.

—— *The Successors of Drake*, London, 1900.

Cotton Manuscripts.

Creighton, Mandell, *Queen Elizabeth*, London, 1906.

Cunningham, W., *Growth of English Industry and Commerce*, 3 vols., Cambridge, 1896–1903.

Dasent, J. R. (see *Acts of the Privy Council of England*).

Devereux, Walter Bourchier, *Lives and Letters of the Devereux, Earls of Essex*, 2 vols., London, 1853.

D'Ewes, Sir Symonds, *A Compleat Journal of the Votes, Speeches and Debate both of the House of Lords, and House of Commons, throughout the whole Reign of Queen Elizabeth*, London, 1693.

Dictionary of National Biography.

Digges, Sir Dudley, *The Compleat Ambassador*, London, 1655.

Dodd, Charles, *Dodd's History from the Commencement of the 16th Century to the Revolution of 1688*, with notes, additions, and a continuation by the Rev. M. A. Tierney, 5 vols., London, 1839–43.

Douay College Diaries. Edited by E. H. Burton and T. L. Williams (Vols. X and XI of the *Catholic Record Society Publications*), 1911.

—— (see Knox, Thomas Francis).

Dudley, Robert (see Leicester, Robert Dudley, Earl of).

Dunlop, R., *Ireland from the Earliest Times to the Present Day*, London, 1922.

Elizabeth, Queen of England, *The Letters of Queen Elizabeth*. Edited by G. B. Harrison, London, 1935.

—— *Letters of Queen Elizabeth and James VI of Scotland*, Camden Society, 1849.

Bibliography

—— (see Margaret of Navarre).

—— (see James VI, King of Scotland).

Ellis, Sir Henry, *Original Letters, Illustrative of English History*, London, 1825.

Encyclopaedia Britannica (Fourteenth Edition).

Fanfani, Amintore, *Catholicism, Protestantism, and Capitalism*, London, 1935.

Fénelon, Bertrand de Salinac, Seigneur de la Mothe, *Correspondance Diplomatique de 1568 à 1575*, 6 vols., Paris, 1838–40.

Fleming, David Hay, *Mary Queen of Scots*, London, 1897.

Foley, Henry, S.J., *Records of the English Province of the Society of Jesus*, 7 vols., London, 1877–84.

Four Masters, The (see *Annals of the Kingdom of Ireland, by the Four Masters*).

Froude, James Anthony, *History of England from the Fall of Wolsey to the Defeat of the Spanish Armada*, 12 vols., London, 1893. (The edition used here is that in the Everyman's Library, comprising 2 vols. on Henry VIII, 1 each on Edward VI and Mary, and 5 on Elizabeth.)

Fugger News Letters (Series I and II, 1568–1605). Edited by Victor von Klarwill, London, 1924–26.

Gairdner, James, *The English Church in the Sixteenth Century, from the Accession of Henry VIII to the Death of Mary*, London, 1904.

—— *Lollardy and the Reformation in England*, 4 vols., London, 1908–13.

Gardiner, Samuel R., and Mullinger, J. B., *Introduction to the Study of English History*, London, 1921.

Gasquet, Francis Aiden, Cardinal, *England Under the Old Religion, and other Essays*, London, 1912.

—— *The Eve of the Reformation*, London, 1900.

—— *A Short History of the Catholic Church in England*, London, 1928.

—— *Henry VIII and the English Monasteries*, 2 vols., London, 1899.

—— and Bishop, Edmund, *Edward VI and the Book of Common Prayer*, London, 1891.

Gee, Henry, *The Elizabethan Clergy and the Settlement of Religion, 1558–1564*, Oxford, 1898.

—— and Hardy, William John, *Documents Illustrative of English Church History*, London, 1896.

Gerson, A. G., "English Recusants and the Spanish Armada," *American Historical Review*, Vol. XXII (1917), pp. 589–594.

Gillow, Joseph, *A Literary and Biographical History, or Biographical Dictionary of English Catholics*, 5 vols., London, 1898.

Giuseppi, M. S., *A Guide to the Manuscripts preserved in the Public Record Office*, 2 vols., London, 1923–4.

Bibliography

Gonzalez, Tomas, editor, *Documents from Simancas relating to the Reign of Elizabeth (1558–1568)*. Translated from the Spanish and edited by Spencer Hall, London, 1865.

Grant, A. J., *A History of Europe from 1494 to 1610*, London, 1931.

Green, John Richard, *Short History of the English People*, London, 1891.

Green, Mary Anne Everett, *Letters of Royal and Illustrious Ladies of Great Britain*, 3 vols., London, 1846.

Gross, Charles, *The Sources and Literature of English History*, 2nd Ed., London, 1915.

Guilday, Peter, *The English Catholic Refugees on the Continent (1558–1795)*, London and New York, 1914.

Guiney, Louise Imogen, *Recusant Poets*, London and New York, 1939.

Gwynn, Stephen, *History of Ireland*, London and New York, 1923.

Hackett, Francis, *Henry VIII*, New York, 1929.

Hakluyt, Richard, *Voyages*, 8 vols., Everyman's Library.

Hale, John Richard, *The Story of the Great Armada*, London, 1913.

Hall, Hubert, *Society in the Elizabeth Age*, 4th ed., London, 1901.

Hardy, William John (see Gee, Henry).

Harington, Sir John, *Nugae Antiquae*, 2 vols., London, 1769.

Harleian MSS.

Harrison, George Bagshawe, *Elizabethan Journals*, three vols. in one, London and New York, 1938.

—— (see Elizabeth, Queen of England).

Hatfield MSS., Historical Manuscripts Commission, 1906.

Haynes, Samuel, editor, *Burghley Papers, 1542–70*, London, 1740.

Hayward, John, *Annals of the First Four Years of the Reign of Queen Elizabeth*. Edited by John Bruce, London, 1840.

Henderson, T. F., *Mary Queen of Scots*, 2 vols., London, 1905.

—— *The Casket Letters and Mary, Queen of Scots*, 2nd. ed., Edinburgh, 1890.

Hennessy, William M. (see *Annals of Loch Cé*).

Hentzer, Paul, *A Journey into England in the Year 1598*, Twickenham, 1757.

Holinshed, Raphael, *Chronicles*, 2nd ed., 3 vols., London, 1587.

Hollis, Christopher, *The Monstrous Regiment*, New York, 1930.

Hosack, John, *Mary Queen of Scots and Her Accusers*, 2 vols., Edinburgh, 1869.

Howell, Thomas Bayly (see Cobbett, William).

Hume, Martin A. S., *Philip II of Spain*, London, 1906.

—— *The Courtships of Queen Elizabeth*, London, 1904.

—— *The Wives of Henry VIII*, New York, 1905.

—— *Treason and Plot. Struggles for Catholic Supremacy in the Last Years of Queen Elizabeth*, London, 1901.

Hyland, St. George K., *A Century of Persecution under Tudor and Stuart Sovereigns, from Contemporary Records*, London, 1920.

Bibliography

in the Reign of Queen Elizabeth, from 1571 to 1596, London, 1759.

Naunton, Sir Robert, *Fragmenta Regalia,* London, 1641.

Neal, Daniel, *The History of the Puritans,* a new edition reprinted from the text of Dr. Toulmin's edition . . . Rev., cor., and enl., 3 vols., London, 1837.

Neale, J. E., *Queen Elizabeth,* New York, 1934.

Nichols, John, *The Progresses and Public Processions of Queen Elizabeth,* 3 vols., London, 1823.

O'Donovan, John (see *Annals of the Kingdom of Ireland, by The Four Masters*).

Pastor, Ludwig von, *Lives of the Popes.* Translated and edited by Ralph Francis Kerr, Vols. XIV to XIX, London, 1930.

Persons, Robert (see Pollen, J. H.).

Phillips, G. E., *The Extinction of the Ancient Hierarchy,* London, 1905.

Pierce, William (see Marprelate, Martin).

Pollard, A. F., *The History of England from the Accession of Edward VI to the Death of Elizabeth (1547–1603),* being Vol. VI of *The Political History of England,* London, 1934.

—— (see *Tudor Tracts*).

Pollen, J. H., S.J., *Sources for the Study of the History of Catholics in England, Ireland, and Scotland,* London, 1921.

—— *The English Catholics in the Reign of Queen Elizabeth,* London, 1920.

—— *Papal Negotiations with Mary Queen of Scots, 1561–67,* Scottish History Society, 1901.

—— *The Institution of the Archpriest Blackwell,* London, 1916.

—— "The Politics of the English Catholics during the Reign of Queen Elizabeth," in the *Month,* Vol. XCIX (1902), pp. 43–60, 131–148, 290–305, 394–411, 600–618; Vol. C. (1902), pp. 176–188.

—— "Mary Stuart and the Babington Plot," in the *Month,* Vol. CII (1903), pp. 430–433; Vol. CVII (1907), pp. 356–366; Vol. CX (1910), pp. 240–254, 363–375.

—— "The Origin of the Appellant Controversy, 1598," in the *Month,* Vol. CXXV (1915), pp. 461–475; Vol. CXXVI (1915), pp. 141–156, 257–271, 480–495.

—— editor, *Mary Queen of Scots and the Babington Plot,* in the *Publications of the Scottish History Society,* Third Series, Vol. III, 1922.

—— editor, *The Memoirs of Father Persons in the Catholic Record Society Publications,* Vol. II (1905), pp. 12–218 and Vol. IV (1907), pp. 1–161.

—— (see Challoner, Richard).

Bibliography

—— and Burton, E. H., *Lives of the English Martyrs*, Second Series, London, 1914.

Power, Eileen (see Tawney, R. H.).

Prescott, H. F. M., *The Life of "Bloody Mary,"* New York, 1940.

Rait, Robert Sangster, and Cameron, Annie I., *King James's Secret: Negotiations between Elizabeth and James VI relating to the Execution of Mary Queen of Scots*, London, 1927.

Read, Conyers, *Mr. Secretary Walsingham and the Policy of Queen Elizabeth*, 3 vols., Oxford, 1925.

—— *Bibliography of Tudor History, Tudor Period, 1485–1603*, Oxford, 1933.

Robinson, Hastings (see *Zurich Letters*).

Rogers, J. E. Thorold, *A History of Agriculture and Prices in England*, 7 vols., Oxford, 1866–1902.

—— *The Economic Interpretation of History*, London, 1921.

Ronan, M. V., *The Reformation in Ireland under Elizabeth, 1558–1580*, London, 1930.

Scargill-Bird, S.R., *Guide to the Principal Classes of Documents Preserved in the Public Record Office*, 3rd ed., London, 1908.

Shakespeare's England: an Account of the Life and Manners of His Age (various authors), 2 vols., Oxford, 1917.

Simpson, Richard, *Edmund Campion: a biography*, London, 1896.

Skelton, John, *Maitland of Lethington*, 2 vols., Edinburgh and London, 1887–88.

Spenser, Edmund, *A View of the Present State of Ireland*, London, 1934.

Stephenson, H. S., *The Elizabethan People*, London, 1910.

Stone, J. M., *Studies from Court and Cloister*, St. Louis, Mo., 1908.

Stow, John, *The Annales of England*, London, 1605.

Strachey, Lytton, *Elizabeth and Essex*, New York, 1928.

Strickland, Agnes, *Life of Queen Elizabeth* (Vols. VI and VII of *Lives of the Queens of England*), London, 1843–45.

Strype, John, *Annals of the Reformation*, 4 vols., London, 1709–31.

Taunton, E. L., *History of the Jesuits in England, 1580–1773*, London, 1901.

Tawney, R. H., *The Agrarian Problem in the Sixteenth Century*, London, 1912.

—— *Religion and the Rise of Capitalism*, London, 1926.

—— and Power, Eileen, *Tudor Economic Documents*, London, 1924.

Tierney, M. A. (see Dodd, Charles).

Traill, H. D., *Social England*, Vols. II and III, London, 1897.

Tudor Tracts, 1532–1588, with an introduction by A. F. Pollard, Westminster, 1903.

Tytler, P. F., *England under the Reigns of Edward VI and Mary*, 2 vols., London, 1839.

Bibliography

Usher, Roland G., *Reconstruction in the English Church*, 2 vols., New York, 1910.

Vertot, René Aubert de, and Villaret, C., *Ambassades de Messieur de Noailles en Angleterre*, 5 vols., Leyden, 1763.

Waldman, Milton, *England's Elizabeth*, Boston and New York, 1933.
Walker, J. C. (see Wernham, R. B.).
Wallis, John P. E. (see Lilly, W. S.).
Walsh, William Thomas, *Philip II*, New York, 1937.
Waugh, Evelyn, *Edmund Campion*, London, 1935.
Weber, Max, *The Protestant Ethic and the Spirit of Capitalism*. Translated by Talcott Parsons, London, 1930.
Wernham, R. S., and Walker, J. C., *England under Elizabeth (1558–1603), illustrated from contemporary sources*, London, 1932.
Wiesener, L., *La Jeunesse d'Elizabeth d'Angleterre*, Paris, 1878. (Translated as *The Youth of Queen Elizabeth* by Charlotte M. Yonge, 2 vols., London, 1879.)
Williams, Charles, *Queen Elizabeth*, London, 1936.
Williams, T. L. (see *Douay College Diaries*).
Williamson, James A., *The Age of Drake*, London, 1938.
Wilson, Elkin Calhoun, *England's Eliza*, Cambridge, Mass., 1939.
Wood, Anthony à, *Athenae Oxoniensis*, 5 vols., London, 1813–20.
Wright, Thomas, *Queen Elizabeth and Her Times*, 2 vols., London, 1838.

Zurich Letters. Edited by Hastings Robinson, 2 vols., Parker Society, 1842–46.

Index

Acton, Lord, 207
Acts and Monuments, 97; *see also Book of Martyrs*
Admiral, Lord, *see* Nottingham, Earl of
Agents provocateurs, 121 f., 124, 263 ff., 267, 276 ff., 282, 335
Aglionby, Edward, 185
Alcazar (Alcacerquiber), battle of, 213
Aldobrandini, Cardinal, 365
Alençon, Francis, Duke of (later Duke of Anjou) 20, 142, 233 ff., 239, 240, 243, 249, 371; arrival of at Greenwich, 238; death of, 246, 252; stand on religion, 244; usefulness to Elizabeth, 235
Allen, William, Cardinal, 2, 214 f., 227, 256, 296, 325, 326, 338, 362, 363; his attack on Elizabeth, 297 f.
Allinga, Ahasuerus, 133
Alva, Duke of, 103, 113, 121, 191, 196, 199, 251; on Ridolfi's plot, 205 f.
Anabaptists, prosecutions of, 330
Andrewes, Lawrence, 372
Angus, Earl of, 22
Anjou, Francis Duke of, *see* Alençon
Anjou, Henry, Duke of (later King Henry III of France), 142, 146, 187, 206, 234; question of Elizabeth's marriage to, 143 ff.
Anne of Denmark, 261, 371
Anticlericalism among the masses, 81
Antonio, Don, Portuguese Pretender, 308
Appellants, 361 ff.; declaration of loyalty to Elizabeth, 366
Appletree, 262
Aquilla, Juan dell', 358
Arden, Edward, 263 f.
Argyle, so-called Countess of, 343
Armada, the, 254, 290 ff., 295 ff.; defeat of, 299 ff.; effect of defeat on Spanish seapower, 307; reason for renewal of persecution after, 335 ff.
Armadas, failure of subsequent, 308; later, 347
Armstrong, Hector, 195

Arran, third Earl of (James Hamilton), 113, 141
Arthington, fanatic, 331
Arundel, Henry Fitzalan, twelfth Earl of, 39, 44, 45, 125, 126, 142, 177, 178, 186, 206, 210, 242; arrest of, 189
Arundel, Philip Howard, first Earl of, (of the Howard family), 284, 325
Ascham, Roger, tutor to Elizabeth, 14, 15, 16, 17
Ashley, Katherine, 14, 30 ff., 371, sent to Tower, 58
Assassination, question of Elizabeth's, 252 ff.
"Association," Leicester's, 275

Babington, Anthony, 228, 276 ff., 282, 335; execution of, 279
Babington conspiracy, 270, 276 ff.
Bacon, Anthony, 226
Bacon, Sir Francis, 226, 322, 340, 341, 351, 352, 353
Bacon, Sir Nicholas, 70, 78, 86, 100, 105, 177, 178, 359
Bagenal, Sir Henry, 348
Bagot, Anthony, on Essex, 341 f.
Bailiff, Sir Christopher Hatton's servant, 265
Baily, Charles, 208
Ballard, John, 276
Baltasar, 252
Baltinglas, Lord, 346
Bancroft, Bishop of London, 355, 365, 367, 373
Barker, Andrew, 292
Barkworth, Father, 334 f.
Barlow, William (later Bishop of Lincoln), 369
Barrow, Henry, 330, 333
Bassett, Mr., 225
Bastard, Thomas, 321
Beauchamp, Lord, 373
Bedford, Earl of, 70, 78, 102, 160, 162
Bedingfield, Sir Henry, 57, 58
Bell, James, 229

Index

Belloc, Hilaire, 110, 120, 126, 135, 192; on excommunication of Elizabeth, 199

Bennett, an imprisoned priest, 325

Bentley, Thomas, 316

Bible, Douay, 214

Bill, William, 71

Bingham, Sir Richard, 304

Bird, James, execution of, 332 f.

Birt, Dom Norbert, 83

Bishops, deprived Elizabethan, the, 91 ff.; Puritan view of, 328 f.

Black, J. B., 231; on Elizabeth and Netherlands, 248

Blackwell, George, 366; appeal against, 365; archpriest, 364

Blisland, Vicar of, 84

Blois, treaty of, 250

"Bloody question," the, 228

Blount, Charles, see Mountjoy, Lord

Blount, Sir Christopher, 341

Bluet, Thomas, 365, 366, 367

Bocher, Joan, 36, 52

Bodmin, the Mayor of, 36

Boleyn, Anne, 1, 15. 65, 101; charges against, 5 f.; imprisonment and death, 4; likeness of Elizabeth to, 8; marriage to Henry pronounced invalid, 6; private marriage to Henry, 2

Boleyn, Mary, 2, 192

Bonner, Bishop, 53, 70, 85, 92, 93, 149; deprived and imprisoned, 90

Book of Martyrs, 51; effect of on Catholic Church, 96 ff.

Bothwell, Earl of, 157, 165, 180; exile of, 169; marriage to Mary Queen of Scots, 167; Mary's marriage to, annulled, 273

"Brag," Campion's, 221

Brantôme, Pierre de Bourdeille, Seigneur and Abbé of, 33, 179

Breuner, Baron, on Elizabeth and Leicester, 133, 136

Brewen, Anne, 330

Brewer, J. S., 98

British Empire, founding of, 309

Browne, Robert, 330

Bryan, Lady Margaret, 9, 10 f.

Bucer, Martin, 37, 38

Buchanan, George, tutor to Mary Queen of Scots, 158, 179

Buckhurst, Lord, see Sackville, Thomas

Bull, Dr. John, Catholic composer, 321, 336

Bunyan, John, 221

Burghley, Lord, see Cecil, William

Burghley, second Lord, see Cecil, Thomas

Burgundy, House of, 247

Burke, Theobald, 346

Byrd, William, Catholic composer, 319, 336

Cadiz, 299, 308, 340

Calais, 111, 116, 117, 244; captured by Spain, 308; loss of to France, 49, 64

Calvin, John, 37

Cambridge University, 149

Camden, William, 16, 83; on Arden's death, 264; on Armada, 301

Campion, Edmund, 220 ff., 225, 230, 233, 267, 368; execution of, 222 f.; his speech in Westminster Hall, 222; *Ten Reasons,* 221

Canterbury, center of heresy, 48

Carberry Hill, 169

Carew, Lady, 185

Carew, Sir George, 305, 358

Carey, Sir George (later second Lord Hunsdon), 216

Carey, Henry, see Hunsdon, Lord

Carey, Robert (later Earl of Monmouth), 374

Carlyle, Thomas, 19

Carne, Sir Edward, 68

Cartwright, Thomas, 330

Casket Letters, 158, 164, 176, 178 ff.; forgery of, 179 f.

Castelnau de Mauvissière, 56, 161, 240; on Elizabeth's virtue, 242

Castiglione, Battista, 58

Castlehaven, 358

Castro, Alphonse, 49

Cateau-Cambrésis, Treaty of, 111, 117

Catesby, John, 352

Catesby, Robert, 352

Catherine de' Medici, 148, 246

Catherine of Valois, 28

Catholic League, 217

Catholicism, and Puritanism, 326 ff.; remnants of in north and west, 336

Catholics, attitude towards Armada, 296, 325; enforcement of laws against, 229 f.; English, attitude towards Elizabeth's excommunication, 199; English, condition of, at death of Norfolk, 212 ff.; English, disloyalty among, 259; English, results for, of Elizabeth's death, 269; number of, in England at beginning of Elizabeth's reign, 82 f.; position of, after the *Regnans in Excelsis,* 213; share of, in repelling Armada, 297; treatment of, after Armada, 325 ff.

Cavalcanti, Guido, 147

Cave, Sir Ambrose, 70

Cecil, Lady, 93

Cecil, Lord Algernon, on William Cecil, 109

388

Index

Index

Index

ff.; courtship with Alençon, 233; death of, 376; denies persecuting Catholics, 226; disingenuous in persecution, 230; Dr. Parry asserts her knowledge of his innocence, 267; education of, 14 f., 16, 18; England under, 321 ff.; English prose style of, 18 f.; Essex falls out of her favor, 349 ff.; excommunicated, 192 f.; the extent of Cecil's influence over her, 110; failure of the Bull of excommunication, 198 f.; first moves in the religious problem, 69 f.; friends of, 371; general attitude towards marriage, 150 f.; gives Quadra to understand she will become a Catholic, 132; granting of monopolies, 360 f.; greed of, 317; guilty of shaking the principle of monarchy, 270; help to rebellious Scots Lords, 154 f.; her attitude towards her right of succession, 65; her Catholic taste in religion, 89; her coronation procession, 73; her death not politically advantageous to Spain, 266; her designs in the Netherlands, 245; her intellectual dishonesty, 335; her lack of clothes in childhood, 11; her personal religious preferences, 68; her policy in the Netherlands, 250 ff.; her speech at Tilbury, 303 f.; her supposititious sons by Thomas Seymour and Leicester, 33; her version of the *Consolation of Philosophy*, 17; her view of her spiritual supremacy, 71; illegitimate, 42; in the Tower, 57; in Thomas Seymour's household, 24, 26 ff.; increasing restlessness, 312; infected with syphilis and other ailments, 134 f.; instructions to Drake, 299; insults monks at Westminster, 77; Katherine Ashley on Seymour's affair with, 26 f.; knowledge of modern languages, 17; last days of, 369 ff.; last illness, 375 f.; last years of, 357 ff.; likeness to Anne Boleyn, 8; likeness to Henry, 7; loses claim to Calais, 117; marriage negotiations with Archduke Charles, 143 ff.; marriage negotiations with Duke of Anjou, 145 f.; mistress of mendacity, 107 f.; neurosis, 139; no actual attempt ever made on her life, 268; nominates James VI, 374; Northumberland attempts to seize her, 44; objections to marriage to Leicester, 140; on murder of Rizzio, 163; on virginity, 133 f.; ordered to court by Mary, 55; orders punishment of rebels of 1569, 193; papal approval of assassination, 207; persecution of Catholics, 216 f.; Philip II offers marriage, 101; plots against, 259 ff.; Pope attempts reconciliation, 106; problem of marriage, 102; "Proclamation against Jesuits and Secular Priests," 367; projects of marriage, 139 ff.; political position of, 100 f.; possible result of Catholic marriage, 151 f.; possibility of blood relationship to Leicester, 136; question of assassination of, 252 ff.; question of legitimacy, 67; question of marriage to Leicester, 125 f.; questioned by Sir Thomas Tyrwhitt, 30 f.; reaction of, to Thomas Seymour's death, 32; relation to Netherlands, 118, 247; relations with Hatton, 237; relations with Leicester, 126; religious policy of, 231; religious settlement, 77 ff.; renewal of project of marriage to Courtenay, 57; responsible for crisis of 1569, 188; right of, to throne, 64 ff.; seeks a French alliance rather than marriage, 235; seizes Spanish treasure ships, 119 ff.; sent to Cheshunt, 22; sent to Hatfield, 15; sent to Hunsdon Hall, 10; sent to Woodstock, 57 f.; sexual abnormality of, 33 ff., 135; Seymour, Thomas, makes love to, 26, 29; Sir James Melville on, 33; Sir Walter Raleigh on, 34 f.; Somerset plans to marry her to his son, 42; strengthened by failure of rebellion of Northern Earls, 196; succeeds to throne, 67; summoned to court, outfits chapel, 58 f.; supports Huguenots in France, 115 ff.; talent of in poetry, 19 f.; tribute of to Anjou's faithfulness to his religion, 148; visits Archbishop Heath, 92; Von Klarwill, on, 32; Wriothesley on, 10

Elizabeth of Valois, 102

Emmanuel Philibert, Duke of Savoy, 60, 142

England, Elizabethan, intellectual life of, 309; state of society in, 321 ff.

Englefield, Sir Francis, 127

Eric, Prince of Sweden, 142

Essex, first Earl of (Walter Devereux), 123, 238

Essex, second Earl of (Robert Devereux), 151, 262, 308, 310, 313, 340 ff.; 371; and Tyrone, 349; character, 355 f.; execution of, 354; his rebellion, 351 f.; in Ireland, 347 ff.; made Governor General of Ireland, 342; on Irish, 348; return to England, 349; rise of, 340; significance of his career, 355 f.; trial of, 352 f.

Index

Index

Index

Index

reported having ceded her rights to Duke of Anjou, 187; treatment of, in England, 271 ff.; trial of, 176 ff., 279 ff.; upshot of enquiries at York and Westminster, 178; Winter ordered to intercept her, 114

Mary Tudor, 13, 42, 65, 93, 98, 111, 123, 160; and burning of heretics, 51 ff.; arouses aid, 44; attitude of, towards Elizabeth, 9 f.; death of, 62; entrance into London, 46; her character, 62; hope of the Catholics, 40 f.; marriage plans of, 47 f.; persecution under, 48 ff., 52 ff.; question of spoliation of Church under, 49; repudiates title as head of English church, 49; sends Elizabeth to Tower, 55 ff.; suspects genuineness of Elizabeth's Catholicism, 59

Mass, regulations concerning, 88 f.; saying of, 215; surreptitious saying of, 184

Massacre of St. Bartholomew's Day, see St. Bartholomew's Day massacre

Mathew, Bishop David, on Elizabethan religious policy, 231; on Gilbert Gifford, 277; on Stanley and York, 257

Mauvisièrre, see Castelnau de Mauvissière

Maximilian, Archduke, 133

Maximilian, Emperor, 143, 144

Maxwell, Sir John, see Herries, Lord

Mayne, Cuthbert, 215 f., 229

M'Cabbe, Melaghlin, 305

Medici, Catherine de', 145, 147, 159, 217, 235, 246

Medina Sidonia, Duke of, 299, 300, 302, 303

Mein Kampf, 99

Melville, Sir James, 33, 136, 160

Mendenez, Pedro, Admiral, 120

Mendoza, Don Bernardino de, 141, 212, 219, 226, 253, 264 ff., 279, 281, 283, 296, 308; on Mary Queen of Scots, 282

Mendoza, Don Pedro de, 304 f.

Metamorphoses of Ajax, 313

Meyer, Arnold Oskar, 83, 198, 253, 290; on Elizabethan church, 368

Michiel, Maffeo, Governor of Zante, 311; on English pirates, 311

Milner, Bishop John, on persecution, 230

Mirror of the Sinful Soul, The, 14

Missionaries, dangers of, in England, 224 f.; dissensions among, 362

Monopolies, 360 f.

Monument of Matrones, 316

Moray, Earl of (James Stewart), 115, 154, 157, 162, 170, 175 ff., 180 f., 188

f., 260; appointed Regent, 170; death of, 192, 252

More, Sir Thomas, 4, 7, 13, 39, 43, 230

Morgan, Thomas, 264, 276 ff.

Morley, Lord, 186

Morton, James Douglas, fourth Earl of, 115, 165, 169, 175 ff., 180, 195, 260

Morton, Nicholas, 200, 296

Moryson, Fynes, on Irish, 346

Mountjoy, Lord, 341, 348, 355, 357, 371, 373

Murdin, William, 272

Mush, John, 338

Music, composers of, 336

"My Dark Rosaleen," 345

Nau, Claude, 280, 282

Naunton, Sir Robert, 110, 125

Naworth castle, 191, 192

Neale, J. E., on Elizabeth, 359 f.

Neri, St. Philip, 215

Netherlands, 118 f., 121 f., 124; Elizabeth's relations to, 247 ff.; Leicester in, 254

Neville, Henry, fifth Earl of Westmoreland, 142

New Testament, Rheims Version, 214

Nichols, John, 317

Noailles, François de, French Ambassador, 45

Nobility, old, power of broken at death of Norfolk, 210

Noble, John, 292

Nombre de Dios, 212

Norfolk, Henry Howard, fourth Duke of, 102, 124, 126, 159, 176, 178, 186, 187, 192, 196, 203, ff., 207, 217, 259, 273, 284, 352, 356; arrest of, 189; death of, 210; effect of death on English Catholics, 212 f.; evidence against, 208; proposal to marry Queen of Scots, 188; trial and conviction of, 209

Norfolk, Thomas Howard, third Duke of, 44

Norris, Sir Henry (later Lord), 272

Northampton, Marquis of, 210; *see also* Parr, William

Northumberland, Countess of, 194

Northumberland, John Dudley, Duke of, 39, 41, 43, 123; arrest of, 45; execution of, 50; plots at death of Edward VI, 44

Northumberland, Thomas Percy, Seventh Earl of, 81, 171, 189, 190, 200, 210, 265; betrayal and death, 195

Norton, Richard, 190, 194, 225

Norton, Thomas, 106

Nottingham, Earl of, Charles Howard,

395

Index

Index

Index

Index